Study Guide
and
Working Papers

for

Advanced Accounting

Tenth Edition

Joe B. Hoyle
University of Richmond

Thomas F. Schaefer
University of Notre Dame

Timothy S. Doupnik
University of South Carolina

Prepared by
Sharon O'Reilly
Saint Mary's University of Minnesota

The *McGraw-Hill* Companies

McGraw-Hill
Irwin

Study Guide and Working Papers for
ADVANCED ACCOUNTING
Joe B. Hoyle, Thomas F. Schaefer, and Timothy S. Doupnik

Published by McGraw-Hill/Irwin, an imprint of The McGraw-Hill Companies, Inc., 1221 Avenue of the Americas, New York, NY 10020. Copyright © 2011, 2009, 2007, 2004 by The McGraw-Hill Companies, Inc. All rights reserved.

1 2 3 4 5 6 7 8 9 0 WDQ/WDQ 1 0 9 8 7 6 5 4 3 2 1 0

ISBN: 978-0-07-726804-6
MHID: 0-07-726804-0

www.mhhe.com

Contents

Chapter 1

The Equity Method of Accounting for Investments

Chapter Outline

Standards Mentioned in This Chapter (note: U.S. standards are now incorporated into the FASB Accounting Standards Codification):

- **APB Opinion 18,** *The Equity Method of Accounting for Investments in Common Stock*
- **ARB No. 51,** *Consolidated Financial Statements*
- **FASB Interpretation 46R,** *Consolidation of Variable Interest Entities*
- **FASB Staff Position 115-1,** *The Meaning of Other-Than-Temporary Impairment and Its Application to Certain Investments*
- **IAS 28,** *Investments in Associates*
- **SFAS No. 115,** *Accounting for Certain Investments in Debt and Equity Securities*
- **SFAS No. 141R,** *Business Combinations*
- **SFAS No. 142,** *Goodwill and Other Intangible Assets*
- **SFAS No. 159,** *The Fair Value Option for Financial Assets and Financial Liabilities*
- **SFAS No. 160,** *Noncontrolling Interests and Consolidated Financial Statements*

I.   *LO1* **The Reporting of Investments in Corporate Equity Securities** – Reporting for an investment depends primarily on the *degree of influence* the investor (stockholder) has over the investee's operating and financial policies. This factor is typically indicated by the relative size of ownership.

There are three approaches to the reporting of investments in corporate equity securities: **fair value**, **consolidation**, and the **equity method**. The following table indicates the typical method of accounting applied to various equity securities.

Criterion	Normal Ownership Level	Applicable Accounting Method
Lack of ability to significantly influence	< 20%	Fair Value (SFAS 115 or 159) or cost
Presence of ability to significantly influence	20% – 50%	Equity method, or fair value option (SFAS 159)
Control through voting interests	> 50%	Consolidated financial statements
Control through variable interests	Primary beneficiary status (no ownership required)	Consolidated financial statements

A.   **Fair value method** (*SFAS 115*) – does not apply to investments in equity securities accounted for under the equity method or to investments in consolidated subsidiaries. It is used when the investor owns a small percentage of the investee stock. The shares are purchased in anticipation of dividends or appreciation of stock market values.

1.   *SFAS 115* is applied when the investor **lacks the ability** to significantly influence the investee's financial and operating policies. Generally, this situation occurs when the investor owns **less than 20%** of a corporation's outstanding voting common stock.

2. *Initial* investments are recorded at cost and periodically adjusted to fair value if fair value is readily determinable; otherwise, the investment remains at cost.

3. *Equity* securities are classified into one of two categories *when significant influence is not present*: (1) *trading securities* or (2) *available-for-sale securities*.

    For both categories of investments, dividends are included in earnings.

    a. *Trading securities* – Equity securities that are purchased and held principally for sale in the short term.

        (1) Trading Securities are reported at **fair value**.
        (2) Unrealized holding gains and losses are included in **earnings**.

    b. *Available-for-sale securities* – Equity securities not classified as trading securities.

        (1) Available-for-sale securities are reported at **fair value**.
        (2) Unrealized gains and losses are excluded from earnings and reported as a separate component of shareholders equity as part of *other comprehensive income*.

    c. *Available-for-sale securities* – Fair Value Option.

        (1) Firms can elect fair value treatment under SFAS 159.
        (2) Balance sheet amounts are reported at fair value.
        (3) Changes in fair value are reported on the income statement, as opposed to other comprehensive income.
        (4) This treatment effectively removes the distinction between trading and available-for-sale securities.

B. **Consolidation of Financial Statements** – Consolidation is required when the investor gains *control* of another entity, usually through ownership of a majority (more than 50%) of the other entity's equity. Generally, the entities are viewed as a single entity for reporting purposes.

1. *Consolidated* financial statements (a single set) are created for external reporting purposes with all assets, liabilities, revenues and expenses being brought together.

2. FASB Interpretation No. 46R expands the use of consolidated financial statements to include entities that are controlled through special contractual arrangements, rather than through voting stock interests. These entities were frequently referred to as "special purpose entities (SPEs)." SPEs provided vehicles for some firms to keep large amounts of assets and liabilities off their consolidated financial statements.

C. *LO2* **Application of the equity method** – The equity method is used when the investor's ownership interest gives it the *ability to exercise significant influence* over the investee's financial and operating policies. Determining the *ability to exercise significant influence* is not always a clear-cut decision – judgment is essential.

1. **General ownership test**: if the investor owns 20% to 50% of the investee's outstanding voting stock, significant influence is normally assumed and the equity method is applied. This assumption can be overcome by prevailing evidence to the contrary.

2. Even if the investor owns less than 20% of the investee, the *ability to exercise significant influence* may still exist. Conditions that indicate the presence of this degree of influence include:

   a. Investor representation on the board of directors of the investee.
   b. Investor participation in the policy-making process of the investee.
   c. Material intra-entity transactions.
   d. Interchange of managerial personnel.
   e. Technological dependency.
   f. Extent of ownership by the investor in relation to the size and concentration of other ownership interests in the investee.

3. It is not required that the investor actually exercise its influence over the investee, only that the ability to exercise significant influence be present.

4. **Limitations of Equity Method Applicability** – the equity method is *not appropriate* for investments that have *any* of the following characteristics regardless of the investor's degree of ownership (no significant influence over the investee):

   a. An agreement exists between investor and investee whereby the investor surrenders significant rights as a shareholder.
   b. A concentration of ownership operates the investee without regard for the views of the investor.
   c. The investor attempts, but fails to obtain representation on the investee's board of directors.

5. If an entity can exercise *control* over the investee without majority ownership, consolidation (rather than the equity method) is appropriate.

6. **Extensions of Equity Method Applicability** – Conditions can also exist where the equity method is appropriate despite a majority voting interest.

   a. The minority owner may be granted approval or veto rights to restrict the powers of the majority owner (such as approval over compensation, hiring, termination and other critical operating and capital spending decisions).
   b. If the minority rights are so restrictive as to call into question whether the majority owner has control, the equity method is used instead of consolidation.

7. **Summary** – In determining whether to apply the equity method, the **sole** criterion is the ability to *significantly influence* (but not control) *the investee*.

8. **International Standards** – Equity method concepts and applications are virtually identical to U.S. standards.

II. **_LO3_ Accounting Procedures Used in Applying the Equity Method** – In applying the equity method, the accounting objective is to report the investor's investment in a way that reflects the close relationship between the companies. The equity method uses the _accrual_ basis for recognizing the investor's share of investee income, thus, the investor recognizes income _as it is earned_ by the investee.

A. The investor maintains the following two accounts when using the equity method:

　1. _Investment in Investee Company_ — a balance sheet account.

　2. _Equity in Investee Income_ — an income statement account.

B. **Recording the basic transactions** is straightforward — the book value of the investment account is adjusted to reflect changes in the book value of the investee's net assets.

　1. The investor **accrues its percentage of the earnings** reported by the investee each period by making the following entry:

　　Investment in Investee Company ....　XX
　　　Equity in Investee Income ....　　　XX

　2. **Dividends** reduce the investment balance to reflect the decrease in the investee's book value. The investor records dividends received from the investee by making the following entry:

　　Cash XX
　　　Investment in Investee Company XX

C. **Reporting a change to the equity method** occurs when the investor's ability to exercise significant influence over an investee is achieved through a series of acquisitions. A **retrospective** adjustment is made to convert all previously reported figures to the equity method at the time the equity method becomes applicable.

　1. This restatement establishes _comparability_ between the financial statements of all years. The investor makes the following entry:

　　Investment in Investee Company ....　XX
　　　Retained Earnings — Prior Period Adjustment
　　　— Equity in Investee Income.................　　XX

　2. An adjustment is made to remove the accounts required by _SFAS 115_ (fair value reporting) that pertain to the investment prior to the obtaining of significant influence. The investor makes the following entry:

　　Unrealized Holding Gain — Shareholders' Equity...　XX
　　　Fair Value Adjustment (Available for Sale).......　　XX

D. **Reporting Investee Income from Sources Other Than Continuing Operations** – If material, the investor's share of investee income from sources other than continuing operations (such as extraordinary items and prior-period adjustments) should be disclosed separately in the investor's income statement.

E. **Reporting investee losses** – the investor's percentage of a loss incurred by the investee is recognized by the investor and reduces the carrying value of the investment account.

    1. **Permanent Losses in Value** – When a *permanent* decline in an equity method investment's value occurs, the investor must recognize an impairment loss and reduce the asset's balance to fair market value.

    2. **Investment Reduced to Zero** – If an investment account is reduced to zero by reported losses or permanent declines in value, the investor should stop using the equity method rather than establish a negative balance. The investment retains a zero balance until subsequent investee profits eliminate all unrealized losses.

F. *LO4* **Reporting the Sale of an Equity Investment** – If the investor sells all or part of its holdings in the investee, the equity method is applied until the transaction date, thus establishing an appropriate carrying value for the investment.

    1. Before recording the sale, the investor makes the following journal entries to (1) record the investor's share of the investee's income for the period and (2) to record the receipt of any dividends from the investee.

Investment in Investee Company	XX	
Equity in Investee Income		XX
Cash	XX	
Investment in Investee Company		XX

    2. The sale of the shares is recorded as follows:

Cash	XX	
Gain (or Loss) on Sale of Investment		XX
Investment in Investee Company		XX

    3. The credit to the investment account is based on the percentage of the investor's interest that is sold. For example, if the investor holds 40,000 shares of the investee's common voting shares, and subsequently sells 4,000 of those shares, then the investor would remove 10% (4,000 shares ÷ 40,000 shares) of the investment account.

    4. **Partial sale** – If only part of the shares are sold, the investor continues to apply the equity method to the remainder of the investment as long as it has significant influence over the investee. If there is not significant influence, the remaining value in the investment account becomes the new carrying value for the investment and the shares are reported according to the fair-value method. There is no restatement of prior periods.

III. *LO5* Excess of Investment Cost over Book Value Acquired

A. The investor's purchase price (cost) seldom equals the underlying book value of the investee company's net assets, and the fair market value of the investee's net assets usually differs from their book value.

A company's fair market value is based on many things including company profitability, perceived worth, expectation of dividends and the general economic conditions.

B. The excess of investment cost over book value can be divided into two general categories:

  1. The investor's share of the excess of fair market value over the book value of the investee's specific assets and liabilities, and
  2. Extra amounts paid because future benefits are expected to accrue from the investment. The additional payment is attributed to an intangible future value referred to as *goodwill* (the excess of cost over fair market value of the investee's identifiable net assets).

C. The investor enters the total cost of the investment in the investment account, and does not show these individual components on its books. However, the asset adjustments and goodwill are tracked so that amortization amounts for the fair market value adjustments can be computed and recorded.

D. Fair value amounts allocated to accounts having limited useful lives are amortized by the investor. Land (which is never amortized or depreciated), goodwill, and other intangible assets considered to have indefinite lives are not amortized.

  1. If the investor is able to relate the excess of cost over book value to the specific assets of the investee, the excess is amortized over the expected useful lives of the assets.

  2. Because the amortization relates to assets held by the investee, the investor does not establish specific expense accounts. The investor makes the following entry:

> Equity in Investee Income ……………………….... XX
>   Investment in Investee Company ……………… XX

  3. Any remaining residual amount that cannot be attributed to a specific asset is considered to be goodwill.

E. **Goodwill** is presumed to have an indefinite life and is carried forward without adjustment until the investment is sold or a permanent decline in value occurs.

  1. Equity method investments are tested in their entirety for permanent declines in value.

  2. However, goodwill arising from a business combination (consolidation) is subject to annual impairment reviews.

IV. *LO6* Elimination of Unrealized Profits in Inventory

A. Gains derived from intra-entity transactions such as inventory sales between the investor and investee are not considered to be earned until the transferred goods are either consumed or resold to unrelated parties. These gains are *deferred* to ensure proper timing of revenue recognition.

B. *Downstream* transfers are sales made by the investor to the investee.

    1. Any unrealized intra-entity gain or loss remaining on the books of the investor at the end of the period (due to investee inventory) is deferred. It is subsequently recognized as income at the time of the inventory's eventual sale to an unrelated party.

    2. The amount of the gain or loss to be deferred is equal to the investor's ownership percentage multiplied by the gain in the merchandise remaining at the end of the year.

    The process may be summarized as follows:

        a. Determine the amount of the transferred inventory that is still present as of the end of the period.
        b. Compute the % intra-entity gain (gross profit) present in the original transfer.
        c. Multiply a. × b. to determine the unrealized portion of the gross profit in the ending inventory.
        d. Multiply c. × the percentage owned by the investor to determine the amount of the unrealized intra-entity gain that must be deferred.

Remaining Transf. Ending Inventory (a)	Gross Profit Percentage (b)	Gross Profit In Ending Inventory (c)	Investor Ownership Percentage	Unrealized Inter-Company Gross Profit (d)
$20,000	25%	$5,000	20%	$1,000

    3. At the end of the period of transfer, the following entry is made on the investor's books:

        Equity in Investee Income XX
                Investment in Investee Company XX

    4. Generally, this entry is reversed in the subsequent period when the remaining transferred inventory is sold to a third party. The remaining unrealized intra-entity profit is recognized with the reversing entry:

        Investment in Investee Company XX
                Equity in Investee Income XX

C. *Upstream* transfers are sales made by the investee to the investor.

    1. They are treated the same as downstream sales for equity method investments (unrealized gains are deferred).
    2. The direction of the sale (upstream or downstream) has consequences in the consolidation of financial statements, as will be seen in later chapters.

V. **Criticisms of the Equity Method** – the equity method is criticized for the following:

   A. Emphasizing the 20-50% of voting stock to determine significant influence, vs. control.

   B. Allowing off-balance sheet financing.

   C. Potentially biasing performance ratios.

VI. *LO7* **Fair Value Reporting Option for Equity Method Investments**

   A. FASB No. 159, *"The Fair Value Option for Financial Assets and Financial Liabilities"*, created a fair value option under which an entity may elect fair value for reporting certain financial assets and liabilities, including investments currently accounted for under the equity method (but not consolidated investments).

   1. The election is irrevocable.

   2. The election date is the date an investment first qualifies for equity method treatment (significant influence).

   3. The fair value option was first available for financial reporting in 2008.

   4. The asset is reported at fair value. Changes in fair value are reported as earnings.

   5. Dividends received from an investee are included in earnings.

   6. Adjustments are not made for excess cost amortizations or intra-entity profits.

   7. The fair value option increases emphasis on fair values for reporting and satisfies a perceived need for consistency across various balance sheet items.

VII. **Additional Equity Method Calculations** often found in problems:

   A. Investor share of Investee Income

Reported income of investee × investor ownership %	$ x
− amortization of excess cost over book value	(x)
− deferred gross profit from intra-entity transfers	(x)
+ gross profit deferred from the prior year	x
= Equity income from investee	xx

   B. Investor Investment Account Balance at Year End

Acquisition cost (or beginning of the year account balance)	$ x
+ Investor share of equity income from investee (from A above)	x
− Investor share of investee dividends	(x)
= Investor Investment Account	xx

   Note: any additional investments in the investee increase the investment account.

Multiple Choice Questions

1. On January 1, 2010, Swanson Company buys 300,000 shares of LifeSys, Inc.'s common stock for $1,800,000, the book value of the shares. This purchase gave Swanson a 30% ownership in LifeSys and the ability to exercise significant influence over operating and financing decisions. During 2010, LifeSys reported net income of $500,000 and paid a $1.20 per share dividend. What is the balance in Swanson's *Investment in LifeSys* account at December 31, 2010?

   A. $1,800,000
   B. $1,590,000
   C. $1,950,000
   D. $2,310,000
   E. $2,010,000

2. On July 1, 2010, West Co. buys 1,000,000 shares of National Water, Inc.'s common stock for $20,000,000, the book value of the shares. This purchase gave West Co. a 28% ownership in National Water and the ability to exercise significant influence over operating and financing decisions. For the fiscal year ending June 30, 2011, National Water reported net income of $1,900,000 and paid a $2.10 per share dividend. What is the balance in West Co's *Investment in National Water* account at June 30, 2011?

   A. $18,432,000
   B. $20,532,000
   C. $22,632,000
   D. $21,568,000
   E. $17,368,000

3. Tara Company owns 22% of Hawkins, Inc. and applies the equity method. During the current year, Tara buys inventory costing $300,000 and sells it to Hawkins for $690,000. At the end of the year, only 15% of this merchandise (at the transfer price) is still being held by Hawkins. What amount of unrealized gain must be deferred by Tara in reporting on the equity method?

   A. $58,500
   B. $85,800
   C. $45,000
   D. $12,870
   E. $22,770

4. What is a downstream sale?

   A. A sale from an investor to its investee
   B. A sale from a producer to its outside supplier
   C. A sale from an investee to its investor
   D. A sale from one manufacturer to another
   E. A sale from a small company to a large one

5. TunaCo purchases 30% of Stanley, Inc. on January 1, 2010 for $1,000,000. This acquisition gives TunaCo the ability to apply significant influence to Stanley's operating and financing policies. Stanley reports assets on that date of $2,500,000 with liabilities of $300,000. One building with a 10-year remaining useful life has a book value of $400,000 and a fair market value of $550,000. During 2010, Stanley reports net income of $340,000 while paying dividends of $150,000. What is the *Investment in Stanley* account balance in TunaCo' accounting records at December 31, 2010?

    A. $1,000,000
    B. $ 947,500
    C. $ 952,000
    D. $1,185,500
    E. $1,052,500

6. Smith Company holds 23% of the outstanding shares of Hello Greeting Cards and appropriately applies the equity method of accounting. For 2011, Hello Greeting Cards reports earnings of $430,000 and pays cash dividends of $180,000. During the year, Hello Greeting Cards acquired inventory for $280,000, which was then sold to Smith for $400,000. At the end of 2011, Smith continues to hold merchandise with a transfer price of $70,000. Assuming no amortization expense related to this investment, what *Equity in Investee Income* should Smith report in 2011?

    A. $ 62,330
    B. $103,730
    C. $ 98,900
    D. $ 52,670
    E. $ 94,070

7. Norbin Company uses the equity method to account for its investment in Stice Company's common stock. After the acquisition date, the investment account reported on Norbin's balance sheet would

    A.   Be increased by Norbin's share of Stice's earnings and decreased by Norbin's share of Stice's losses.
    B.   Be increased by Norbin's share of Stice's earnings but not be affected by Norbin's share of Stice's losses.
    C.   Not be affected by Norbin's share of Stice's earnings and losses.
    D.   Not be affected by Norbin's share of Stice's earnings but be decreased by Norbin's share of Stice's losses.
    E.   Be decreased by Norbin's share of Stice's earnings and increased by Norbin's share of Stice's losses.

8. Emmy Company buys 32% of Soupy, Inc.'s common stock on January 1, 2010 for $4,600,000. The equity method of accounting is to be used. Soupy's net assets on that date totaled $8,500,000. All of the excess of cost over book value is attributed to a copyright owned by Soupy, which is amortized over ten years. Soupy immediately begins selling inventory to Emmy as follows:

Year	Cost to Soupy	Transfer Price	Amount Held by Emmy at Year End (at Transfer Price)
2010	$ 680,000	$ 800,000	$ 200,000
2011	900,000	1,500,000	825,000

Inventory held at the end of one year is sold at the beginning of the next. Soupy reports net income of $740,000 in 2010 and $920,000 in 2011 while paying $500,000 in dividends each year. What is *Equity in Soupy's Income* to be reported by Emmy in 2010?

A. $236,800
B. $ 39,200
C. $415,200
D. $ 58,400
E. $434,400

9.   Refer to the information in #8 above. What is *Equity in Soupy's Income* to be reported by Emmy in 2011?

A. $ 10,400
B. $ 800
C. $202,400
D. $106,400
E. $198,400

10.   Refer to the information in #8 above. What is the balance in Emmy's *Investment in Soupy* account at December 31, 2011?

A. $4,811,200
B. $4,435,200
C. $4,649,600
D. $4,329,600
E. $4,280,000

11.   Generally, what percentage of another company's stock must be owned to cause us a change in the method of accounting for the investment from the Fair Value Method to the Equity Method?

A.   10%
B.   20%
C.   25%
D.   51%
E.   100%

12.   Which of the following is the best theoretical justification for consolidated financial statements?

A.   In form, the companies are separate; in substance, they are one entity.
B.   In form the companies are one entity; in substance they are separate.
C.   In form and substance the companies are one entity.
D.   In form and substance, the companies are separate entities.
E.   Consolidation is required by federal law.

13.   Which of the following cannot be presented at fair value on the financial statements?

A.   Investments accounted for under the equity method.
B.   Investments classified as available-for-sale securities.
C.   Investments where the investor has control of the investee.
D.   Investments classified as held-to-maturity securities.
E.   All of the above can be presented at fair value.

Brief Essay Questions

1. How should amortization related to an equity method investment be recorded in the investor's accounting records?

2. Under what conditions can an investment of less than 20% be accounted for using the equity method?

3. Under what conditions can a company hold more than 20% of another company's common voting stock and yet not be allowed to use the equity method of accounting?

4. Exactly what is Goodwill? When do we record it, and what does it represent?

5. Under what condition can a company report equity method investments at fair value?

Problems

1. Pees Inc. purchased 80,000 shares of Q-Corp's 320,000 outstanding shares for $4.20 per share. As a result of this purchase, Pees was able to place one of its managers on the Q-Corp's board of directors. At the time of the acquisition on January 1, 2011, the book value of Q-Corp's net assets was $1,210,000, which approximated their fair market value. During 2011, Q-Corp earned $60,000 of net income and paid a $.15 per share dividend.

   Required:

   A. Provide the entry to be made by Pees to record its investment in Q-Corp.

   B. Provide the entries which Pees should make to record the income resulting from its investment in Q-Corp and the dividends received from Q-Corp.

   C. What is the appropriate year-end balance in Pees' Investment in Q-Corp account?

2. In January 2010, Clark Corporation acquired 45% of the outstanding common stock of Lois Company for $2,800,000. This investment provided Clark with the ability to exercise significant influence over Lois. The book value of Lois on the acquisition date was $5,000,000. Lois' primary asset was a patent having a book value of $4,500,000 and a fair market value of $5,700,000. The patent has a remaining useful life of five years. The remaining excess of purchase price of book value was allocated to Goodwill.

   For the year ended December 31, 2010, Lois reported net income of $860,000 and paid cash dividends of $400,000 on its common stock.

   Required:

   What is the carrying value of Clark's investment in Lois at December 31, 2010?

3. Toy Corp. purchased a 30% interest in Tennessee Plastic Wheels Corp. (TPW) on January 1, 2010. At the time, the book value of TPW's net assets equaled the purchase price paid for the investment. During 2010, Toy Corp. sold inventory costing $360,000 to TPW for $500,000. At the end of 2010, TPW still had $160,000 of the inventory purchased from Toy Corp. on hand. TPW reported net income of $890,000 for 2010 and paid no dividends.

Required:

A. What entries should be made on the books of Toy Corp. at the end of 2010 as a result of the inventory sale to Tennessee Plastic Wheels Corp.?

B. What entry should be made in 2011 as a result of the 2010 sale?

Solutions to Multiple Choice Questions

1. **B**
Cost of purchase	$ 1,800,000
+ Income accrual ($500,000 × 30%)	150,000
− Dividend received (300,000 × $1.20)	(360,000)
= Investment in LifeSys Company	$ 1,590,000

2. **A**
Cost of purchase	$ 20,000,000
+ Income accrual ($1,900,000 × 28%)	532,000
− Dividend received (1,000,000 × $2.10)	(2,100,000)
= Investment in National Water Company	$ 18,432,000

3. **D**
Inventory at year-end ($690,000 × .15)	$ 103,500.00
Gross profit markup ($390,000 ÷ $690,000)	× 565
Unrealized gain	$ 58,500.00
Ownership share	× .22
Intra-entity unrealized gain — deferred	$ 12,870.00

4. **A**

5. **E**

   Goodwill Computation

	%	BV		Useful Life	Amort.
TunaCo's Cost			1,000,000		
Stanley's Book Value	30.00%	2,200,000	660,000		
Excess of cost over book value			340,000		
Building	30.00%	150,000	45,000	10	4,500
Goodwill			295,000	N/A	-
Total Amortization					4,500

Cost of purchase	$ 1,000,000
Income accrued ($340,000 × 30%)	102,000
Annual amortization	(4,500)
Dividend received ($150,000 × 30%)	(45,000)
Investment in Stanley	$ 1,052,500

6. E

Remaining year-end inventory	$ 70,000.00
Gross profit markup ($120,000 ÷ $400,000)	× .30
Profit in remaining inventory	$ 21,000.00
Ownership share	× 23%
Unrealized intra-entity gain	$ 4,830.00
Equity in income accrual ($430,000 × 23%)	$ 98,900.00
Unrealized intra-entity gain (see above)	(4,830.00)
Equity in investee income	$ 94,070.00

7. A

8. B

Purchase price of Soupy stock	$ 4,600,000
Soupy's book value ($8,500,000 × 32%)	– (2,720,000)
Copyright	= 1,880,000
Life of copyright in years	÷ 10
Annual copyright amortization	$ 188,000

2010 % of Inventory on Hand = $200,000 ÷ $800,000 = 25%

2010 Income accrual ($740,000 × 32%)	$ 236,800
Annual copyright amortization	(188,000)
Deferral of 2010 unrealized gain ($120,000 × 25% × 32%)	(9,600)
Equity income in Soupy Company	$ 39,200

9. A

Purchase price of Soupy stock	$ 4,600,000
Soupy's book value ($8,500,000 × 32%)	– (2,720,000)
Copyright	= 1,880,000
Life of copyright in years	÷ 10
Annual copyright amortization	$ 188,000

Additional calculations follow.

2010 % of Inventory on Hand = $200,000 ÷ $800,000 = 25%
2011 % of Inventory on Hand = $825,000 ÷ $1,500,000 = 55%

2011 Income accrual ($920,000 × 32%)	$ 294,400
Annual copyright amortization	(188,000)
Recognition of 2010 unrealized gain ($120,000 × 25% × 32%)	9,600
Deferral of 2011 unrealized gain ($600,000 × 55% × 32%)	(105,600)
Equity income in Soupy Company	$ 10,400

10.	**D**	Cost of purchase at January 1, 2010	$ 4,600,000
		+ Equity in Soupy Net Income, 2010	39,200
		+ Equity in Soupy Net Income, 2011	10,400
		− 2010 Dividend (500,000 × 32%)	(160,000)
		− 2011 Dividend (500,000 × 32%)	(160,000)
		= Investment in Soupy, December 31, 2011	$ 4,329,600

11.   B

12.   A

13.   C   Investments required to be consolidated (the investor has control) cannot be presented at fair value (SFAS 159).

Answers to Brief Essay Questions

1.   The investor should report any amortization arising out of an equity method investment in another company as an adjustment of its *Equity in Investee Income* account.

2.   There are several circumstances that, when present, can indicate that a less-than-20% investor has the ability to exercise *significant influence* over the investee. Included in those circumstances are:

- Investor representation on the board of directors of the investee.
- Investor participation in the policy-making process of the investee.
- Material intra-entity transactions.
- Interchange of managerial personnel.
- Technological dependency.
- Extent of ownership by the investor in relation to the size and concentration of other ownership interests in the investee.

3.   Several conditions exist that would prevent the use of the equity method of accounting when stock ownership exceeds 20%. *FASB Interpretation 35* states that the equity method is not appropriate for investments that have any of the following characteristics regardless of the investor's degree of ownership because the investor is unable to exercise significant influence over the investee:

- An agreement exists between investor and investee whereby the investor surrenders significant rights as a shareholder.
- A concentration of ownership operates the investee without regard for the views of the investor.
- The investor attempts but fails to obtain representation on the investee's board of directors.

Further, the presence of a majority stockholder (50% or greater) would generally preclude any significant influence on the investor's part. In addition, the oversight of a government authority that exercises control or influence can negate any influence the investor might have. Finally, any documentation or contractual relationship that precludes the ability of the investor to exercise significant influence over the investee would mean the equity method could not be used to account for the investment.

4. Goodwill is the excess of an investment's cost over the fair market value of the identifiable net assets acquired. Goodwill can only be recorded following a business acquisition, when a value can be assigned. In addition, Goodwill is never amortized, in accordance with SFAS No. 142.

5. A company can report equity method investments at fair value by making an irrevocable election to do so under the fair value reporting option in SFAS 159. The fair value election was first available for financial reporting in 2008.

Solutions to Problems

1. Analysis of the purchase price:

Price paid to acquire a 25% interest (80,000 × $4.20)	$ 336,000
Book value of the interest acquired ($1,210,000 × 25%)	(302,500)
Goodwill — excess of cost over fair market value	$ 33,500

    A. Note: All investments in the stock of other companies should be recorded at historical cost.

Investment in Q-Corp	336,000	
Cash		336,000
To record the investment in Q-Corp		

    B. Note: The presence of one of Pees' managers on the board of directors of Q-Corp is an indication that Pees has the ability to exercise significant influence over Q-Corp. Therefore, the equity method of accounting is appropriate for this investment.

Cash	12,000	
Investment in Q-Corp		12,000
To record the receipt of dividends of $.15 per share		

Investment in Q-Corp	15,000	
Equity in Q-Corp's Income		15,000
To recognize Pees's share of Q-Corp's net income		

    C.

Cost	$ 336,000
Investment income ($60,000 × 25%)	15,000
Dividends received (80,000 × $.15)	(12,000)
Year-end balance in Investment in Q-Corp	$ 339,000

2. Goodwill and the ending balance in Clark's *Investment in Lois, Inc.* are calculated as follows:

    ### Goodwill Computation

	%	BV		Useful Life	Amortization
Clark's Cost			2,800,000		
Q-Corp 's Book Value	45.00%	5,000,000	2,250,000		
Difference			550,000		
Patent	45.00%	1,200,000	540,000	5	108,000
Goodwill			10,000	N/A	-
Total Amortization					108,000

Computation of Year-end Investment Account Balance:

Cost		$2,800,000
Equity in Lois Company's Net Income:		
Clark's share of Net Income ($860,000 × 45%)	$387,000	
Amortization of Lois's Patent (see above)	(108,000)	279,000
Dividends paid by Lois ($400,000 × 45%)		(180,000)
Year-end balance in Investment in Lois Company		$2,899,000

3.

Selling price of inventory	$500,000
Cost of inventory	(360,000)
Profit	$140,000

Year-end remaining inventory	$160,000
Mark-up % ($140,000 ÷ $500,000)	× 28%
Profit in inventory	$ 44,800
Toy Corp.'s ownership percentage	× 30%
Profit to be deferred	$ 13,440

A. Equity in TPW's Net Income 13,400
      Investment in TPW Corp. 13,400
      To record deferred profit

B. Investment in TPW Corp. 13,400
      Equity in TPW Net Income 13,400
      To reverse profit deferral from 2010

Chapter 2

Consolidation of Financial Information

Chapter Outline

Standards Mentioned in This Chapter (Note: U.S. standards are incorporated into the FASB Accounting Standards Codification – Business Combinations, Topic 805 and Consolidation, Topic 810):
- **IFRS 3,** *Business Combinations*
- **SFAS No. 141R,** *Business Combinations*
- **SFAS No. 157,** *Fair Value Measurements*
- **SFAS No. 160,** *Noncontrolling Interests and Consolidated Financial Statements*

I. *LO1* **Expansion through Corporate Takeovers** – the combining of two or more businesses into a single entity under common management and ownership control occurs frequently in today's business world.

    Reasons for Firms to Combine Include:

    A.   Business combinations can be part of an overall managerial strategy to maximize shareholder value.

    B.   Many business combinations share one or more of the following characteristics that potentially enhance profitability:

        1.   Vertical integration of one firm's output and another firm's distribution or further processing.

        2.   Cost savings through elimination of duplicate facilities and staff.

        3.   Quick entry for new and existing products into domestic and foreign markets.

        4.   Economies of scale allowing greater efficiency and negotiating power.

        5.   The ability to access financing at rates that are more attractive. As a firm's size increases, negotiating power with financial institutions can also increase.

        6.   Diversification of business risk.

    C.   The principal motivation for many business combinations can be traced to an increasingly competitive environment.

II. *LO2* **The Consolidation Process** – the consolidation of financial information into a single set of statements becomes necessary when the business combination of two or more companies creates a single economic entity.

A. *LO3* **Business Combinations – Creating a Single Economic Entity** – a business combination refers to a transaction or other event in which an acquirer obtains *control* over one or more businesses.

Combinations are formed by a variety of transactions or events:

1. **Statutory Merger** – A business combination in which only one of the original companies continues to exist.

    a. **Asset acquisition**: One company acquires the assets (and often the liabilities) of a second company. The second company then dissolves, ceasing to exist.

    b. **Capital stock acquisition**: One company acquires the capital stock of a second company. The second company's assets and liabilities are transferred to the acquiring company, and the acquired company is dissolved (but often remains as a division of the acquiring company).

2. **Statutory Consolidation** – Two or more companies transfer either their net assets or their capital stock to a newly formed corporation.

    a. Both of the original companies are dissolved.

    b. The term "consolidation" is used here as a legal term, and should not be confused with the use of "consolidation" when referring to the accounting process of combining the financial information of two companies.

3. **Acquisition of more than 50% of the Voting Stock** – A company acquires enough equity interest in a second company to exercise control over it. (Usually this is > 50%.)

    a. Both companies continue to exist. Separate incorporation allows the acquired company to take advantage of any accrued intangible benefits as well as to enhance its potential market value as a standalone entity.

    b. The controlled company is referred to as the subsidiary.

    c. The company holding the controlling interest is referred to as the parent.

    d. Each company maintains a separate accounting system.

4. **Control through ownership of variable interests**

    a. A sponsoring firm creates an entity, often referred to as a *variable interest entity* (VIE), to engage in a specific activity.

    b. The acquired company remains in existence as a separate entity – often as a trust or partnership.

    c. Control is exercised through contractual arrangements with the sponsor, referred to as the *primary beneficiary*, rather than through equity control.

     d.   Prior to 2004, a VIE could be excluded from consolidation when the sponsor owned less than a controlling equity interest, even though control was effectively achieved through other means. This allowed *off-balance-sheet financing* for the sponsoring firm.

B.   **Consolidation of Financial Information**

    1.   The objectives of consolidation are straightforward – the asset, liability, equity, revenue and expense accounts of the companies are combined.

    2.   Reciprocal accounts and intra-entity transactions must be adjusted or eliminated to ensure that all reported balances represent the single entity.

    3.   Procedures vary significantly depending on the legal format used to create the business combination.

        a.   When the acquired company is dissolved, only one accounting consolidation occurs. This consolidation is on the date of the combination.

        b.   When the acquired company is not dissolved and both the controlling company and the acquired company continue to exist as legal entities, no permanent consolidation is made. The consolidation process is done on a worksheet each time the reporting entity prepares financial statements for external reporting purposes.

III. *LO4* **Financial Reporting for Business Combinations – Acquisition Method**

    A.   The fundamental characteristic of any asset acquisition is a change in ownership.

    B.   Fair value is the measurement attribute used to recognize aspects of a business combination. Fair values for both the items exchanged and received can enter into the acquirer's accounting valuation of the acquired firm.

    C.   Applying the acquisition method involves recognizing and measuring:

        1.   The consideration transferred for the acquired business.

        2.   The separately identified assets acquired, liabilities assumed and any noncontrolling interest.

        3.   Goodwill or gain from a bargain purchase.

    D.   **Consideration Transferred for the Acquired Business**

        1.   The fair value of the consideration transferred, including cash, securities and other property is the starting point in valuing a business combination.

        2.   *Fair value* is defined as "the price that would be received to sell an asset or paid to transfer a liability in an orderly transaction between market participants at the measurement date" (SFAS 157).

3. *Contingent consideration* is sometimes negotiated as part of the acquisition. It is treated as part of the fair value of the consideration transferred, consistent with the fair value measurement attribute. Determining the fair value of contingent consideration typically involves probability and risk assessments based on circumstances on the acquisition date as well as the time value of money.

E. **Fair Values of the Assets Acquired, Liabilities Assumed, and Noncontrolling Interest**

1. The fair value of identifiable assets acquired and liabilities assumed in the business combination are recognized and measured at their acquisition-date fair values, with only a few exceptions.

2. Deciding on acquisition-date fair values of individual assets and liabilities is challenging because there is typically only one overall valuation amount (the consideration transferred).

3. Therefore, the overall fair value must be allocated across acquired assets and liabilities.

4. Three valuation techniques are typically employed to estimate fair values for individual items:

   a. *Market approach* – fair values are estimated using other market transactions involving similar assets or liabilities. This approach is used for marketable securities and some tangible assets with established markets as well as many liabilities.

   b. *Income approach* – fair values are estimated using estimated future cash flows discounted to reflect the time value of money. This approach is often useful for estimating the fair value of intangible assets and acquired in-process research and development.

   c. *Cost approach* – fair values are estimated using replacement cost (less the effects of obsolescence). This approach is often used for tangible assets such as property, plant and equipment.

F. **Goodwill and Gains on Bargain Purchases**

1. Goodwill is an asset representing the future economic benefits arising in a business combination that are not individually identified and separately recognized.

2. For combinations resulting in 100% ownership by the acquirer, goodwill is the excess of consideration transferred over the collective fair values of the net identifiable assets acquired and liabilities assumed.

3. If the collective fair values of the net identifiable assets acquired and liabilities assumed exceed the consideration transferred, the acquirer recognizes a "gain on bargain purchase." In this case, the fair value of the net assets acquired becomes the valuation basis.

IV. **Procedures for Consolidating Financial Information**

    A. *LO5, LO6* **Acquisition Method when *Dissolution* Takes Place.**

        1. **Consideration Transferred = Net Fair Value of Assets Acquired & Liabilities Assumed**

            a. The assets and liabilities being acquired are recorded by the buyer at fair value on the date of acquisition, and a consolidation entry is made directly in the financial records of the surviving company.

            b. Revenue, expense, dividend, and equity accounts are not recorded.

        2. **Consideration Transferred > Net Fair Value of Assets Acquired & Liabilities Assumed**

            a. All of the acquired company's identifiable assets and liabilities are consolidated at fair market value.

            b. The excess is allocated to an unidentifiable asset known as goodwill.

        3. **Consideration Transferred < Net Fair Value of Assets Acquired & Liabilities Assumed**

            a. If the consideration transferred is less than the total fair market value, a *bargain purchase* exists.

            b. Bargain purchases most often occur in forced or distressed sales.

            c. The assets acquired and liabilities assumed are recorded at their individual fair values.

            d. The excess of the fair value acquired and the consideration transferred is recorded as a *Gain on Bargain Purchase*. This gain is recognized in the income statement in the acquisition period.

        4. **Related Expenses of Business Combinations**

            a. **Direct combination expense**s such as accounting, legal, investment banking and appraisal fees are expensed as incurred.

            b. **Indirect combination expenses** such as internal costs of allocated secretarial or managerial time are expensed as incurred.

            c. **Amounts incurred to register and issue securities** reduce the value assigned to the fair value of the securities issued (typically debited to additional paid-in capital).

B. *LO7* **The Acquisition Method When** *Separate Incorporation* **is Maintained**.

1. Many consolidation procedures are the same as when dissolution takes place. Fair value remains the basis for initial consolidation of the subsidiary's net assets.

2. Since dissolution does not occur, independent record keeping is maintained by each company.

3. A worksheet and consolidation entries are used to simulate the consolidation process when preparing consolidated financial statements.

4. Consolidation entries are made only on the worksheet and do not actually change the books of either the parent company or the subsidiary.

5. The fair value of consideration transferred and the net fair value of assets acquired and liabilities assumed are determined as of the acquisition date, as is any resulting goodwill or a gain on bargain purchase.

6. Worksheet steps on acquisition date:

   a. A fair value allocation schedule as of the acquisition date is prepared. Goodwill or a gain on bargain purchase may need to be recognized. See the Step 1 schedule in the book following Exhibit 2.6.

   b. Enter the acquisition date financials for the Parent and the Subsidiary in the first two columns of the consolidation worksheet. Pre-combination subsidiary revenues, expenses, and dividends are not included.

   c. **Entry S** – Make an entry on the worksheet to eliminate the subsidiary's beginning stockholders' equity accounts. (The **S** is a reference to **S**tockholder's equity.) The accounts to be eliminated (debited) include the subsidiary's Common Stock and Additional Paid-In Capital accounts, and the subsidiary's Retained Earnings balance (after any pre-combination revenue, expense and dividend accounts have been closed).

   d. **Entry S** – Credit the *Investment in Subsidiary* account for the total of the subsidiary's stockholders' equity accounts (same as the net book value of the subsidiary).

   e. **Entry A** – (Allocations) removes (credits) any excess payment in the *Investment in Subsidiary* account and assigns it to the specific accounts indicated in the fair-value allocation schedule.

   f. Extend the account balances and adjustments across the worksheet into the Consolidated Totals column.

   g. Totals are now calculated vertically (vs. being extended across the columns) in the Consolidated Totals column.

> **(1)** Consolidated expenses are subtracted from consolidated revenues to arrive at consolidated net income. (On an acquisition-date worksheet, these figures are identical to the parent's figures.)
>
> **(2)** Consolidated net income is carried down the worksheet to the statement of retained earnings and used to compute the ending balance of retained earnings.
>
> **(3)** The ending balance of retained earnings is carried down to the retained earnings in the stockholders' equity portion of the balance sheet.

h. As of the acquisition date, after the worksheet entries are made:

> **(1)** The balance in the Investment account = 0.
>
> **(2)** The stockholders' equity accounts reflect the parent's balances only.
>
> **(3)** Consolidated assets = the book value of the parents assets + the fair value of the subsidiary's assets.

V. *LO8* Acquisition-Date Fair Value Allocations – Additional Issues

A. Intangibles

1. Intangible assets may be the largest proportion of the fair value of an acquired firm. Intangible assets are nonfinancial assets that lack physical substance.

2. Two essential attributes to determine whether to recognize an intangible asset:

a. Does the intangible asset arise from contractual or other legal rights?

b. Is the asset capable of being sold or otherwise separated from the acquired enterprise?

3. Examples of intangible assets to which excess cost can be allocated:

a. Trademarks and trade names

b. Internet domain names

c. Non-competition agreements

d. Customer lists

e. Books, magazines, other literary works

f. Musical works such as compositions, song lyrics, and advertising jingles

g. Pictures and photographs

h. Licensing, royalty, standstill agreements

i. Franchise agreements

j. Operating and broadcast rights

k. Use rights such as landing, drilling, water, air, mineral, timber cutting, and route authorities.

l. Patented and unpatented technology

m. Computer software

n. Databases

o. Trade secrets

A more complete list is shown in Exhibit 2.7 in the textbook.

4. Amounts assigned to goodwill should be those amounts that cannot be assigned to identifiable, separable intangible assets.

B. Pre-existing Goodwill on Subsidiary's Books

1. An acquired firm may have goodwill recorded on its books from a previous business combination. This pre-existing goodwill is not considered identifiable by the parent; therefore, it is simply ignored in allocating the purchase price.

2. Only the goodwill reflected in the business fair value of the current acquisition is brought forward in the financial reports of the consolidated entity.

C. Acquired In-Process Research and Development (IPR&D)

1. IPR&D acquired in a business combination is assigned a fair value and recognized as an asset.

2. Acquired IPR&D assets are considered indefinite-lived until the project is completed or abandoned. An indefinite-lived intangible asset is tested for impairment, but is not amortized until its useful life is determined to be no longer indefinite.

3. Research and development expenditures after the date of acquisition are expensed.

VI. Convergence Between U.S. and International Accounting Standards

A. SFAS 141R *"Business Combinations"*, SFAS 160 *"Noncontrolling Interests and Consolidated Financial Statements"* and IFRS 3 *"Business Combinations"* are the outcomes of a joint FASB and IASB project to develop a single high-quality standard that can be used for both domestic and cross-border financial reporting.

B. These statements effectively converged the international accounting for business combinations.

C. However, differences can result in noncontrolling interest valuations and other limited applications.

VII.   *LO9* **Legacy Methods of Accounting for Business Combinations**

   A.   **Background**.

     1.   Beginning in 2009, the acquisition method is used for new business combinations.

     2.   From 2002 – 2008, the purchase method was used exclusively for business combinations. For decades prior to this most consolidated financial statements used the purchase method, although some used the pooling of interests method.

     3.   The acquisition method is applied prospectively (for new business combinations), thus the purchase and pooling of interest methods continue to provide the basis for reporting for pre-2009 business combinations and will remain relevant for many years.

   B.   **The Purchase Method: An Application of the Cost Principal**

     1.   Prior to the recent emphasis on fair values, a basic accounting principal was to record transactions at cost. Thus, the acquisition cost of the new owners provided the valuation basis for the net assets acquired.

     2.   Differences from the fair-value acquisition method:

         a.   **Acquisition-Date Cost Allocations** – cost allocations made using the purchase method were based on the acquisition-date fair values of the acquired assets and liabilities. Also similar to the acquisition method was the assignment of any excess of cost over the sum of the net asset fair values to goodwill.

         b.   **Bargain Purchases** – under the purchase method, bargain purchases were not recognized as gains. Instead, certain long-term assets were recorded at amounts below their assessed fair values. An extraordinary gain on purchase was recorded only if these long-term assets were adjusted down to zero value.

         c.   **Direct Combination costs** were included in the cost basis for the acquired firm.

         d.   **Contingent consideration** obligations were accounted for as post-combination adjustments to the purchase cost (or stockholder's equity if the contingency involved the parent's equity share value) upon resolution of the contingency.

         e.   **Acquired In-Process Research and Development (IPR&D)** – acquired IPR&D was immediately expensed, consistent with the treatment for ongoing R&D.

   C.   **The Pooling of Interests Method: Continuity of Previous Ownership**

     1.   Prior to 2002 both the purchase and pooling of interest methods were allowed.

     2.   Strict criteria were required in order to use the pooling method.

     3.   The criteria had two overriding objectives:

         a.   To ensure the complete fusion of the two organizations, one company had to obtain substantially all (90% or more) of the voting stock of the other.

b. To prevent managers from engaging in purchase transactions and reporting them as poolings of interest (usually to increase reported earnings).

4. A business combination accounted for as a pooling of interests in the past continues to be accounted for as a pooling of interests.

5. The Pooling of Interest Method Applied

    a. In theory, a *pooling* involves *the uniting of the ownership interests of two or more companies* by the exchange of voting shares so that *continuity of ownership* is maintained.

    b. The book values of the assets and liabilities of both companies were combined into the book values reported by the combined entity. Fair values were ignored.

    c. Previously unrecognized intangibles continue to be reported at a zero value.

    d. Because of the combination of book values, no new goodwill was recorded.

    e. The revenue and expense accounts were combined *retrospectively* as well as prospectively.

    f. Using book values under the pooling method typically resulted in a smaller asset values, producing lower depreciation and amortization expenses, and therefore higher future net income.

    g. Financial ratios such as Net Income/Total Assets were dramatically inflated. The denominator is understated by not recognizing certain intangibles and the fair values of assets. The numerator is overstated by lower depreciation and amortization expenses.

Multiple Choice Questions

1. South Port, Inc. and Wet Dock Corporation were joined into a new company called Sowet, Inc. Both companies transferred their assets and liabilities to the new company and then both companies were dissolved. Which of the following terms best describes this event?

   A. Statutory Consolidation
   B. Statutory Merger
   C. Acquisition of Majority Interest
   D. Business Combination

2. How would each of the following types of costs be accounted for under the Purchase method?

	Direct Combination Fees	Stock Issuance Costs
A.	Increase Acquisition Cost	Expense as incurred
B.	Increase Paid-In Capital	Increase Acquisition Cost
C.	Expense as Incurred	Decrease Paid-In Capital
D.	Increase Acquisition Cost	Decrease Paid-In Capital
E.	Decrease Acquisition Cost	Decrease Paid-In Capital

3. Using the Acquisition Method, how would each of the following types of costs be accounted for?

	Direct Combination Fees	Stock Issuance Costs
A.	Increase Acquisition Cost	Expense as incurred
B.	Increase Paid-In Capital	Increase Acquisition Cost
C.	Expense as Incurred	Decrease Paid-In Capital
D.	Increase Acquisition Cost	Decrease Paid-In Capital
E.	Decrease Acquisition Cost	Decrease Paid-In Capital

4. In accounting for a business combination, a *bargain purchase* exists when

   A. Consideration transferred > book value of net assets acquired.
   B. Fair value of net assets acquired > consideration transferred.
   C. Fair value of net assets acquired < book value.
   D. Fair value of net assets acquired > book value.
   E. Fair value of net assets acquired < consideration transferred.

5. On the consolidated financial statements of a business combination accounted for as an acquisition, which one of the following is the appropriate basis for valuing fixed assets of a wholly-owned subsidiary on the date of acquisition?

   A. Fair value.
   B. Book value as shown on the books of the subsidiary.
   C. Book value plus any excess of purchase price over book value of the acquired assets and liabilities.
   D. Historical cost as shown on the books of the subsidiary.
   E. Current carrying value.

6. Generally, what was done with In-Process Research and Development when using the purchase method?

    A.   Write off the accumulated costs as an expense on the consolidation worksheet.
    B.   Reduce Goodwill by the fair value of the capitalized IPR&D.
    C.   Allocate a portion of the purchase price to an expense item equal to the fair value of the IPR&D.
    D.   Record the fair value of the IPR&D as an Extraordinary Item.
    E.   Record the fair value of the IPR&D as an asset.

7. Shaw Company has the following account balances:

Cash	$ 450,000
Receivables	600,000
Inventory	450,000
Land	200,000
Building — net	550,000
Liabilities	350,000
Common stock	1,100,000
Additional paid-in capital	150,000
Retained earnings	650,000

Shaw's land has a fair value of $350,000 while its building has a fair value of $600,000. Shaw's liabilities have a fair value of $325,000. Brooks Company obtains all of the outstanding shares of Shaw for $2,300,000 cash. Shaw has no intangible assets. In the financial statements prepared immediately after the business combination, what is the amount of goodwill?

    A. $175,000
    B. $225,000
    C. $200,000
    D. $400,000
    E. $ 0

Items 8 through 10 are based on the following information:

On December 31, Sam Company was acquired by Paul Company. In carrying out the business combination, Paul Company issued 60,000 shares of its $10 par value common stock, with a fair market value of $15 per share, for all of Sam Company's outstanding common stock. The business fair value was equal to the fair value of the net assets acquired. The stockholders' equity section of the two companies immediately before the business combination was:

	Paul Company	Sam Company
Common Stock	$ 500,000	$ 400,000
Additional Paid-in Capital	200,000	100,000
Retained Earnings	300,000	200,000

8. On the December 31 consolidated balance sheet, the *Additional Paid-In Capital* account should be reported at:

    A. $100,000.
    B. $200,000.
    C. $300,000.
    D. $400,000.
    E. $500,000.

9. Building on the previous question, assume that Paul Company included contingent consideration in the deal. Paul Company agrees to pay an additional $100,000 to Sam Company's shareholders in three years, if Sam Company achieves its revenue projections. The present value of the $100,000 payment at a discount rate of 4% is $88,710. There is a 75% chance that Sam Company's estimates will prove correct. Using the Acquisition Method, what would Paul Company record as the acquisition cost on the date of acquisition?

    A. $ 988,710.00
    B. $ 966,532.50
    C. $ 983,532.50
    D. $1,005,710.00
    E. $1,000,000.00

10. Assume that in addition to the 60,000 shares of stock that Paul Company issued to acquire Sam Company, Paul Company also incurred $17,000 in direct combination costs and $23,000 in costs related to the issuance of stock. Using the acquisition method, the *Additional Paid-In Capital* account should be reported at:

    A. $100,000.
    B. $200,000.
    C. $460,000.
    D. $477,000.
    E. $500,000.

11. Generally, what should be done with In-Process Research and Development when using the acquisition method?

    A. Write off the accumulated costs as an expense on the consolidation worksheet.
    B. Allocate a portion of the consideration transferred to an asset equal to the fair value of the IPR&D.
    C. Allocate a portion of the consideration transferred to an expense item equal to the fair value of the IPR&D.
    D. Record the fair value of the IPR&D as an Extraordinary Item.

Brief Essay Questions

1. What is a business combination? Distinguish between a statutory merger and a statutory consolidation.

2. How does the treatment of contingent consideration differ under the Purchase Method (SFAS 141) and the Acquisition Method (SFAS 141R)?

3. How is the amount of goodwill at the acquisition date determined? Explain.

4. In preparing the consolidated balances for a parent company and its subsidiary, what are the major steps in the process?

Problems

1. On January 1, Chester Inc. acquires 100% of Festus Corp.'s outstanding common stock by issuing 100,000 shares of Chester's $1 par value common voting stock. In addition, Chester paid $1,800,000 in cash. Chester also incurred direct combination costs of $350,000 and stock issuance costs of $650,000.

   On January 1, Chester's voting common stock had a market value of $38.50 per share. Festus' voting common shares were selling for $12.50 per share. Festus' balances on the acquisition date, just prior to acquisition are listed below.

	Book Value	Market Value
Cash	$ 530,000	$ 530,000
Receivables	610,000	650,000
Inventory	400,000	400,000
Land	600,000	700,000
Building (net)	500,000	580,000
Equipment (net)	375,000	300,000
Payables	(280,000)	(280,000)
Common Stock, $1 par value	(1,800,000)	(2,250,000)
Paid-In Capital	(660,000)	
R/E (January 1)	(275,000)	

   Required:

   A. Using the Purchase Method, compute the value of Chester's investment account on January 1, the date of acquisition.

   B. Assume that Chester allocates $160,000 of the purchase price to a database that was created by Festus, but not previously recorded on Festus's books. Using the Purchase Method, compute the value of the Goodwill account on the date of acquisition.

2. Using the same numbers in the problem above, answer the following two questions:

   Required:

   A. Using the Acquisition Method, compute the value of Chester's investment account on the date of acquisition, January 1.

   B. Assume that Chester allocates $160,000 of the purchase price to a database that was created by Festus, but not previously recorded on Festus's books. Using the Acquisition Method, compute the value of the Goodwill account on January 1, the date of acquisition.

3. In a business combination occurring on April 1, Big Company issued 50,000 shares of its $10 par value common stock in exchange for all of the outstanding common stock of Bitty Company. On that date Big's Common stock had a market value of $18.75 per share. In addition, Big incurred $235,000 in stock issuance costs. The following information was available concerning the two companies immediately before the acquisition:

	Big Company	Bitty Company
Common stock, $10 par value	$ 1,000,000	
Common stock, $5 par value		$ 500,000
Additional paid-in capital	$ 30,000	$ 50,000
Retained Earnings	$ 170,000	$ 120,000

Required:

A. Using the purchase method, determine the amount of the consolidated common stock, additional paid-in capital, and retained earnings immediately after the combination.

B. How would your answer to part (A) above change using the Acquisition Method?

4. West Corp. acquires 100% of Barns Construction on July 1. The acquisition involves West issuing 75,000 shares of its $10 par value, voting common stock in exchange for all of Barns Construction's outstanding voting common stock. In addition, West Corp. agrees to pay an additional $100,000 on July 1 of the following year, if Barns Construction is the winning bidder on a large state construction contract (the present value of the $100,000 payment at an interest rate of 6% is $94,190). There is a 50% chance of receiving the contract.

There are $20,000 in direct combination costs and $45,000 in stock issuance costs. On the acquisition date, West's common shares are trading for $32.50 per share. The balances for West Corporation and Barns Construction just prior to the combination are as follows:

Account	West Corporation	Barns Construction BV	Barns Construction FMV
Cash	$ 260,000	$ 175,000	$ 175,000
Accounts Receivable	850,000	265,000	265,000
Inventory	625,000	300,000	325,000
Land	1,700,000	500,000	780,000
Buildings	8,500,000		
Building #1		120,000	250,000
Building #2		170,000	340,000
Equipment (net)	2,650,000	1,295,500	850,500
Accounts Payable	(215,000)	(275,000)	(275,000)
Notes Payable	(800,000)	(400,000)	(400,000)
Common Stock	(5,000,000)	(1,000,000)	
Paid-In-Capital	(7,300,000)	(250,000)	
Retained Earnings, June 30	(950,000)	(900,500)	
Revenues	(13,300,000)		
Expenses	12,980,000		

Required:

A. Using the Purchase Method, prepare the consolidation worksheet for West and Barns as of the July 1 acquisition date.

B. Using the Acquisition Method, prepare the consolidation worksheet for West and Barns as of the July 1 acquisition date.

Solutions to Multiple Choice Questions

1. A

2. D

3. C

4. B

5. A

6. C

7. A

Purchase price of Shaw Company common stock	$ 2,300,000
Book value of Shaw Company	(1,900,000)
Cost in excess of book value	400,000
Excess assigned to:	
Undervalued land	(150,000)
Undervalued building	(50,000)
Overvalued liabilities	(25,000)
Goodwill	$ 175,000

8. E   Sam Company's Paid-In Capital is eliminated in the consolidation process. Paul Company's Paid-In Capital account consists of the $200,000 in the account prior to the issuance of stock. The issuance of 60,000 shares at a fair market value $5 in excess of par value results in an additional $300,000 being added to the account.

9. B   Using the Acquisition Method, Paul Company should include the fair value of the stock issued on the acquisition date (60,000 shares× $15 per share = $900,000) and the fair value contingent consideration on the date of acquisition, adjusted for expected value ($88,710 × 75% = $66,532.50).

10. D   Sam Company's Paid-In Capital is eliminated in the consolidation process. Paul Company's Paid-In Capital account consists of the $200,000 in the account prior to the issuance of stock. The issuance of 60,000 shares at a fair market value $5 in excess of par value results in an additional $300,000 being added to the account. The stock issuance costs of $23,000 are treated as a reduction of Paul Company's Additional Paid-In Capital account, thus Additional Paid-In Capital is $477,000.

11. B

Answers to Brief Essay Questions

1. A business combination occurs when two or more companies join together under common control. A business combination results in the creation of a single economic entity. The consolidation of financial information into a single set of financial records is required whenever one of the companies in the group directly or indirectly has a controlling financial in the other enterprises.

    In a statutory merger, the acquiring company absorbs the acquired company so that only one company (the acquiring company) survives as a legally incorporated business. In a statutory consolidation, the net assets or capital stock of two or more companies are transferred to a newly formed corporation. Only the newly formed company exists as a legal entity after the business combination.

2. Under the Purchase Method, contingent consideration is not accounted included in the determination of acquisition cost. Such costs are recognized as post-acquisition adjustments when the contingency is finally resolved. Under the Acquisition Method, the fair value of the contingent consideration is included in the acquisition cost. The determination of fair value includes consideration of the time-value of money and an estimate of the likelihood that the contingency will be resolved in favor of the subsidiary.

3. Goodwill is defined as the excess of the consideration transferred over the fair value of the net assets acquired. The amount allocated to goodwill should be a residual allocation that represents the amount of the purchase price that cannot be attributed to any other identifiable asset.

4. The major steps in preparing the consolidated balances for a parent company and its subsidiary are:

    - Enter the final adjusted trial balance amounts for the parent company and the subsidiary company on the worksheet.
    - **Entry S** – Make an entry on the worksheet to eliminate the subsidiary's stockholders' equity accounts as of the beginning of the most recent period of ownership and credit the *Investment in Subsidiary* account for the book value of the subsidiary's net assets.
      Entry A – removes (credits) any excess payment in the *Investment in Subsidiary* account and assigns it to the specific accounts indicated in the fair-value allocation schedule.
    - Subtract consolidated expenses from consolidated revenues to arrive at Net Income. Compute the ending Retained Earnings balance from the calculated Net Income, beginning Retained Earnings and dividends.
    - Combine the remaining balances and adjustments across the worksheet to determine the consolidated balances.

Solutions to Problems

1. **A.** Under the Purchase Method, the value in the investment account (Chester's Cost of the acquisition of Festus) is computed as follows:

Cash Paid by Chester			$ 1,800,000
Fair Value of Common Stock Issued by Chester:	100,000	shares	
	$ 38.50	per share	3,850,000
Direct Combination Costs			350,000
Chester's Cost of Investment			$ 6,000,000

B.   Under the Purchase Method, Chester's Goodwill computation is as follows:

Chester's Cost			6,000,000
Portion of Festus' Book Value			
Purchased by Chester	100%	2,735,000	2,735,000
Difference to be allocated			3,265,000
Inventory	100%	40,000	40,000
Land	100%	100,000	100,000
Building	100%	80,000	80,000
Equipment	100%	(75,000)	(75,000)
Database	100%	160,000	160,000
Goodwill			2,960,000

2.   **A.**   Under the Acquisition Method, the value of the investment account (at acquisition-date, the fair value of the consideration transferred by Chester) is computed as follows:

Cash paid by Chester			$ 1,800,000
Fair Value of Common Stock			
Issued by Chester:	100,000	shares	
	$ 38.50	per share	3,850,000
Chester's Investment account balance			$ 5,650,000

Under the Acquisition Method, Direct Costs are not part of the computation of the acquisition price.

B.   Under the Acquisition Method, Chester's Goodwill computation is as follows:

Fair value of consideration transferred by Chester		5,650,000
Festus' Book Value		2,735,000
Excess of fair value over book value		2,915,000
Allocations made to specific accounts:		
Inventory	40,000	
Land	100,000	
Building	80,000	
Equipment	(75,000)	
Database	160,000	305,000
Goodwill		2,610,000

3.   **A.**   Bitty Company's Common Stock, Additional Paid-in Capital, and Retained Earnings are all eliminated during the consolidation process. Big Company's Common Stock will increase for the number of shares issued × the par value (50,000 shares × $10 par value per share). Big Company's Additional Paid-In Capital will increase by the number of shares issued × the excess of market value over par value (50,000 shares × $8.75) per share. In addition, Big Company will charge the $235,000 in stock issuance costs to the Additional Paid-In Capital account. Big Company's Retained Earnings will not change.

Consolidated Equity Balances:

Common stock	$1,500,000
Additional paid-in capital	232,500
Retained earnings	170,000
Total	$1,092,500

B. There is no difference between the Acquisition Method and the Purchase Method with regard to determining the consolidated balances for Common Stock, Additional Paid-In Capital, or Beginning Retained Earnings.

The only difference that might have occurred in this case would be if there was a contingent consideration involving Big Company's common stock. In such a case, the Acquisition method would adjust Common Stock and Addition Paid-In Capital for the equity-based contingent consideration, whereas the Purchase Method would make no recognition of the contingent consideration until such time in the future where the contingent consideration is actually paid.

4. A. The consolidation Spreadsheet for West and Barns using the purchase method appears as follows:

Purchase Method

Account	West Corp.	Barns Construction	DR	CR	Consolidated Balance
Income Statement					
Revenues	(13,300,000)				(13,300,000)
Expenses	12,980,000				12,980,000
Net Income	**(320,000)**				**(320,000)**
Statement of Retained Earnings					
Ret. Earnings 6/30	(950,000)				(950,000)
Net Income	(320,000)		-	-	(320,000)
Dividends paid	-				-
Ret. Earnings 7/1	**(1,270,000)**				**(1,270,000)**
Balance Sheet					
Cash	$ 195,000	$ 175,000			$ 370,000
Accounts Rec.	850,000	265,000			1,115,000
Inventory	625,000	300,000	25,000		950,000
Land	1,700,000	500,000	280,000		2,480,000
Buildings (net)	8,500,000	290,000	300,000		9,090,000
Equipment (net)	2,650,000	1,295,500		445,000	3,500,500
Investment	2,457,500			2,457,500	-
Goodwill			147,000		147,000
Total Assets	**16,977,500**	**2,825,500**			**17,652,500**
Accounts Payable	(215,000)	(275,000)			(490,000)
Notes Payable	(800,000)	(400,000)			(1,200,000)
Common Stock	(5,750,000)	(1,000,000)	1,000,000		(5,750,000)
Paid-in-Capital	(8,942,500)	(250,000)	250,000		(8,942,500)
Ret. Earnings 7/1	(1,270,000)	(900,500)	900,500		(1,270,000)
Total Liab. And Eq.	**(16,977,500)**	**(2,825,500)**			**(17,652,500)**

Consolidating entries and computations are shown on the following page.

The computation of West's initial acquisition cost using the purchase method is as follows:

Cash Paid by West			$ -
+ Fair Value of Common Stock			
Issued by West:	75,000	shares	
	$ 32.50	per share	2,437,500
Direct Combination Costs			20,000
West's Cost of Investment			$ 2,457,500

Goodwill is computed as follows:

West's cost of investment			2,457,500
Barn's Book Value	100%	2,150,500	2,150,500
Difference to be allocated			307,000
Allocations:			
Inventory		25,000	
Land		280,000	
Building #1		130,000	
Building #2		170,000	
Equipment		(445,000)	160,000
Goodwill			147,000

Consolidation Entries on the Acquisition Date

Date	Accounts	Debit	Credit
S	Common Stock - Barns	1,000,000	
	Paid-In Capital - Barns	250,000	
	Retained Earnings	900,500	
	Investment in Barns		2,150,500
A	Inventory	25,000	
	Land	280,000	
	Building #1	130,000	
	Building #2	170,000	
	Goodwill	147,000	
	Equipment		445,000
	Investment in Barns		307,000

Note that after posting the consolidation entries to the consolidation spreadsheet, the Investment in Barns account has a zero balance. In addition, on the date of acquisition, the amounts in Entry A can come directly from the Goodwill Computation Worksheet.

B. The Consolidation Spreadsheet for West and Barns using the acquisition method appears as follows:

Acquisition Method

Account	West Corp.	Barns Construction	DR	CR	Consolidated Balance
Income Statement					
Revenues	(13,300,000)				(13,300,000)
Expenses	13,000,000				13,000,000
Net Income	**(300,000)**				**(300,000)**
Statement of Retained Earnings					
Ret. Earnings 6/30	(950,000)				(950,000)
Net Income	(300,000)				(300,000)
Ret. Earnings 7/1	**(1,250,000)**				**(1,250,000)**
Balance Sheet					
Cash	$ 195,000	$ 175,000			$ 370,000
Accounts Rec.	850,000	265,000			1,115,000
Inventory	625,000	300,000	25,000		950,000
Land	1,700,000	500,000	280,000		2,480,000
Buildings (net)	8,500,000	290,000	300,000		9,090,000
Equipment (net)	2,650,000	1,295,500		445,000	3,500,500
Investment	2,484,595			2,484,595	-
Goodwill			174,095		174,095
Total Assets	**17,004,595**	**2,825,500**			**17,679,595**
Accounts Payable	(215,000)	(275,000)			(490,000)
Contingent Liability	(47,095)				(47,095)
Notes Payable	(800,000)	(400,000)			(1,200,000)
Common Stock	(5,750,000)	(1,000,000)	1,000,000		(5,750,000)
Paid-in-Capital	(8,942,500)	(250,000)	250,000		(8,942,500)
Retained Earnings	(1,250,000)	(900,500)	900,500		(1,250,000)
Total Liab. & Equity	**(17,004,595)**	**(2,825,500)**			**(17,679,595)**

The computation of West's initial acquisition cost is as follows:

Cash Paid by West			$	-
+ Fair Value of Common Stock				
Issued by West:	75,000	shares		
	$ 32.50	per share		2,437,500
Fair Value of Contingent Consideration				47,095
West's Consideration transferred				$ 2,484,595

Consolidating entries are shown on the following page.

The fair value allocation and computation of Goodwill is as follows:

West's Consideration transferred			2,484,595
Barn's Book Value	100%	2,150,500	2,150,500
Excess of fair value over book value			334,095
Fair value allocations			
Inventory		25,000	
Land		280,000	
Building #1		130,000	
Building #2		170,000	
Equipment		(445,000)	160,000
Goodwill			174,095

Consolidation Entries on the Acquisition Date

Date	Accounts	Debit	Credit
S	Common Stock - Barns	1,000,000	
	Paid-In Capital - Barns	250,000	
	Retained Earnings	900,500	
	Investment in Barns		2,150,500
A	Inventory	25,000	
	Land	280,000	
	Building #1	130,000	
	Building #2	170,000	
	Goodwill	174,095	
	Equipment		445,000
	Investment in Barns		334,095

Note that after posting the consolidation entries to the consolidation spreadsheet, the Investment in Barns account has a zero balance. In addition, on the date of acquisition, the amounts in Entry A can come directly from the acquisition-date fair value allocation schedule.

The Acquisition Method requires that the present value of the contingent consideration be added to the acquisition cost and that a corresponding "Contingent Consideration Liability" be added to the parent's balance sheet.

Chapter 3

Consolidations – Subsequent to the Date of Acquisition

Chapter Outline

Standards Mentioned in This Chapter:
- **FASB Concepts Statement No. 7,** *Using Cash Flow Information and Present Value in Accounting Measurements*
- **IAS 8,** *Operating Segments*
- **IAS 36,** *Impairment of Assets*
- **SEC Staff Accounting Bulletin No. 54,** *Application of "Push Down" Basis of Accounting in Financial Statements of Subsidiaries Acquired by Purchase*
- **SEC Staff Accounting Bulletin No. 73,** *"Push Down" Basis of Accounting for Parent Company Debt Related to Subsidiary Acquisitions*
- **SFAS No. 131,** *Disclosures about Segments of an Enterprise and Related Information*
- **SFAS No. 141R,** *Business Combinations* (replaces SFAS 141)
- **SFAS No. 142,** *Goodwill and Other Intangible Assets*

I. *LO1* **Consolidation — the Effects Created by the Passage of Time**

    A. This chapter examines consolidation procedures for periods after acquisition when separate incorporation of the subsidiary is maintained.

    B. A worksheet and consolidation entries continue to be used for preparing financial statements for the combined entity.

    C. Consolidation objectives remain the same, but additional complications are encountered.

        1. The parent must select an accounting method for its books to account for the relationship between the two companies. The method chosen affects the investment account balance and the income from the subsidiary recorded in its accounts.

        2. Regardless of the accounting method chosen,

            a. The parent's investment balance is eliminated on the worksheet so the subsidiary's actual assets and liabilities can be consolidated.

            b. The income figure accrued by the parent is excluded each period so the subsidiary's revenues and expenses can be included in the consolidated income statement.

    D. Objectives of the consolidation process:

        1. The subsidiary's assets and liabilities are adjusted to reflect the allocations originating from their acquisition-date fair values.

        2. The income effects (amortization) of these allocations are recognized.

        3. Reciprocal or intra-entity accounts are eliminated.

II. **LO2 Investment Accounting by the Acquiring Company**

   A. **Internal Investment Accounting Alternatives** — Consolidation of a subsidiary becomes necessary for *external* reporting whenever control exists; but, for *internal* record keeping, the parent has a choice of three alternatives:

      1. **Equity Method**

        a. Uses *full accrual accounting* in maintaining the investment account and the related income from the subsidiary.

        b. The investment account changes over time to recognize changes in the book value of the subsidiary (the parent's underlying equity).

          (1) Dividends received are recorded as a reduction of the *Investment* account.

          (2) The parent recognizes its share of the subsidiary's income in an account called *Equity in Subsidiary Earnings* and credits the *Investment* account.

          (3) Fair market value adjustments identified during the acquisition process are amortized, and charged to *Equity in Subsidiary Earnings*.

          (4) Unrealized gains on intra-entity transactions are deferred (Chapter 5).

          (5) Advantage: parent company accounts give a true representation of consolidation figures.

      2. **Initial Value Method** (formerly the cost method)

        a. Uses the *cash basis* for income recognition.

        b. Investment account always remains at the initial value recorded for the acquisition.

        c. Dividends received are recorded as dividend revenue.

        d. Income earned by the subsidiary and amortization of fair market value adjustments are not recorded.

        e. This method might be selected because the parent does not require an accrual-based income measure of subsidiary performance.

        f. Advantages: easy to apply and measures cash flows.

      3. **Partial Equity Method.**

        a. The investment account is adjusted over time for dividends received and the parent's share of the subsidiary's income, the same as the equity method.

        b. No other adjustments, including amortization of fair market value adjustments or deferral of unrealized gains are recognized. This differs from the equity method.

        c. Advantages: easier to apply than the full equity method, but earnings figures on the parent's books approximate consolidated totals.

B. *LO3* The parent's choice of accounting method does not affect the figures reported in the consolidated financial statements – the consolidated figures always reflect the equity method.

1. At the acquisition date, the investment account begins with the same amount.

2. The balances on the parent's books for the investment in subsidiary, income from subsidiary and retained earnings accounts differ based upon the method applied.

3. Because the investment and subsidiary income accounts are eliminated in the consolidation, the parent's accounting method for the investment does not affect the totals ultimately reported for the combined companies (under the equity method).

III. *LO4* **Subsequent Consolidation — Investment Recorded by the Equity Method**

A. The Allocation of Subsidiary Fair Values and Amortization schedules are used in several of the consolidation entries.

B. For a consolidation after the acquisition date, certain "*elimination*" procedures are required to avoid double counting of items related to the combination.

1. The *Investment in Subsidiary* account is eliminated so that the subsidiary's assets and liabilities can be added to the consolidation without double counting them.

2. The *Equity in Subsidiary Income* is eliminated so the subsidiary's revenue and expense accounts can be combined with the parent's accounts without double counting them.

3. Prior to posting any of the elimination entries to the consolidation worksheet, the parent updates its own records for the equity method adjustments to the investment account.

4. Elimination entries are posted ONLY to the consolidated worksheet, and do not impact the general ledger accounts of either company.

C. **Determination of Consolidated Totals** — the objectives of the consolidation process:

1. The subsidiary's assets and liabilities are adjusted to reflect their acquisition date fair-values, and amortization of the allocations is recognized due to the passage of time.

2. Reciprocal or intra-entity accounts such as receivables and payables are eliminated.

3. Consolidated totals can be determined without a worksheet:

   a. *Revenues* = parent + subsidiary revenues (since acquisition date if mid-year).

   b. *COGS and expenses* = Parent + subsidiary costs (since acquisition) + amortization of fair-value allocations. COGS is adjusted for intra-entity transactions such as sales of inventory between entities.

   c. *Equity in subsidiary earnings* = 0 as this account is eliminated.

   d. *Net income* = consolidated revenues minus consolidated expenses (including amortization).

   e. *Assets and liabilities* = parent + subsidiary book values + fair value allocations (as of the beginning of the year) less the current year's amortization.

   f. *Investment in subsidiary* = 0 as this account is eliminated.

   g. *Retained earnings, beginning balance* = parent book value (subsidiary account is eliminated in Entry S) (+- adjustments if the initial value or partial equity method is used by the parent).

h. *Retained earnings, end of the year* = consolidated retained earnings, beginning of the year + consolidated net income.

i. *Capital stock and additional paid-in capital* = parent balances only (subsidiary balances are eliminated).

D. Consolidation Worksheet

1. *Consolidation Entry S* eliminates the subsidiary's stockholders' equity accounts (as of the acquisition date, or the beginning of the period when other than the period of acquisition). The Investment in Subsidiary account is credited.

   <u>*Consolidation Entry S* (for **S**tockholders' Equity)</u>

Common Stock (Subsidiary)	XX	
Additional Paid-In Capital (Subsidiary)	XX	
Retained Earnings, 1/1/0X (Subsidiary)	XX	
Investment in Subsidiary		XX

2. *Consolidation Entry A* recognizes the unamortized allocations of fair market value adjustments associated with the subsidiary's assets as of the beginning of the period (or the acquisition date if this is the period of acquisition).

   <u>*Consolidation Entry A* (for **A**llocations)</u>

Land (if undervalued on the Sub's books)...............	XX	
Patents (if undervalued on the Sub's books)..........	XX	
Goodwill	XX	
Equipment (if overvalued on the Sub's books).......		XX
Investment in Subsidiary		XX

3. *Consolidation Entry I* eliminates the *Equity in Subsidiary Earnings* (or income) accrued by the parent.

   <u>*Consolidation Entry I* (for **I**ncome)</u>

Equity in Subsidiary Earnings	XX	
Investment in Subsidiary		XX

4. *Consolidation Entry D* removes intra-entity dividends received from the subsidiary.

   <u>*Consolidation Entry D* (for **D**ividends)</u>

Investment in Subsidiary	XX	
Dividends Paid		XX

5. *Consolidation Entry E* records the excess amortization expense for the current period on the allocations from the original adjustments to fair value.

   (Remember that the fair market value difference associated with Land is never amortized. Also, some intangibles such as trademarks may have indefinite lives and therefore are not amortized.)

   <u>*Consolidation Entry E* (for **E**xcess amortization)</u>

Amortization Expense	XX	
Equipment (*if originally overvalued*)	XX	
Patents		XX
Intangibles		XX

6. *Consolidation Entry P* eliminates any intra-entity payable/receivable balances.

*Consolidation Entry **P*** (for intra-entity **P**ayable)

Payable …………………………………	XX	
Receivable ………………………………….		XX

E. **Consolidation Subsequent to Year of Acquisition – Equity Method** – If the acquisition was made during a previous period, most of the consolidation entries remain applicable.

   1. The amount of the subsidiary's stockholders' equity to be removed in *Consolidation Entry S* will differ each period to reflect the balances as of the beginning of the current period.

   2. The allocations established by *Consolidation Entry A* also change with each subsequent consolidation as only the *unamortized* balances remaining as of the beginning of the current period are recognized in this entry.

IV. **Subsequent Consolidations — Investment Recorded Using Initial Value or Partial Equity Method**

A. When the parent does not use the equity method for its accounting, the consolidation procedures previously described are modified. There are few differences, and only three of the parent's accounts vary because of the method applied:

   1. The investment account.

   2. The income recognized from the subsidiary.

   3. The parent's retained earnings (in periods after the initial year of the combination).

B. *LO4b* **Initial Value Method Applied — Consolidation**

   1. In the year of acquisition, only entries *I* and *D* differ from the equity method.

      a. On its books, the parent company recognizes dividends received as *dividend income*, rather than as a reduction of the investment account, and therefore, does not change the Investment in Subsidiary account.

      b. Since dividends received from the subsidiary are recorded as income under the Initial Value Method, the intra-entity income eliminated in *Consolidation Entry I* consists only of the dividend income from the subsidiary.

      c. No separate *Consolidation Entry D* is needed (as the intra-entity dividends are eliminated in Entry I).

      d. Under the initial value method, the parent does not recognize its share of *Equity in Subsidiary Earnings* or *Amortization Expense*.

   2. After the year of acquisition, *Consolidation Entry *C* (**C** for **C**onversion to the Equity Method, * to indicate the entry relates to prior periods) is used to update the *Investment in Subsidiary* and *Retained Earnings* balances and convert all prior amounts into equity method balances.

      a. Record *Consolidation Entry *C* **before** the other consolidation entries are made, to align beginning balances with the equity method.

      b. Since no *Equity in Subsidiary Income* has been recognized by the parent, the parent's beginning retained earnings each year will be understated (or overstated if there has been a net cumulative loss since the acquisition).

      c.   Entry *C is a catch-up entry which records a cumulative computation of the parent's share of all the subsidiary's net income since acquisition and any amortization that would have been recorded under the equity method.

*Consolidation Entry *C*

    Investment in Subsidiary.........................XX
        Retained Earnings, Beg............................XX

    3.   **Summary**: when the parent uses the initial value method, the only entries that differ from when the parent uses the equity method are I and D in the year of acquisition; and I, D and *C in subsequent years.

C.   *LO4c* **Partial Equity Method Applied — Consolidation**

    1.   In the year of acquisition, only entry *I* differs from the equity method.

        a.   Under the partial equity method, the parent's records only two periodic journal entries: the annual accrual of subsidiary income and the receipt of dividends.

        b.   The intra-entity income to be removed in *Consolidation Entry I* is the equity accrual only; no amortization expense is included.

    2.   Intra-entity dividends are eliminated as usual with *Consolidation Entry D*.

    3.   After the year of acquisition, *Consolidation Entry *C* (**C** for **C**onversion to the Equity Method, * to indicate the entry relates to prior periods) is used to update the *Investment in Subsidiary* and beginning *Retained Earnings* balance and convert all prior amounts into equity method balances.

        a.   Record *Consolidation Entry *C* **before** the other consolidation entries are made, to align beginning balances with the equity method.

        b.   Since the parent does not record amortization expense, Consolidation *Entry *C* converts the appropriate account balances to the equity method by recognizing the amortization expense that relates to all of the past years.

        *Consolidation Entry *C*

        Retained Earnings, Beg XX
            Investment in Subsidiary............................XX

    4.   **Summary**: when the parent uses the partial equity method, the only entries that differ from when the parent uses the equity method are *I* in the year of acquisition; and *I* and *C in subsequent years.

D.   To solve a consolidation problem, you may need to determine which method the parent used to account for the investment by examining the balance in the *Investment in Subsidiary* account or the amount recorded as *Equity in Subsidiary Earnings*.

V.   *LO5* **Goodwill and Intangible Assets**

   A.   Amortization of intangible assets:

    1.   All identified intangible assets are to be amortized over their useful economic life unless their life is considered *indefinite*.

2.   An asset with an indefinite life (which is not the same as an infinite life) should not be amortized unless and until its life is determined to be finite.

3.   The method of amortization should reflect the pattern of decline in economic usefulness of the asset. If there is not an apparent pattern, the straight-line method should be used.

4.   In most cases, the residual value is presumed to be zero.

B.   Intangible assets with indefinite lives are not amortized, but are tested for impairment on an annual basis.

C.   Goodwill

1.   Goodwill is never amortized (SFAS 142). Goodwill does not decrease over time in a "rational and systematic manner" that periodic amortization implies.

2.   Prior to SFAS 142, amortization of goodwill was allowed under GAAP.

3.   The unamortized portion of Goodwill existing on a company's books as of the beginning of annual reporting periods in 2002 was carried forward at the unamortized amount.

4.   Goodwill is tested at least annually for impairment.

5.   Goodwill is only reduced if there is an impairment loss, a sale or a partial sale of the subsidiary.

VI.   *LO6* **Goodwill Impairment**

A.   Goodwill is considered impaired when the fair value of its related reporting unit falls below its carrying value. Goodwill should ***not*** be amortized, but should be tested for impairment at the *reporting unit level* (operating segment or lower identifiable level).

1.   An annual test for goodwill impairment is required.

2.   However, if one or more indicators of a potential impairment are present, testing must be performed more frequently. Indicators include adverse changes in the business climate or market, legal factors, regulatory action, introduction of competition, or loss of key personnel.

B.   **Testing Goodwill for Impairment** uses a two-step approach.

Step 1 – Is the Fair Value of a Reporting Unit Less Than Its Carrying Value?

If the fair value of the reporting unit exceeds or equals its carrying value, goodwill is not considered impaired and no further analysis is necessary.

If the fair value of the reporting unit is less than its carrying value, a potential for goodwill impairment exists and step 2 must be performed to determine if there is an impairment of goodwill.

Step 2 – Is Goodwill's Implied Value Less Than Carrying Value?

If Step 1 indicates a potential goodwill impairment for a reporting unit, goodwill's implied and carrying values are compared for that reporting unit.

    a.   To determine the *Implied Value* of the Goodwill, use the most recently determined fair value of the reporting unit as a replacement for the acquisition-date fair value – as if the reporting unit were being acquired.

    b.   Then the replacement acquisition-date fair value is allocated to the reporting unit's identifiable assets and liabilities with any remaining excess considered as the implied fair value of goodwill.

    c.   This allocation is performed only for purposes of testing goodwill for impairment and is not used to adjust the values of any other assets or liabilities.

    d.   If the implied value of goodwill is less than the carrying value, goodwill must be written down. The *Goodwill Impairment Loss* is recorded as a separate line item in the operating section of the income statement.

C.   Assigning Values to Reporting Units

    1.   Identify the reporting units resulting from the acquisition.

    2.   All acquired assets and liabilities (including goodwill) are assigned to reporting units.

    3.   Total acquired goodwill is often divided among a number of reporting units.

D.   Determining the Fair Value of Reporting Units Periodically

    1.   Fair value can be determined using any of the following techniques:

        a.   Quoted market prices, if they exist.

        b.   Comparable businesses may exist that can help in the determination of fair value.

        c.   Present value techniques to determine the fair value of an identifiable set of future cash flows.

    2.   A previously determined fair value can continue to be used if *all* of the following conditions are met:

        a.   The assets and liabilities that compose the reporting unit have not changed significantly since the most recent fair-value determination.

        b.   The most recent fair-value determination resulted in an amount that exceeded the carrying amount of the reporting unit by a substantial margin.

        c.   Based on an analysis of events that have occurred and circumstances that have changed since the most recent fair-value determination, it is remote that a current fair-value determination would be less than the current carrying amount of the reporting unit.

E. Comparisons with International Accounting Standards

    1. Similarities:

        a. Goodwill is recognized when the fair value of the consideration transferred exceeds the net fair values of the assets acquired and liabilities assumed.

        b. Goodwill is tested for impairment at least annually, and more frequently when potential impairment indicators exist.

    2. Differences exist in the way goodwill impairment is tested for and recognized.

    3. **Goodwill allocation** — IFRS requires goodwill to be allocated to cash-generating units or groups of cash-generating units vs. the reporting units used in U.S. GAAP.

    4. **Impairment testing** — IFRS uses a one-step approach comparing the fair value of the cash-generating unit with the carrying value of the cash-generating unit vs. the two-step approach used by U.S. GAAP.

    5. **Determination of the impairment loss** — under IFRS, any excess carrying amount over fair value for a cash-generating unit first reduces goodwill. If goodwill is reduced to zero, other assets of the cash-generating unit are reduced pro-rata based on the carrying value of the assets.

    6. The FASB and IASB are including impairment recognition and reporting as a future convergence project.

VII. *LO7* **Contingent Consideration**

    A. The final price paid by an acquiring company may ultimately depend on some future event such as the earnings of the subsidiary or the market value of the parent's common stock.

    B. **Accounting for Contingent Consideration in Business Combinations**

        1. Under the acquisition method, contingent consideration is recognized as part of the initial value assigned in a business combination, consistent with the fair-value concept.

        2. The fair value of the contingent consideration must be estimated. The FASB recommends a *probability-weighted* approach such as expected cash flow. This approach may include calculations of the time value of money.

        3. A cash contingency is recognized as a contingent liability.

        4. A contingent stock payment is recorded as an element of stockholders' equity such as *APIC – Contingent Equity Outstanding*.

        5. Obligations classified as liabilities are subsequently re-measured at fair value, with adjustments recognized in income as a *Gain* or *Loss from Revaluation of Contingent Performance Obligation*.

        6. Obligations classified as equity are not subsequently re-measured.

VIII.   *LO8* **Push-Down Accounting** – push-down accounting is the direct recording of fair-value allocations and subsequent amortization by a subsidiary in its books.

A.   **External Reporting** – Currently, primary guidance comes from the SEC.

1.   As a general rule, the SEC requires push-down accounting in the separate financial statements of a "substantially wholly owned" subsidiary when the ownership change is greater than 95% (no substantial outside ownership), and objects to it when the ownership change is less than 80%.

2.   However, if the acquired subsidiary has outstanding public debt or preferred stock, push down accounting is encouraged by the SEC, but not required.

3.   Currently, push-down accounting is required only when the subsidiary desires to issue securities to the public, as regulated by the SEC.

B.   **Internal Reporting**

1.   At the time of acquisition, the subsidiary records the fair-value adjustments directly into its own financial records rather than a worksheet. Subsequent amortization expense is also recorded by the subsidiary.

2.   Proponents argue that a change in ownership creates a new basis for the subsidiary's assets. Push-down accounting reports the assets and liabilities of the subsidiary at the fair-value (generally the consideration transferred). It also assists the new owner in evaluating the profitability that the subsidiary is adding to the business combination.

3.   Push-down accounting can also make the consolidation process easier since fair value allocations and amortization don't need to be included as worksheet entries.

Multiple Choice Questions

Items 1 through 4 are based on the following information.

On January 1, 2010, Parkway Corporation acquired all of the outstanding common stock of Shaw Company for $3,650,000 cash. On that date, Shaw's net assets had a book value of $2,800,000. Equipment with a 10-year life was undervalued by $260,000 in Shaw's financial records. Goodwill resulting from this combination equals $590,000. Shaw reported net income of $620,000 in 2010, $700,000 in 2011, and $630,000 in 2012. Dividends of $300,000 were declared and paid in each of the three years. Select account balances as of December 31, 2012 for the two companies are:

	Parkway	Shaw
Revenues	$ 9,600,000	$ 2,630,000
Expenses	9,150,000	2,000,000
Equipment (net)	800,000	680,000
Retained Earnings, 1/1/12	720,000	182,000
Dividends Paid	800,000	300,000

1. For each of the three methods discussed in the chapter, what should be the *Investment in Shaw Company* account balance in the records of Parkway Corporation at December 31, 2012?

	Equity Method	Partial Equity Method	Initial Value Method
A.	$4,622,000	$3,650,000	$4,700,000
B.	$4,318,000	$4,370,000	$3,650,000
C.	$4,622,000	$4,700,000	$3,650,000
D.	$4,700,000	$4,700,000	$3,650,000
E.	$4,648,000	$4,700,000	$2,750,000

2. What is *consolidated net income* for 2012 if the parent company uses the partial equity method?

   A. $1,054,000
   B. $1,080,000
   C. $1,106,000
   D. $ 450,000
   E. $ 424,000

3. What is *consolidated retained earnings* at January 1, 2012 if the parent company is using the equity method?

   A. $ 902,000
   B. $ 876,000
   C. $ 694,000
   D. $1,170,000
   E. $ 720,000

4. What would **Parkway's** *retained earnings* be at January 1, 2012 if the parent company had used the partial equity method?

    A. $694,000
    B. $668,000
    C. $772,000
    D. $746,000
    E. $642,000

5. When testing goodwill for impairment, the appropriate level of testing is at the

    A. Consolidated entity level
    B. Parent company level
    C. Operating unit level
    D. Subsidiary company level
    E. Reporting unit level

6. Powell Company buys all of the outstanding common shares of South Bay Company on January 1, 2011 for $1,500,000 cash. This price resulted in goodwill of $300,000. If the subsidiary earns sufficiently high profits over the next two years, Powell will be required to pay South Bay's previous owners an additional $450,000 cash on January 1, 2013.

    How should Powell report the contingent consideration on January 1, 2011?

    A. The $450,000 contingent consideration will be included in the cost of the acquisition.
    B. The $450,000 contingent consideration should be expensed when it is paid in 2013.
    C. The $450,000 contingent consideration should be ignored. If it is paid in 2013, it should increase the balance in the Goodwill account.
    D. The probability-adjusted present value of the $450,000 contingent consideration should be included in the cost of the acquisition.
    E. The probability-adjusted future value of the $450,000 contingent consideration should be added to Goodwill when it is paid in 2013.

Use the following information for number 7 and 8.

Bowling & Sons, Inc. buys all of the outstanding shares of Gaspard Construction on July 1, 2011 for $1,500,000 cash. Gaspard Construction's book value at the acquisition date was $1,100,000.

At the acquisition date, Gaspard Construction has equipment with a book value of $360,000 and a fair value of $325,000. The equipment has a remaining useful life of 3 years. Building #1 has a book value of $125,000 and a fair value of $200,000, and a remaining useful life of 8 years. Building #2 has a book value of $240,000 and a fair value of 380,000, with a remaining useful life of 10 years. Gaspard Construction has four building lots with a book value of $23,000 each, and a fair value of $28,000 each. During the negotiation process, it was determined that Gaspard Construction has developed a patentable construction process that has a market value of $200,000, and a useful life of 5 years.

Bowling & Sons fiscal year ends on June 30th.

7.   Bowling & Sons incurred $75,000 in legal costs related directly to the combination. They use Acquisition Method accounting and apply the equity method to investments. How much Goodwill will be reported in the consolidated financial statements on June 30, 2012?

    A. $ 0
    B. $400,000
    C. $ 75,000
    D. $200,000
    E. $275,000

8.   What is the amortization expense for the period ending June 30, 2012?

    A. $11,708
    B. $51,708
    C. $75,042
    D. $42,333
    E. $ 0

Brief Essay Questions

1.   On January 1, 2011, Patrick Company purchases 100 percent of the outstanding common shares of Sportswear Inc. for $1,500,000. On that date, Patrick reported retained earnings of $150,000 while Sportswear reported an $80,000 balance. Patrick reported net income of $75,000 in 2011 and $90,000 in 2012, and paid $25,000 in dividends each year. Sportswear reported net income of $50,000 in 2011 and $65,000 in 2012, and paid $5,000 in dividends each year. Annual amortization of $7,000 results from the combination.

If Patrick applies the equity method, calculate the *Investment in Sportswear Inc.* account balance on December 31, 2012.

How would your answer differ if Patrick uses the partial equity method?

2.   What is the SEC's rationale for requiring the use of push-down accounting for the separate financial statements of any subsidiary where no substantial outside ownership exists of the company's common stock, preferred stock, and publicly held debt?

3.   What are the primary differences between the Purchase Method, as described in SFAS No. 141, and the Acquisition Method as described SFAS 141R?

4.   Identify the five primary worksheet entries used in the consolidation of financial statements where the parent uses the equity method. Identify the function of each of those entries.

Problems

1. On January 1, 2011, Giant Inc. purchased all of the outstanding common shares of Tiny Co. for $3,600,000 cash. In addition, Giant incurred $100,000 of costs that related directly to the combination.

    On January 1, 2011, Tiny's equity accounts had the following balances: *Common Stock* — $500,000; *Additional Paid-In Capital* — $1,800,000; and *Retained Earnings* — $700,000. All of Tiny's assets were fairly stated except for equipment having a book value of $180,000 and a fair value of $270,000, and a building having a book value of $600,000 and a fair value of $800,000. The equipment is estimated to have a remaining useful life of five years, and the building has a ten-year remaining useful life. Tiny also had a copyright with a fair value of $310,000 and an expected useful life of 5 years on January 1, 2011.

    During 2011, Tiny reported net income of $1,325,000 and paid dividends of $850,000. During 2012, Tiny reported net income of $900,000 and paid dividends of $1,100,000.

    Required:

    A. Prepare an *Allocation of Subsidiary Fair Value* and an *Amortization Schedule.*

    B. Assume that Giant uses the equity method to account for its investment in Tiny. Prepare all entries to be made *on the books* of Giant for 2011 regarding its investment in Tiny.

    C. Prepare the consolidation worksheet entries for the year ended December 31, 2011 assuming Giant uses the equity method of accounting.

2. *Required:*

    Assuming that Giant Inc. uses the equity method to account for its investment in Tiny Co., prepare the consolidation worksheet entries for the year ended December 31, 2012.

3. *Required:*

    Assuming that Giant Inc. uses the partial equity method to account for its investment in Tiny Co., prepare the consolidation worksheet entries for the year ended December 31, 2012.

4. *Required:*

    Assuming that Giant Inc. uses the initial value method to account for its investment in Tiny Co., prepare the consolidation worksheet entries for the year ended December 31, 2012.

5. On January 1, 2011, Old Guy Shoes acquired 100% of a sport shoe company, Viagrunners, for $820,000 cash. At that date, the book value of Viagrunners was $630,000. Viagrunners was carrying land on January 1, 2011 that had a book value of $15,000 and a market value of $40,000. All other assets were carried at fair value.

The following balances existed for Old Guy Shoes and its wholly owned sport shoe subsidiary, Viagrunners, at December 31, 2011:

Account	Old Guy Shoes BV	Viagrunners BV	Viagrunners FMV
Cash	$ 860,000	$ 70,000	$ 70,000
Accts Receivable	460,000	120,000	110,000
Inventory	725,000	195,000	125,000
Investment in Viagrunner	640,000		
Land	400,000	15,000	55,000
Building (net)	900,000	90,000	120,000
Equipment (net)	1,200,000	210,000	150,000
Acct. Pay.	(235,000)	(250,000)	(110,000)
Common Stock	(600,000)	(100,000)	
PIC	(3,900,000)	(350,000)	
R/E - January 1	(680,000)	(180,000)	
Dividends	250,000		
Revenues	(6,800,000)	(1,500,000)	
Expenses	6,600,000	1,680,000	
Equity in Viagrunner NI	180,000		

The fair market value of Old Guy's investment in Viagrunners has dropped to $540,000 as of December 31, 2011.

Required:

Is Goodwill related to Old Guy's investment in Viagrunners impaired at December 31, 2011? Assume that Viagrunners is a unique reporting unit.

6. On January 1, 2011, Pet Corp. bought a 100% interest in FeedCor for $3,000,000 million in cash. In addition, Pet Corp. issued 350,000 shares of its $1 par value stock. Pet Corp.'s stock had a market value of $20.00 per share on January 1. On the acquisition date, FeedCor had a book value of $7,800,000.

On the date of acquisition, FeedCor had assets with the following book values and fair values:

Account	Book Value	Fair Value	Remaining Useful Life
Accounts Receivable	387,000	412,000	1
Inventory	298,000	378,000	1
Land	2,150,000	2,400,000	Indefinite
Buildings (net)	2,600,000	3,000,000	10
Equipment (net)	3,250,000	2,850,000	5

Pet Corp. and FeedCor each have a December 31 year-end. FeedCor has a trademark valued at $900,000 (estimated useful life = 10 years) and a database valued at $600,000 (estimated useful life = 5 years). Pet Corp. and FeedCor's balances at December 31, 2011 were as follows:

Account	Pet Corporation	FeedCor
Cash	$ 6,800,000	$ 950,000
Accounts Receivable	9,600,000	680,000
Inventory	4,160,000	500,000
Land	2,400,000	3,000,000
Buildings (net)	8,500,000	3,200,000
Equipment (net)	7,500,000	5,499,000
Investment in Barns	14,825,000	
Accounts Payable	(4,860,000)	(529,000)
Notes Payable	(5,000,000)	(400,000)
Common Stock	(4,550,000)	(700,000)
Paid-In-Capital	(18,550,000)	(4,250,000)
Retained Earnings, 1/1	(6,200,000)	(2,850,000)
Dividends	4,000,000	300,000
Revenues	(225,600,000)	(32,400,000)
Expenses	212,100,000	27,000,000
Equity in Subsidiary Income	(5,125,000)	

Required:

Prepare a Consolidation Worksheet for the period ending December 31, 2011. Pet Corp uses the equity method on its books.

7. Refer to the information in Problem 6 above. Prepare consolidation entries for Pet Corp. at December 31, 2012 (the year after the acquisition of FeedCor), using the following information.

The general ledger balances for FeedCor at December 31, 2012 are as follows:

Account	FeedCor
Cash	$ 750,000
Accounts Receivable	800,000
Inventory	750,000
Land	3,000,000
Buildings (net)	3,050,000
Equipment (net)	7,400,000
Accounts Payable	(890,000)
Notes Payable	(360,000)
Common Stock	(700,000)
Paid-In-Capital	(4,250,000)
Retained Earnings, Jan. 1	(7,950,000)
Dividends	4,000,000
Revenues	(40,500,000)
Expenses	34,900,000
Equity in Subsidiary Income	

Solutions to Multiple Choice Questions

1.   C   Allocation of the fair value of consideration transferred as of January 1, 2010:

Consideration transferred	3,650,000		
BV of Shaw	2,800,000		
Excess of fair value over book value	850,000	years	amort.
Equipment	260,000	10	26,000
Goodwill	590,000		-
Annual Amortization Expense			26,000

Equity method:

	Investment in Shaw		
Consideration	3,650,000	300,000	2010 Dividend
NI, 2010	620,000	300,000	2011 Dividend
NI, 2011	700,000	300,000	2012 Dividend
NI, 2012	630,000	26,000	2010 Amortization
		26,000	2011 Amortization
		26,000	2012 Amortization
	4,622,000		

Partial equity method:

	Investment in Shaw		
Consideration	3,650,000	300,000	2010 Dividend
NI, 2010	620,000	300,000	2011 Dividend
NI, 2011	700,000	300,000	2012 Dividend
NI, 2012	630,000		
	4,700,000		

Initial value method: No entries are made to reflect the income earned, amortization, or dividends received. Therefore, the investment account remains at its original value.

Investment in Shaw Company — 12/31/2012 $3,650,000

2.   A   Consolidated net income:

	Parkway		Shaw		Consolidated Net Income
Revenues	$ 9,600,000	+	$ 2,630,000	=	$ 12,230,000
Expenses	9,150,000	+	2,000,000	=	(11,150,000)
Amortization Exp.					(26,000)
					$ 1,054,000

3. **E**   In a consolidation, the subsidiary's earnings prior to the date of acquisition are not reflected in the consolidated totals. Consolidation Entry S eliminates all of the subsidiary's retained earnings as of the beginning of the period (which represents the past net earnings of the company). Therefore, under the equity method, Parkway's January 1, 2012 retained earnings balance of $720,000 also represents consolidated retained earnings.

4. **C**   If Parkway Corporation uses the partial equity method; its retained earnings balance at January 1, 2012 will be the same as the equity method except that amortization was not recorded.

Parkway's retained earnings – equity method (above)	$ 720,000
Amortization for 2010-2011 ($26,000 × 2 years)	52,000
Parkway's retained earnings – partial equity method	$ 772,000

5. **E**

6. **D**   Under the acquisition method, contingent consideration is included in the acquisition cost. The FASB recommends the use of probability-adjusted discounted cash flows as a means of determining the current fair value of the contingent consideration. At the time of the acquisition, a contingent liability is recorded.

7. **A**   Under the acquisition method, direct combination costs are expensed immediately, and are not part of the acquisition costs.

Consideration transferred	1,500,000
Book Value	1,100,000
Consideration in excess of book value	400,000
Land	20,000
Building #1	75,000
Building #2	140,000
Equipment	(35,000)
Construction Process	200,000
Goodwill	-

8. **B**

	Allocation		Years		Amort.
Building #1	75,000	÷	8	=	9,375
Building #2	140,000	÷	10	=	14,000
Equipment	(35,000)	÷	3	=	(11,667)
Construction Process	200,000	÷	5	=	40,000
					51,708

Answers to Brief Essay Questions

1. If Patrick Company uses the equity method, the *Investment in Sportswear Inc.* account balance on December 31, 2012 is $1,591,000.

Consideration transferred on January 1, 2011	$ 1,500,000
Sportswear net income — 2011	50,000
Sportswear net income — 2012	65,000
Dividends paid by Sportswear ($5,000 × 2)	(10,000)
Amortization — 2011-2012 ($7,000 × 2)	(14,000)
Investment in Sportswear Inc. at December 31, 2012	$ 1,591,000

    If Patrick Company uses the partial equity method, the *Investment in Sportswear Inc.* account balance on December 31, 2012 is $1,605,000.

Consideration transferred on January 1, 2011	$ 1,500,000
Sportswear net income — 2011	50,000
Sportswear net income — 2012	65,000
Dividends paid by Sportswear ($5,000 × 2)	(10,000)
Investment in Sportswear Inc. at December 31, 2012	$ 1,605,000

2. The SEC's rationale for requiring push-down accounting is based on the idea that when the form of ownership is within the control of the parent company, the accounting basis should be the same whether the entity continues to exist or is merged into the parent's operations. Consequently, the SEC believes that a change in ownership justifies a new basis of accounting for the subsidiary's assets and liabilities.

3. The Purchase Method and the Acquisition Method differ in several significant ways. First, the Purchase Method includes direct combination costs as part of the acquisition cost in a combination, while the Acquisition Method expenses the direct combination costs when they occur. A second difference is in the way the two methods treat contingent consideration. Generally, the Purchase Method does not include contingent consideration in computation of acquisition cost. At the date of the acquisition, any contingent consideration is ignored. Under the Acquisition Method, the contingent consideration is included in the computation of the acquisition cost. The FASB recommends a probability-adjusted time value approach.

    In addition, the treatment of IPR&D and bargain purchases differ under the two approaches. Under the purchase method, IPR&D that has not reached technological feasibility and has no alternative future use is expensed. Under the acquisition method, the IPR&D is measured at its fair value and capitalized. Consistent with its emphasis on fair values, with the Acquisition method, assets and liabilities acquired in a bargain purchase are valued at fair market value and a bargain purchase price is recognized where the acquisition price is less than the fair value of net assets acquired. Under the purchase method, a gain on bargain purchase is only recognized if the amount of the fair value of net assets acquired minus the acquisition price exceeds the fair value of all noncurrent assets that are eligible to be reduced to zero under the purchase method.

4. *Consolidation Entry S* – In this entry, the equity accounts of the subsidiary are eliminated as of the beginning of the consolidation period.

Consolidation Entry A – In this entry, the unamortized portions of the original fair value allocations as of the beginning of the year are added to the consolidated balance sheet.

Consolidation Entry I – In this entry, the balance in the parent's Equity in Subsidiary Net Income account is eliminated.

Consolidation Entry D – In this entry, the balance in the subsidiary's dividends account is eliminated.

Consolidation Entry E – In this entry, the current year amortization expense related to the original fair value allocations is recorded.

Solutions to Problems

1. **A.**

Giant Inc.
Allocation of Subsidiary Fair Values
January 1, 2011

			years		Amortization
Giant's consideration transferred	$ 3,600,000				
Tiny's Book Value	3,000,000				
Difference to be allocated	600,000				
Equipment	90,000	÷	5	=	18,000
Buildings	200,000	÷	10	=	20,000
Copyright	310,000	÷	5	=	62,000
Total	$ -				100,000

B.   Entries on the books of Giant Inc.:

Date	Accounts	Debit	Credit
1/1/2011	Investment in Tiny	3,600,000	
	Cash		3,600,000
	to record investment in Tiny		
12/31/2011	Investment in Tiny	1,325,000	
	Equity in Tiny Income		1,325,000
	to record Giant's share of Tiny's Income		
12/31/2011	Cash	850,000	
	Investment in Tiny		850,000
	to record receipt of dividends from Tiny		
12/31/2011	Equity in Tiny Income	100,000	
	Investment in Tiny		100,000
	to record amortization expense		

C. **Consolidation** worksheet entries for the year ended *December 31, 2011* – **Equity Method** (**Hint** — use the mnemonic device *SAIDE*)

Date	Accounts	Debit	Credit
12/31/2011	**ENTRY S**		
	Common Stock - Tiny	500,000	
	Paid-In Capital - Tiny	1,800,000	
	Retained Earnings - beginning	700,000	
	Investment in Tiny		3,000,000
12/31/2011	**ENTRY A**		
	Equipment	90,000	
	Building	200,000	
	Copyright	310,000	
	Investment in Tiny		600,000
12/31/2011	**ENTRY I**		
	Equity in Tiny Income	1,225,000	
	Investment in Tiny		1,225,000
12/31/2011	**ENTRY D**		
	Investment in Tiny	850,000	
	Dividends		850,000
12/31/2011	**ENTRY E**		
	Amortization Expense	100,000	
	Equipment		18,000
	Building		20,000
	Copyright		62,000

2. Consolidation worksheet entries for the year ended *December 31, 2012* — **Equity Method**:

ENTRY	Accounts	Debit	Credit
ENTRY S	Common Stock - Tiny	500,000	
	Paid-In Capital - Tiny	1,800,000	
	Retained Earnings - beginning *	1,175,000	
	Investment in Tiny		3,475,000
ENTRY A	Equipment	72,000	
	Building	180,000	
	Copyright	248,000	
	Investment in Tiny		500,000
ENTRY I	Equity in Tiny Income	800,000	
	Investment in Tiny		800,000
ENTRY D	Investment in Tiny	1,100,000	
	Dividends		1,100,000
ENTRY E	Amortization Expense	100,000	
	Equipment		18,000
	Building		20,000
	Copyright		62,000

*Note: the beginning balance of retained earnings for Tiny is: Tiny - retained earnings 1/1/2011 of $700,000 + Tiny's 2011 income $1,325,000 less Tiny's 2011 dividends $850,000 = $1,175,000.

3. Consolidation worksheet entries for the year ended *December 31, 2012* — **Partial Equity Method**:

ENTRY	Accounts	Debit	Credit
ENTRY *C	Retained Earnings	100,000	
	Investment in Tiny		100,000
	to adjust the balances to what they would have been if Giant had used the equity method.		
ENTRY S	Common Stock - Tiny	500,000	
	Paid-In Capital - Tiny	1,800,000	
	Retained Earnings - beginning	1,175,000	
	Investment in Tiny		3,475,000
ENTRY A	Equipment	72,000	
	Building	180,000	
	Copyright	248,000	
	Investment in Tiny		500,000
ENTRY I	Equity in Tiny Income	900,000	
	Investment in Tiny		900,000
ENTRY D	Investment in Tiny	1,100,000	
	Dividends		1,100,000
ENTRY E	Amortization Expense	100,000	
	Equipment		18,000
	Building		20,000
	Copyright		62,000

Entry *C adjusts the parent's beginning balances to reflect the amortization that would have been recorded for 2011 if the parent had used the equity method.

4. Consolidation worksheet entries for the year ended *December 31, 2012* — **Initial value method**:

ENTRY	Accounts	Debit	Credit
ENTRY *C	Investment in Tiny	375,000	
	Retained Earnings		375,000
ENTRY S	Common Stock - Tiny	500,000	
	Paid-In Capital - Tiny	1,800,000	
	Retained Earnings - beginning	1,175,000	
	Investment in Tiny		3,475,000
ENTRY A	Equipment	72,000	
	Building	180,000	
	Copyright	248,000	
	Investment in Tiny		500,000
ENTRY I	Dividend Income	1,100,000	
	Dividends		1,100,000
ENTRY D	*Not applicable in the inital value method*		
ENTRY E	Amortization Expense	100,000	
	Equipment		18,000
	Building		20,000
	Copyright		62,000

Entry *C adjusts the parent's beginning balances to reflect the change in the investment account that would have been recorded for 2011 if the parent had used the equity method. (2011 income of $1,325,000 less dividends of $800,000 less amortization of $100,000 = the $375,000 retained earnings adjustment.

If the equity method had been used, the balance in the investment account would be $3,975,000 (acquisition fair value + income – dividends – amortization). Under the initial value method, the balance would equal the acquisition fair value amount of $3,600,000; therefore, the adjustment is $375,000.

5. **Step 1: Is FMV of the investment < Carrying amount of the investment?**

In this case, the FMV of the investment is $540,000. The book, or carrying value, of the investment is $640,000. Therefore, since $540,000 < $640,000, we must go to Step #2.

Step 2: Is the Implied Goodwill < the carrying amount for Goodwill?

To determine this, we must first know the carrying amount for Goodwill. In the original acquisition, Old Guy paid $820,000 for 100% of Viagrunners.

Acquisition fair-value	$ 820,000
Book Value of Viagrunners	630,000
Acquisition fair-value in Excess of BV	$ 190,000
Fair market value adjustment for Land	25,000
Goodwill	$ 165,000

Next, we must compare the "implied" goodwill to the carrying amount for goodwill ($165,000). In our problem, we know that the current value of the investment is $540,000.

Current Fair Value	$ 540,000
Fair Value of Viagrunners' Net Assets	520,000
Implied Goodwill	$ 20,000

Now, compare "implied" goodwill to the carrying amount for goodwill:

$20,000 (implied goodwill) < $165,000 (carrying amount for goodwill)

Therefore, we conclude that goodwill is impaired and must be adjusted downward by $145,000.

6. **Pet Corp Acquisition of FeedCor – Year One.**

Computation of Pet Corp's Acquisition Cost			
Cash paid by Pet Corp			$ 3,000,000
Fair Value of Common Stock			
Issued by Pet Corp:	350,000	shares	
	$ 20.00	per share	7,000,000
Pet Corp's Cost of Investment			$ 10,000,000

Goodwill Calculation and Computation of Amortization Expense for year one:

Pet Corp's Investment Cost	$ 10,000,000					
FeedCor's Book Value	7,800,000					
Difference to be allocated	2,200,000					
				years		Amortization
Accounts Receivable	25,000	÷	1	=	25,000
Inventory	80,000	÷	1	=	80,000
Land	250,000	÷	NA		
Buildings	400,000	÷	10	=	40,000
Equipment	(400,000)	÷	5	=	(80,000)
Trademark	900,000	÷	10	=	90,000
Database	600,000	÷	5	=	120,000
Goodwill	$ 345,000				275,000

The consolidation worksheet follows.

Account	Pet Corp.	FeedCor	DR	CR	Consolidated Balance
Income Statement					
Revenues	(225,600,000)	(32,400,000)			(258,000,000)
Expenses	212,100,000	27,000,000	275,000		239,375,000
Equity in Barns NI	(5,125,000)		5,125,000		-
Net Income	**(18,625,000)**	**(5,400,000)**			**(18,625,000)**
Statement of Retained Earnings					
Beg. Ret. Earnings	(6,200,000)	(2,850,000)	2,850,000		(6,200,000)
Net Income	(18,625,000)	(5,400,000)			(18,625,000)
Dividends	4,000,000	300,000		300,000	4,000,000
Ending Ret. Earnings	**(20,825,000)**	**(7,950,000)**			**(20,825,000)**
Balance Sheet					
Cash	$ 6,800,000	$ 950,000			$ 7,750,000
Accounts Rec.	9,600,000	680,000	25,000	25,000	10,280,000
Inventory	4,160,000	500,000	80,000	80,000	4,660,000
Land	2,400,000	3,000,000	250,000		5,650,000
Buildings (net)	8,500,000	3,200,000	400,000	40,000	12,060,000
Equipment (net)	7,500,000	5,499,000	80,000	400,000	12,679,000
Investment	14,825,000		300,000	15,125,000	-
Trademark			900,000	90,000	810,000
Database			600,000	120,000	480,000
Goodwill			345,000		345,000
Total Assets	**53,785,000**	**13,829,000**			**54,714,000**
Accounts Payable	(4,860,000)	(529,000)			(5,389,000)
Notes Payable	(5,000,000)	(400,000)			(5,400,000)
Common Stock	(4,550,000)	(700,000)	700,000		(4,550,000)
Paid-in-Capital	(18,550,000)	(4,250,000)	4,250,000		(18,550,000)
Retained Earnings	(20,825,000)	(7,950,000)			(20,825,000)
Total Liab + Stk Eq	(53,785,000)	(13,829,000)			(54,714,000)

7. Consolidation entries included in the worksheet:

ENTRY	Accounts	Debit	Credit
ENTRY S	Common Stock - FeedCor	700,000	
	Paid-In Capital - FeedCor	4,250,000	
	Retained Earnings - 1/1	2,850,000	
	Investment in FeedCor		7,800,000
ENTRY A	Accounts Receivable	25,000	
	Inventory	80,000	
	Land	250,000	
	Buildings	400,000	
	Trademark	900,000	
	Database	600,000	
	Goodwill	345,000	
	Equipment		400,000
	Investment in FeedCor		2,200,000
ENTRY I	Equity in FeedCor Net Income	5,125,000	
	Investment in FeedCor		5,125,000
ENTRY D	Investment in FeedCor	300,000	
	Dividends (FeedCor)		300,000
ENTRY E	Amortization Expense	275,000	
	Equipment	80,000	
	Accounts Receivable		25,000
	Inventory		80,000
	Buildings		40,000
	Trademark		90,000
	Database		120,000

8. Pet Corp Consolidation Calculations and Entries – Year Two

Amortization Computation
For the year ending December 31, 2012

	Original Balance				Amortization Expense	Unamortized Balance
Acct. Rec.	25,000				-	-
Inventory	80,000				-	-
Land	250,000				-	250,000
Building	400,000	÷	10	=	40,000	360,000
Equipment	(400,000)	÷	5	=	(80,000)	(320,000)
Trademark	900,000	÷	10	=	90,000	810,000
Database	600,000	÷	5	=	120,000	480,000
					170,000	1,580,000

Note that the accounts receivable and inventory allocations were completely amortized in 2011, so there are no amounts in Entry A for them. The unamortized balances used in Entry A, for the December 31, 2012 consolidation, equal the original allocation amounts less the 2011 amortization.

ENTRY	Accounts	Debit	Credit
ENTRY S	Common Stock - FeedCor	700,000	
	Paid-In Capital - FeedCor	4,250,000	
	Retained Earnings (Beginning)	7,950,000	
	Investment in FeedCor		12,900,000
ENTRY A	Land	250,000	
	Buildings	360,000	
	Trademark	810,000	
	Database	480,000	
	Goodwill	345,000	
	Equipment		320,000
	Investment in FeedCor		1,925,000
ENTRY I	Equity in FeedCor Net Income	5,430,000	
	Investment in FeedCor		5,430,000
ENTRY D	Investment in FeedCor	4,000,000	
	Dividends (FeedCor)		4,000,000
ENTRY E	Amortization Expense	170,000	
	Equipment	80,000	
	Buildings		40,000
	Trademark		90,000
	Database		120,000

Chapter 4

Consolidated Financial Statement and Outside Ownership

Chapter Outline

Standards Mentioned in This Chapter:
- **IFRS 3,** *Business Combinations*
- **SFAS No. 141R,** *Business Combinations (replaces SFAS 141)*
- **SFAS No. 160,** *Noncontrolling Interests and Consolidated Financial Statements*

I. **Consolidated Financial Reporting in the Presence of a Noncontrolling Interest**

   A. *LO1* **Reasons** – There are many reasons for a company to own < 100% of a subsidiary:

      1. The parent may not have sufficient resources to obtain all of the outstanding stock.

      2. Several stockholders of the subsidiary could have elected to retain their ownership.

      3. This situation is frequent with foreign subsidiaries. Some countries prohibit foreign companies from maintaining complete control of domestic business enterprises.

   B. **Definition** – The FASB defines a *noncontrolling interest* as "The ownership interests in the subsidiary that are held by owners other than the parent is a noncontrolling interest." They may also be referred to using the traditional term *minority* interest.

   C. **Control and Accountability**

      1. When a parent company acquires a controlling interest, it is responsible for managing all the subsidiary's assets and liabilities.

      2. The parent must account for the noncontrolling shareholders' interest in its consolidated financial statements.

      3. Fair-value is used to measure both the subsidiary and the individual assets and liabilities. At acquisition date, the acquirer measures the:

         a. Identifiable assets acquired and liabilities assumed at their full fair values.

         b. Noncontrolling interest at fair value.

         c. Goodwill or a gain from a bargain purchase.

   D. *LO2* **Subsidiary Acquisition–Date Fair Value in the Presence of a Noncontrolling Interest**

      1. The total fair value of an acquired firm when there is a noncontrolling interest is the sum of the following at acquisition date:

         The fair value of the controlling interest +
         The fair value of the noncontrolling interest.

2. The fair value of the controlling interest in the majority of cases is measured by the consideration transferred.

3. However, the parent must use other valuation techniques to estimate the fair value of the noncontrolling interest.

    a. Market Trades – Usually a parent can use readily available market trading prices for the noncontrolling interest shares in the weeks before and after the acquisition for an objective measure of their fair value.

    b. *Control premium* – often acquirers pay a premium price per share to obtain sufficient shares to gain a controlling interest. These control premiums are included in the fair value of the controlling interest, but usually do not affect the fair value of the noncontrolling interest.

    c. Implied by Parent's Consideration Transferred – In a limited number of cases, especially when the parent purchases a large percentage of the voting stock, the consideration paid by the parent reflects the acquiree's total fair value (and the price per share paid by the controlling interest is equal to the fair value per share of the noncontrolling interest).

E. *LO3* **Allocating Acquired Goodwill to the Controlling and Noncontrolling Interests**

1. Goodwill is allocated across the controlling and noncontrolling interests.

2. The parent first allocates goodwill to its controlling interest:

    Fair value of the parents interest at acquisition date
    <u>– Relative fair value of the parents share of identifiable net assets</u>
    = Goodwill allocated to the controlling interest

3. Any remaining goodwill is then attributed to the noncontrolling interest.

4. Thus, goodwill allocated to the controlling and noncontrolling interests will not always be proportional. (However, where the same per share value is used for the fair value of the controlling and noncontrolling interests (see I.D.3.c), goodwill is allocated proportionately.)

5. *Bargain purchase* – If the total fair value of the consideration transferred is less than the total fair value of the acquired firm's net identifiable assets, a bargain purchase occurs (rare).

    a. The parent recognizes the entire gain on bargain purchase in current income.
    b. No gain is allocated to the noncontrolling interest.

II. *LO4* **Allocating the Subsidiary's Net Income to the Parent and Noncontrolling Interests**

A. The subsidiary's net income must be allocated to the parent and noncontrolling interest, but the FASB did not provide detailed guidance.

B. The textbook assumes that the relative ownership percentages of the parent and noncontrolling interest are the appropriate basis for allocating all elements of subsidiary income (including excess acquisition date fair-value amortizations).

C. The noncontrolling interest in the subsidiary's current year income = (subsidiary net income minus excess amortizations) × noncontrolling interest %.

D. The parent's interest in the combined entity's consolidated net income = consolidated net income – noncontrolling interest share of subsidiary income.

III. *LO5* Partial Ownership Consolidations (Acquisition Method)

A. Consolidation Involving a Noncontrolling Interest – Subsequent to Acquisition

1. The acquisition method focuses on incorporating 100% of the subsidiary's assets and liabilities at their acquisition date fair values in the consolidated financial statements.

   a. Note that the parent's *internal* accounting for the investment in the subsidiary is based on its % ownership.

2. Subsequent to acquisition, changes in the fair values are not recognized (except when required by GAAP for all firms, such as for marketable equity securities).

3. Most consolidation procedures do not change, but a separate noncontrolling interest column is added to the consolidation worksheet. The noncontrolling interest is calculated in the worksheet at the end of the year by adding four noncontrolling interest balances:

   % share of the subsidiary's book value as of the *beginning* of the current year
   + % share of the *beginning* of the year unamortized excess fair-value allocations
   + % share in the subsidiary's current year net income
   <u>– % share of the subsidiary's dividend payments</u>
   = Noncontrolling interest as of the end of the year.

4. The end of the year noncontrolling interest is reported in the owners' equity section of the balance sheet.

B. Alternative Calculation of Noncontrolling Interest – Subsequent to Acquisition

1. The noncontrolling interest as of the end of the year can also be calculated by adding the noncontrolling interests:

   % share in the fair value of the subsidiary at *acquisition date*
   + % share in changes to retained earnings *since acquisition* (from prior years)
   – % share of excess fair-value amortizations (*prior years*)
   + % share in the subsidiary's current net income
   <u>– % share of the subsidiary's current year dividend payments</u>
   = Noncontrolling interest as of the end of the year.

C. **_LO6_ Consolidated Financial Statement Presentations of Noncontrolling Interest**

   1. Prior to *SFAS 160*, the placement of the noncontrolling interest on the consolidated balance sheet varied across entities.

   2. Noncontrolling interests in the equity of subsidiaries are reported in the owners' equity section of the balance sheet. The amount should be clearly distinguished from the parent's controlling interest in the subsidiaries.

   3. Consolidated net income (or loss) and each component of other comprehensive income is allocated to the noncontrolling and controlling interest.

   4. The consolidated statement of changes in owners' equity also shows the allocation of consolidated net income to the parent and subsidiary as well as the allocation of dividends to the parent and subsidiary.

D. **_LO7_ Alternative Fair-Value Specification – Evidence of a Control Premium**

   1. Often acquirers pay a premium price per share (control premium) to obtain sufficient shares to gain a controlling interest.

   2. However, the additional amount paid might not be reflected in the market value of the noncontrolling interest.

   3. The total fair value is computed as follows:

   Consideration transferred by the parent
   + Noncontrolling interest fair value
   = Total fair value of the company.

   4. Identifiable assets acquired and liabilities assumed are adjusted to fair value.

   5. Because the parent paid an amount in addition to the fair value of the non-controlling interest shares, more goodwill is allocated to the parent.

   6. The presence of a control premium affects goodwill in the consolidated financial statements, and little else.

IV. **Consolidation Involving a Noncontrolling Interest – Worksheet Process**

   A. The acquisition method focuses on consolidating 100% of the subsidiary's fair value as of the *acquisition* date.

   B. Noncontrolling interest amounts are shown in a separate column in the worksheet. The year end noncontrolling interest is the *sum* of:

   1. The noncontrolling percentage of the subsidiary's book value at the beginning of the consolidation period, plus

2. The noncontrolling percentage of the unamortized fair value allocations as of the beginning of the year, plus

3. The noncontrolling percentage of the subsidiary's income for the period less the current period amortization of allocations,

4. Less the share of the subsidiary's dividends paid to the noncontrolling shareholders.

C. The worksheet entries are as follows (**SAIDE**):

1. *Consolidation Entry S*

   a. Eliminate (debit) the subsidiary's beginning of period equity accounts.

   b. Credit the *Investment in Subsidiary* account for the parent's share of the beginning of period equity accounts.

   c. Credit *Noncontrolling Interest* with the noncontrolling interest share of the beginning of period equity accounts.

2. *Consolidation Entry A*

   a. Make debit and credit adjustments to assets and liabilities for 100% of the unamortized fair value allocations as of the beginning of the year.

   b. Credit *Investment in Subsidiary* for the parent's share of the total unamortized fair value adjustments.

   c. Credit *Noncontrolling Interest* for the noncontrolling shareholders' percentage of the total unamortized fair value adjustments.

3. Enter the total of 1.c. and 2.c. in the separate Noncontrolling Interest column of the worksheet (corresponding to the line titled "noncontrolling interest in subsidiary (beginning of year)").

4. *Consolidation Entry I*

   a. Eliminate the *Equity in Subsidiary Earnings* account and credit the *Investment in Subsidiary* account (assuming positive income).

   b. The *Noncontrolling Interest in Subsidiary Income* is computed as the noncontrolling shareholders' percentage of the subsidiary's net income less the fair value allocation amortization for the period. It is added in the separate Noncontrolling Interest column of the worksheet.

5. *Consolidation Entry D*

   a. Eliminate (credit) the subsidiary's *Dividends Paid* to the parent company.

   b. Debit the parent's share of the dividends to the *Investment in Subsidiary* account.

c. The noncontrolling shareholders' portion of the dividends is entered in the separate Noncontrolling Interest column of the worksheet.

6. *Consolidation Entry E*

   a. Recognize the amortization expense on the fair value allocations.

   b. Debit or credit the related asset or liability accounts.

   c. Note: the noncontrolling shareholders' share of the fair value allocations is already included in the computation of *Noncontrolling Interest in Subsidiary Income* (see IV.C.4.b above).

7. The total of the balances in the Noncontrolling Interest column is calculated, and extended over to the Consolidated Balance Sheet totals. This is the noncontrolling interest at the end of the year.

8. Extend account balances across the worksheet.

9. Continue the process from the previous chapters – calculate net income and ending retained earnings and carry them down the worksheet.

D. Effects Created by Alternative Investment Methods

   1. Conversion to Equity Method from Initial Value Method

   a. The parent recognizes dividend income rather than equity income accruals. The *I* entry eliminates the dividend income and subsidiary dividends paid to the parent. No separate *D* entry is needed.

   b. The parent does not recognize equity income, excess amortization expense or prior dividends paid, thus, *Entry *C* is needed to convert the previously recorded balances for beginning Retained Earnings and the Investment in Subsidiary account to the equity method.

   c. The *Entry *C* adjustment amount is:

   (1) The increase for the *prior* years since the acquisition in the subsidiary's retained earnings (income less dividends) × the parent's ownership percentage

   (2) + the parent's percentage × total amortization expense for the *prior* years.

   2. Conversion to Equity Method from Partial Equity Method

   a. The parent does not recognize excess amortization expense, thus, Entry *C* is needed to convert the previously recorded balances for beginning Retained Earnings and the Investment in Subsidiary account to the equity method.

   b. The Entry *C* adjustment amount is for the parent's percentage × total amortization expense for the prior years.

V. *LO8* Revenue and Expense Reporting for Mid-Year Acquisitions

A. **Consolidating Postacquisition Subsidiary Revenue and Expenses** – changes are needed when a company gains control at mid-year.

   1. The parent calculates the subsidiary's book value at the acquisition date to determine the excess total fair value over book value allocations.

   2. Excess amortization expenses as well as any equity accrual and dividend collections are recognized for a period of less than a year.

   3. Only *postacquisition* revenues and expenses are included in consolidated totals.

   4. Additional adjustments:

      a. The year-end balances the subsidiary submits for consolidation (trial balance) typically include income and expenses for the entire period.

      b. The noncontrolling interest is viewed as coming into being as of the parent's acquisition date.

      c. Preacquisition subsidiary revenues, expenses and dividends, through *Entry S*, are:

         (1) Eliminated as part of the subsidiary book value elimination in the year of acquisition.

         (2) Included as components of the beginning value of the noncontrolling interest.

         (3) Excluded from the consolidated income statement and statement of retained earnings.

         Consolidation Entry S (for Stockholders' Equity)

Common Stock - Subsidiary ………………………....	XX	
Additional Paid-In Capital - Subsidiary ……………	XX	
Retained Earnings, 1/1/0X - Subsidiary ……………	XX	
Revenues, preacquisition - Subsidiary …………….	XX	
Dividends paid - Subsidiary …………………… ..		XX
Expenses, preacquisition - Subsidiary ………….......		XX
Noncontrolling interest (acquisition date) ………..		XX
Investment in Subsidiary …………………………		XX

B. **Acquisition Following an Equity Method Investment**

   1. Often, a parent company owns a noncontrolling equity interest in a firm prior to obtaining control. Upon gaining control, the parent consolidates only post-acquisition revenues and expenses of its new subsidiary.

   2. The parent also accrues and reports on its income statement the *equity in earnings of the investee* up to the date control was obtained.

   3. In the year of acquisition, the consolidated income statement reports both combined revenues and expenses (post-acquisition) of the subsidiary and equity method income (preacquisition).

---

4. In subsequent years, the parent needs to make sure that excess amortizations correctly reflect the mid-year acquisition.

VI. *LO9* Step Acquisitions

A. Control Achieved in Steps – Acquisition Method

1. The acquisition method measures the acquired firm at fair value, including the noncontrolling interest.

2. If the parent previously held a noncontrolling interest in the acquired firm, the parent remeasures that interest to fair value and recognizes a gain or loss in current income.

3. If after obtaining control, the parent increases its ownership interest in the subsidiary, no further remeasurement takes place – the additional subsidiary shares acquired are treated as an equity transaction.

4. Note that the acquisition method views a multiple step acquisition as essentially the same as a single step acquisition. Once control is obtained, the only relevant values in consolidating the subsidiary accounts are the fair values at acquisition date.

B. Step Acquisition Resulting after Control is Obtained

1. Once control is obtained, the acquisition method focuses exclusively on acquisition date fair values. A parent's subsequent subsidiary stock acquisitions do not affect these initially recognized fair values as long as control is maintained.

2. Any further purchases are treated as equity transactions.

3. The difference between the fair value of the consideration transferred and the underlying subsidiary valuation is recognized as an adjustment to additional paid-in capital.

C. *LO10* Parent Company Sales of Subsidiary Stock – Acquisition Method

1. Principles

   a. Current standards reflect the economic unit concept, in which transactions in the stock of a subsidiary, whether purchases or sales, are considered to be transactions in the equity of the consolidated equity.

   b. To account for sales of subsidiary shares, the valuation basis of acquisition-date fair value adjusted for subsequent changes in the subsidiary's net assets is maintained.

   c. The "income" effect (difference between proceeds and the carrying amount of the shares sold) from the sale of subsidiary shares depends on whether the parent continues to maintain control after the sale.

2. **Sale of Subsidiary Shares with Control Maintained**

   a. If the parent *maintains control*, no gain or loss is recognized when a portion of the subsidiary's stock is sold, because under the economic unit concept, transactions in a subsidiary's stock are considered to be transactions in the equity of the consolidated entity.

   b. The difference between the proceeds and the carrying amount of the shares sold is reported as an adjustment to owner's equity in an account such as *Additional paid-in capital from noncontrolling interest transaction*.

3. **Sale of Subsidiary Shares with Control Lost**

   a. The loss of control of a subsidiary is a *remeasurement* event that can result in gain or loss recognition.

   b. If the parent loses control of the subsidiary upon sale of subsidiary shares, the parent recognizes any resulting gain or loss on the sale of the investment (proceeds minus carrying value) in consolidated net income.

   c. If the parent retains any of its former subsidiary's shares, the retained investment should be remeasured to fair value on the date control is lost. A gain or loss on the revaluation is included in the parent's net income.

4. **Cost-Flow Assumptions**

   a. If a parent sells part of its shares in a subsidiary and has made more than one purchase, it must select an appropriate cost-flow assumptions.

   b. Use of specific identification based on serial numbers is acceptable. Averaging or FIFO assumptions are also often applied. Use of averaging is appealing because shares are truly identical.

5. **Accounting for Shares That Remain** – if a parent sells part of its shares in a subsidiary, it must determine the proper method of accounting for the shares that remain.

   a. If the parent no longer controls the subsidiary or has significant influence, consolidation is no longer applicable.

      (1) In the period prior to the sale, the equity method is used to report the investment.

      (2) After the sale, the market-value method is used for the remaining shares.

   b. If the parent still has significant influence, the parent utilizes the equity method for the entire year based upon the different percentages owned during the year.

   c. If the parent maintains control, consolidated financial statements are still required.

      (1) The process after the sale is based on the end-of-year ownership percentage.

      (2) The parent separately recognizes any current year income accruing to it from the shares it sold.

VII. Comparisons with International Accounting Standards

A. The accounting and reporting for business combinations has largely converged though the issuance of SFAS 141R and IFRS 3R, both titled *"Business Combinations"*.

B. Similarities:

1. The acquisition method is required.

2. A fair value model is embraced.

3. Exchanges between the parent and the noncontrolling interest are treated as equity transactions unless control is lost.

C. Differences in accounting for the noncontrolling interest:

1. U.S. GAAP – Acquisition-date fair value provides a basis for reporting the noncontrolling interest, which is adjusted for its share of subsidiary income and dividends subsequent to acquisition.

2. IFRS – The noncontrolling interest may be measured at either its acquisition-date fair value, which can include goodwill, or a proportionate share of the acquiree's identifiable net asset fair value, which excludes goodwill. This proportionate share option effectively assumes that goodwill created through the business combination applies to the controlling interest.

VIII. *LO11* SFAS 141 Purchase Method – Consolidated Financial Reporting With a Noncontrolling Interest

A. *SFAS 141R* and *SFAS 160* provisions for 100% fair-value measurements for all acquisitions are applied prospectively; therefore, there will be long lasting financial statement effects from past applications of the purchase method to business combinations.

B. Valuation of subsidiary assets and liabilities:

1. In the purchase method, the parent recognized the fair values of acquired subsidiary assets and liabilities only to the extent of the parent's % ownership.

2. In the presence of a noncontrolling interest, subsidiary assets and liabilities were thus measured partially at fair value and partially at the subsidiary's book value.

3. This dual valuation was viewed as being consistent with the cost principle.

C. Four noncontrolling interest figures are determined for reporting purposes:

1. Noncontrolling interest in the subsidiary as of the beginning of the current year.

2. Noncontrolling interest in the subsidiary's current year income.

Note: amortizations of cost in excess of book value are based on the parent's ownership % and are attributed solely to the parent company.

3. Noncontrolling interest in the subsidiary's dividend payments.

4. Noncontrolling interest as of the end of the year is found by combining the three balances above.

D. Noncontrolling interest balances are accumulated in a separate Noncontrolling Interest column in the consolidation worksheet. Consolidation entries for the Purchase method (entries SAIDE) are as follows:

1. *Consolidation Entry S*

   a. Eliminate (debit) the subsidiary's beginning of period equity accounts.

   b. Credit the *Investment in Subsidiary* account for the parent's share.

   c. Credit *Noncontrolling Interest* with the noncontrolling interest percentage of the subsidiary's book value at the beginning of the consolidation period.

2. *Consolidation Entry A*

   a. Set up adjustments for the *parent's percentage* of the unamortized fair value allocations.

   b. Credit the *Investment in Subsidiary* account for the total.

3. *Consolidation Entry I*

   a. Eliminate (debit if positive income) the *Equity in Subsidiary* Income account.

   b. Credit the *Investment in Subsidiary* account for the parent's share (assuming positive income).

   c. The Noncontrolling Interest in Subsidiary Income is computed as the noncontrolling shareholders' percentage of the subsidiary's net income. It is added to the separate, Noncontrolling Interest column of the worksheet.
   Note: amortizations of cost in excess of book value are attributed to the parent company.

4. *Consolidation Entry D*

   a. Eliminate (credit) the dividends paid to the *parent* company.

   b. Debit *Investment in Subsidiary* for the parent's share.

   c. The noncontrolling shareholders' portion of the dividends is entered in the separate, Noncontrolling Interest column of the worksheet.

5. *Consolidation Entry E*

    a.   Recognize the current amortization expense(s) based on the fair value allocations. (The calculations of the amortization are based on the parent's % ownership of the subsidiary.)

    b.   Debit or Credit the related asset and liability accounts.

6. The end-of-year noncontrolling interest total is the sum of the three noncontrolling amounts above (1.c., 3.c., and 4.c.).

7. The end-of-year noncontrolling interest is reported in the stockholders' equity section of the consolidated balance sheet (*SFAS 160*). Prior to *SFAS 160*, the location of the noncontrolling interest balance varied, and the noncontrolling interest could be shown as a liability, in stockholders' equity, or as a "mezzanine" item between liabilities and stockholders' equity.

E.   Criticisms of the Purchase Method in the Presence of a Noncontrolling Interest

1. Dual valuation of subsidiary balance sheet accounts.

2. The previous "mezzanine" categorization of the noncontrolling interest in consolidated balance sheets (between liabilities and stockholders' equity).

3. The valuation basis for the noncontrolling interest.

4. Accounting for the parent's transactions in the ownership shares of its subsidiary.

Multiple Choice Questions

Questions 1 through 5 are based on the following information.

On January 1, 2012, Cobb Enterprises acquired 80% of Bob's Bricks Inc.'s outstanding common shares. The acquisition price was considered proportionate to Bob Brick's total fair value. In acquiring this interest, Cobb paid a total of $3,000,000. Bob's Bricks' net assets had a book value of $2,600,000 at the time. A building with a ten-year life and a book value of $200,000 was worth $350,000. Any other excess amount was attributed to goodwill. Cobb reports net income for 2012 of $700,000 (without regard for its ownership in Bob's Bricks), while Bob's Bricks has $350,000 in earnings.

1. On a consolidated balance sheet as of 12/31/2012, what is the amount of goodwill?

    A. $1,030,000
    B. $1,000,000
    C. $1,550,000
    D. $ 800,000
    E. $1,150,000

2. What is the amount of consolidated net income for the year ended 12/31/2012?

    A. $1,050,000
    B. $ 980,000
    C. $ 993,000
    D. $ 968,000
    E. $1,035,000

3. What is the amount of consolidated net income attributable to the controlling interest for the year ended 12/31/2012?

    A. $1,050,000
    B. $ 980,000
    C. $ 993,000
    D. $ 968,000
    E. $1,035,000

4. What value should be attributed to the building in a consolidated balance sheet at the date of the business combination?

    A. $335,000
    B. $200,000
    C. $310,000
    D. $320,000
    E. $350,000

5. What value should be attributed to the building in a consolidated balance sheet as of 12/31/2012?

    A. $335,000
    B. $200,000
    C. $310,000
    D. $320,000
    E. $350,000

Items 6 and 7 are based on the following information:

On January 1, 2008, Ashley Inc. acquires 60% of Mask Co.'s outstanding common stock by issuing common stock with a market value of $180,000. Mask reported common stock on that date of $150,000 with retained earnings of $80,000. Equipment, which had a five-year remaining life, was undervalued in Mask's financial records by $20,000. Previously unrecorded franchise agreements valued at $50,000 are to be amortized over 10 years.

During 2008, Mask earns income of $90,000 and pays cash dividends of $30,000.

6. Under the purchase method, what is the noncontrolling interest in Mask's 2008 income?

    A. $24,000
    B. $54,000
    C. $60,000
    D. $36,000
    E. $44,000

7. Under the purchase method, what is the *noncontrolling interest* in Mask at the end of 2008?

   A. $ 92,000
   B. $254,000
   C. $116,000
   D. $ 92,000
   E. $128,000

8. On January 1, 2008, Pierce Inc. acquired 80% of the outstanding common stock of Sloan Co. for $580,000 cash. Sloan's net assets had a book value of $600,000 on that date. Sloan had land with a book value of $30,000 and a fair value of $50,000 on the acquisition date. In addition, Sloan had a database with a fair value of $80,000 and a remaining useful life of 4 years. The remaining purchase price was allocated to Goodwill. On December 31, 2008, Sloan reports revenues of $125,000 and expenses of $50,000 while Pierce reports operating revenues of $400,000 and expenses of $250,000. Using the Purchase Method, what is consolidated net income for 2008?

   A. $209,000
   B. $225,000
   C. $212,200
   D. $205,000
   E. $194,000

9. Using the information from # 9 above, what is consolidated net income if all events including the acquisition took place in 2011, and Pierce uses the acquisition method?

   A. $209,000
   B. $225,000
   C. $212,200
   D. $205,000
   E. $194,000

10. Which consolidation entry is used to eliminate pre-acquisition revenues and expenses?

   A. Consolidation Entry S
   B. Consolidation Entry A
   C. Consolidation Entry I
   D. Consolidation Entry D
   E. Consolidation Entry E

11. The noncontrolling owners' interest in a subsidiary is shown on the balance sheet:

   A. In the assets section
   B. In the liabilities section
   C. In the owners' equity section
   D. Between the liabilities and the owners' equity section
   E. This account is not shown on the balance sheet

12. Allen, Inc. buys all of the outstanding shares of Cookeville Ice Cream Company on April 1, 2012 for $860,000 cash. Cookeville Ice Cream's book value at the acquisition date was $600,000.

At the acquisition date, Cookeville Ice Cream has equipment with a book value of $140,000 and a fair value of $110,000. The equipment has a remaining useful life of 3 years. Cookeville Ice Cream also has a building with a book value of $175,000 and a fair value of $260,000. The building has a remaining useful life of 10 years. Cookeville Ice Cream is carrying land on its books with a fair value of $60,000. The original cost of the land was $26,000. Allen, Inc. incurred $5,000 in legal costs related directly to the combination.

How much Goodwill will be reported in the consolidated financial statements on December 31, 2012, the end of Allen's fiscal year?

A. $111,000
B. $171,000
C. $181,000
D. $198,250
E. $260,000

13. Referring to the information for #11 above, what is the excess amortization expense for the period ending December 31, 2012?

A. $ (1,500)
B. $ 8,500
C. $ (1,125)
D. $10,000
E. $ 0

14. Referring to the information in #11 above, what will the excess amortization expense be for the period ending December 31, 2017?

A. $10,000
B. $ 8,500
C. $ 6,375
D. $(1,500)
E. $ 0

Brief Essay Questions

1. What is the primary complicating factor when a consolidation involves ownership of less than 100% of a subsidiary?

2. Where do you find the Noncontrolling Interest account on a set of consolidated financial statements?

Problems

1. Bream Inc. pays $2,400,000 for 75% of Sockeye's outstanding common stock. Sockeye Co. has net assets with a book value of $2,350,000. Sockeye has land that was originally purchased for $320,000 is now worth $680,000. The remainder of the business combination's purchase price is allocated to Goodwill. Bream, Inc. accounts for its investment in Sockeye using the equity method.

   Required:

   A. Using the Purchase Method for consolidation, determine the amount that should be attributed to goodwill.

   B. Using the Acquisition Method for consolidation, determine the amount that should be attributed to goodwill.

2. On April 1, 2011, Tiger Inc. acquires 60% of Stripes & Spots Co.'s (S&S) outstanding common stock by issuing 45,000 shares of its $1 par value common stock. Tiger's stock has a $42 per share market value. Consolidation costs of $210,000 were also paid. Tiger uses the equity method to account for its investment in S&S.

   S&S has equipment (with an 8-year remaining useful life) undervalued on its books by $400,000. Land on S&S's books is undervalued by $500,000. S&S has franchise contracts valued at $250,000. The contracts are to be amortized over 5 years. The remainder of the purchase price is allocated to Goodwill. Prior to the business combination, the financial records of the two companies show the following account balances:

	Tiger	S&S
Current Assets	$ 1,800,000	$ 400,000
Land	$ 3,200,000	$ 600,000
Equipment	$ 5,800,000	$ 800,000
Other Fixed Assets	$ 12,500,000	$ 950,000
Liabilities	$ 6,200,000	$ 750,000
Common Stock	$ 10,000,000	$ 1,800,000
Additional Paid-In Capital	$ 6,800,000	$ 100,000
Retained Earnings	$ 300,000	$ 100,000

   Required:

   Using the acquisition method for consolidations, determine the consolidated balance sheet figures immediately after the business combination.

3. Assume the same facts as in number 2 above, except that the acquisition took place on April 1, 2008 and therefore, the purchase method was appropriate.

   Required:

   Using the purchase method for consolidations, determine the consolidated balance sheet figures immediately after the business combination.

Solutions to Multiple Choice Questions

1. B

Book value of Bob's Bricks = $2,600,000
Fair value of Bob's Bricks' net assets* = $2,750,000
Fair value of Bob's Bricks company ($3,000,000 ÷ 80%) = $3,750,000
includes the adjustment for the buildings.

Fair Value of Bob's Bricks	$ 3,750,000			
BV of Bob Bricks' net assets	2,600,000			
Difference to be allocated	1,150,000			
Allocated to Buildings	150,000	÷	10 =	15,000
Goodwill	$ 1,000,000			
Total Amortization Expense				15,000

2. E Basic information derived from this item and the above solution follows:

Cobb Enterprises Net Income	$ 700,000
Bob's Bricks Inc. Net Income	350,000
Amortization Expense	(15,000)
Consolidated Net Income	1,035,000

3. D

Cobb Enterprises Net Income			$ 700,000	
Bob's Bricks Inc. Net Income	100%	350,000	350,000	
Amortization Expense			(15,000)	
Consolidated Net Income			1,035,000	
Net Income - noncontrolling interest	20%	335,000	$ (67,000)	
Net Income - controlling interest			968,000	

4. E

Book value of building	$200,000
Allocation based on FMV	150,000
Consolidated Value	$350,000

5. A $335,000 – Initial consolidated value of $350,000 less 1 year amortization of $15,000.

6. D Noncontrolling interest in Mask's 2008 income is:

($90,000 × 40%) = $36,000

7. **C**   Under the purchase method, to calculate the noncontrolling interest in Mask Co. at the end of 2008, start with the noncontrolling interest in Mask's book value at the acquisition date, add the noncontrolling interest share of Mask's income for the year and then subtract the dividends paid to outside owners.

Mask Co.'s book value at the acquisition date — January 1, 2008:

Common stock	$ 150,000	
Retained earnings	80,000	$230,000
40% of Mask Co.'s 1/1/2008 Book Value		$ 92,000
+ 40% of Mask Co.'s 2008 Income		36,000
– 40% of Mask Co.'s Dividends		(12,000)
= Noncontrolling Interest in Mask Co.		$116,000

8. **E**

Purchase Price			$ 580,000			
BV of Sloan Co.'s net assets	80%	600,000	480,000			
Difference to be allocated			100,000			
Allocated to Land	80%	20,000	16,000	years	amortization	
Allocated to Database	80%	80,000	64,000	÷ 4 =	16,000	
Goodwill			$ 20,000			
Total Amortization Expense						$ 16,000

2008 Income of Pierce	$ 150,000
2008 Income of Sloan	75,000
Less: Amortization Expense	(16,000)
Less: Noncontrolling interest ($75,000 × 20%)	(15,000)
Consolidated Net Income	$ 194,000

9. **E**

Implied Value of Sloan ($580,000 ÷ 80%)	$ 725,000			
BV of Sloan Co.'s net assets	600,000			
Difference to be allocated	125,000			
Allocated to Land	20,000	years	amortization	
Allocated to Database	80,000	÷ 4 =	20,000	
Goodwill	$ 25,000			
Total Amortization Expense			$ 20,000	

2011 Income of Pierce	$ 150,000
2011 Income of Sloan	75,000
Less: 2011 Amortization Expense	(20,000)
Less: Noncontrolling interest ($55,000 × 20%)	(11,000)
Consolidated Net Income – 2011	$ 194,000

10. **A**

11. **C**

12. B   Allen Inc.'s Goodwill computation is as follows:

Consideration transferred	860,000
BV	600,000
Cost over book value	260,000
Land	34,000
Building	85,000
Equipment	(30,000)
Goodwill	171,000

13. C   When computing annual amortization for Allen Inc.'s consolidation, remember that the acquisition did not take place at the beginning of the year. The acquisition took place on April 1, which means we only compute amortization expense for 9 months, or 75% of the year.

Account	Allocation		years	× part. pd.		amort.
Building	85,000	÷	10 ×	0.75	=	6,375
Equipment	(30,000)	÷	3 ×	0.75	=	(7,500)
						(1,125)

14. B   In 2017, the allocation to the equipment will have been fully amortized. There is a full year of amortization on the remaining unamortized portion of the allocation to the building.

Building	85,000	÷	10 ×	1	=	8,500

Answers to Brief Essay Questions

1.   The primary complicating factor when a consolidation involves ownership of less than 100% of a subsidiary is accounting for the noncontrolling interest. When a parent company owns less than 100% of a subsidiary, the consolidation process requires making allowance for the portion of the subsidiary that is still owned by third party stockholders. While 100% of the subsidiary's balances are consolidated with the parent company, an account called Noncontrolling Interest is added to the Balance Sheet.

2.   *SFAS 160* requires noncontrolling interests in the equity of subsidiaries be reported in the owners' equity section of the consolidated statement of financial position. It should be clearly identified, labeled, and distinguished from the parent's controlling interests in its subsidiaries.

   Prior to *SFAS 160*, the purchase method allowed several locations for the noncontrolling interest: liabilities, equity, or as a mezzanine item between liabilities and equity.

   The portion of income allocated to the noncontrolling interest is shown on the consolidated income statement.

Solutions to Problems

1. **A.** Computation of Goodwill (Purchase Method):

Purchase Price			$ 2,400,000
BV of net assets	75%	2,350,000	1,762,500
Difference to be allocated			637,500
Allocated to land	75%	360,000	270,000
Goodwill			$ 367,500

B. Computation of Goodwill (Acquisition Method):

Implied Fair Value of Sockeye ($2,400,000 / .75)	$ 3,200,000
BV of net assets	2,350,000
Difference to be allocated	850,000
Allocated to land	360,000
Goodwill	$ 490,000

2. Computation of goodwill under the acquisition method: (Remember, under the acquisition method, direct combination costs are expensed.)

Implied Fair Value of S&S ($1,890,000 ÷ 60%)		$ 3,150,000
Book Value of net assets		2,000,000
Difference to be allocated		1,150,000
Allocated to land	500,000	
Allocated to equipment	400,000	
Allocated to franchise contracts	250,000	1,150,000
Goodwill		-

Date	Accounts	Debit	Credit
4/1/2011	**ENTRY S**		
	Common Stock - S&S	1,800,000	
	Paid-In Capital - S&S	100,000	
	Retained Earnings - 4/1/08	100,000	
	Investment in S&S		1,200,000
	Noncontrolling Interest in S&S		800,000
4/1/2011	**ENTRY A**		
	Land	500,000	
	Equipment	400,000	
	Franchise Contracts	250,000	
	Noncontrolling Interest in S&S		460,000
	Investment in S&S		690,000

CONSOLIDATION WORKSHEET - Tiger Inc. & Stripes and Spots Co.
Date of Consolidation = 4/1/2011

Account	Tiger	S&S	Consolidation Entries DR	Consolidation Entries CR	Noncontrolling Interest	Consolidated Balance
Current Assets	1,590,000	400,000				1,990,000
Land	3,200,000	600,000	500,000			4,300,000
Equipment	5,800,000	800,000	400,000			7,000,000
Other Fixed Assets	12,500,000	950,000				13,450,000
Investment in S&S	1,890,000			1,200,000 690,000		-
Franchise Contracts			250,000			250,000
Total Assets	24,980,000	2,750,000				26,990,000
Liabilities	(6,200,000)	(750,000)				(6,950,000)
Noncontrolling Interest				800,000 460,000	(800,000) (460,000)	(1,260,000)
Common Stock	(10,045,000)	(1,800,000)	1,800,000			(10,045,000)
Additional Paid-in Capital	(8,645,000)	(100,000)	100,000			(8,645,000)
Retained Earnings	(90,000)	(100,000)	100,000			(90,000)
Total Liab. & Owners Equity	(24,980,000)	(2,750,000)				(26,990,000)

3. Computation of Goodwill (Purchase Method):

Remember, under the purchase method, the combination costs of $210,000 are included in the investment cost.

Purchase Price ((45,000 shares x $42/share) + $210,000)			$ 2,100,000
Book Value of net assets	60%	2,000,000	1,200,000
Difference to be allocated			900,000
Allocated to land	60%	500,000	300,000
Allocated to equipment	60%	400,000	240,000
Allocated to franchise contracts	60%	250,000	150,000
Total to goodwill			210,000

Date	Accounts	Debit	Credit
4/1/2008	**ENTRY S**		
	Common Stock - S&S	1,800,000	
	Paid-In Capital - S&S	100,000	
	Retained Earnings - 4/1/08	100,000	
	Investment in S&S		1,200,000
	Noncontrolling Interest in S&S		800,000
4/1/2008	**ENTRY A**		
	Land	300,000	
	Equipment	240,000	
	Franchise Contracts	150,000	
	Goodwill	210,000	
	Investment in S&S		900,000

CONSOLIDATION WORKSHEET - Tiger Inc. & Stripes and Spots Co.
Date of Consolidation = 4/1/2008

Account	Tiger	S&S	Consolidation Entries DR	CR	Noncontrolling Interest	Consolidated Balance
Assets						
Current Assets	1,590,000	400,000				1,990,000
Land	3,200,000	600,000	300,000			4,100,000
Equipment	5,800,000	800,000	240,000			6,840,000
Other Fixed Assets	12,500,000	950,000				13,450,000
Investment in S&S	2,100,000			1,200,000		-
				900,000		
Franchise Contracts			150,000			150,000
Goodwill			210,000			210,000
Total Assets	**25,190,000**	**2,750,000**				**26,740,000**
Liabilities	(6,200,000)	(750,000)				(6,950,000)
Noncontrolling Interest				800,000	(800,000)	(800,000)
Common Stock	(10,045,000)	(1,800,000)	1,800,000			(10,045,000)
Additional Paid-in Capital	(8,645,000)	(100,000)	100,000			(8,645,000)
Retained Earnings	(300,000)	(100,000)	100,000			(300,000)
Total Liab + Owners Equity	**(25,190,000)**	**(2,750,000)**				**(26,740,000)**

Chapter 5

Consolidated Financial Statements – Intra-entity Asset Transactions

Chapter Outline

Standards Mentioned in This Chapter:
- **FASB Interpretation 46R,** *Consolidation of Variable Interest Entities, an Interpretation of ARB No. 51*
- **SFAS No. 160,** *Noncontrolling Interests and Consolidated Financial Statements*
- **SFAS No. 167,** *Amendments to FASB Interpretation 46R*

I. *LO1* **Principles**

   A. Since consolidated financial statements report results for the consolidated entity as if it were a single company, the effects of gain or loss transactions among the entities must be eliminated because the transactions do not occur with an unrelated outside party.

   B. Intra-entity transactions are common, especially in vertically integrated organizations. These transactions were often called intercompany transactions.

II. **Intra-entity Inventory Transactions**

   A. *LO2* **Sales and Purchase Accounts**

      1. Intra-entity inventory sales are frequent transactions. The individual accounting systems of the two companies record the transfer as a sale by one party and as a purchase by the other.

      2. Because the transaction did not involve an unrelated outside party, the sales and purchases balances created by the transfer must be eliminated in the consolidation process using *Entry TI*.

      <u>*Consolidation Entry **TI*** (for **T**ransferred **I**nventory)</u>

      Sales ……………………......…………………………….XX
            Cost of Goods Sold (purchases component) ……………XX

   B. *LO3* **Unrealized Gross Profit – Year of Transfer (Year 1)**

      1. Any transferred inventory that is held at the end of the year is recorded at its transfer price, which will often include unrealized gross profit. This overstatement created by the gross profit in the transfer price remains in:

         a. Ending Inventory

         b. Gross profit

      2. Unrealized intra-entity gross profit must be eliminated as long as the inventory remains unsold to an outside third party.

      3. The consolidation process shifts the gain from the period of transfer into the period in which the goods are sold to unrelated parties or consumed.

---

4. For consolidation purposes, the unrealized intra-entity gross profit remaining in *unsold* inventory is deferred by eliminating the amount from the *Inventory* account on the *balance sheet* and from the ending inventory figure in *Cost of Goods Sold* on the *income statement*.

*Consolidation Entry **G*** (for Unrealized **G**ross profit)

Cost of Goods Sold (ending inventory component) XX
      Inventory ....…………......………...………......……......…..XX

C. *LO4 Unrealized Gross Profit – Year Following Transfer (Year 2)*

1. Since the effects of the transfer carry over to the subsequent fiscal period, the unrealized gain must be removed a second time — from the *beginning inventory component of Cost of Goods Sold* and from the *beginning Retained Earnings balance* using *Entry *G*.

*Consolidation Entry ***G*** (for Unrealized **G**ross profit, * for prior year)

Retained Earnings (*seller's* beginning balance) XX
      Cost of Goods Sold (beginning inventory) ...…………XX

2. **Intra-entity Beginning Inventory Profit Adjustment – Downstream Sales When Parent Uses Equity Method**

   a. When the parent uses the equity method and the transfer was *downstream*, the beginning Retained Earnings balance is correct; therefore, the debit is to the *Equity in Subsidiary Earnings* account instead of retained earnings to recognize the previously deferred unrealized gross profit as part of current year income.

   b. This application of the equity method differs from that presented in chapter 1 when there is only a significant influence, in which case the investor company defers unrealized intra-entity gross profits only to the extent of its percentage ownership.

3. **Equity Method Not Applied by Parent** – when the equity method is not applied by the parent company, *Entry *C* converts the parent's beginning retained earnings to its value under the equity method. *Entry *C* is adjusted for upstream transfers made in the prior period because the transfers affected the prior year's income from the subsidiary.

D. *LO5 Unrealized Gross Profit – Effect on Noncontrolling Interest Valuation*
The FASB codification indicates that alternative approaches are available in calculating the noncontrolling interest's share of a subsidiary's net income; recognition of outside ownership *may or may not* be affected by unrealized gains resulting from intra-entity transfers.

1. In the text, noncontrolling interest balances are adjusted only on *upstream* sales from the subsidiary to the parent.

2. In the text, *downstream* sales are made by the parent and viewed as having no effect on the outside interest, as any gain will be earned by the parent.

E. *Relationship between Gross Profit Rate and Markup on Cost*

1. Gross profit rate (GPR) = gross profit / sales *or* markup on cost / (1 + markup on cost)

2. Markup on cost (MC) = gross profit / COGS *or* GPR / (1 - GPR)

III.   **Intra-entity Asset Transactions**

A.   **Asset valuation** and **revenue/expense recognition** issues arise in consolidation when assets are transferred at an amount other than book value.

B.   The selling company's books will include a gain or loss that has not been earned in an arm's length transaction with an unrelated third party.

1.   From the perspective of the consolidated entity, the income is not correctly stated in the year of the sale due to the intra-entity gain/loss. The gain/loss must be eliminated from consolidated income in the period of transfer.

2.   In subsequent periods, the gain/loss will reside in the selling company's retained earnings, and must be eliminated in each of those periods as long as the asset is still held by the consolidated entity.

3.   The buying company records the asset at its acquisition cost.

4.   If the asset acquired is depreciable, the depreciation expense on the buyer's books for each year of the asset's remaining economic life (unless the asset is sold), will need to be adjusted on the consolidation worksheet to account for the difference between the original "*cost*" to the combined entity and the new "*carrying value*" on the buyers books (the acquisition cost of the buyer, which includes an unrealized gain or loss).

IV.   *LO6* **Intra-entity Land Transfers**

A.   **Accounting for Land Transactions**

1.   The original seller of the land reports a gain (losses are rare in intra-entity asset transactions), even though the transaction occurred between related parties. The acquiring company records the inflated transfer price for the land vs. the land's historical cost.

2.   The seller's gain is closed into retained earnings at the end of the year, which is now overstated from a consolidated perspective.

3.   From a consolidated perspective, the gain on the original transfer is actually earned when the land is sold to an outside party.

4.   **Eliminating Unrealized Gains – Land Transfers**

a.   *Consolidated income* in the year of the sale and *retained earnings* in subsequent years are overstated and the *Land* account of the buyer is overstated in each year until the land is sold to an outside party.

b.   *Entry TL* (for **T**ransfer **L**and) is needed in the year of the sale to remove the unrealized gain and reduce land to its original cost.

Consolidation Entry TL (for **T**ransfer **L**and)

Gain on Sale of Land ....…......……......XX
        Land…......…..…...…...….............…..………XX

c.   *Entry *GL* is made in subsequent years until the land is sold or otherwise disposed of to an outside third party.

*Consolidation Entry *GL* (for prior **G**ain on **L**and)

Retained Earnings (seller) ……...……..…...XX
       Land …….....…..…..…...…....…………..….…XX

Exception: If the parent uses the equity method and the transfer was downstream, the *beginning Retained Earnings balance* will be correct; therefore, the adjustment is to the *Investment* account.

5. If the land is sold to an outside party, the intra-entity gain is recognized in the period of sale.

*Consolidation Entry *GL* (for prior **G**ain on **L**and)

Retained Earnings (seller)……..…..…..…..XX
       Gain on Sale of Land....……………………......XX

V. *LO7* Intra-entity Transfers of Depreciable Assets

A. The unrealized gain must be deferred for consolidation purposes to establish the appropriate historical cost balances.

B. The difference between the transfer-based accounting value and the historical cost of the asset will change each year due to the effects of depreciation.

  1. The unrealized gain amount in *Retained Earnings* is reduced annually since *excess depreciation expense* is recognized annually (and closed to *Retained Earnings*) based on the inflated transfer price.

  2. Consequently, the unrealized gain eliminated from *Retained Earnings* and the reduction of the asset value to historical cost differ from one year to the next.

  3. Within the consolidation process, the recorded *Depreciation Expense* must be adjusted every period to the appropriate amount based on the asset's original acquisition price.

C. The following *consolidation worksheet elimination entries* are made:

  1. *Entry TA* is made in the year of transfer to remove the unrealized gain and return the asset account to the original historical cost balance.

*Consolidation Entry **TA*** (for **T**ransfer **A**sset)

Gain on Sale of Equipment……..…….…..……..………XX
Equipment……..……..……..……..……..……..……..…..…..XX
       Accumulated Depreciation…..……..…..…..…..…..…..…..XX

Note: the above entry assumes the sale of equipment for more than the seller's book value.

  2. *Entry ED* eliminates the current year overstatement of *depreciation expense* caused by the inflated transfer price. This entry is repeated each year over the economic life of the depreciable asset.

*Consolidation Entry **ED*** (for **E**xcess **D**epreciation)

Accumulated Depreciation……..…….……..……..………XX
       Depreciation Expense…..……..……..……..……..…..……XX

3. In the year of the intra-entity depreciable asset transfer, *entries TA* and *ED* are applicable whether the transfer was upstream or downstream.

4. *Entry *TA* (for prior year effect of **T**ransfer of **A**ssets) is made in the years following the transfer, and eliminates the remaining effect of the previous transfer so that consolidated account balances are based on the original historical cost.

    *Consolidation Entry *TA* (for prior year effect of **T**ransfer of **A**sset)*

    Equipment XX
    Retained Earnings, 1/1/XX.....................................XX
         Accumulated Depreciation...XX

5. If the transfer is *downstream* and the *equity method is applied*, a slight modification is made to *entry *TA* because the parent has already eliminated the unrealized gain. *The Investment in Subsidiary* account is debited instead of Retained Earnings.

6. In this textbook, upstream transfers are assumed to affect the noncontrolling interest in income, whereas downstream transfers do not.

Summary of Worksheet Elimination Entries
For Intercompany Asset Transactions

CODE	ENTRY	PURPOSE
TI	Sales Cost of Goods Sold	To eliminate intercompany sales & purchases balances in the year the sale occurs
G	Cost of Goods Sold (End. Inv.) Inventory	To remove unrealized gross profit created by an intercompany sale in the year the sale occurs
*G	Retained Earnings (seller) Cost of Goods Sold (Beg. Inv)	To remove the unrealized gross profit from beginning figures so it can be recognized in the current period. Used when the sale is UPSTREAM, and when sale is DOWNSTREAM and the parent has not applied the equity method.
*G	Equity in Subsidiary Earnings Retained Earnings	To recognize the previously deferred unrealized gross profit in DOWNSTREAM sales where the parent applied the equity method.
*C	Investment in Subsidiary Retained Earnings	To recognize the change in the book value of the subsidiary and amortization related to the investment in the subsidiary. (Equity method not used by parent.)
TL	Gain on Sale of Land Land	To eliminate the effects of an intercompany transfer of land in the year that the transfer occurs.
*GL	Retained Earnings Land	To eliminate the effects of an intercompany transfer of land that occurred in a previous year. Make this entry every year until the land is sold to a third party.
TA	Gain on Sale of Equipment Equipment (*or other asset*) Accumulated Depreciation	To remove the unrealized gain created by an intercompany sale of a fixed asset in the year the sale occurs, and to return fixed asset balances to historical cost basis.
*TA	Retained Earnings Equipment (*or other asset*) Accumulated Depreciation	To remove the unrealized gain created by an intercompany sale of a fixed asset in a previous period, and to return fixed asset balances to historical cost basis.
ED	Accumulated Depreciation Depreciation Expense	To eliminate excess depreciation expense caused by an inflated transfer price.

Note: In the case of *downstream* sales where the *parent applies the equity method*, the entries shown above for *GL* and *TA* are modified: the *Investment* account is used instead of Retained Earnings, as the parent will have already adjusted retained earnings on its books.

Multiple Choice Questions

1. Redstone owns 60% of Granite Co.'s outstanding common stock. Redstone reports *cost of goods sold* in 2011 of $1,400,000 while Granite Co. reports $460,000. During 2011, Redstone sold inventory costing $250,000 to Granite Co. for $400,000. 30% of these goods are not resold by Granite Co. until the following year. What is *consolidated cost of goods sold*?

   A. $1,860,000
   B. $1,460,000
   C. $1,505,000
   D. $1,415,000
   E. $1,721,000

2. McKnight Inc. owns 80% of Horse Co.'s common stock. On January 2, 2011, McKnight Inc. sold Horse Co. some equipment for $640,000. The equipment had a carrying amount of $400,000. At the acquisition date, the equipment has a remaining useful life of 8 years. Horse Co. uses the straight-line method. The net adjustments to calculate 2011 and 2012 *consolidated net income* would be an increase (decrease) of

	2011	2012
A.	$(240,000)	$ 50,000
B.	$ 210,000	$ 30,000
C.	$ 240,000	$ 30,000
D.	$(210,000)	$(30,000)
E.	$(210,000)	$ 30,000

   Items 3 through 7 are based on the following information.

   Presented below are several figures reported for Park Inc. and Masters Co. as of December 31, 2012.

	Park Inc.	**Masters Co.**
Inventory	$ 400,000	$ 200,000
Sales	900,000	500,000
Cost of Goods Sold	300,000	180,000
Expenses	180,000	140,000

   Park Inc. acquired 75% of Masters Co.'s outstanding common stock on January 1, 2011. Land use rights valued at $281,250 were owned by Masters Co. and should be amortized over twenty years. During 2011, Masters sold Park inventory costing $80,000 for $100,000. 30% of this inventory was not sold to external parties until 2012. During 2012, Masters sold inventory costing $100,000 to Park for $150,000. Of this inventory, 25 % remained unsold on December 31, 2012.

3. What is the 2012 *consolidated sales* figure?

   A. $1,400,000
   B. $1,550,000
   C. $1,050,000
   D. $1,350,000
   E. $1,250,000

4. What is the 2012 *consolidated cost of goods sold* figure?

   A. $480,000
   B. $336,500
   C. $337,000
   D. $330,500
   E. $370,000

5. What is the *consolidated inventory* on December 31, 2012?

   A. $603,500
   B. $593,500
   C. $619,500
   D. $587,500
   E. $546,500

6. What is the 2012 *consolidated expenses* figure?

   A. $320,000
   B. $309,453
   C. $330,547
   D. $334,063
   E. $328,250

7. What is the *noncontrolling interest's share* of Masters Co.'s 2012 net income?

   A. $39,859
   B. $43,375
   C. $45,000
   D. $46,625
   E. $40,375

8. On January 1, 2011, Rogers Inc. sold equipment costing $3,150,000 with accumulated depreciation of $1,890,000 to Cooper Corp., a wholly owned subsidiary, for $1,500,000. Rogers had owned the equipment for six years and was depreciating the equipment using the straight-line method over ten years with no salvage value. Cooper will continue to use the straight-line method over the remaining four years of the equipment's economic life. In the consolidated statements at December 31, 2011, the cost and accumulated depreciation, respectively, should be:

   A. $3,150,000 and $1,890,000
   B. $1,500,000 and $ 375,000
   C. $1,500,000 and $1,050,000
   D. $3,150,000 and $ 375,000
   E. $3,150,000 and $2,205,000

9. In 2007, Ennis Inc. purchased land from its 70%-owned subsidiary for $125,000. The subsidiary originally paid $75,000 for the land several years earlier. In 2008, Ennis Inc. needed to raise some cash and sold the land to an unrelated third party for $150,000. What amount of gain or loss on the sale of the land should be reported in the *consolidated income statement* in 2007 and 2012?

	2007	2012
A.	$ 50,000 gain	$ 25,000 gain
B.	$ –0–	$ 50,000 gain
C.	$ 50,000 gain	$ 75,000 loss
D.	$ –0–	$ 75,000 gain
E.	$ –0–	$ 25,000 gain

10. Granville Manor Inc. owns 80% of Carrboro Condos Co. On January 1, 2004, Granville Manor Inc. acquired equipment with a ten-year life for $4,200,000. No salvage value was anticipated and the equipment was to be depreciated on the straight-line basis. On January 1, 2011, Granville Manor sold the equipment to Carrboro Condos for $3,000,000. At that time, the equipment had a remaining useful life of three years, but still had no expected salvage value. In preparing financial statements for 2011, how does this transfer affect the calculation of *consolidated net income*?

    A. Consolidated net income must be increase by $580,000.
    B. Consolidated net income must be decreased by $580,000.
    C. Consolidated net income must be increased by $420,000.
    D. Consolidated net income must be decreased by $1,000,000.
    E. Consolidated net income must be increased by $1,000,000.

Brief Essay Questions

1. How does the consolidation process for the intra-entity transfer of a depreciable asset differ from that for inventory and land, assuming the depreciable asset is transferred at a gain?

2. Bazley Inc. sold some of its heavy equipment to Cleave Co., its subsidiary, for an amount over its book value. When will the gain on this sale be earned?

3. What is the impact on the consolidation process if parties agree to transfer all assets between companies at book value, without any markup?

Problems

1. Slik Brick Manufacturing Inc. owns 70% of the outstanding common stock of Clay Pot Co. Clay Pot reports net income for 2012 of $400,000. Since being acquired, Clay Pot has regularly supplied inventory to Slik Brick. Inventory costing $450,000 was sold to Slik Brick for $600,000 in 2011. In 2012, Clay Pot sold inventory costing $250,000 for $420,000. Typically, 20% of the inventory that Slik Brick purchases from Clay Pot during any one year is not used until the following year.

    Required:

    A. What is the noncontrolling interest's share of Clay Pot's income in 2012?

    B. Prepare the 2012 consolidation entries that would be required by the above intra-entity inventory transfers.

2. Angel Inc. has a 75% interest in Halo Corporation. On January 1, 2011, land having an historical cost of $240,000 is sold in an intra-entity transaction for $300,000.

Required:

A. If Angel sold the land to Halo, what would be the appropriate consolidation worksheet entries at the end of 2011 and 2012 as a result of the transaction?

B. If Halo sold the land to Angel, what would be the appropriate consolidation worksheet entries at the end of 2011 and 2012 as a result of the transaction?

3. Portland Inc. owns 60% interest in Sherman Co. On January 1, 2011, equipment having a historical cost of $100,000 and a book value of $70,000 is sold in an intra-entity transfer for $80,000. The equipment has a remaining useful life of four years. Sherman Co. reports *net income* of $140,000 in 2011 and $160,000 in 2012.

Required:

A. If Portland Inc. sold the equipment to Sherman Company, what would be the appropriate consolidation worksheet entries for 2011 and 2012?

B. What effect, if any, would the transaction in part A. have on the valuation of the noncontrolling interest in Sherman's 2011 and 2012 income?

C. If Sherman sold the equipment to Portland, what would be the appropriate consolidation worksheet entries for 2011 and 2012?

D. What effect, if any, would the transaction in part C have on the valuation of the noncontrolling interest in Sherman's 2011 and 2012 income?

4. Porter Inc. holds a 70% interest in Stevenson Co. During 2011, Porter sold inventory costing $30,000 to Stevenson for $40,000. During 2011, Stevenson reports net income of $120,000, and during 2012, reports net income of $140,000. Porter uses the partial equity method.

Required:

A. Prepare the consolidation worksheet entries required in 2011 and 2012 if 40% of the intra-entity inventory is still on hand at the end of 2011.

B. What is the noncontrolling interest in income for 2011 and 2012?

C. Prepare the required consolidation worksheet entries if Stevenson had sold the inventory to Porter.

Solutions to Multiple Choice Questions

1. C

Intra-entity gain ($400,000 – $250,000)	$ 150,000
Inventory remaining at year-end	× 30%
Unrealized intra-entity gain at December 31	$ 45,000

Cost of goods sold – Redstone, Inc.	$1,400,000
Cost of goods sold — Granite Co.	460,000
Remove intra-entity transfer	(400,000)
Defer unrealized gain	+ 45,000
Consolidated cost of goods sold	$1,505,000

2. E   In 2011, the consolidated entity has a gain of $240,000 to eliminate. In addition, while McKnight's depreciation expense is now $80,000 ($640,000 ÷ 8 years), it would have only been $50,000 ($400,000 ÷ 8 years) if the transfer had not taken place. Therefore, we also have to eliminate $30,000 in depreciation expense in 2011. If we eliminate a gain of $240,000 (Consolidation Entry TA) and we eliminate the excess depreciation (Consolidation Entry ED), the net income effect would be to reduce consolidated net income by $210,000.

In 2012, the original gain is still on the seller's records, but it is now in Retained Earnings. Therefore the original gain should be removed from retained earnings, and there is no income effect related to the original gain. In addition, last year's excess depreciation is removed with Consolidation Entry *TA. Finally, there is still the need to remove the excess depreciation for this year. Consolidation Entry ED is repeated to eliminate the excess depreciation. The net effect on income in 2012 is an increase of $30,000.

3. E

Park Inc.'s reported sales	$ 900,000
Masters Co.'s reported sales	500,000
Elimination of intra-entity sales	(150,000)
Consolidated sales	$1,250,000

4. B

Cost of goods sold — Park Inc.	$ 300,000
Cost of goods sold — Masters Co.	180,000
Elimination of 2012 intra-entity purchases/sales	(150,000)
Deferral of 2012 unrealized gain ($50,000 × 25%)	12,500
Recognition of 2011 unrealized gain ($20,000 × 30%)	(6,000)
Consolidated cost of goods sold for 2012	$ 336,500

5. D

Inventory — Park Inc.	$ 400,000
Inventory — Masters Co.	200,000
2012 unrealized gross profit	(12,500)
Consolidated inventory	$ 587,500

6. D

Expenses — Park Inc.	$ 180,000	
Expenses — Masters Co.		140,000
2012 amortization of land use rights		
($281,250 × 75% ÷ 20 years)		14,063
Consolidated expenses		$ 334,063

7. A

Masters Co.'s reported income for 2012	$ 180,000
Unrealized gain deferred in 2011	6,000
Unrealized gain deferred in 2012	(12,500)
Amortization of land use rights	(14,063)
Realized income of Masters Co.	159,437
Noncontrolling interest percentage	× 25%
Noncontrolling interest's share of Masters Co. income	$ 39,859

8. **E** Historical cost of the equipment $ 3,150,000
Accumulated depreciation at 12/31/2011 ($1,890,000 + $315,000) = $2,205,000

9. **D** In 2007, no sale to an unrelated third party occurred. Thus, no gain is recognized in the 2007 *consolidated income statement*.

In 2012, a sale to an unrelated third party occurred. For the consolidated entity, the historical cost of the land is $75,000. Since Ennis Inc. sold the land for $150,000, a $75,000 gain ($150,000 – $75,000) is reported on the 2012 *consolidated income statement*.

10. **A** The equipment was not sold to an unrelated third party. Thus, from the point of view of the consolidated entity, depreciation expense must be based on the original historical cost of the equipment. Since the parent sold the equipment to the subsidiary at a gain, the subsidiary will record excess depreciation expense that must be eliminated in consolidation. The elimination of excess depreciation has the effect of *increasing consolidated net income*. Excess depreciation is calculated below:

Annual depreciation based on transfer price ($3,000,000 ÷ 3 years)	$ 1,000,000
Annual depreciation based on original cost ($4,200,000 ÷ 10 years)	(420,000)
Excess depreciation	$ 580,000

Answers to Brief Essay Questions

1. Like other intra-entity inventory and land transfers, unrealized gains created by intra-entity transfers of depreciable assets must be eliminated along with the overstatement of the asset. However, because of subsequent depreciation, these adjustments systematically change from period to period. Following the transfer of the depreciable asset, the buyer calculates depreciation expense based on the new inflated transfer price. Thus, expense is recorded that reduces the carrying value of the asset at a rate in excess of appropriate depreciation; book value moves closer to the historical cost figure each time that depreciation is recorded. Additionally, since the excess depreciation is closed annually to retained earnings, the overstatement of the equity account resulting from the unrealized gain is constantly reduced. To produce consolidated figures at any point in time, the remaining inflation in these figures (as well as in the current depreciation expense) must be determined and removed.

The consolidation process differs from that related to the intra-entity sale of land or inventory in several ways. The intra-entity gain resulting from a sale of land does not change from period to period and there is no related depreciation or amortization. An unrealized gain in inventory is generally short term, and is removed the following year due to the sale of the inventory to unrelated parties. The sale of a fixed asset generally has a long-term effect.

2. A gain on sale will be realized if the equipment is sold to an outside third party. However, the effect of the intra-entity gain is reduced over the remaining useful life of the equipment as Blaze Co. depreciates it. At the end of the equipment's useful life, the effect of the transfer is zero.

3. Setting the transfer price for all asset transfers at book value eliminates the need to account for deferred unrealized gains and losses, and allows us to ignore concerns about excess depreciation expense. However, in the case of inventory, the transfers will still create inflated sales and cost of goods sold numbers that need to be adjusted. With the tendency of companies to try to get financial statement information users to focus on the "top line" instead of the "bottom line", engaging in transaction that inflate revenues could be tempting. Therefore, intra-entity sales of inventory are eliminated.

Solutions to Problems

1. **A.**

Reported 2012 income of Clay Pot Co.	$ 400,000
2011 intra-entity gain realized in 2012 ($150,000 × 20%)	30,000
2012 intra-entity gain to be realized in 2013 ($170,000 × 20%)	(34,000)
Realized 2012 income of Clay Pot Co.	396,000
Outside ownership percentage	× 30%
Noncontrolling interest's share of Clay Pot Co.'s 2012 income	$ 118,800

B. Consolidation entries for 2012 are as follows:

Consolidation Entry *G

Retained Earnings 1/1/2012 (Clay Pot Co.) ………………	30,000	
Cost of Goods Sold ……………………………………..		30,000

To remove intra-entity gain from balances carried over from 2011 so that it can be recognized.

Consolidation Entry TI

Sales ……………………………………………………………	420,000	
Cost of Goods Sold (purchases) ……………………		420,000

To eliminate effects of intra-entity transfer of inventory.

Consolidation Entry G

Cost of Goods Sold ………………………………………….	34,000	
Inventory ……………………………………………………..		34,000

To remove intra-entity gain from 2012 so that it can be appropriately recognized in 2013.

2. **A.** Consolidation Entry TL — 2011

Gain on Sale of Land ………………………………………..	60,000	
Land ………………………………………………………		60,000

To eliminate effects of intra-entity land sale.

Consolidation Entry *GL — 2012

Retained Earnings (Angel Inc.) …………………………..	60,000	
Land ………………………………………………………		60,000

To eliminate the effects of intra-entity land sale in a previous year.

Note: if Angel applied the equity method, the gain would have been eliminated on Angel's books in 2011 and therefore would not be included in Retained Earnings. The debit in this case would be to *Equity in Halo's Earnings.*

B. Consolidation Entry TL — 2011

Gain on Sale of Land …………………………………………	60,000	
Land …………………………………………………………		60,000

To eliminate effects of intra-entity land sale.

Consolidation Entry *GL — 2012

Retained Earnings (Halo Corp.) …………………………	60,000	
Land ………………………………………………………		60,000

To eliminate the effects of intra-entity land sale in a previous year.

3. **A.** Consolidation Entry TA — 2011

Gain on Sale of Equipment ………………………………..	10,000	
Equipment ……………………………………………………...	20,000	
Accumulated Depreciation — Equipment ………….		30,000

To remove unrealized gain and restore historical cost balances.

<u>Consolidation Entry ED — 2011</u>

Accumulated Depreciation — Equipment …………………..	2,500	
Depreciation Expense …………………………………..		2,500

To eliminate the overstatement of depreciation expense caused by a price in excess of historical cost.

<u>Consolidation Entry *TA — 2012</u>

Retained Earnings ……………………………………………..	7,500	
Equipment ………………………………………………………..	20,000	
Accumulated Depreciation — Equipment ………….		27,500

To eliminate the effects of the 2011 intra-entity sale of assets.

<u>Consolidation Entry ED — 2012</u>

Accumulated Depreciation — Equipment …………………..	2,500	
Depreciation Expense …………………………………..		2,500

To eliminate the overstatement of depreciation expense caused by a price in excess of historical cost.

B. Because the sale is downstream, the noncontrolling interest is unaffected by the gain.

C. The *consolidation worksheet entries* TA, ED, and *TA will be the same as in Solution A. Note that the direction of the sale does not affect these entries.

D. The noncontrolling interest valuation is affected by these entries because this was an upstream sale from the subsidiary to the parent. The unrealized gain needs to be removed in 2011, and excess depreciation removed in 2011 and 2012.

<u>Allocation of Noncontrolling Interest in Income — 2011</u>

Income reported by Sherman Co.	$ 140,000
Less unrealized gain	(10,000)
Add excess depreciation	2,500
Realized income	132,500
Noncontrolling Interest percentage	× 40%
Income allocated to Noncontrolling Interest	$ 53,000

In 2012, Consolidation Entry *TA will debit *Retained Earnings* of the seller for $7,500, having no effect on the noncontrolling interest in income. Entry ED, however, will increase the interest on noncontrolling interest income by reducing the depreciation expense.

<u>Allocation of Noncontrolling Interest in Income — 2012</u>

Income reported by Sherman Co.	$ 160,000
Add excess depreciation	2,500
Realized income	162,500
Noncontrolling Interest percentage	× 40%
Income allocated to Noncontrolling Interest	$ 65,000

4. A. *Consolidation Entry TI — 2011*

Sales………………………………………………………………..	40,000	
Cost of Goods Sold (purchases) ……………………		40,000

To eliminate effects of intra-entity transfer of inventory.

Consolidation Entry G — 2011

Cost of Goods Sold (ending inventory component) ………....	4,000	
Inventory (balance sheet account) …………………		4,000

To eliminate unrealized gain on intra-entity inventory sale.
Note: gross profit = 10,000 × 40% = $4,000.

Consolidation Entry *G — 2012

Retained Earnings (Porter Inc.) 4,000
Cost of Goods Sold (beginning inventory component) ...   4,000
To remove unrealized gain from cost of goods sold so that it may be realized in the current period.

B. Because the inventory sale is downstream, the noncontrolling interest is unaffected by the sale.

2011 income	$ 120,000
Noncontrolling interest percent	× 30%
Noncontrolling interest in 2011 income	$ 36,000
2012 income	$ 140,000
Noncontrolling interest percent	× 30%
Noncontrolling interest in 2012 income	$ 42,000

C. Consolidation worksheet entries would be the same as in Solution A except that the $4,000 in Consolidation _Entry *G_ for 2012 would be associated with the Retained Earnings of Stevenson Co., not Porter. On the consolidation worksheet, the noncontrolling interest in Stevenson's income would change to reflect the unrealized gross profit.

Chapter 6

Variable Interest Entities, Intra-entity Debt, Consolidated Cash Flows, and Other Issues

Chapter Outline

Standards Mentioned in This Chapter:
- **ARB No. 51,** *Consolidated Financial Statements*
- **FASB Interpretation 46R,** *Consolidation of Variable Interest Entities*
- **SFAS No. 141R,** *Business Combinations*
- **SFAS No. 160,** *Noncontrolling Interests and Consolidated Financial Statements*
- **SFAS No. 167,** *Amendments to FASB Interpretation 46R*

I. *LO1* **Consolidation of Variable Interest Entities**

    A. **Background**

        1. Many firms establish separate business structures for specific purposes such as favorable financing. These structures are known as *special purpose entities* (SPEs), *special purpose vehicles*, or *off-balance sheet structures*. In the text, these entities are referred to collectively as *variable interest entities* or VIEs.

        2. VIEs can help accomplish legitimate business purposes.

        3. However, some firms used VIEs to avoid consolidation and provide off-balance sheet financing.

        4. In December 2003, the FASB issued FASB Interpretation 46R (FIN 46R), *Consolidation of Variable Interest Entities,* in response to previous abuses.

        5. In June, 2009 the FASB issued SFAS 167, *Amendments to FASB Interpretation 46R,* which expanded and changed several of the financial reporting requirements for firms using VIEs.

    B. **What is a Variable Interest Entity (VIE)?**

        1. Can be a trust, partnership, joint venture, or corporation.

        2. Typically has neither independent management nor employees.

        3. Firms often sponsor VIEs to accomplish limited, well-defined, valid business purposes and to provide low-cost financing.

        4. Examples of VIE activities include transfers of financial assets, leasing, hedging financial instruments and R&D.

    C. **How does a VIE provide low-cost financing and lower risk?**

        1. A company sets up or *sponsors* a VIE.

        2. The VIE acquires an asset.

3. Since the VIE's risk is isolated from the overall risk of the sponsor, the creditor lowers their risk by taking a specific collateral interest in the asset, which lowers the financing cost of the transaction.

4. The sponsor often guarantees the debt.

5. The VIE leases the asset back to the sponsor.

D.   Control of the VIE

1. A VIE frequently has little or no voting stock.

2. The sponsor company may not exercise equity control over the SPE, as control is often achieved through contractual means.

3. Prior to current consolidation requirements, since the sponsor company did not own a majority of the voting stock, the VIEs were not consolidated.

E.   Characteristics of Variable Interest Entities

1. Unlike in most businesses, the role of the equity investors can be fairly minor and they are typically provided only a small rate of return.

2. Typically, another party (often the sponsor) must contribute substantial resources (often loans and / or guarantees) to enable the VIE to secure the necessary financing.

3. Other contractual arrangements may limit returns to equity holders, while participation rights provide increased profit potential and risks to the sponsor.

4. These risks and rewards cause the sponsor's economic interest to *vary* depending on the VIE's success – thus the term *variable interest entity*.

F.   Consolidation of Variable Interest Entities

1. Prior to FIN 46R, since many of these entities had no voting stock, they were not consolidated with the sponsor because there was technically no equity control.

2. Companies must first identify a VIE that is not subject to control through voting ownership interests, but is subject to their control through other means and therefore is subject to consolidation.

3. **Identification of a Variable Interest Entity** – an entity qualifies as a VIE if *either* of the following conditions exist:

   a. The total equity at risk is not sufficient to permit the entity to finance its activities without additional subordinated financial support. Generally, this applies if the equity at risk is less than 10%.

   b. The equity investors in the VIE *lack any one* of the following three characteristics:

      (1) The power, through voting rights or similar rights, to direct the activities of an entity that most significantly impact the entity's economic performance.

      (2) The obligation to absorb the expected losses of the entity (i.e. the principal beneficiary may guarantee a return to the equity investee).

      (3) The right to receive the expected residual returns of the entity.

4. **Identification of the Primary Beneficiary of the VIE**

    a. If a firm has a relationship with a VIE it must determine if it qualifies as the primary beneficiary.

    b. The primary beneficiary must consolidate the assets, liabilities, revenues, expenses and noncontrolling interest of the VIE.

    c. An enterprise with a controlling financial interest in a VIE will have *both* of the following characteristics:

        (1) The power to direct the activities of a VIE that most significantly impact the entity's economic performance.

        (2) The obligation to absorb losses of the entity that could potentially be significant to the VIE or the right to receive benefits from the entity that could potentially be significant to the VIE.

G. **Procedures to Consolidate Variable Interest Entities**

    1. **Initial measurement issues** — initial valuations are based on fair values with few exceptions.

        a. When determining the consolidation amount for a VIE, the total business value of the VIE is the sum of:

            (1) Consideration transferred by the primary beneficiary, and

            (2) The fair value of the noncontrolling interest.

        b. The fair value principle applies to consolidating VIEs in the same way as in other business combinations. Thus, goodwill or a bargain purchase may be recognized.

            (1) **Total Business Fair Value of VIE Equals Assessed Net Asset Value** – Neither goodwill nor a gain on bargain purchase is recognized, and all assets and liabilities are consolidated at their fair values.

            (2) **Total Business Fair Value of VIE is Less Than Assessed Net Asset Value** – a gain on bargain purchase is recognized in the current year.

            (3) **Total Business Fair Value of VIE is Greater Than Assessed Net Asset Value** – if the VIE is a business, the excess is reported as goodwill.

    2. **Consolidation of VIEs Subsequent to Initial Measurement** – the consolidation process proceeds.

        a. Eliminate all intra-entity transactions between the sponsor and VIE.

        b. Income of the VIE must be allocated among the parties involved (equity holders and the primary beneficiary).

H. **Other Variable Interest Entity Disclosure Requirements**

    1. Current accounting standards require enhanced disclosures for any enterprise that holds a variable interest in a VIE.

    2. Enhanced disclosures for primary beneficiaries consolidating a VIE include:

        a. The nature, purpose, size, and activities of the VIE.

        b. The significant judgments and assumptions made by an enterprise in determining whether it must consolidate a VIE and/or disclose information about its involvement in a VIE.

        c. The nature of restrictions on a consolidated VIE's assets and on the settlement of its liabilities reported by an enterprise in its statement of financial position, including the carrying amounts of such assets and liabilities.

        d. The nature of, and changes in, the risks associated with an enterprise's involvement with the VIE.

        e. How an enterprise's involvement with the VIE affects the enterprise's financial position, financial performance, and cash flows.

    3. Enterprises that hold a significant variable interest in a VIE, but are not the primary beneficiary must disclose:

        a. Significant quantitative and qualitative information about the VIE.

        b. The enterprise's maximum exposure to loss as a result of its involvement with the VIE.

I. **Comparisons with International Accounting Standards**

    1. IFRS does not specifically mention VIEs, but an interpretation addresses when a special purpose entity (SPE) should be consolidated.

    2. Similarities – SPEs may be controlled despite a lack of ownership interest.

    3. Differences – control of an SPE is defined differently in IFRS than control of a VIE is defined in U.S. GAAP.

    4. The IASB has a project on its agenda to reconsider all of its consolidation guidance, including VIEs.

II. *LO2* **Intra-entity Debt Transactions**

    A. When one member of a business combination loans money to another (a *direct* loan), the resulting receivable/payable accounts, as well as the interest income/expense balances, are identical and can be directly offset in the consolidation process.

    B. **Acquisition of Affiliate's Debt from an Outside Party** – an *indirect* loan – requires special handling so that consolidated financial statements can be produced.

1. From a consolidation viewpoint, the liability is *retired* as of the acquisition date.

2. Since the cost to purchase the debt will usually differ from the book value of the liability, a gain or loss has been created with respect to the business combination. The difference is a gain or a loss because the debt acquisition effectively *retires* the debt (since no third party owns it).

3. This gain or loss is not recorded within the individual records of either company, but must be recognized in the consolidated financial statements.

4. Because of the amortization of any associated discounts and/or premiums, the interest income being reported by the buyer will not be the same as the interest expense of the debtor.

5. In the consolidation process, all balances are adjusted to reflect the effective retirement of the debt.

C. In the year of acquisition, all intra-entity accounts (the liability, the receivable, interest income, and interest expense) are eliminated during the consolidation process, and the gain or loss on the retirement of the debt (which produced the discrepancies) is recognized. This is done using entry *B* for **B**onds.

Consolidation Entry B (for **B**onds)

```
Bonds Payable ……. ..… …........ ............ .............................XX
Interest Income ............ ............ ............ .............................XX
Loss on Retirement of Bonds .... ............ .............................XX
          Investment in Subsidiary Bonds ........................…........XX
          Interest Expense ........... ............ ............................. ..........XX
```

D. **Assignment of Retirement Gain or Loss**

1. From a practical perspective, the assignment of the gain or loss is important only in calculating noncontrolling interest.

2. Theoretically, several approaches are possible in assigning the gain or loss.

3. The FASB has not set an official standard.

4. In the text, unless otherwise noted, all income effects relating to intra-entity debt transactions are assigned to the parent.

5. Therefore, the noncontrolling interest is not affected by the adjustments to consolidate intra-entity debt.

E. **Intra-entity Debt Transactions – Subsequent to Year of Acquisition**
   After the year of retirement, all intra-entity accounts must be eliminated in each subsequent consolidation. The beginning retained earnings of the parent company is adjusted for the previous gain or loss amount.

1. The change in retained earnings is needed from a consolidated perspective because a gain or loss was created in a prior year by the retirement of the debt, however, only interest income and interest expense were recognized on the books by the two parties. Use entry **B*.

2. The amount of the change made to Retained Earnings at any point in time is the original gain or loss adjusted for the subsequent amortization of discounts or premiums.

III. **LO3 Subsidiary Preferred Stock**

    A.   The existence of subsidiary preferred shares does little to complicate consolidation.

    B.   Any preferred shares not owned by the parent are included in the subsidiary business fair-value calculation and become a component of the noncontrolling interest.

    C.   If an entity has both common and preferred subsidiary shares, combining the consolidation entries S and A avoids an unnecessary allocation of the subsidiary's retained earnings across these equity shares.

    D.   **Allocation of Subsidiary Income**

        1.   The company's income must be allocated between the two types of stock.

        2.   This division must be made for every period subsequent to the takeover to:

            a.   Compute the noncontrolling interest's share of income, and

            b.   The parent's income recognition.

IV. **LO4 Consolidated Statement of Cash Flows** – the statement is produced from the *consolidated balance sheet and income statement,* not from the separate cash flow statements of the component companies.

    A.   **Background**

        1.   A Statement of Cash Flows is required in consolidated financial reports.

        2.   The main purpose of the statement is to provide information about the entity's cash receipts and cash payments during a period.

        3.   It also shows why an entity's net income is different from its operating cash flows.

        4.   The cash flows relate to the entire business combination (parent and all subsidiaries).

        5.   The statement uses three separate categories:

            a.   Cash flows from operating activities – using either the indirect approach or the direct approach.

            b.   Cash flows from investing activities.

            c.   Cash flows from financing activities.

    B.   **Acquisition Period Statement of Cash Flows**

        1.   **Business Acquisitions in Exchange for Cash** – the *net* cash outflow to acquire a business (cash paid less subsidiary cash acquired) is reported as an amount paid in a business acquisition under investing activities.

2. **Operating Cash Flow Adjustments**

   a. Consolidated net income is the starting point for the indirect calculation of consolidated operating cash flows.

   b. Changes in operating balance sheet accounts (working capital accounts) must be computed net of the amounts acquired in the acquisition.

3. **Excess Fair Value Amortizations** – amortization adjustments must reflect only post-acquisition amounts.

4. **Subsidiary Dividends Paid**

   a. The cash outflow from a dividend paid by a subsidiary only leaves the consolidated entity when it is paid to a noncontrolling interest. Therefore, dividends paid by a subsidiary to the parent do not appear as financing outflows.

   b. Subsidiary dividends paid to the noncontrolling interest are shown as cash outflows from financing activities.

5. **Intra-entity Transactions**

   a. The consolidated Statement of Cash Flows should not include the impact of intra-entity transfers.

   b. Since the Statement of Cash Flows is derived from the consolidated balance sheet and income statement, the impact of transfers has been removed and no special adjustments are required for intra-entity transfers.

V.   *LO5* **Consolidated Earnings Per Share (EPS)**

A.   **Basic earnings per share** – Consolidated net income, less a reduction for preferred stock dividends, is divided by the weighted-average number of parent shares outstanding.

B.   **Diluted earnings per share**

   1. If convertibles (such as bonds or warrants) exist for the parent shares, their weight must be included — if they can possibly dilute EPS.

   2. If the subsidiary has dilutive equity convertibles, the subsidiary earnings figure is not necessarily applicable to the diluted earnings per share computation.

      a. The accountant must separately determine the amount of subsidiary income that should be used in deriving diluted EPS for the business combination.

      b. The focus is on EPS for the parent company stockholders, even if there is a noncontrolling interest.

      c. For both basic and diluted EPS, if one or more less-than-wholly-owned subsidiaries are included in the consolidated group, income from continuing operations and net income shall exclude the income attributable to the noncontrolling interest in subsidiaries (*SFAS 160*).

d. Thus, consolidated income attributable to the parent's interest is the basis for the numerator in all EPS calculations for consolidated EPS.

VI. *LO6* **Subsidiary Stock Transactions**

A. If the subsidiary issues new shares of stock or reacquires its own shares (treasury stock), a nonoperational increase or decrease occurs in the company's fair value and book value.

B. Because the transaction may not involve the parent, the parent's investment account does not automatically reflect the effect of this change.

1. A change is created in the book value underlying the parent's *Investment* account, and the increase or decrease should be reflected by the parent as an adjustment to their investment account, and in this textbook, to *Additional Paid in Capital* (APIC).

2. The effect on the parent depends on whether the price received (or paid) is greater or less than the per share subsidiary adjusted fair value at that point in time. The book value of the subsidiary that corresponds to the parent's ownership is measured before and after the transaction with any adjustment recorded directly to the investment account and APIC.

C. Treasury stock acquired by the subsidiary may also necessitate a similar adjustment to the parent's investment account. Subsidiary treasury stock is eliminated during the consolidation process.

Multiple Choice Questions

1. Teccom Inc. holds a 65% interest in its subsidiary, Iota Corporation. On January 1, 2011, Teccom acquires $2,000,000 of bonds originally issued by its subsidiary in 2006. The 10-year bonds, which pay 5% interest every December 31, were originally issued to earn a 6% effective interest rate. The original discount of $103,041 is amortized by Iota using the straight-line approach. The bonds had a book value of $1,948,480 on January 1, 2011. Teccom pays $2,001,074 for the bonds, based on the current market rate of interest of 5.25%. Teccom will amortize its $1,074 premium using the straight-line method over the next 5 years. What amount of interest expense should be eliminated in Consolidation Entry B for the year ending December 31, 2011?

   A. $100,000
   B. $ 97,424
   C. $116,909
   D. $ 89,696
   E. $110,304

2. Using the information above, how much interest revenue should be eliminated in Consolidation Entry B for the year ending December 31, 2011?

   A. $100,000
   B. $ 99,785
   C. $100,215
   D. $ 98,926
   E. $101,074

3. Using the information in #1 above, what is the Loss or Gain on Retirement of Bonds to be recorded in Consolidation Entry B for the year ending December 31, 2011?

   A. $ 52,594 Gain
   B. $ 52,594 Loss
   C. $104,115 Gain
   D. $104,115 Loss
   E. $ 0 (no gain on loss)

4. Gaw Properties invests $5 million into RSR, a variable interest entity. RSR qualifies as a business entity. RSR's assets and liabilities have the following fair values:

   Cash.....................................$2,000,000
   Land......................................$7,000,000
   Long-term Debt.....................$2,500,000
   Gaw Properties Equity.............$5,000,000
   Noncontrolling Interest............$1,500,000

   At what amount is the land consolidated on Gaw Properties books?

   A. $5,000,000
   B. $7,000,000
   C. $9,000,000
   D. $ 0

5. Refer back to the information in #6 above. Assume that Gaw Properties invested $7,500,000 into the VIE. The business fair value of the VIE exceeds the assessed fair value of the assets by $2,500,000. How should the $2,500,000 excess be treated?

   A.   Recognize an extraordinary loss of $2,500,000 on the consolidated income statement.
   B.   Recognize an extraordinary gain of $2,500,000 on the consolidated income statement.
   C.   The land account should be reduced by $2,500,000 on the consolidated balance sheet.
   D.   The consolidated balance sheet should show Goodwill of $2,500,000
   E.   The land account should be increased by $2,500,000 on the consolidated balance sheet.

6. Which of the following is NOT a characteristic of Variable Interest Entities?

   A.   A VIE can be a trust, a partnership, a joint venture, or a corporation.
   B.   A VIE usually has a narrowly defined purpose.
   C.   A VIE usually has a "sponsor" company that controls decision-making for the VIE
   D.   Generally, in most cases, VIE's can be excluded from the consolidation process of the "sponsor" company.
   E.   FIN 46R outlines the conditions that would require the consolidation of a VIE.

7. A company holding a "significant" interest in a Variable Interest Entity, must disclose all of the following, except

   A.   The nature of the variable interest entity.
   B.   The purpose of the variable interest entity.
   C.   The names of the officers of the variable interest entity
   D.   The size of the variable interest entity.
   E.   The primary activities of the variable interest entity

8. Big Dan Fabrics recently acquired $6,000,000 of the bonds of Karen's Remnant Rack, Inc., one of its subsidiaries, paying more than the carrying value of the bonds. To whom would the loss probably be attributed?

   A. To Karen's Remnant Rack because the bonds were issued by Karen's Remnant Rack.
   B. The loss should be amortized over the life of the bonds and need not be attributed to either party.
   C. The loss should be deferred until it can be determined to whom the attribution can be made.
   D. To Big Dan Fabrics because Big Dan Fabrics is the controlling party in the business combination.
   E. The loss should be allocated between Big Dan Fabrics and Karen's Remnant Rack based on the purchase price and the original face value of the debt.

9. Which of the following is NOT identified by FASB FIN 46R as a characteristic of a "primary beneficiary" of a VIE?

   A. Ownership of a controlling equity interest in the VIE.
   B. The ability to make decisions about the VIE's activities.
   C. The obligation to absorb expected losses of the VIE.
   D. The right to receive expected residual returns from the VIE.
   E. All of the above are characteristics of a "primary beneficiary".

10. When one business acquires another, how is the cash paid for the acquisition reported in the statement of cash flows?

   A. The net cash outflow is reported as an investing activity.
   B. The net cash outflow is reported as an operating activity.
   C. The net cash outflow is reported as a financing activity.
   D. The acquisition amount is reported as a significant non-cash transaction.

11. Which of the following characteristics must be present to indicate a controlling interest in a variable interest entity?

   I. The direct or indirect ability to make decisions about the entity's activities.
   II. The obligation to absorb the expected losses of the entity if they occur.
   III. The right to receive the expected residual returns of the entity if they occur.

   A. I only.
   B. II only.
   C. III only.
   D. Any one of the above is sufficient to indicate a controlling interest in a variable interest entity.
   E. All of the above must be present to indicate a controlling interest in a variable interest entity.

Brief Essay Questions

1. A parent company purchases bonds from a third party that had been issued originally by one of its subsidiaries. From a consolidation perspective, what accounting issues arise as a result of the purchase?

2. A parent company acquires the outstanding bonds of a subsidiary from a third party. Explain how the parent company calculates the gain or loss on the acquisition.

3. CableCo has developed the technology to offer high-speed broadband internet service to its customers over a wireless broadcast system. The system was recently tested during an outdoor music concert attended by over 1,000,000 people. However, the commercial market simply does not exist. It may take up to 5 years to develop the market to the point where the service is profitable. CableCo sets up Pita Properties with the sole purpose of developing the market for the new wireless broadband service. CableCo sells the technology to Pita Properties for $100 million. Pita Properties obtains funding from a local bank to pay CableCo for the technology. However, the local bank requires CableCo to guarantee the loan to the Pita Properties. CableCo puts up its own stock as collateral against the loan.

Is Pita Properties a variable interest entity? In this circumstance, is CableCo a "primary beneficiary"?

4. Under what circumstances would a variable interest entity be subject to consolidation?

Problems

1. Palmer Inc. obtained controlling interest in Stewart Co. on January 1, 2011 for total consideration of $5,000,000. At that time, Stewart had the following equity accounts:

8% cumulative, participating preferred stock, $100 par value, 5,000 shares outstanding	$ 500,000
Common stock, $1 par value, 2,000,000 shares outstanding	2,000,000
Retained earnings	4,000,000

There were no dividends in arrears on the preferred stock. Palmer purchased 30% of the outstanding shares of preferred stock for $450,000. The remainder of the $5,000,000 acquisition was for 80% of the common stock. The acquisition-date fair value of the noncontrolling interest in the common shares was $1,250,000 and was $1,050,000 for the preferred stock.

All assets and liabilities were fairly valued on Stewart's books at the date of acquisition except for one building, which was undervalued by $200,000. The building has a remaining useful life of ten years. During 2011, Stewart reported net income of $1,600,000 and paid dividends of $280,000.

Required:

What amount is attributed to goodwill on the date of acquisition?

2. The following data applies to Parker Inc. and its subsidiary Stansbury Co. Parker Inc. acquired 80,000 shares of Stansbury Co. several years ago. Stansbury reports the following information about its shares and book values:

Shares outstanding	100,000 shares
Book value of company	$ 1,200,000

Note: Round any percentage calculations to the nearest whole percent.

Required:

A. Stansbury issues 10,000 shares of previously unissued common stock to the public for $10 per share. Parker purchased none of this stock. What journal entry should Parker make to recognize the impact of this stock transaction?

B. Stansbury issues 10,000 shares of previously unissued common stock to the public for $15 per share. Parker purchased none of this stock. What journal entry should Parker make to recognize the impact of this stock transaction?

Solutions to Multiple Choice Questions

1. **D**   Iota Corporation's Interest Expense to be eliminated is:
    Interest Payment ($2,000,000 × 5%)   = $100,000
    Less Discount Amortization of ($103,041 ÷ 10) = (10,304)
    Interest Expense to be eliminated   = $ 89,696

2. **B**   Teccom, Inc.'s Interest Revenue to be eliminated is:
    Interest Received ($2,000,000 × 5%)   = $100,000
    Less Premium Amortization of ($1,074 ÷ 5) = (215)
    Interest Revenue to be eliminated   = $ 99,785

3. **B**   Since Teccom paid $52,594 ($2,001,074 – $1,948,480), a loss of $52,594 must be recorded.

4. **B**   The land is consolidated at its full fair market value.

5. **D**   Since RSR has been identified as a business entity, the excess should be recorded as Goodwill.

6. **D**

7. **C**

8. **D**

9. **A**

10. **A**

11. **D**

Answers to Brief Essay Questions

1. Since the bonds were purchased from an outside party, the acquisition price is likely to differ from the book value of the bonds as found in the subsidiary's records. The difference creates accounting problems in handling the intra-entity transaction. From a consolidated perspective, the bonds have been retired; a gain or loss should be reported with no further interest being recorded. In reality, each company will continue to maintain these bonds in their individual financial records. In addition, since discounts or premiums are likely to be present, both of these account balances, as well as the interest income or expense will change from period to period because of amortization. For reporting purposes, all individual accounts must be eliminated with the gain or loss being reported so that the events are shown from the point of view of the consolidated entity.

2. The gain or loss to be reported is the difference between the price paid and the book value of the debt on the date of acquisition.

3. Pita Properties will qualify as a variable interest entity, because it has less than 10% of its equity at risk. In this case, the VIE has effectively none of its equity at risk. The risk is actually born 100% by the primary beneficiary.

    CableCo will be considered a primary beneficiary, because it has the obligation to absorb any expected losses of Pita Properties. If the broadband service does not generate sufficient cash to pay off the loan, then the lender will seek recourse against CableCo. CableCo's stock will be sold to pay off the debt. Furthermore, CableCo's stock value will likely suffer in the event of a failure of the VIE, resulting in the necessity of selling even more stock than originally anticipated due to the depressed value.

4. A variable interest entity is subject to consolidation if an enterprise determines that it is the primary beneficiary of the VIE. A primary beneficiary with a controlling financial interest in a VIE will have these characteristics: The power to direct the activities of a VIE that most significantly impact the entity's economic performance; and the obligation to absorb losses or the right to receive benefits of the entity that could potentially be significant to the VIE. The primary beneficiary must consolidate the assets, liabilities, revenues, expenses and noncontrolling interest of the VIE.

Solutions to Problems

1.

Consideration transferred for common stock	$5,000,000
Consideration transferred for preferred stock	450,000
Noncontrolling interest in common stock	1,250,000
Noncontrolling interest in preferred stock	1,050,000
Total acquisition-date fair value	$7,750,000
Book value of Stewart	6,500,000
Excess acquisition date fair value over book value	$1,250,000
Assigned to building	$ 200,000
Assigned to goodwill	$1,050,000

2. A. Analysis:

Adjusted book value ($1,200,000 + $100,000)	$ 1,300,000
Current parent ownership % (80,000 ÷ 110,000)	73%
Book value equivalency of ownership	$ (949,000)
Current book value of investment	960,000
Required investment reduction	$ 11,000

Date	Accounts	Debit	Credit
	REQUIRED ENTRY		
	Additional Paid-In Capital - Parker Inc.	11,000	
	Investment in Stansbury Co.		11,000

Note: the parent's ownership % was rounded to the nearest whole percentage.

B. Analysis

Adjusted book value ($1,200,000 + $150,000)	$ 1,350,000
Current parent ownership % (80,000 ÷ 110,000)	73%
Book value equivalency of ownership	$ (985,500)
Current book value of investment	960,000
Required investment reduction	$ (25,500)

Date	Accounts	Debit	Credit
	REQUIRED ENTRY		
	Investment in Stansbury Co.	25,500	
	Additional Paid-In Capital - Parker Inc.		25,500

Note: the parent's ownership % was rounded to the nearest whole percentage.

Chapter 7

Consolidated Financial Statements – Ownership Patterns and Income Taxes

Chapter Outline

I. *LO1* **Indirect Subsidiary Control**

    A.   Control can be achieved indirectly by controlling the parent company of another subsidiary(s).

    B.   One of the most common corporate structures is the *father-son-grandson* configuration where each subsidiary in turn owns one or more subsidiaries.

    C.   **Consolidation Process – When Indirect Control is Present**

        1.   Indirect ownership affects the mechanics of consolidation, not conceptual issues.

        2.   **Calculation of Subsidiary Income** is essential as it serves as the basis for calculating equity income accruals and the noncontrolling interest's share of consolidated income.

            a.   When there is indirect control, at least one company within the business combination holds both a parent and a subsidiary position.

            b.   Any company in that position must first recognize the equity income that accrues from subsidiaries.

            c.   Second, determine accrual-based income for the parent.

            d.   Start at the lowest levels of the father-son-grandson configuration, and work up to the highest-level parent.

    D.   **Consolidation Worksheet Process – Indirect Control**

        1.   Each corporate ownership layer effectively doubles the worksheet entries – first for the son's investment in the grandson and then for the father's ownership of the son.

        2.   Enter the balances of all companies on the consolidation worksheet.

        3.   Eliminate prior year unrealized intra-entity gains between the various companies using Consolidation Entry **G*. (It may be helpful to label the entries for each company.)

        4.   If something other than the equity method was used, then Consolidation Entry *C* (or **C*) is necessary for each company that accounted for a subsidiary using the initial value or partial equity method.

        5.   Prepare each of the consolidation entries for each of the parent/subsidiary relationships in the father-son-grandson configuration.

6. Determining *Noncontrolling Interest in Consolidated Income* requires a systematic approach to allocating subsidiary income *up the chain* to each successive parent and to the noncontrolling interest based on the accrual-based earnings of the subsidiary. Begin with the furthest subsidiary down the chain. Then, move up a level and do the same until you have calculated the noncontrolling income for each subsidiary.

II. *LO2* **Indirect Subsidiary Control — Connecting Affiliation**

A. A *connecting affiliation* exists whenever two or more companies within a business combination hold an equity interest in another member of that organization. (Think of a triangle.)

1. Often, neither investing party holds a controlling equity interest in the affiliated company.

2. The combined ownership interests of the various investing parties can be combined to effectively control the investee, thus, consolidation is required.

3. The valuation basis for the subsidiary in the consolidated statements is established on the date the parent obtains control.

B. The consolidation process is essentially the same for a connecting affiliation as for a father-son-grandson organization, however, more than two investments are always present.

C. Accrual-based income figures must be determined for each individual company.

III. *LO3* **Mutual Ownership**

A. **Mutual Affiliation** exists whenever two companies within a business combination hold an equity interest in each other. This occurs when:

1. A subsidiary owns shares of its parent company.

2. Mutual ownership exists between two subsidiary companies.

B. **Treasury Stock Approach**

1. According to the FASB codification, shares of the parent held by a subsidiary should not be treated as outstanding shares on the consolidated balance sheet.

2. Thus, a treasury stock treatment is required for parent shares held by a subsidiary.

3. This approach treats the stock as treasury stock, focusing on the parent's control over the subsidiary.

4. The purchase of the parent's shares by any of the affiliated members is reported as treasury stock in the consolidated financial statements. The shares are reclassified during the consolidation process to a treasury stock account.

5. Any dividend payments on this stock are considered intra-entity cash transfers that must be eliminated.

IV. Indirect Control — Comparisons with International Accounting Standard

A. Under U.S. GAAP the consolidation process for indirectly controlled subsidiaries begins with the lowest firm in the organization and proceeds upwards until the parent consolidates its direct subsidiaries.

B. Under IFRS, the method for consolidating indirectly controlled subsidiaries is not specifically addressed, which could lead to differences.

V. *LO4* Income Tax Accounting for a Business Combination

A business combination may elect to file a consolidated tax return for all companies that qualify as part of an *affiliated group* according to IRS guidelines.

A. Affiliated Groups

   1. Determining the Affiliated Group:

      a. A subsidiary may be included in an affiliated group for tax purposes if the parent company (either directly or indirectly) owns at least 80% of the voting stock of the subsidiary and 80% of each class of its nonvoting stock.

      b. Subsidiaries in the affiliated group must be domestic companies.

      c. Any subsidiaries that are not part of the affiliated group must file separate tax returns.

      d. An 80-100% owned domestic subsidiary may file as part of a consolidated return, or may file separately.

   2. The filing of a consolidated tax return provides several potential advantages to the members of an affiliated group.

      a. Intra-entity profits are not taxed until realized. Similarly, losses (rare) are not deducted until intra-entity realized.

      b. Intra-entity dividends are not taxed (these distributions are nontaxable for all members of an affiliated group whether a consolidated return or a separate return is filed).

      c. Losses of one affiliated company can be used to reduce the taxable income earned by other members of the group.

B. *LO5* Deferred Income Taxes

   1. Some of the differences between GAAP and income tax laws produce *temporary differences* – differences between an asset's accounting and tax basis. This results in taxable or deductible amounts in future years, requiring recognition of a deferred tax asset or liability for accounting purposes.

2. The specific amount of the deferred tax depends somewhat on whether consolidated or separate tax returns are filed.

3. **Dividends**

   a. For financial reporting, intra-entity dividends are always eliminated as they represent intra-entity cash transactions.

   b. In tax accounting, dividends are removed (and are nontaxable) from income if at least **80%** of the subsidiary's stock is owned. Therefore, there is no temporary difference.

   c. If less than 80% of the subsidiary is owned, 20% of the dividends received from the subsidiary are taxed because the dividends-received deduction (nontaxable portion) is only 80%. In addition, deferred taxes are required for any of the subsidiary's income that is not paid currently as dividends.

      (1) A current tax liability is recorded based on dividends received.

      (2) A deferred tax liability is recorded for the taxable portion of any income not paid as dividends.

4. **The Impact of Goodwill**

   a. For tax purposes, goodwill can be written off over a 15-year period.

   b. For financial purposes, goodwill is reduced or written off if impaired or if all or part of the related business unit is sold.

   c. This creates a temporary timing difference requiring the recognition of deferred income taxes.

   d. The same is true for other purchased intangibles if a life other than 15 years is used for financial reporting.

5. **Unrealized Intra-entity Gains**

   a. For financial purposes, unrealized intra-entity gains resulting from transfers are deferred. For consolidated tax returns, the treatment is the same.

   b. If separate returns are filed, taxes must be paid on intra-entity profits in the period of transfer. This temporary timing difference, which for accounting purposes is a prepayment of taxes, creates a deferred income tax asset.

C. *LO5* **Income Tax Expense Assignment – Consolidated Return**

   1. If a consolidated tax return is filed, an allocation of the income tax expense must be made to each of the component companies. The expense is also used in noncontrolling interest calculations.

      a.   **Percentage Allocation Method** – One method of allocating the tax expense is using a percentage of the total taxable income coming from each company.

      b.   **Separate Return Method** – Income tax expense can also be assigned to each subsidiary based on the amounts that would have been paid on separate returns.

D.   *LO6* **Filing of Separate Tax Returns**

    1.   Mandatory for foreign subsidiaries.

    2.   Required for domestic subsidiaries that do not qualify for inclusion in an affiliate group (less than 80% owned).

    3.   Members of an affiliate group can choose to file separately.

      a.   This may be advantageous if all companies are profitable and there are few intra-entity transactions.

      b.   Filing separately allows more flexibility in the choice of accounting methods and fiscal years.

      c.   Once a choice is made to file as part of a consolidated return, it is difficult to get IRS permission to file separately.

      d.   The filing of a separate return often creates temporary differences because of:

        (1)   Immediate taxation of unrealized gains (and losses).

        (2)   Possible future tax effect of subsidiary income > dividend payments (*undistributed income*). This part of a **domestic** subsidiary's income is not taxed until a later date, therefore, a deferred tax liability is created.

        (3)   **Exception** to the recognition of deferred income taxes on a subsidiary's undistributed income: a deferred tax liability is not recognized for the excess amount for financial reporting over the tax basis of an investment in a **foreign** subsidiary that is essentially permanent in duration.

E.   *LO7* **Temporary Differences Generated by Business Combinations**

    1.   Purchase combinations may be taxable or nontaxable, based on the nature of the transaction. In most tax-free purchases and a few taxable purchases, the tax basis of a subsidiary's assets and liabilities (cost) may differ from their consolidated values, which are based on the fair market values on the date the combination is created.

      a.   If additional taxes will result in future years (for example — if the tax basis of an asset is lower than its consolidated value so that future depreciation expense for tax purposes will be less), a *deferred tax liability* is created by a combination.

  b. The deferred tax liability is then written off, creating a reduction in income tax expense in future years so that the net expense recognized matches the combination's book income (a lower number because of the extra depreciation on the consolidated value).

 2. The deferred tax liability or asset is on the balance sheet of the consolidated entity.

F. *LO8* **Business Combinations and Operating Loss Carryforwards**

 1. Net operating losses (NOLs) recognized by a company can be used to reduce taxable income from the previous two years (a *carryback*) or for the future twenty years (a *carryforward*).

 2. NOL carryforwards can only be used by the company recording the loss under U.S. law, so acquisition of companies with an NOL carryforward is no longer a popular business strategy.

 3. If a company in a newly created combination has an *operating loss carryforward*, the future income tax benefits are recognized as a *deferred income tax asset*.

 4. However, a *valuation allowance* is also recorded to reduce the deferred tax asset to the amount that is *more likely than not* to be realized if it is more likely than not (>50%) that some portion or all of the deferred tax assets will not be realized.

 5. If a company established a valuation allowance, but was subsequently able to use the carryforward to successfully reduce taxes, the valuation allowance must be removed.

  a. Any changes in a valuation allowance for an acquired entity's deferred tax asset are reported as a reduction or increase to income tax expense.

  b. However, changes within the measurement period that result from new information about facts and circumstances that existed at the acquisition date are recognized with an adjustment to goodwill.

G. **Income Taxes and Business Combinations — Comparisons with International Accounting Standard**

 1. Similarities: both require business combinations to recognize current tax effects and anticipated future tax consequences using deferred tax assets and liabilities.

 2. Difference: taxes on intra-entity asset transfers within the consolidated group.

  a. U.S. GAAP prohibits the recognition of deferred taxes on intra-entity profits. Any tax impacts to the selling firm are deferred until the asset is sold to a third party.

  b. International standards require recognition of deferred taxes on intra-entity profits at the buying firm's tax rate. Tax impacts to the selling firm are recognized as incurred.

Multiple Choice Questions

1. Perview Inc. owns 70% of Software Co. Software Co. owns 80% of Bronston Co. Operating income figures for the current year are presented below, which contain no investment income. Included in both Software's and Bronston's income is a $120,000 *unrealized gain on intra-entity transfers* to Perview.

	Perview Inc.	Software Co.	Bronston Co.
Operating Income	$1,250,000	$720,000	$400,000

    What is Perview Inc.'s accrual-based income for the current year?

    A. $1,826,800
    B. $1,910,800
    C. $2,194,000
    D. $2,333,000
    E. None of the above

2. Palmroy Inc. owns 70% of Sport Co., which, in turn, owns 60% of Frank Co. Operating income figures (without investment income) as well as unrealized gains that are included within the income for the year are presented below.

	Palmroy Inc.	Sport Co.	Frank Co.
Operating Income	$870,000	$600,000	$420,000
Unrealized Gains	$ 60,000	$100,000	$ 75,000

    On the *consolidated income statement* for the year, what balance is reported for the noncontrolling interest in the subsidiaries' income?

    A. $316,000
    B. $254,000
    C. $138,000
    D. $350,100
    E. $212,100

3. For companies that comprise an affiliated group, which of the following is a benefit associated with the filing of a consolidated tax return?

    A. Intra-entity profits are taxed before they are realized.
    B. Intra-entity dividends are taxed at a lower rate that applies to all dividends between members of an affiliated group, regardless of whether a consolidated return is filed.
    C. Intra-entity profits are never taxed, even when they are realized.
    D. Intra-entity profits may be taxed twice in certain cases.
    E. Losses incurred by one affiliated company can be used to reduce taxable income earned by other members of that group.

4. Which one of the following statements is true?

   A. The amortization of goodwill affects the calculation of income taxes on a consolidated return only if the goodwill is amortized over a thirty-year period.
   B. The FASB codification requires the recording of a deferred income tax asset for any NOL carryforward.
   C. Goodwill is deductible for income tax purposes as long as a company exports a significant amount of its domestic production.
   D. Net operating losses may be carried back for twenty years and applied as a reduction to taxable income figures previously reported.
   E. When a consolidated income tax return is filed, separate returns must always be filed by all of the component corporations.

5. Alton Inc. owns 80% of the voting stock of Edinburg Co. The purchase price exceeded the underlying book value of Edinburg Co.'s assets and liabilities by $30,000. At the same time, Edinburg holds a 30% interest in the outstanding common stock of Alton. The Alton stock was purchased at a price that exceeds the underlying book value by $20,000. Each company uses the cost method to account for its investment in the other. During 2011, the following information was obtained:

	Operating Income	Dividend Income	Total Income
Alton Inc.	$160,000	$32,000	$192,000
Edinburg Co.	$ 60,000	$30,000	$ 90,000

   All dividend income recognized by the two companies is due to investment in the other company. If the *treasury stock method* is used, what amount would be recorded in the *consolidated financial statements* as the *noncontrolling interest in Edinburg's income*?

   A. $ 6,400
   B. $18,000
   C. $ 6,000
   D. $12,000
   E. $10,600

6. If a subsidiary owns shares of its parent, a mutual affiliation is said to exist. Which one of the following statements is true?

   A. This investment is not considered to be intra-entity in nature; therefore, it does not have to be eliminated for consolidation purposes.
   B. The amount of the investment eliminated and the income allocated to the subsidiary can only be calculated by using the treasury stock approach.
   C. The treasury stock approach reclassifies the cost of the shares as treasury stock with an equity accrual being recorded.
   D. This investment is intra-entity in nature and therefore must be eliminated for consolidation purposes. The amount to be eliminated and the income allocated to the subsidiary can be calculated in two different ways.

7. On January 3, Packer Inc. purchases all of Silver River Co.'s outstanding common stock for $3,200,000 in cash. On that date, the subsidiary has net assets with a $2,600,000 fair market value, but with a $2,100,000 income tax basis. The income tax rate is 32%. Neither company has reported any *deferred income tax assets* or *deferred income tax liabilities*. What amount of goodwill should be recognized on the date of the business combination?

    A. $ –0–
    B. $760,000
    C. $440,000
    D. $160,000
    E. $600,000

Items 8 and 9 are based on the following information.
The following figures are reported by Payne Inc. and its 80% owned subsidiary, Shelley Co., for the year ended December 31, 2011. Shelley paid dividends of $25,000 during 2011.

	Payne Inc.	Shelley Co.
Sales	$ 400,000	$ 300,000
Cost of Goods Sold	(200,000)	(200,000)
Operating Expenses	(100,000)	(50,000)
Dividend Income	20,000	-
Net Income	$ 120,000	$ 50,000

Amortization expense relating to Payne's takeover of Shelley is $5,000 per year, and is related to a database owned by Shelley. In 2010, unrealized gains of $20,000 on upstream transfers were deferred to 2011. In 2011, unrealized gains of $10,000 on upstream sales were deferred to 2012.

8. Assuming a 30% income tax rate, what *income tax expense* should be shown in the *consolidated income statement* if a *consolidated income tax return* is filed in 2011?

    A. $48,000
    B. $44,400
    C. $42,900
    D. $51,600
    E. $46,500

9. Assuming a 30% income tax rate, what is the amount of income tax currently payable in 2011?

    A. $51,600
    B. $46,500
    C. $48,000
    D. $44,400
    E. $42,900

Brief Essay Questions

1. According to current income tax laws, a business combination may elect to file a consolidated income tax return encompassing all companies that comprise an affiliated group. What are the essential criteria for including a subsidiary within an affiliated group?

2. What are the advantages of a business combination filing a consolidated income tax return?

3. In accounting for a mutual ownership, what unique conceptual issues are raised?

4. What is the difference between mutual ownership and indirect subsidiary control through a connecting affiliation?

Problems

1. Dakota Inc. purchased 80% of the outstanding stock of Tennessee, Inc. on January 1, 2011 for $800,000. Tennessee Inc. purchased 70% of Knoxville Co. on January 1, 2011 for $500,000. All assets and liabilities were fairly valued on Tennessee Inc.'s books and on Knoxville Co.'s books. Each of the parent companies used the cost method to account for its subsidiary and no dividends were paid by either Knoxville or Tennessee during the year. Net income for 2011 for each company separately was Dakota $300,000, Tennessee $100,000 and Knoxville $100,000.

   Required:

   Determine the *consolidated net income* to be reported by the business combination.

2. Oregon Inc. owns 90% of the outstanding stock of Florida Co. Oregon reported income for the current year, exclusive of any income accrued from Florida, of $100,000. Florida reported income of $60,000 and paid dividends of $10,000. There were no intra-entity transactions during the period. Florida's assets and liabilities were fairly valued at the time of purchase and there was no goodwill recognized.

   Required:

   A. Assuming that the companies qualify as an affiliated group and that they elect to file a consolidated income tax return, how much would consolidated income taxes be if the group pays taxes at a 40% marginal tax rate?

   B. What would the total income tax be if each company filed separately?

Solutions to Multiple Choice Questions

1. B

Bronston's Operational Income	$ 400,000
Unrealized Gain Deferred	(120,000)
Bronston's Accrual-Based Income	$ 280,000

Software's Operational Income	$ 720,000
Investment Income ($280,000 × 80%)	224,000
Software's Accrual-based Income	$ 944,000

Perview's Operational Income	$ 1,250,000
Investment Income ($944,000 × 70%)	660,800
Perview's Accrual-based Income	$ 1,910,800

2. D

Frank's Operational Income	$ 420,000
Unrealized Gain Deferred	(75,000)
Frank's Accrual-based Income	$ 345,000
Outside Ownership Percentage	40%
Noncontrolling Interest in Frank Co.	$ 138,000

Sport's Operational Income	$ 600,000
Unrealized Gain Deferred	(100,000)
Investment Income ($345,000 × 60%)	207,000
Sport's Accrual-based Income	$ 707,000
Outside Ownership Percentage	30%
Noncontrolling Interest in Sport Co.	$ 212,100
Noncontrolling Interest in Frank Co.	$ 138,000
Total Noncontrolling Interest	$ 350,100

3. E

4. B

5. B   The noncontrolling interest is based on total income (operating income + dividend income). Therefore:

Total Edinburg Co. income	$ 90,000
Noncontrolling interest percentage	20%
Noncontrolling interest in Edinburg Co. income	**$ 18,000**

6. B

7. B   A *deferred tax liability* is created by the temporary timing difference of $500,000 ($2,600,000 fair market value less $2,100,000 tax basis). Given a 32% income tax rate, a *deferred income tax liability* of $160,000 ($500,000 × 32%) must be recognized by the newly formed business combination.

Consequently, in a consolidated balance sheet prepared immediately after Packer obtains control over Silver River, the *net assets* would be recorded at a fair market value of $2,600,000. In addition, the new *deferred income tax liability* of $160,000 is recognized. Since the net value of these two accounts is $2,440,000, goodwill of $760,000 is also recorded as the figure remaining from the $3,200,000 purchase price. The goodwill is calculated as follows:

Consideration transferred		$3,200,000
Fair market value	$2,600,000	
Deferred income tax liability	(160,000)	(2,440,000)
Goodwill		$ 760,000

8. A   On consolidated statements, the unrealized gains are deferred until realized. Since 80% of the subsidiary's stock is owned, the dividends are nontaxable and no *deferred income tax liability* is required on the income not distributed by the subsidiary.

Calculation of Shelley Co.'s Realized Income:

Reported Income	$ 50,000
2010 Deferred Gains	20,000
2011 Deferred Gains	(10,000)
Accrual-based Income	$ 60,000
Outside Ownership Percentage	20%
Noncontrolling Interest	$ 12,000

Income Tax Expense:

Paynes Income	$ 100,000
Shelley's Accrual-based Income (above)	60,000
Income to be Taxed	$ 160,000
Income Tax Rate	30%
Income Tax Expense	$ 48,000

9. C

Current Tax Payable (as per Consolidated Return)

Paynes Income	$ 100,000
Shelley's Accrual-based Income (above)	60,000
Income to be Taxed	$ 160,000
Income Tax Rate	30%
Income Tax Payable	$ 48,000

On consolidated income tax returns, the unrealized gains are deferred until realized. Since 80% of the subsidiary's stock is owned, the dividends are nontaxable. Any allocation of income to a noncontrolling interest is not deductible; therefore, income tax payable is calculated on the entire amount of the subsidiary net income. In this case, financial and tax accounting are the same for tax expense and tax payable.

Answers to Brief Essay Questions

1. According to present income tax laws, an affiliated group can be comprised of all domestic corporations in which a parent holds 80% ownership. More specifically, the parent must own (directly or indirectly) 80% of the voting stock of the subsidiary corporation as well as at least 80% of each class of nonvoting stock.

2. There are several advantages to business combinations that file a consolidated income tax return. **First**, intra-entity profits are not taxed until realized. For companies with large amounts of intra-entity transactions, the deferral of unrealized gains causes a delay in the making of significant tax payments. **Second**, losses incurred by one company can be used to reduce or offset taxable income earned by other members of the affiliated group. **Third**, intra-entity dividends are not taxable, but that exclusion applies to the members of an affiliated group regardless of whether a consolidated tax return or separate return is filed.

3. If a subsidiary owns shares of its parent, a mutual ownership is said to exist. The unique concerns raised by mutual ownership center on the handling of any parent company stock owned by a subsidiary. Shares of the parent held by a subsidiary are not treated as outstanding stock in the consolidated balance sheet. Under the *treasury stock approach,* the FASB codification requires reclassification of the cost of these shares as treasury stock with no equity accrual being recorded.

4. "Mutual Ownership" occurs when a subsidiary owns shares of its parent. The existence of mutual ownership complicates the computation of noncontrolling interest in the subsidiary's net income. A "connected affiliation" occurs whenever two or more companies within a business combination hold an equity interest in another member of that combination. Often, neither party holds a controlling interest on their own, but the combination of interests results in effective control.

Solutions to Problems

1.

Tennessee Inc.'s Income	$ 100,000
70% of Knoxville Co.'s Reported Income	70,000
Tennessee Inc.'s Adjusted Income	$ 170,000
Dakota Inc.'s Ownership Percentage	80%
Dakota Inc.'s Accrual of Tennessee Inc.'s Income	$ 136,000
Dakota Inc.'s Reported Income	300,000
Consolidated Income	$ 436,000

2.   A.

Oregon Inc.'s Income	$ 100,000
Florida Co.'s Income	60,000
Total Taxable Income	$ 160,000
Income Tax Rate	40%
Consolidated Income Tax Expense	$ 64,000

B. In this case, the total tax if separate returns are filed would also be $64,000. Since more than 80% of the subsidiary's stock is owned, the amount distributed that is less than current earnings is not taxed immediately, and taxes are not required for the dividend payments as the transfer is nontaxable even on a separate return.

Oregon Inc.'s Income	$ 100,000
Income Tax Rate	40%
Oregon Inc.'s Income Tax Expense	$ 40,000
Florida Co.'s Income	$ 60,000
Income Tax Rate	40%
Florida Co.'s Total Income Tax Expense	$ 24,000

Chapter 8

Segment and Interim Reporting

Chapter Outline

Standards Mentioned in This Chapter:

- **APB Opinion No. 28,** *"Interim Financial Reporting"*
- **IAS 34,** *"Interim Financial Reporting"*
- **IFRS 8,** *"Operating Segments"*
- **FASB Interpretation No. 18, "***Accounting for Income Taxes in Interim Periods: an interpretation of APB Opinion No. 28"*
- **SFAS No. 14,** *"Financial Reporting for Segments of a Business Enterprise"*
- **SFAS No. 131,** *"Disclosures about Segments of an Enterprise and Related Information"*
- **SFAS No. 154,** *"Accounting Changes and Error Corrections"*

I. **Segment Reporting**

   A. *SFAS 14* required extensive disclosures pertaining to industry segments, domestic and foreign operations, export sales, and major customers.

   B. *SFAS 131* was issued later to improve segment reporting.

II. *LO1* **Operating Segments**

   A. According to *SFAS 131, Disclosures about Segments of an Enterprise and Related Information,* the objective of segment reporting is to provide information about the different business activities in which an enterprise engages and the different economic environments in which it operates to help users of financial statements:

   1. Better understand the enterprise's performance.

   2. Better assess its prospects for future net cash flows.

   3. Make more informed judgments about the enterprise as a whole.

   B. The *management approach* for determining segments is based on the way that management disaggregates the enterprise for making operating decisions.

   1. The disaggregated components are *operating segments*, which will be evident from the enterprise's organization structure.

   2. An *operating segment* is a component of an enterprise if:

      a. It engages in business activities from which it earns revenues and incurs expenses.

    b.   Its operating results are regularly reviewed by the chief operating decision maker to assess performance and make resource allocation decisions.

    c.   Discrete financial information is available for it.

  3. However, in some cases, business activities are disaggregated in more than one way and the chief operating decision maker uses multiple sets of reports (i.e. reports by geographic reasons *and* reports by product line). In those cases, two additional criteria must be considered to identify operating segments:

    a.   The segment has a segment manager who is directly accountable to the chief operating decision maker for its financial performance.

    b.   If segment managers exist for two or more overlapping sets of organization units (i.e. matrix form of organization), the nature of the business activities must be considered, and the organizational units based on products and services constitute the operating segments.

III.   *LO2* **Determining Reportable Operating Segments**

  A. After identifying operating segments, management must decide which segments should be reported separately.

    1. Generally, information must be reported separately for each operating segment meeting one or more quantitative thresholds.

    2. However, if two or more operating segments have essentially the same business activities and economic environments, information may be combined.

  B. In determining whether business activities and environments are similar, and thus could be reported together, management must consider these aggregation criteria:

    1. The nature of the products and services provided by each operating segment.

    2. The nature of the production process.

    3. The type or class of customer.

    4. The distribution methods.

    5. If applicable — the nature of the regulatory environment.

  C. Segments must be similar in all of the above areas to be combined. Aggregation is not required.

  D. **Quantitative Thresholds**

    1. The FASB established three tests for identifying *significant* operating segments for which separate disclosure is required.

2. An operating segment is considered significant (reportable) if it meets any *one* of the following:

    a. *Revenue test* — determine if segment revenues, both external and intersegment, are 10 percent or more of the combined revenue, internal and external, of all reported operating segments.

    b. *Profit or loss test* — Determine if segment profit or loss is 10 percent or more of the greater (in absolute terms) of the combined reported profits of all profitable segments or the combined reported loss of all segments incurring a loss.

    c. *Asset test* — determine if segment assets are 10 percent or more of the combined assets of all operating segments.

IV. Other Guidelines

A. FASB rules for disclosure of operating segment information are designed to ensure that the disaggregated data is *consistent* from year to year and *relevant* to the needs of financial statement users.

B. If an operating segment qualifies for the first time for disclosure in the current year, prior period segment data presented for comparative purposes must be restated to reflect the newly reportable segment as a separate segment (for comparability).

C. A *substantial* portion of a company's operations must be presented individually to enhance the value of the disaggregated information.

    1. A sufficient number of segments are presumed to be included only if their combined sales to unaffiliated customers are at least 75% of total company sales made to outsiders.

    2. If the combined sales are less than 75%, additional segments must be disclosed separately even thought they do not meet any of the three tests (revenue, profit or loss, or asset test).

D. If several segments individually meet the conditions to be reportable, but are otherwise *identical*, they can be combined.

E. The FASB suggests there may be a practical upper limit to the number of segments that should be reported separately, as beyond that information becomes too detailed. The FASB suggests that 10 separately reported segments might be the practical limit.

V. *LO3* Information to be Disclosed by Operating Segment

A. *General information* about the operating segment:

    1. Factors used to identify operating segments.

    2. Types of products and services from which each operating segment derives its revenues.

B. *Segment profit or loss* and the following revenues and expenses included in segment profit or loss:

   1. Revenues from external customers.

   2. Revenues from transactions with other operating segments.

   3. Interest revenue and interest expense (reported separately); net interest revenue may be reported for finance segments if this measure is used internally for evaluation.

   4. Depreciation, depletion, and amortization expense.

   5. Other significant noncash items included in segment profit or loss.

   6. Unusual items (discontinued operations and extraordinary items).

   7. Income tax expense or benefit.

C. *Total segment assets* and the following related items:

   1. Investment in equity method affiliates.

   2. Expenditures for additions to long-lived assets.

D. The FASB does not specifically require cash flow information to be reported for each operating segment since this information often is not generated by segments for internal reporting purposes.

E. Immaterial items need not be disclosed.

F. If the internal financial reporting system does not generate information for an item on a segment basis, the item does not need to be disclosed.

G. **Reconciliations to Consolidated Totals:**

   1. Disaggregated information does not need to be based on GAAP.

   2. Preparing segment information using the accounting standards used at the consolidated level would be difficult because some standards are not intended to apply at the segment level. Allocation of these items to operating segments is not required. Examples include accounting for:

      a. Inventory on a LIFO basis when inventory pools include inventory items in more than one segment.

      b. Companywide pension plans.

      c. Purchased goodwill.

3. However, certain items must be reconciled to consolidated totals, including:

   a. The total of the reportable segments' revenues must be reconciled to consolidated revenue totals.

   b. The total of the reportable segments' profit or loss must be reconciled to consolidated income before tax.

   c. The total of the reportable segments' assets must be reconciled to the enterprises' total assets.

   d. Immaterial operating segments — in reconciling the total of segments' revenues, profit or loss, and assets to the enterprise totals, the aggregate amount of those items from immaterial operating segments must be disclosed.

4. Total amounts from components of the enterprise that are not operating segments must be disclosed, including:

   a. Assets
   b. Revenues
   c. Expenses
   d. Gains and Losses
   e. Interest Expense
   f. Depreciation, depletion, and amortization

VI. Enterprise-wide Disclosures

A. **Information about products and services** – Revenues derived from transactions with external customers from each product or service must be disclosed, if operating segments have not been determined based on differences in products or services.

B. *LO4* **Information about geographic areas** must be reported for (1) the domestic country, (2) all foreign countries in total in which the enterprise derives revenues or holds assets, and (3) for each foreign country in which a *material* amount of revenues is derived or assets are held:

   1. Revenues from external customers.

   2. Long-lived assets.

C. Information for each *material country* must be disclosed.

   1. There is no specific FASB guidance on how to determine if a country is material, and variations exist as to how this rule is applied.

   2. Management needs to use judgment as to whether the information's omission could change a user's decision about the enterprise as a whole.

D. The FASB changed the reporting requirements from geographic regions to individual countries believing there are benefits from reporting based on countries versus geographical areas:

    1. It reduces the burden on companies preparing the information because most companies only have material operations in a few countries.

    2. Country-specific information is easier to interpret and therefore more useful to investors and others in assessing risk associated with foreign operations.

E. *LO5* **Information about Major Customers**

    1. When more than 10% of a company's revenues are derived from a single customer, reliance on that customer must be disclosed.

    2. The amount of revenues from all major customers and the operating segment earning those revenues must be disclosed.

    3. The identity of the customer(s) need not be revealed.

    4. The FASB requires this information even if a company operates in only one segment and therefore does not provide segment information.

VII. **IFRS — Segment Reporting**

    1. IFRS 8, "*Operating Segments*", substantially converges IFRS with U.S. GAAP.

    2. Differences:

        a. IFRS 8 requires disclosure of total assets and total liabilities by operating segment if this information is provided to the chief operating decision maker. U.S. GAAP is silent with respect to the disclosure of liabilities.

        b. IFRS 8 includes intangible assets in the long-lived assets to be disclosed that are attributable to geographic segments. SFAS 131 is silent with respect to this issue.

        c. Matrix form of organization — IFRS 8 indicates operating segments can be based on either products and services or geographic areas. In a matrix organization, SFAS 131 stipulates that segments must be based on products and services.

VIII. *LO6* **Interim Reporting**

A. The SEC requires publicly traded companies to provide quarterly financial statements.

B. Interim periods must be treated as *integral* parts of an annual period, rather than *discrete*, or stand-alone periods.

C. Generally, interim statements should follow the same accounting principles used for annual statements.

D. **Special rules:**

1. **Revenues** should be recognized as earned, using the same method as used annually (for example, percent of completion).

2. **Inventory and Cost of Goods Sold**

    a. **LIFO Liquidation:** If a company experiences a LIFO liquidation at the end of an interim period, but the company expects to replace the inventory by year-end, the temporary LIFO liquidation should not be reflected in the interim period.

    b. **Lower-of-cost-or-market rule:** If market value has fallen at the end of an interim period, but is expected to recover by year-end, no lower-of-cost-or-market adjustment is required.

    c. **Standard costing:** If planned variances arising from a standard cost system are expected to be absorbed by the end of the year, they should not be reflected in the interim statements. Unplanned variances should be reported, as they would be in the annual statements.

    d. **Other costs and expenses:** Costs and expenses not matched directly with revenue should be charged in the period in which they occur, unless they can be identified with the activities or benefits of other interim periods, in which case they should allocated among interim periods.

3. **Extraordinary items** are reported fully in the interim period in which they occur.

4. **Income taxes** are computed each interim period using an estimated annual effective rate.

5. **Change in accounting principle** — *retrospective* application is required, as follows:

    a. The cumulative effect of the change in accounting principle on periods prior to those presented is reflected in the carrying amounts of the assets and liabilities as of the beginning of the *first* period presented.

    b. An offsetting adjustment is made to the beginning balance of Retained Earnings if needed.

    c. Financial statements for each individual prior period are adjusted to reflect the period-specific effects of applying the new principle.

    d. In *rare* situations where retrospective treatment is impracticable, the accounting change is not made in the interim period, but at the beginning of the next fiscal year.

6. **Seasonal items:** For companies with significant seasonal variations, the seasonal nature of the business should be disclosed, and the interim reports supplemented with reports covering the 12-month period ending at the interim date.

IX. *LO7* **Minimum Disclosures in Interim Reports**

    A.   Current accounting standards require the following minimum disclosures:

        1.   Sales or gross revenues, provision for income taxes, extraordinary items, and net income.

        2.   Earnings per share.

        3.   Seasonal revenues and expenses.

        4.   Significant changes in estimates or provisions for income taxes.

        5.   Disposal of a segment of a business and unusual or infrequently occurring items.

        6.   Contingent items.

        7.   Changes in accounting principles or estimates.

        8.   Significant changes in financial position.

    B.   Balance Sheet and Cash Flow Information

        1.   Current standards encourage but don't require this information in interim periods.

        2.   If not included, significant changes since the last period in cash and cash equivalents, networking capital, long-term liabilities and stockholders' equity must be disclosed.

X.   **Segment Information in Interim Reports**

    A.   SFAS No. 131 requires the following **segment information** in interim reports:

        1.   Revenues from external customers.

        2.   Intersegment revenues.

        3.   Segment profit or loss.

        4.   Total assets, if there has been a material change from the last annual report.

        5.   A reconciliation of the total segments' profit or loss to the company's total income before taxes and disclosure of any change from the last annual report in the basis for measuring segment profit or loss.

XI.   *LO8* **IFRS — Interim Reporting**

    A.   Unlike U.S. GAAP, in IAS 34, "*Interim Financial Reporting*", minimum reporting requirements include condensed statements of financial position (balance sheet), statement of comprehensive income, statement of changes in equity, statement of cash flows and selected explanatory notes.

    B.   Other differences in accruals:

        1.   Each interim period is treated as a *discrete* period in determining the amounts to be recognized, which means that expenses incurred in one quarter are recognized in full that quarter even though the expenditure benefits the entire year.

        2.   There is no accrual in earlier quarters for expenses expected to be incurred in a later quarter of the year (exception: income tax, which is accrued at the end of each quarter).

Multiple Choice Questions

1. Pennwick Inc. identified 6 segments. The Sports Segment appropriately determined *segment revenue* of $2,100,000 on sales to outsiders and $600,000 on sales to other segments. In addition, Pennwick identified the following expenses associated with its *sporting segment:*

Operating expenses (on sales to outsiders)	$ 1,750,000
Operating expenses (on sales to other segments)	380,000
Total interest expense for the company	180,000
Total income tax expense for the company	65,000
Cumulative effect of a change in accounting principal	10,000

    What is the appropriate *segment profit?*

    A. $315,000
    B. $325,000
    C. $390,000
    D. $570,000
    E. $950,000

2. Which of the following disclosures is required?

    A. The identity of any major customer that represents more than 10% of total revenues.
    B. The existence of a major customer (without disclosure of the customer's identity) that represents more than 10% of total revenues.
    C. Specific countries that account for more than 10% of total company revenues.
    D. Earnings per share for each reportable segment
    E. Total revenues for any segment that passes both the Revenue Test and the Identifiable Assets Test

3. Under current U.S. accounting standards, a company is required to disclose the following information for each *reportable operating segment*, except for

    A. revenues
    B. gross profit
    C. total segment assets
    D. expenditures for additions to long-lived assets
    E. income tax expense or benefit

4. Which one of the following items of information is required to be included in *interim reports* for each operating segment?

    A. revenues from external customers
    B. intersegment revenues
    C. revenues from internal customers
    D. segment profit or loss
    E. total assets, if there has been a material change from the last annual report

5. Which one of the following is a test for identifying operating segments for which separate disclosure is required?

   A. asset test
   B. liability test
   C. expense test
   D. gross profit test
   E. equity test

6. Reed Inc. has three operating segments with the following information:

	Boats	Aircraft	Publishing	Total
Sales to Outsiders	$4,000,000	$1,200,000	$5,200,000	$10,400,000
Intersegment Transfers	500,000	60,000	1,200,000	$1,760,000
Interest Income (outsiders)	200,000	0	400,000	$600,000
Interest Income (insiders)	160,000	16,000	100,000	$276,000
Expenses	3,600,000	735,000	4,800,000	$9,135,000
Assets	10,000,000	7,200,000	12,000,000	$29,200,000

   Using the revenue test, what is the minimum amount of revenue that a segment can have and still be considered reportable?

   A. $1,040,000
   B. $1,216,000
   C. $1,303,600
   D. $1,276,000
   E. $ 362,500

7. Using the information in #6 above, which segments are reportable using the revenue test?

   A. Boats and Publishing
   B. Boats and Aircraft
   C. Aircraft and Publishing
   D. Aircraft only
   E. Boats, Aircraft, and Publishing

8. Ashley Inc. has a publishing industry operating segment. Which one of the following is included in calculating the segment's operating profit or loss?

   A. intersegment revenues
   B. interest expense
   C. extraordinary losses
   D. income taxes
   E. intersegment interest income

9. Masten Inc. has four identifiable industry segments:

	Paper	Wood	Furniture	Toys
Revenues	$30,000	$25,000	$23,000	$10,000
Intersegment Revenues	6,000	4,000	2,000	7,000
Intersegment COGS	4,000	2,000	1,000	5,000
Operating Expenses	10,000	8,000	12,000	18,000
Allocation of Common Costs	3,000	2,000	3,000	1,000
Interest Expense (outsiders)	1,000	3,000	4,000	2,000
Income Taxes (Savings)	4,500	4,000	1,200	(2,000)

What is the minimum operating profit or loss that a segment must have in order to be considered significant?

A. $3,200
B. $1,100
C. $2,700
D. $4,500
E. $4,600

10. A company is required to disclose the following information for each *reportable industry segment*, except for:

A. identifiable liabilities
B. revenues
C. operating profit or loss
D. capital expenditures
E. equity in net income from an investment in the net assets of equity investees

11. Which one of the following is not a difference between U.S. GAAP and IFRS with respect to operating segment reporting?

A. IFRS 8 requires intangible assets to be included in the disclosure of long-lived assets by geographic area.
B. IFRS 8 requires the disclosure of liabilities if reported to the chief operating decision maker.
C. IFRS 8 requires condensed balance sheet and cash flow information for segments.
D. IFRS 8 allows companies with matrix organizations to define operating segments based on either products and services or geographic areas.

Brief Essay Questions

1. How are changes in accounting principles made in an interim period reported?

2. What three attributes does an operating segment that is a component of an enterprise have?

Problems

1. Examine the following information for Faru Co., and determine which segments are reportable.

Faru Co.

Business Segments

	Plastics	Metals	Lumber	Paper	Finance
Total Assets	$ 1,772,000	$ 4,351,000	$ 408,000	$ 791,000	$ 700,000
Sales to Outside Parties	8,215,000	2,787,000	827,000	451,000	-
Intersegment Revenues	138,000	170,000	125,000	140,000	-
Interest Income	-	25,000	8,000	-	242,000
Cost of Goods Sold	5,088,000	2,096,000	1,191,000	753,000	21,000
Other Expenses	79,000	21,000	66,000	40,000	113,000

2. Examine the following information for Hoyle Inc., and determine which segments are reportable.

Hoyle Inc.

Business Segments

	Textbooks	Study Guides	Tapes	Videos	Lecture
Total Assets	$ 50,000	$ 50,000	$ 25,000	$ 370,000	$ -
Sales to Outside Parties	250,000	180,000	72,000	450,000	1,960,000
Intersegment Revenues	400,000	20,000	8,000	-	-
Interest Income (external)	30,000	-	2,000	-	-
Cost of Goods Sold	425,000	140,000	15,000	185,000	-
Other Expenses	170,000	80,000	30,000	27,000	490,000

3. Examine the following information for American Sales, Inc., and determine which segments are reportable.

Business Segments

	Retail	Parts	Delivery	Auto	Clothing
Total Assets	120,000	100,000	400,000	600,000	300,000
Sales to Outside Parties	90,000	70,000	265,000	700,000	140,000
Sales to Clothing Segment	-	30,000	-	30,000	-
Sales to Parts Segment	5,000	-	-	125,000	-
Sales to Delivery Segment	10,000	50,000		100,000	
Sales to Auto Segment	15,000	-	-	-	-
Cost of Goods Sold	112,000	106,000	175,000	600,000	70,000
Other Operating Expenses	25,000	40,000	75,000	350,000	110,000

Solutions to Multiple Choice Questions

1. D

Segment revenue	$2,700,000
Operating expenses (on sales to outsiders)	(1,750,000)
Operating expenses (on sales to other segments)	(380,000)
Segment profit	$ 570,000

2. B

3. B

4. C

5. A

6. D

	Boats	Aircraft	Publishing	Total
Sales to Outsiders	$4,000,000	$1,200,000	$5,200,000	$10,400,000
Intersegment Transfers	500,000	60,000	1,200,000	1,760,000
Interest Income (outsiders)	200,000	0	400,000	600,000
Total Revenues for Purposes of the Revenue Test	$4,700,000	$1,260,000	$6,800,000	$12,760,000
Materiality Threshhold %				10%
Minimum Segment Profit				$1,276,000

7. A   Boats and Publishing are reportable. The total revenues for Boats ($4,700,000) and for Publishing ($6,800,000) exceed the $1,276,000 threshold and would therefore be *reportable segments*. The Aircraft segment ($1,260,000) falls below the threshold and does not pass the revenue test.

8. A

9. D   The operating profit or loss test does not include interest expense or income taxes. Therefore, the operating profit or loss of a segment is its revenues and intersegment revenues less the cost of intersegment transfers, operating expenses, and common costs.

Operating Profits:		Operating Losses:	
Paper	$19,000	Toys	$7,000
Wood	17,000		
Furniture	9,000		
Total	$45,000		$7,000

Total operating profits for segments with profits is $45,000. Total operating losses for segments with losses are $7,000. $45,000 > $7,000. We use 10% of the larger number. Therefore, any segment where the absolute value of the segment's operating gain or loss exceeds $4,500 will be a *reportable segment*.

10.   A

11.   C

Answers to Brief Essay Questions

1.   Changes in accounting principles made in interim periods are given retrospective treatment. The cumulative effect of the change in accounting principle on periods prior to those presented is reflected in the carrying amounts of the assets and liabilities as of the beginning of the *first* period presented (they are restated), and an offsetting adjustment is made to the beginning balance of Retained Earnings if needed.

Financial statements for each individual prior period are adjusted to reflect the period-specific effects of applying the new principle. In *rare* situations where retrospective treatment is impracticable, the accounting change is not made in the interim period, but at the beginning of the next fiscal year.

2.   An operating *segment* is a component of an enterprise:

   A.   that engages in business activities from which it earns revenues and incurs expenses,

   B.   whose operating results are regularly reviewed by the chief operating decision maker to assess performance and make resource allocation decisions, and

   C.   for which discrete financial information is available.

Solutions to Problems

1. Plastics and Metals each pass at least one test. The 75% rule is met, so no additional segments need to be added.

Revenue Test

	Revenues per Segment	Total Revenues	10% of Revenues	Does this segment pass this test?
Plastics	8,353,000	13,128,000	1,312,800	YES
Metals	2,982,000	13,128,000	1,312,800	YES
Lumber	960,000	13,128,000	1,312,800	NO
Paper	591,000	13,128,000	1,312,800	NO
Finance	242,000	13,128,000	1,312,800	NO

Identifiable Assets Test

	Assets per Segment	Total Assets	10% of Assets	Does this segment pass this test?
Plastics	1,772,000	8,022,000	802,200	YES
Metals	4,351,000	8,022,000	802,200	YES
Lumber	408,000	8,022,000	802,200	NO
Paper	791,000	8,022,000	802,200	NO
Finance	700,000	8,022,000	802,200	NO

Profit or Loss Test

	Gain or Loss per Segment	Greater of Total Profits or Total Losses	10% of Total Gains or Total Losses	Does this segment pass this test?
Plastics	3,186,000	4,159,000	415,900	YES
Metals	865,000	4,159,000	415,900	YES
Lumber	(297,000)	4,159,000	415,900	NO
Paper	(202,000)	4,159,000	415,900	NO
Finance	108,000	4,159,000	415,900	NO

75% Test

Total Revenues (external)	75% of Total Revenues (external)	Total External Revenues + Interest	Is 75% test met?
$ 12,555,000	$ 9,416,250	$ 11,027,000	YES

2. Textbooks, Study Guides, Videos, and Lectures each pass at least one test. The 75% rule is met, so no additional segments need to be added.

Revenue Test

	Revenues per Segment	Total Revenues	10% of Revenues	Does this segment pass this test?
Textbooks	680,000	3,372,000	337,200	YES
Study Guides	200,000	3,372,000	337,200	NO
Tapes	82,000	3,372,000	337,200	NO
Videos	450,000	3,372,000	337,200	YES
Lectures	1,960,000	3,372,000	337,200	YES

Identifiable Assets Test

	Assets per Segment	Total Assets	10% of Assets	Does this segment pass this test?
Textbooks	50,000	495,000	49,500	YES
Study Guides	50,000	495,000	49,500	YES
Tapes	25,000	495,000	49,500	NO
Videos	370,000	495,000	49,500	YES
Lectures	-	495,000	49,500	NO

Profit or Loss Test

	Gain or Loss per Segment	Greater of Total Profits or Total Losses	10% of Total Gains or Total Losses	Does this segment pass this test?
Textbooks	85,000	1,830,000	183,000	NO
Study Guides	(20,000)	1,830,000	183,000	NO
Tapes	37,000	1,830,000	183,000	NO
Videos	238,000	1,830,000	183,000	YES
Lectures	1,470,000	1,830,000	183,000	YES

75% Test

Total Revenues (external)	75% of Total Revenues (external)	Total External Revenues + Interest	Is 75% test met?
$ 2,944,000	$ 2,208,000	$ 2,870,000	YES

3. Retail, Delivery, Auto, and Clothing each pass at least one test. The 75% rule is met, so no additional segments need to be added.

Revenue Test

	Revenues per Segment	Total Revenues	10% of Revenues	Does this segment pass this test?
Retail	120,000	1,630,000	163,000	NO
Parts	150,000	1,630,000	163,000	NO
Delivery	265,000	1,630,000	163,000	YES
Auto	955,000	1,630,000	163,000	YES
Clothing	140,000	1,630,000	163,000	NO

Identifiable Assets Test

	Assets per Segment	Total Assets	10% of Assets	Does this segment pass this test?
Retail	120,000	1,520,000	152,000	NO
Parts	100,000	1,520,000	152,000	NO
Delivery	400,000	1,520,000	152,000	YES
Auto	600,000	1,520,000	152,000	YES
Clothing	300,000	1,520,000	152,000	YES

Profit or Loss Test

	Gain or Loss per Segment	Greater of Total Profits or Total Losses	10% of Total Gains or Total Losses	Does this segment pass this test?
Retail	(17,000)	57,000	5,700	YES
Parts	4,000	57,000	5,700	NO
Delivery	15,000	57,000	5,700	YES
Auto	5,000	57,000	5,700	NO
Clothing	(40,000)	57,000	5,700	YES

75% Test

Total Revenues (external)	75% of Total Revenues (external)	Total External Revenues for Reportable Segments	Is 75% test met?
$ 1,265,000	$ 948,750	$ 1,195,000	YES

Chapter 9

Foreign Currency Transactions and Hedging Foreign Exchange Risk

Chapter Outline

Standards Mentioned in This Chapter:
- **IAS 21,** *The Effects of Changes in Foreign Exchange Rates*
- **IAS 39,** *Financial Instruments: Recognition and Measurement*
- **SFAS No. 52,** *Foreign Currency Translation*
- **SFAS No. 133,** *Accounting for Derivative Instruments and Hedging Activities*
- **SFAS No. 138,** *Accounting for Certain Derivative Instruments and Certain Hedging Activities*

I.   *LO1* **Foreign Exchange Markets** – Introduction

    A.   Merchandise may be imported or exported with prices denominated in a foreign currency.

    B.   For the reporting purposes of a U.S. company, each transaction denominated in a foreign currency must be re-stated in U.S. dollars using an exchange rate that represents the value of the U.S. dollar relative to the foreign currency.

    C.   Exchange rates tend to fluctuate as the strength of the U.S. economy changes relative to the economies of other countries.

II.   **Exchange Rate Mechanisms**

    A.   Exchange rates have not always fluctuated.

    B.   From 1945-1973, foreign currency exchange rates were fixed to the U.S. dollar, which was in turn tied to the value of gold.

        1.   Called the *"Gold Standard"*.

        2.   The U.S. ended reliance on the "Gold Standard" in 1973.

    C.   There are several different approaches to setting currency exchange rates.

        1.   *Independent Float* – The value of currency is allowed to fluctuate freely.

        2.   *Pegged to Another Currency* – The value of currency is fixed to the value of another currency.

        3.   *European Monetary System* – 12 European countries agreed to use a single common currency called the euro (€) in 2002. Today 16 countries are part of the euro area.

III.   **Foreign Exchange Rates**

    A.   **Foreign Exchange Rates** – quotes can be obtained from many sources:

        1.   Wall Street Journal, internet, newspapers, banks, currency exchanges.

        2.   *Direct Quotes* = the number of U.S. $ needed to purchase one unit of a foreign currency.

        3.   *Indirect Quotes* = the number of foreign currency units required to purchase one (1) U.S. $.

    B.   **Spot and Forward Rates** – Foreign currency trades can be executed on a *spot* basis or *forward* basis.

        1.   The *spot rate* is the price at which a foreign currency can be purchased or sold today.

        2.   The *forward rate* is the price today at which foreign currency can be purchased or sold sometime in the future.

    C.   **Option Contracts** – A *foreign currency option* gives its holder the right, but not the obligation, to trade foreign currency in the future.

        1.   The sale of foreign currency by the holder of the option is accomplished with a *put* option.

        2.   The exchange rate at which the option will be executed if the holder decides to exercise the option is the *strike price*.

        3.   Options are purchased by paying an *option premium*, which is a function of two components:

            a.   The *intrinsic value* of an option is equal to the gain that could be realized by immediately exercising the option.

            b.   The *time value* of an option relates to the possibility that the spot rate will change over time.

IV.   *LO2* **Foreign Currency Transactions**

    A.   Export sales and import purchases are international transactions that are components of a trade. These transactions have exposure to foreign exchange risk.

        1.   *Export sale* — a *transaction exposure* exists when the exporter allows the buyer to pay in a foreign currency and also allows the buyer to pay sometime after the sale has been transacted.

        2.   *Import purchase* — a *transaction exposure* exists when the importer is required to pay in a foreign currency and is allowed to pay sometime after the purchase has been transacted.

B.   Accounting Issue

1.   Sales made in a foreign currency – how to treat the changes in the U.S. dollar value of the sale and accounts receivable when the foreign currency changes in value between the time of the export sale and the collection of the receivable.

2.   Purchases made in a foreign currency – how to treat the changes in the U.S. dollar value of the purchase and account payable when the foreign currency changes in value between the time of the import purchase and the payment for the purchase.

C.   Accounting Alternatives – Transaction Perspective – two alternative approaches:

1.   *One-transaction perspective:* assumes that an export sale (or other transaction denominated in foreign currency) is not complete until the foreign currency receivable has been collected and converted into U.S. dollars; any change in the dollar value of the foreign currency is accounted for as an adjustment to *Accounts Receivable* and *Sales*. This method is not acceptable under U.S. GAAP.

2.   *Two-transaction perspective:* required by the FASB, companies treat an export sale and the subsequent cash collection as two separate transactions.

    a.   The U.S. dollar value of an export sale is recorded as of the date the sale.

    b.   Any difference between the U.S. dollar amount that could have been received at the date of sale and the U.S. dollars actually received at the date of payment due to fluctuations in the exchange rate is treated as a *Foreign Exchange Gain or Loss* and reported separately from Sales in the *income statement*.

D.   Accounting Alternatives – two alternative approaches to accounting for unrealized foreign exchange gains and losses.

1.   *Deferral approach:* unrealized foreign exchange gains and losses are deferred on the *balance sheet* until cash is actually paid or received. This approach is not acceptable under U.S. GAAP.

2.   *Accrual approach:* required by the FASB to account for unrealized foreign exchange gains and losses.

    a.   Unrealized foreign exchange gains and losses due to changes in the exchange rate are included in income for the period in which the exchange rate changes.

        (1)   Any change in the exchange rate from the date of sale to the balance sheet date results in a *foreign exchange gain or loss* to be reported in income for that period.

        (2)   Any change in the exchange rate from the balance sheet date to the date of payment results in a second *foreign exchange gain or loss* that would be reported in the second accounting period.

    b.   This approach is criticized for violating the principle of conservatism because it recognizes *unrealized foreign exchange gains* when present at the balance sheet date.

V.   *LO3* **Hedges of Foreign Exchange Risk**

    A.   Companies engaged in foreign currency transactions often enter into hedging arrangements to reduce foreign exchange risk as soon as they receive a noncancelable sales order or place a noncancelable purchase order.

    B.   **Foreign Currency Forward Contracts**

        1.   Forward contracts are agreements to exchange foreign currency for U.S. dollars at a predetermined exchange rate on a specified date in the future.

        2.   Forward contracts are non-cancelable.

        3.   Foreign currency forward contracts can be used to hedge foreign exchange risk by locking in the exchange rate for buying or selling a foreign currency to satisfy a payable or to exchange proceeds from a receivable. Thus, the U.S. dollar amount of the transaction is not subject to future foreign currency fluctuations.

    C.   **Foreign Currency Options** – A *foreign currency option* gives its holder the right, but not the obligation, to trade foreign currency in the future.

        1.   Essentially, these are forward contracts that the company can use or not use, at their option.

        2.   The option contract has a cost, whether it is executed or not.

        3.   Options establish a price at which a company is able, but is not required, to sell or buy the foreign currency. Thus, it can take advantage of any foreign exchange gains while eliminating future foreign exchange losses.

VI.   **Derivatives Accounting**

    A.   Current U.S. standards provide guidance for hedges of the following sources of foreign exchange risk:

        1.   Recognized foreign currency denominated assets and liabilities.

        2.   Unrecognized foreign currency firm commitments.

        3.   Forecasted foreign currency denominated transactions.

        4.   Net investments in foreign operations (chapter 10).

    B.   **Fundamental Requirements of Derivatives Accounting**

        1.   All derivatives are reported on the balance sheet at their fair value.

        2.   Derivatives are reported as assets when they have a positive fair value and liabilities when they have a negative fair value.

C. **Determination of Fair Value of Derivatives** – the fair value is determined by measuring changes in the forward rate over the life of the contract.

    1. Three pieces of information are needed:

        a. The forward rate when the forward contract was entered into.

        b. The current forward rate for a contract that matures on the same date as the forward contract entered into.

        c. A discount rate (typically the company's incremental borrowing rate).

    2. The value of a foreign currency option is determined by obtaining a price quote from an option dealer (such as a bank) or, if dealer quotes are unavailable, by using a pricing model such as the Black-Scholes pricing model.

D. **Accounting for Changes in the Fair Value of Derivatives**

    1. Changes in the fair value of derivatives must be included in *comprehensive income*.

    2. Current standards modified the treatment of changes in the fair value of derivatives used as hedges.

        a. *Speculative Derivatives* – gains/losses arising from the change in fair value of derivatives are recognized in net income.

        b. *Derivatives Used for Hedging*

            (1) Gains/losses arising from the change in fair value of fair value hedges are recognized in *net income*.

            (2) Gains/losses arising from the change in fair value of cash flow hedges are recognized in *Accumulated Other Comprehensive Income* (AOCI).

VII. Hedge Accounting

A. Hedge relationships are created when a company uses a foreign currency derivative to minimize the adverse effect that changes in exchange rates have on cash flows and net income.

B. Hedge accounting can only be used if three conditions are met:

    1. The derivative is used to hedge either a fair value exposure or a cash flow exposure to foreign exchange risk.

    2. The derivative is *highly effective* in offsetting changes in the fair value or cash flows related to the hedged item.

    3. The derivative is properly documented as a hedge.

C. **Nature of Hedged Risk**

    1. A *fair value exposure* exists when changes in exchange rates can affect the fair value of an asset or liability reported on the balance sheet.

        a. The transaction must have the potential to impact net income if it is not hedged.

2. A *cash value exposure* exists if changes in exchange rates affect the amount of cash flow to be realized from a transaction.

   a. Recognized foreign currency assets and liabilities.

   b. Foreign currency firm commitments.

   c. Forecasted foreign currency transactions.

3. A foreign currency account receivable has both a fair value exposure and a cash flow exposure.

4. A hedge of a forecasted foreign currency transaction can only qualify as a cash flow hedge.

VIII. *LO4* **Hedges of Foreign Currency Denominated Assets and Liabilities**

A. Hedges of foreign currency denominated assets and liabilities such as accounts receivable and accounts payable can qualify as either *cash flow hedges* or *fair value hedges*.

   1. Cash flow hedge – to qualify, the hedging instrument must completely offset the variability in the cash flows associated with the foreign currency or payable.

   2. If the hedging instrument does not qualify as a cash flow hedge or the company elects not to designate the instrument as a cash flow hedge, the hedge is a fair value hedge.

B. **Cash Flow Hedges Procedures**

   1. Adjust the hedged asset/liability to fair value based on changes in the spot rate. A foreign exchange gain/loss is recognized in net income.

   2. Adjust the derivative to fair value. The resulting gain/loss is recorded as part of *Accumulated Other Comprehensive Income* (AOCI).

   3. Transfer an amount equal to the foreign exchange gain/loss on the hedged asset/liability from AOCI to net income.

   4. An additional amount is removed from AOCI and recognized in net income to reflect:

      a. The current period's amortization of the original discount/premium on the forward contract, or

      b. The change in the time value of the option, depending on which is being used.

C. **Fair Value Hedge Procedures**

   1. Adjust the hedged asset/liability to fair value based on changes in the spot exchange rate. A foreign exchange gain/loss is recognized in net income.

   2. The derivative hedging instrument is adjusted to fair value. The resulting gain/loss is reporting in net income.

IX.   **Using a Forward Contract to Hedge a Foreign Currency Denominated Asset**

A.   **Forward Contract Designated as a Cash Flow Hedge**

    1.   On the date the forward contract is taken, the value is $0, because the agreement is an *executory* contract.

    2.   On the balance sheet date, determine the fair value of the forward contract.

        a.   Record the forward contract asset or liability.

            (1)   Determine the U.S. dollar equivalent of the amount hedged by the forward contract using the contract exchange rate.

            (2)   Determine the U.S. dollar equivalent of the amount hedged by the forward contract using a currently available contract with a maturity date that is the same as the original forward contract rate.

            (3)   The difference is the undiscounted value of the forward contract.

                i. If (1) > (2), then record a forward contract asset.
                ii. If (1) < (2), then record a forward contract liability.

            (4)   Discount (3) using the pre-established discount rate and the forward contract due date as the future maturity date.

        b.   Record the other side of the entry to *Accumulated Other Comprehensive Income* (AOCI).

        c.   Remove enough from the AOCI account to offset any gain/loss recognized in the income statement related to the re-measurement of the underlying foreign currency asset.

        d.   Record the amortization of the forward contract discount/premium. The other side of the entry is debited or credited to AOCI.

            (1)   Compare the U.S. dollar amount of the original foreign currency asset to the U.S. dollar amount that will be realized when the forward contract matures.

            (2)   The difference is identified as the "*forward contract discount/premium*"

    3.   On the date that the forward contract matures:

        a.   Adjust the forward contract to the fair value on the maturity date.

            (1)   Determine the fair value by comparing the forward contract rate to the current spot rate.

            (2)   Record an adjustment to the Forward Contract account.

            (3)   Record the other side of the entry in AOCI.

        b.   Remove enough from AOCI to offset any foreign exchange gain/loss realized from the re-measurement of the underlying foreign currency asset.

c. Amortize the remaining Forward Contract Discount

d. **Note:** If this is done properly, these entries will cause the AOCI account to zero out on the maturity date.

B. Forward Contract Designated as a Fair Value Hedge

1. On the date the forward contract is taken, the value is $0, because the agreement is an executory contract.

2. On the balance sheet date, determine the fair value of the forward contract.

    a. Record a forward contract asset or liability.

        (1) Determine the U.S. dollar equivalent of the amount hedged by the forward contract using the contract exchange rate.

        (2) Determine the U.S. dollar equivalent of the amount hedged by the forward contract using a currently available contract with a maturity date that is the same as the original forward contract rate.

        (3) The difference is the undiscounted value of the forward contract.

        (4) Discount (3) using the pre-established discount rate and the forward contract due date as the future maturity date.

    b. Record the other side of the entry to *Gain/Loss on Forward Contract*.

3. On the date that the forward contract matures:

    a. Adjust the Forward Contract to fair value on the maturity date.

    b. Record the settlement of the forward contract.

C. Cash Flow Hedge versus Fair Value Hedge

1. When a forward contract hedge completely offsets the variability in cash flows associated with the hedged item it can be designated as either a cash flow hedge or fair value hedge.

2. The *total* impact on income (which may affect more than one reporting year) is the same regardless of the designation.

3. A benefit to the cash flow hedge designation is that the company knows the forward contract's effect on net income for each year as soon as the contract is signed. (The net impact on income is the amortization of the forward contract discount or premium.)

4. Fair value hedges have a potential for greater volatility in periodic net income, so companies may prefer to designate forward contracts as cash flow hedges.

X. **Foreign Currency Option Used to Hedge a Foreign Currency Denominated Asset**

    A. **Steps for an Option designated as a Cash Flow Hedge**

        1. The foreign currency option contract is recorded at cost on the date it is purchased.

        2. On the balance sheet date:

            a. Adjust the value of the option contract based on a quote or pricing model. The adjustment amount is recorded in AOCI.

            b. Remove enough from the AOCI account to offset any gain/loss recognized in the income statement related to the re-measurement of the underlying foreign currency asset.

            c. Record the change in the time value of the option as an adjustment to AOCI.

        3. On the date the foreign currency option matures:

            a. Adjust the option contract to the fair value on the maturity date.

            b. Remove enough from AOCI to offset any foreign exchange gain/loss realized from the re-measurement of the underlying foreign currency asset.

            c. Record the change in the time value of the option as an adjustment to AOCI.

            d. Amortize the remaining cost of the option to expense.

            e. If exercised, record the exercise of the option.

    B. **Steps for an Option designated as a Fair Value Hedge**

        1. The foreign currency option contract is recorded at cost on the date it is purchased.

        2. On the balance sheet date, adjust the fair value of the option contract. Record a gain/loss on the income statement.

        3. On the date the foreign currency option matures, adjust the option contract to fair value.

        4. If exercised, record the exercise of the option.

XI. *LO5* **Hedges of Unrecognized Foreign Currency Firm Commitments**

    A. Companies engaging in foreign currency transactions often enter into hedging arrangements as soon as an order has been accepted.

    B. The FASB originally indicated that only *Fair Value Hedges* were appropriate for a hedge of a foreign currency firm commitment, however, the FASB's Derivatives Implementation Group subsequently concluded cash flow hedge accounting could also be used. *Note*: cash flow hedge accounting for unrecognized foreign currency firm commitments is not covered by the text, as fair value results are more appealing.

C. Executory Contracts

    1. A firm commitment is an *executory* contract, which normally would not be recognized in the financial statements.

    2. However, when a derivative financial instrument is used to hedge a firm commitment, explicit recognition on the balance sheet at the fair value of both the derivative financial instrument (forward contract or option) and the firm commitment is required.

    3. The change in fair value of the firm commitment results in a gain or loss that offsets the loss or gain on the hedging instrument, thus achieving the goal of the hedge accounting.

    4. To measure the fair value of the firm commitment:

        a. For a forward contract – fair value is determined by changes in the forward exchange rate.

        b. For a foreign currency option – use the change in the spot rate.

D. **Forward Contract Used as Fair Value Hedge of a Firm Commitment**

    1. The hedging instrument must be reported as either an asset or a liability on the balance sheet.

        a. Changes in the fair value of the hedging instrument are recognized as gains and losses in income.

    2. Although there is no transaction to account for, gains and losses on the foreign currency commitment must be recognized in income to offset gains and losses on the forward contract (achieving the goal of the hedge accounting).

E. Options can also be used as hedge instruments for firm foreign currency commitments.

XII. *LO6* **Hedge of Forecasted Foreign Currency Denominated Transactions**

    A. Current accounting standards allow the use of *hedge accounting* for forward contracts hedging *forecasted* transactions (also known as a *cash flow hedge*) and for options used for the same purpose.

    B. The accounting for a *cash flow hedge* differs from the accounting for a *fair value hedge* in two ways:

        1. There is no recognition of gains and losses on a forecasted transaction, unlike the accounting for a firm commitment.

        2. The foreign currency option is reported at *fair value*, but because there is no gain or loss on the forecasted transaction to offset against, changes in the fair value of the foreign currency option are not reported as gains or losses in net income.

a. They are reported as part of *Accumulated Other Comprehensive Income* (AOCI).

b. On the projected date of the forecasted transaction, the *cumulative change in fair value* is transferred from *AOCI* (balance sheet) to *net income* (income statement).

XIII. Use of Hedging Instruments

A. Some companies require hedging of all foreign currency transactions.

B. Others require the use of a foreign contract hedge when the *forward rate* results in a greater cash inflow or smaller cash outflow than with the *spot rate*.

C. *Proportional hedging policies* requiring hedging of some predetermined percentage of transaction exposure.

D. **The Euro** – the use of the euro as a common currency in much of Europe reduces the need for hedging in that part of the world. This is also true for U.S. based companies having euro accounts receivables from sales in one country and euro accounts payables from purchases in another. These offsetting transactions act as a natural hedge.

XIV. *LO7* Foreign Currency Borrowing

A. Companies borrow foreign currency from foreign lenders to:

1. Finance foreign operations, or

2. Take advantage of more favorable interest rates.

B. Accounting is complicated by:

1. The denomination of both the principal and interest in foreign currency and

2. The resulting exposure to foreign exchange risk from *both* the foreign currency note payable and the accrued foreign currency interest payable.

C. Differences are recorded as foreign exchange gains or losses.

D. **Foreign Currency Loan** – Companies at times lend foreign currency to related parties.

1. Fluctuations in U.S. dollar values of principal and interest lead to foreign exchange gains and losses.

2. *Exception:* foreign exchange gains and losses on *intra-entity foreign currency transactions that are of a long-term investment nature* are deferred in the stockholders' equity section of the balance sheet until the loan is repaid.

XV. IFRS-Foreign Currency Transactions and Hedges

A. Similarities:

1. Use of the two-transaction perspective in accounting for foreign currency transactions.

2. There are no substantive differences in the accounting for foreign currency transactions.

3. Generally the standards for hedge accounting are consistent.

B. Differences:

1. Under U.S. GAAP only derivative financial instruments can be used as a cash flow hedge.

2. Under IFRS non-derivative financial instruments, such as foreign currency loans, may be designated as a cash flow hedge.

Multiple Choice Questions

1. The foreign exchange rate for the immediate delivery of currencies exchanged is called the

   A. Forward rate.
   B. Historical rate.
   C. Market rate.
   D. Swap rate.
   E. Spot rate.

2. When a foreign currency exchange rate is expressed as the number of foreign currency units required to purchase one (1) U.S. $, this is called a(n)

   A. Derivative quote
   B. Forward quote
   C. Direct quote
   D. Indirect quote
   E. Market quote

3. When a foreign currency exchange rate is expressed as the number of U.S. $ required to purchase one (1) unit of foreign currency, this is called a(n)

   A. Derivative quote
   B. Forward quote
   C. Direct quote
   D. Indirect quote
   E. Market quote

4. According to current U.S. standards, for which of the following can the resultant hedge gains/losses be recorded in Comprehensive Income, rather than on the income statement?

A. Gains/losses arising from the change in fair value of hedges using speculative derivatives.
B. Gains/losses arising from the change in fair value of Fair Value Hedges.
C. Gains/losses arising from the change in fair value of Cash Flow Hedges.
D. Gains/losses arising from a hedge of a forecasted foreign currency transaction accounted for as a Fair Value Hedge.
E. Gains/losses arising from a hedge of an Option Contract that is accounted for as a Fair Value Hedge.

5. For which of the following hedges does U.S. GAAP allow hedge accounting to be used to record gains and losses related to the hedge instrument in net income?

	Forward Contract Hedge	Option Used as a Hedge of a Foreign Currency Firm Commitment	Foreign Currency Option Used as a Cash Hedge
A.	Yes	Yes	Yes
B.	Yes	No	Yes
C.	Yes	Yes	No
D.	No	Yes	No
E.	Yes	No	No

6. A U.S. exporter has a 90-day account receivable denominated in Euros (€) as a result of an export sale made on May 1, 2011, to a German customer. The exporter signed a 90-day forward contract on May 1, 2011, to sell Euros. The spot rate was $1.305 on that date and the 90-day forward rate was $1.250. On June 30, 2011, the exporter's fiscal year-end, the spot rate was $1.320 and the 30-day forward rate was $1.275. Which one of the following would the U.S. exporter have reported in income for the year ending June 30, 2011?

A. Net Exchange Loss
B. Net Exchange Gain
C. No Exchange Gain or Loss
D. Net Credit Adjustment to Beginning Retained Earnings
E. Net Debit Adjustment to Beginning Retained Earnings

7. Barger Co. ordered parts costing £250,000 from a British supplier on March 12 when the spot rate was $1.55 per£. A one-month forward contract, which was properly designated as a fair value hedge of the firm commitment, was signed on that date to purchase £250,000 at a forward rate of $1.52. On April 12, when the parts were received, the spot rate was $1.56. At what amount should the parts be carried on Barger's books?

A. $387,500
B. $390,000
C. $380,000
D. $388,750
E. $250,000

Items 8 and 9 are based on the following information.

NOD Corp. (a U.S.-based company) sold parts to an Indian customer on December 15, 2011, with payment of 720,000 rupee's to be received on January 15, 2012. The following exchange rates apply:

Date	Spot Rate	Forward Rate to January 15
December 15, 2011	$0.0225	$0.0228
December 31, 2011	$0.0230	$0.0231
January 15, 2012	$0.0232	N/A

8. Assuming no forward contract was entered into, how much foreign exchange gain or loss should NOD report on its 2011 income statement with regard to this transaction?

   A. no gain or loss
   B. $ 360 gain
   C. $ 360 loss
   D. $ 144 gain
   E. $ 144 loss

9. Assume that a forward contract was entered into to hedge this foreign currency transaction, and that NOD wants to account for the forward contract as a fair value hedge. NOD uses a discount rate of 6%. The present value factor for 30 days is .9950. The present value factor for 15 days is .9975. What is the total net exchange gain or loss for 2011?

   A. $ 144.54 net loss
   B. $ 144.54 net gain
   C. $ 575.46 net loss
   D. $ 575.46 net gain
   E. $ 576.00 net gain

Items 10 through 12 are based on the following information.

On November 15, 2011, Duster places an order for inventory items from their Japanese supplier. On the same date, Duster Inc. entered into a forward contract to purchase ¥1,500,000 in ninety days to hedge the inventory purchase, which is payable on February 15, 2012. The relevant exchange rates are as follows:

Date	Spot Rate	Forward Rate to February 15
November 15, 2011	$ 0.009250	$ 0.009380
December 15, 2011	$ 0.009320	$ 0.009400
December 31, 2011	$ 0.009352	$ 0.009450
February 15, 2012	$ 0.009420	$ 0.009410

10. Duster uses a discount rate of 5%. The present value factor for 90 days is .9876. The present value factor for 60 days is .9917. The present value factor for 45 days is .9938. The present value factor for 30 days is .9958. On November 15, 2011, what is the fair value of this forward contract?

    A. $ 0.00 - no value
    B. $ 195.00 asset
    C. $ 195.00 liability
    D. $ 192.58 asset
    E. $ 192.58 liability

11. Referring to #10 above, what is the fair value of the forward contract on December 31?

    A. $ 153.00 asset
    B. $ 153.00 liability
    C. $ 104.35 asset
    D. $ 104.35 liability
    E. $ 105.00 asset

12. Referring again to the information in #10 above, what is the amount of gain or loss that Duster should record on February 15, 2012 assuming Duster accounted for the forward contract as a fair value hedge?

    A. $ 44.35 loss
    B. $ 44.35 gain
    C. $ 60.00 loss
    D. $ 60.00 gain
    E. $ 0.00 – no gain or loss

13. The exchange rate at which an option will be executed if the holder decides to exercise the option is called the

    A.   Strike price.
    B.   Intrinsic value.
    C.   Spot rate.
    D.   Forward rate.
    E.   Option price.

Brief Essay Questions

1. Briefly list and describe the three *currency arrangements* (exchange rate mechanisms).

2. Contrast the definitions of a *spot rate* and a *forward rate*.

3. According to the text, why is the *one-transaction perspective* criticized?

4. Current accounting standards require the *accrual approach* be used to account for foreign exchange gains and losses. What basic principle of accounting does the use of this approach depart from?

Problems

1. Johnson Inc., a U.S.-based firm, sold some of its inventory to a foreign firm on November 27, 2011 when the exchange rate was $1.7500 to the local currency unit (LCU). The agreement called for the foreign firm to remit 140,000 LCUs on January 26, 2012. Additional information regarding exchange rates is shown below:

December 1, 2011	$1.7800
December 31, 2011	1.8125
January 26, 2012	1.8220

   Required:

   A. Show the entry (or entries) to be made (if any) on Johnson's books on December 31, 2011 and provide supporting calculations.

   B. Show the entry to be made on Johnson's books on January 26, 2012 when it receives payment from the foreign firm.

2. On December 2, 2011, Norton Inc. (a U.S. company) purchases inventory from a foreign supplier for 5,000,000 local currency units (LCUs). Payment will be made in two months. To hedge the transaction, Norton signs a forward contract to buy 5,000,000 LCUs in sixty days. Norton uses a discount of 6%, resulting in a one-month present value factor of .9950. Norton uses the straight-line method for amortizing discounts.

   The appropriate LCU exchange rates are as follows:

Date	Spot Rate	Forward Rate to 1/31/2012
December 2, 2011	0.009252 = 1 LCU	0.009375 = 1 LCU
December 31, 2011	0.009352 = 1 LCU	0.009420 = 1 LCU
January 31, 2012	0.009415 = 1 LCU	N/A

   Required:

   Prepare all journal entries for Norton Inc. in connection with the purchase and payment. Assume that Norton wants to account for this as a *cash flow hedge*.

3. Refer to the information in #2 above. Assume that Norton accounts for this as a *fair value hedge*.

   Required:

   Record the journal entries in connection with the purchase and payment.

4. New York Chili, Inc. (a U.S. company in Montana) has the following import/export transactions in 2012:

August 1   Sold inventory for 2,200,000 pesos, on account, to a foreign customer. Payment is due on November 1. New York Chili took a forward contract to hedge this transaction.

November 1   Received payment for the August 1 sale.

New York Chili has a September 30 year-end. The company uses an 8% discount rate, resulting in a 30-day present value factor of .9934. Currency exchange rates are as follows:

Date	Spot Rate	Forward Rate to 11/1/12
August 1, 2012	$0.0900 = 1 peso	$0.0930 = 1 peso
September 30, 2012	$0.0920 = 1 peso	$0.0928 = 1 peso
November 1, 2012	$0.0925 = 1 peso	$0.0927 = 1 peso

Required:

Assume New York Chili accounts for this transaction as a fair value hedge. Record the journal entries in connection with the purchase of inventory and sale of goods for New York Chili.

Solutions to Multiple Choice Questions

1.   **E**

2.   **D**

3.   **C**

4.   **C**

5.   **C**

6.   **A**   Since the exporter is going to be receiving €'s, it means they will selling €'s and receiving U.S. $ on the maturity date in 30 days. They currently have a contract that will pay them $1.250 per €. The currently available 30-day forward contract would pay them $1.275 per €. They will recognize a loss of $.025 per € on the value of the forward contract. However, they have a gain of only $.015 per € on the account receivable. Therefore, there will be a net loss recorded on June 30 of $.010 per €.

7.   **B**   When there is a forward contract which is properly designated as a fair value hedge of a firm commitment, the parts inventory is recognized at the spot rate at the date of purchase (£250,000 × $1.56) = $390,000.

8.   **B**

Dollar value of receivable @ 12/31/11 (720,000 rupees × $.0230)	$ 16,560
Dollar value of receivable @ 12/15/11 (720,000 rupees × $.0225)	(16,200)
Increase	$ 360 gain

9. B   @ the Contracted Forward Rate (720,000 rupees × $.0228) $16,416.00
         @ the Currently Available Rate (720,000 rupees × $.0231) (16,632.00)
         Net change in value (Loss) $ (216.00) loss
         Present Value Factor for 15 days @ 6%   ×   .9975
         Fair Value of Forward Contract on 12/31/11 $ (215.46) loss
         Plus Gain on Original Receivable   360.00 gain
         Net gain $ 144.54 gain

10. A   On November 15, 2011, the contracted rate for a February 15, 2012 delivery and the
         currently available forward rate to February 15, 2012 are both the same. Since there is no
         difference, there is no fair value recorded for the forward contract on November 15,
         2011. This is considered to be an executory contract.

11. C   @ the Currently Available Rate (1,500,000 ¥ × $.00945) $ 14,175.00
         @ the Contracted Forward Rate (1,500,000 ¥ × $.00938)   14,070.00
         Net change in value $ 105.00 gain
         Present Value Factor for 45 days @ 5%   ×   .9938
         Fair Value of Forward Contract on 12/31/11 $ 104.35 asset

         The ¥1,500,000 will be purchased on February 15, 2012 at the contracted rate of
         $.00938, or $14,070.00. If the company had waited until December 31, 2011 to hedge the
         inventory purchase, it could have obtained a forward rate of $.009450, resulting in the
         ¥1,500,000 costing $14,175.00 on February 15, 2012. The difference is $105.
         The present value of that $30 over 45 days (to Feb. 15), using a discount rate of 5%,
         is $104.35; an asset.

12. A   The value of the forward contract on December 31, 2011, was a $104.35 debit balance
         (an asset). The fair value of the forward contract on February 15, 2012, is determined by
         comparing the dollars that Duster is required to pay on the forward contract ($14,070)
         to the dollars Duster would have had to pay if they had not hedged the transaction
         (¥1,500,000 × .00942 = $14,130). The current fair value is a $60.00 debit balance.
         Therefore, a loss of $44.35 is recognized (fair value at 2/15 of $60.00 less the fair value
         at 12/31 of $104.35).

13. A

Answers to Brief Essay Questions

1. Three currency arrangements:

    A. *Independent float* — the value of the currency is allowed to fluctuate freely according to
        market forces with little or no intervention from the central bank.

    B. *Pegged to another currency* — the value of the currency is fixed (pegged) in terms of a
        particular currency and the central bank intervenes as necessary to maintain the fixed value.

    C. *European monetary System (EMS)* — the currencies of most of the members of the European
        Union float jointly against non-EMS currencies.

2. The *spot rate* is the price at which a foreign currency can be purchased or sold today. In contrast, the *forward rate* is the price today at which foreign currency can be purchased or sold sometime in the future.

3. The *one-transaction perspective* is criticized because it sometimes hides the difference in what a company would have collected on a sale, or paid for a purchase, on the transaction date vs. the settlement date of the transaction. For example, the fact that a company could have received a larger dollar amount if the foreign customer had been required to pay at the time of the sale is hidden in an adjustment to sales using the one-transaction perspective.

4. Using the accrual approach results in the recognition of unrealized gains on the income statement. This departs from the principle of conservatism.

Solutions to Problems

1. Entries to be made on Johnson Inc.'s books:

Date	Accounts	Debit	Credit
A			
12/31/2011	Accounts Receivable (LCU)	8,750	
	Foreign Exchange Gain		8,750
	(1.8125 – 1.75) × 140,000		
1/26/2012	Cash (140,000 × 1.8220)	255,080	
	Accounts Receivable (LCU) (140,000 × 1.8125)		253,750
	Foreign Exchange Gain		1,330

2. Entries to record Norton's purchase of inventory and accompanying hedge entries when the hedge is accounted for as a **cash flow hedge**.

Date	Accounts	Debit	Credit
12/2/2011	Inventory	46,260.00	
	Accounts Payable (LCU)		46,260.00
	To record payable at the 12/2 spot rate		
	Note: There is no entry on 12/2 to record the forward contract.		
12/31/2011	Foreign Exchange Loss	500.00	
	Accounts Payable (LCU)		500.00
	To adjust the payable to the 12/31 spot rate		
	(.009352 – .009252) × 5,000,000		

(continued on the following page)

Date	Accounts	Debit	Credit
12/31/2011	Forward Contract	223.87	
	AOCI		223.87
	to record the fair value of the forward contract		
	(.009375 − .00942) × 5,000,000 × .995		
	AOCI	500.00	
	Gain on Forward Contract		500.00
	To record an offsetting gain against the foreign		
	exchange loss associated with the A/P		
	Premium Expense	307.50	
	AOCI		307.50
	To allocate the $615 forward contract premium over the term of the		
	forward contract. (12/2 forward rate of .009375 less the 12/2 spot rate		
	of .009292) × 5,000,000 = $615. $615 × 30/60 = $307.50.)		
1/31/2012	Foreign Exchange Loss	315.00	
	Accounts Payable (LCU)		315.00
	To adjust accounts payable to the current exchange		
	rate value ((.009415 − .009352) × 5,000,000).		
	AOCI	23.87	
	Forward Contract		23.87
	To adjust forward contract to fair value		
	Fair value at 12/31 = 223.87		
	Fair value at 1/31 = 200.00 (forward rate at 12/2 of		
	.009375 less spot rate at 1/31 of .009415)		
	Change in fair value = 23.87		
	AOCI	315.00	
	Gain on Forward Contract		315.00
	To record an offsetting gain to the foreign exchange loss		
	Premium Expense	307.50	
	AOCI		307.50
	To recognize the remainder of the forward contract premium.		
	Foreign Currency (LCU)	46,875.00	
	Cash		46,875.00
	to acquire LCUs at the contracted exchange rate of $.009375		
	Accounts Payable (LCU)	47,075.00	
	Forward Contract		200.00
	Foreign Currency LCU)		46,875.00

Note that after all entries on 1/31/2012, the balance in AOCI is zero (0).

Advanced Accounting – 10/e

3. Entries to record Norton's purchase when the hedge is accounted for as a **fair value hedge**.

Date	Accounts	Debit	Credit
12/2/2011	Inventory	46,260.00	
	Accounts Payable (LCU)		46,260.00
	To record payable at the 12/2 spot rate		
	Note: There is no entry on 12/2 to record the forward contract.		
12/31/2011	Foreign Exchange Loss	500.00	
	Accounts Payable (LCU)		500.00
	To adjust the payable to the 12/31 spot rate		
	Forward Contract	223.87	
	Gain on Forward Contract		223.87
	To record the fair value of the forward contract.		
1/28/2012	Foreign Exchange Loss	315.00	
	Accounts Payable (LCU)		315.00
	To adjust A/P to current spot rate value		
	Loss on Forward Contract	23.87	
	Forward Contract		23.87
	To adjust forward contract to fair value		
	Foreign Currency (LCU)	46,875.00	
	Cash		46,875.00
	to acquire LCUs at the contracted exchange rate of $.009415		
	Accounts Payable (LCU)	47,075.00	
	Forward Contract		200.00
	Foreign Currency (LCU)		46,875.00

4. Entries to record New York Chili's sale. The hedge is accounted for as a fair value hedge.

Date	Accounts	Debit	Credit
8/1/2012	Accounts Receivable (Peso)	198,000.00	
	Sales		198,000.00
	to record sale to foreign customer		
	Note: There is no entry on 8/1 to record the forward contract.		
9/30/2012	Accounts Receivable (Peso)	4,400.00	
	Foreign Exchange Gain		4,400.00
	to adjust the A/R to the 9/30 spot rate		
	Forward Contract	437.10	
	Gain on Forward Contract		437.10
	to record the fair value of the forward contract.		
11/1/2012	Accounts Receivable (Peso)	1,100.00	
	Foreign Exchange Gain		1,100.00
	to adjust A/R to the 11/1 spot rate value		
	Forward Contract	662.90	
	Gain on Forward Contract		662.90
	to adjust forward contract to fair value		
	Foreign Currency (Peso)	203,500.00	
	Accounts Receivable (Peso)		203,500.00
	to record receipt of pesos (2,200,000 x .0925)		
	Cash	204,600.00	
	Forward Contract		1,100.00
	Foreign Currency (Peso)		203,500.00
	to record conversion of pesos into U.S. $		

Chapter 10

Translation of Foreign Currency Financial Statements

Chapter Outline

Standards Mentioned in This Chapter:
- **IAS 21,** *The Effects of Changes in Foreign Exchange Rates*
- **IAS 29,** *Financial Reporting in Hyperinflationary Economies*
- **SFAS No. 1,** *Disclosure of Foreign Currency Translation Information*
- **SFAS No. 8,** *Accounting for the Translation of Foreign Currency Transactions and Foreign Currency Financial Statements*
- **SFAS No. 52,** *Foreign Currency Translation*
- **SFAS No. 105,** *Disclosure of Information about Financial Statements with Off-Balance Sheet Risk and Financial Instruments with Concentrations of Credit Risk*
- **SFAS No. 133,** *Accounting for Derivative Instruments and Hedging Activities*

I. **Exchange Rates Used in Translation**

    A. Two types of exchange rates are used in translating foreign currency financial statements into U.S. $.

        1. *Historical exchange rate* — the exchange rate that exists when a transaction occurs.

        2. *Current exchange rate* — the exchange rate that exists at the balance sheet date.

    B. **Translation Adjustments**

        1. *Positive Translation Adjustment* – assets translated at the current exchange rate, when the foreign currency has appreciated, generate a positive (credit) translation adjustment. The adjustment is a *credit* in the equity section of the balance sheet.

        2. *Negative Translation Adjustment* – liabilities translated at the current exchange rate, when the foreign currency has appreciated, generate a negative translation adjustment. The adjustment is a *debit* in the equity section of the balance sheet.

    C. **Balance Sheet Exposure**

        1. Balance sheet items translated at the *current exchange rate* change from period to period simply as a result of a change in the exchange rate. These items are *exposed* to translation adjustment (also called balance sheet, translation or accounting exposure).

        2. Balance sheet items translated at *historical exchange rates* do not change in dollar value from period to period and are not exposed to translation adjustment.

        3. Translation adjustments arising from balance sheet exposure do not directly result in cash inflows or outflows.

4. Transaction exposure arising when a company has foreign currency receivables and payables (as seen in Chapter 9) results in foreign exchange gains and losses that are ultimately realized in cash.

5. A foreign operation has a *net asset balance sheet exposure* when assets translated at the current exchange rate are greater than the liabilities translated at the current exchange rate.

6. A foreign operation has a *net liability balance sheet exposure* when liabilities translated at the current exchange rate are greater than the assets translated at the current exchange rate.

II.   *LO1* Translation Methods

A.   The Current Rate Method

1. Required by *SFAS 52* for foreign subsidiaries that:

   a. Use something other than the U.S. $ as their *functional currency* (discussed later).

   b. Operate fairly independently of the U.S. parent company.

2. The basic assumption underlying the *current rate method* is that a company's *net investment* in a foreign operation is *exposed* to foreign exchange risk.

3. The balance sheet exposure under the current rate method is equal to the foreign operation's net asset (assets minus liabilities) position.

   Total assets – total liabilities = net asset exposure

4. All assets of the foreign subsidiary are converted to U.S. $ using the rate in effect on the date of the translation (current rate).

5. All revenues and expenses are converted to U.S. $ using the rate in effect on the date of the transaction (historical rate).

   a. For revenues and expenses that are earned throughout the period, where using the historical rate would be impractical, *the weighted average rate* for the period is acceptable.

   b. For revenues and expenses that occur at a readily identifiable point in time, the exchange rate on that date should be used.

6. Capital Accounts (such as Common Stock and Paid-In Capital) are converted using the historical rates in effect at the date the stock was originally issued.

7. Beginning Retained Earnings is defined by the U.S. $ Retained Earnings from the previous period.

8. Ending Retained Earnings is determined:

    Start with beginning retained earnings (which is already in U.S. $)
    + Net income (from the translated Income Statement), and
    – Dividends (translated at the historical rate from the date the dividends are declared).

9. Any imbalance between the translated net assets and the translated equity section of the balance sheet is recorded in an account called *Cumulative Translation Adjustment*.

    a. This account is usually located in the equity section of the translated balance sheet and is reported as a component of *Other Comprehensive Income*.

B. The Temporal Method

1. Established originally by *SFAS 8* and required by *SFAS 52* for foreign subsidiaries that:

    a. Use the U.S. $ as their *functional currency* (discussed later).

    b. Use the U.S. $ for most of their transactions.

    c. Also required for foreign subsidiaries operating in a high inflation economy.

2. The basic objective of the *temporal method* is to produce a set of U.S. dollar translated financial statements as if the foreign subsidiary had used U.S. dollars in conducting its operations.

3. *Assets and liabilities* on the foreign operation's balance sheet at *historical cost* are translated at *historical* exchange rates to yield an equivalent historical cost in U.S. dollars.

4. *Assets and liabilities* carried at a *current or future value* are translated at the *current* exchange rate to yield an equivalent current value in U.S. dollars.

5. All revenues and expenses are converted to U.S. $ using the rate in effect on the date of the transaction (historical rate).

    a. For revenues and expenses earned throughout the period, where using the historical rate would be impractical, the weighted average rate for the period is acceptable.

    b. For revenues and expenses that occur at a readily identifiable point in time, the actual historical rate is used.

6. Capital Accounts (such as Common Stock and Paid-In Capital) are converted using the historical rates in effect at the date the stock was originally issued.

7. Beginning Retained Earnings is defined by the U.S. $ Retained Earnings from the previous period.

a. Ending Retained Earnings is determined:

Beginning retained earnings (already in U.S. $)
+ Net income (from the translated Income Statement),
– Dividends (translated at the historical rate in effect on the date the dividends were declared).

8. Any imbalance between the translated net assets and the translated equity section of the balance sheet is recorded in an account called *Translation Gain or Loss,* which is a gain or loss account reported on the income statement.

III. Complicating Aspects of the Temporal Method (and comparisons to the current rate method)

A. With the *temporal method,* but not the *current rate method*, some items are translated at the *historical* exchange rate in effect when the item was acquired. For these items, a record must be kept of the *historical* exchange rate:

1. Inventory

2. Prepaid expenses

3. Fixed assets

4. Intangible assets

B. **Cost of Goods Sold (COGS)**

1. **Current Rate Method** – translate the balance in COGS using an average-for-the-period exchange rate.

2. **Temporal Method** – decompose COGS into its component parts.

a. Beginning Inventory is translated at the historical exchange rate.

b. Purchases are translated at the average exchange rate.

c. Ending Inventory is translated at the historical exchange rate.

C. **Application of the Lower-of-Cost-or-Market Rule**

1. **Current Rate Method**

a. Ending inventory reported on the foreign currency balance sheet is translated at the current exchange rate.

b. This is regardless of whether it is carried at cost or a lower market value.

2. **Temporal Method**

    a.   The inventory's foreign currency cost and foreign currency market value are translated into U.S. $ at appropriate exchange rates.

    b.   The lower of the dollar cost and dollar market value is reported on the consolidated balance sheet.

    c.   As a result, inventory can be carried at cost on the foreign currency balance sheet and at market on the U.S. $ consolidated balance sheet and vice versa.

D.   **Fixed Assets, Depreciation, and Accumulated Depreciation**

    1.   **Current Rate Method**

        a.   Fixed assets are translated at the current exchange rate.

        b.   Accumulated Depreciation is translated at the current exchange rate.

        c.   Depreciation Expense is translated at the average exchange rate.

    2.   **Temporal Method**

        a.   Each fixed asset is translated at its respective historical exchange rate.

        b.   Accumulated Depreciation is translated at the same historical exchange rate as the asset to which it is related.

        c.   Depreciation Expense is translated at the same historical exchange rate as the asset to which it is related.

E.   **Gain or Loss on the Sale of an Asset**

    1.   **Current Rate Method** – The gain/loss is translated at the exchange rate in effect on the date of disposition.

    2.   **Temporal Method** – The cash received (use exchange rate in effect on the date of disposition) and the asset sold (use historical exchange rate when the asset was acquired) are translated separately. The gain/loss is determined based on those two translated amounts.

IV.   **U.S. Rules**

A.   SFAS 8 required the use of the *temporal method* with *translation gains and losses* being reported in the income statement by all companies for all foreign operations.

    1.   Required the use of the U.S. $ perspective.

        a.   This perspective assumed that there is a close relationship between the foreign subsidiary and the parent.

        b.   It also assumed that the foreign subsidiary uses the U.S. $ for operations and accounting.

    2.   SFAS 8 was criticized, and in 1978 as a result of the negative feedback, the FASB reconsidered the translation issue. SFAS 52 overhauled U.S. GAAP reporting.

B.   *LO2* **Two Translation Combinations** – in developing current standards, the FASB recognized two types of foreign entities

    1.   Closely integrated entities that do much of their business in U.S. dollars. The *temporal method* is appropriate for these entities.

    2.   Foreign entities that are relatively self-contained and integrated with the local economy. These entities use a foreign currency in daily operations. Accounting standards require the *local currency perspective* for these types of subsidiaries. Thus, the *current rate method* replaced the *temporal method* in most cases where the accounts of the foreign subsidiary are being reported.

V.   **Disposition of Translation Adjustment**

A.   There are two major issues relating to foreign currency financial statement translation.

    1.   Selecting the appropriate method.

    2.   Deciding where the resulting translation adjustment should be reported in the consolidated financial statements.

B.   There are two prevailing schools of thought regarding the second issue.

    1.   *Translation gain or loss* — the translation adjustment is considered to be a gain or loss similar to a gain or loss arising from foreign currency transactions and should be reported as income in the period in which the fluctuation in the exchange rate occurs (required by the Temporal Method).

    2.   *Cumulative translation adjustment in stockholders' equity* — the translation adjustment is taken directly to stockholders' equity as a part of *Other Comprehensive Income* (required by the Current Rate Method).

C.   **Functional Currency**

    1.   The *functional currency* is the currency a foreign subsidiary uses to conduct most of its operating and financing functions.

    2.   The *functional currency* may be:

        a.   The foreign entity's local currency, or

        b.   The parent's currency (the U.S. $).

3. The functional currency orientation results in the following:

Functional Currency	Translation Method	Translation Adjustment
U.S. dollar	Temporal method	Gain (loss) in Net Income
Foreign currency	Current rate method	Separate component of Other Comp. Income (Stockholders' Equity)

4. Indications for determining the functional currency are found in the books Exhibit 10.2

D. **Highly Inflationary Economies** — the temporal method is required for subsidiaries located in a highly inflationary economy.

E. *LO3* **Translation of Financial Statements — Current Rate Method**

1. First, all account balances are recorded in the foreign subsidiary's functional currency.

2. Next, the financial statements of the subsidiary are adjusted to comply with U.S. GAAP.

3. *All* of the subsidiary's asset and liability balances are *translated* into the parent company's *reporting currency* based on the exchange rate at the balance sheet date.

4. Other accounts are translated at the historical exchange rate that was in effect at the time of original accounting recognition.

5. Any increases or decreases created by translating assets and liabilities at new currency rates will be accumulated over the years and reported as a separate *translation adjustment* in the *stockholders' equity section* of the *balance sheet*; no income effect is created by a translation.

   a. The *translation adjustment* is determined by monitoring the change in value of the *exposed net asset or liability position* held by the subsidiary.

   b. All changes made in the *net asset or liability position* during the period are identified along with the corresponding value at that time.

   c. The total is compared to the translated balance of the assets and liabilities at year-end.

F. *LO4* **Remeasurement of Financial Statements — Temporal Method**

1. *Remeasurement* (rather than *translation*) is mandated in several specific situations.

2. Remeasurement is required for:

   a. Recording of individual transactions that are carried out by a company (parent or subsidiary) in a currency other than its own *functional currency*.

      b. Restating a foreign subsidiary's account balances into the parent's *reporting currency* (in anticipation of consolidation) when the subsidiary operates in a highly inflationary environment.

      c. Restating a foreign subsidiary's account balances into the parent's *reporting currency* when both companies have the same *functional currency*.

    3. *Remeasurement* applies the rules of the *temporal method* to foreign currency account balances.

      a. Cash, monetary receivables, monetary liabilities, and market-valued assets are remeasured at *current* exchange rates whereas all other accounts are remeasured at *historical* rates as of the date of the original transaction.

      b. *Remeasurement gains and losses* are reported as a component of income.

VI.   *LO1* **Comparison of the Results from Applying the Two Different Methods**

    A. The current rate method does not always result in greater net income and a larger amount of equity than the temporal method.

    B. The determination of the functional currency and the resulting translation method can have a material impact on the amounts reported by a parent company in its consolidated financial statements.

    C. The temporal method distorts financial ratios as measured in the foreign currency.

    D. Conceptually, when the *current rate method* is used, *income statement items* can be translated at either the *average* or the *current* exchange rate.

VII.   *LO5* **Hedging Balance Sheet Exposure**

    A. Some companies hedge balance sheet exposures to avoid reporting remeasurement losses in net income and/or negative translation adjustments in Other Comprehensive Income.

    B. Translation adjustments and remeasurement gains or losses are a function of two factors:

      1. Changes in the exchange rate and

      2. Balance sheet exposure.

    C. Parent companies can hedge balance sheet exposure by using a derivative financial instrument, such as a forward contract or foreign currency option or other hedging instrument.

    D. *SFAS 133* provides that the gain or loss on a hedging instrument used to hedge net investments in foreign operations are reported in the same manner as the translation adjustment being hedged.

VIII. Disclosures Related to Translation

A. Current standards require firms to present an analysis of the change in the *Cumulative Translation Adjustment* account in either the

    1. Financial statements, or

    2. Notes to the financial statements.

B. Many companies comply with this requirement by including a *translation adjustment* column in the *Statement of Stockholders' Equity*.

C. Other firms provide separate disclosure in the notes.

IX. *LO6* Consolidation of a Foreign Subsidiary

A. Special attention needs to be paid to the treatment of the *excess of fair value over book value*.

B. A *cumulative translation adjustment* will be required to balance the *trial balance (Entry T* for **T**ranslation is used).

C. The following consolidation entries are made on the consolidation worksheet (SAIDE + T):

Entry S — eliminates the subsidiary's *stockholders' equity* accounts as of the beginning of the current year and credits the *Investment* account.

Entry A — allocates the *excess of fair value over book value* at the date of acquisition to asset (and liability) accounts and debits (credits) that amount from the *Investment* account.

Entry I — eliminates equity income recognized by the parent in the current year and included in the *Investment* account under the equity method.

Entry D — eliminates the subsidiary's dividends that reduced the *Investment* account under the equity method.

Entry T — eliminates the *cumulative translation adjustment* included in the *Investment* account under the equity method and the *cumulative translation adjustment* on the parent's books.

Entry E — revalues the *excess fair value over book value* for the change in exchange rate since the date of acquisition with the counterpart recognized as an increase in the *consolidated cumulative translation adjustment*.

X.   **IFRS — Translation of Foreign Currency Financial Statements**

A.   IAS 21, *"The Effects of Changes in Foreign Exchange Rates",* generally follows the functional currency approach used by U.S. GAAP. A foreign subsidiary's financial statements are translated using the current rate method when the foreign currency is the functional currency, and are translated using the temporal method when the parent company's currency is the functional currency.

B.   Significant differences relate to:

1.   The hierarchy of factors used to determine the functional currency. Because of this it is *possible* that a different functional currency for foreign subsidiary could be determined under IFRS than under U.S. GAAP.

2.   The method used to translate the foreign currency statements of a subsidiary located in a country with hyperinflation.

   a.   First, financial statements are restated for local inflation in accordance with IAS 29, *"Financial Reporting in Hyperinflationary Economies."*

   b.   Second, each financial statement line item (already restated for local inflation) is translated using the current exchange rate.

   c.   Thus, *neither the temporal method nor current rate method* is used for a subsidiary located in a country experiencing hyperinflation.

   d.   Because all balance sheet accounts, including retained earnings, are translated at the current exchange rate, there is no translation adjustment.

   e.   U.S. GAAP requires the temporal method for a subsidiary located in a country experiencing hyperinflation.

   f.   Characteristics indicating hyperinflation differ between the two sets of standards.

XI.   **Summary of Steps** — the functional currency is determined first, as it determines the method and process to use.

Determine the functional currency	U.S. Dollar	Foreign Currency
Determine the method to use based on the functional currency	Temporal Method	Current Rate Method
Determine applicable exchange rates	Textbook Exhibit 10.1	Textbook Exhibit 10.1
Process	Remeasure the balance sheet first. Calculate the ending retained earnings balance so that the balance sheet balances!	Translate the income statement first.
	Remeasure the statement of retained earnings. Ending retained must be the same as on the balance sheet. Dividends are remeasured at the historical rate. Determine net income (so beginning retained earnings + income – dividends = ending retained earnings).	Net income is carried down to the retained earnings statement.
	The remeasurement gain or loss is the gain or loss needed to adjust income on the income statement so it is equal to net income per the statement of retained earnings.	Ending retained earnings is carried to the balance sheet.
	Finish the remeasurement of the income statement.	The translation adjustment is needed to make the balance sheet balance.
Adjustment	Remeasurement gain or loss	Cumulative translation adjustment
Financial Statement	Income Statement	Separate component of Other Comprehensive Income in the Stockholders' Equity section of Balance Sheet

Multiple Choice Questions

1. Which method for translating the financial statements are foreign subsidiaries of U.S. parent companies that operate in highly inflationary economies required to use?

    A. Temporal Method, with the *Translation Gain or Loss* to be reported as part of *Comprehensive Income*.
    B   Current Rate Method, with the *Cumulative Translation Adjustment* to be reported as part of *Comprehensive Income*.
    C. Temporal Method, with the *Translation Gain or Loss* to be reported as part of Net Income.
    D. Current Rate Method, with the *Cumulative Translation Adjustment* to be reported as part of Net Income.
    E. Equity Method, with the *Translation Gain or Loss* to be reported as part of *Noncontrolling Interest in Subsidiary*.

2. A subsidiary of Stephen Inc. is located in Germany. The *functional currency* of this subsidiary is the Euro (€). The subsidiary acquires inventory on October 31, 2010 for 300,000 €. The inventory is sold on January 15, 2011 for 420,000 €. Collection of the money takes place on February 4, 2011. Applicable exchange rates are as follows:

Date	Spot Rate	
October 31, 2010	1.3500 =	1 €
December 31, 2010	1.3650 =	1 €
January 15, 2011	1.3750 =	1 €

    What amount is reported for this inventory on the December 31, 2010 U.S. $ consolidated balance sheet?

    A. $219,780
    B $405,000
    C. $412,500
    D. $409,500
    E. $222,222

3. A subsidiary of Shaw Inc. has one asset (*Inventory*) and one liability (*Accounts Payable*). The *functional currency* of this subsidiary is the Kuwaiti dinar. The inventory was acquired for 90,000 dinars when the *exchange rate* was $3.2500 = 1 dinar. *Accounts Payable*, which has a balance of 50,000 dinars, was established when the *exchange rate* was $3.2875 = 1 dinar. At year-end, the *exchange rate* was $3.3000 = 1 dinar. What type of exposure does Shaw have?

    A. Net asset balance sheet exposure.
    B. Net liability balance sheet exposure.
    C. Translation adjustment exposure.
    D. Transaction exposure.
    E. Currency rate fluctuation exposure.

4. A U.S.-based company has a subsidiary located in Germany. The Euro (€) is the *functional currency* of the subsidiary. What exchange rate should be used to translate the following items reported in the subsidiary's year-end financial statements?

	Inventory	Machinery	Depreciation Expense
A.	Current rate	Current rate	Average rate
B.	Historical rate	Current rate	Current rate
C.	Current rate	Historical rate	Average rate
D.	Average rate	Historical rate	Current rate
E.	Average rate	Current rate	Current rate

5. If a company has no foreign subsidiaries, then the issues related to hedging of receivables and payables denominated in foreign currencies are irrelevant.

   A. True
   B. False

6. At what point in the process should the parent company adjust the foreign subsidiary's accounts to bring them in accordance with GAAP?

   A. Prior to the beginning of the translation process.
   B. After translation, but prior to consolidation.
   C. After consolidation, but prior to reporting.
   D. No adjustments are necessary, since most foreign countries already use GAAP.
   E. No adjustment should be necessary. Foreign subsidiaries are required by the SEC to have an accounting system that is consistent with GAAP.

7. Which one of the following translation methods has as its basic assumption the premise that a company's *net investment* in a foreign operation is *exposed* to foreign exchange risk?

   A. current rate method
   B. average rate method
   C. current/noncurrent method
   D. monetary/nonmonetary method
   E. temporal method

8. The primary currency of the foreign entity's operating environment is known as the

   A. translation currency.
   B. functional currency.
   C. reporting currency.
   D. temporal currency.
   E. prime-time currency.

9. Packstone Inc. owns a subsidiary in England. The subsidiary's *functional currency* is the pound. The subsidiary began 2010 with £500,000 in cash and no other assets or liabilities. On March 1, 2010, the subsidiary used £100,000 to purchase equipment. On April 20, 2010, the subsidiary used cash to purchase inventory costing £80,000. The inventory was sold on May 16, 2010, for £120,000 in cash. On November 1, 2010, the subsidiary paid a cash dividend to Packstone of £60,000 and recorded depreciation on the equipment for the year of £50,000. The appropriate exchange rates were as follows:

Date	Spot Rate
January 1, 2010	1.8500 = £1
March 1, 2010	1.8600 = £1
April 20, 2010	1.8650 = £1
May 16, 2010	1.8500 = £1
November 1, 2010	1.8450 = £1
December 31, 2010	1.8550 = £1
Average for 2010	1.8520 = £1

What is the *translation adjustment* to be reported in the *stockholders' equity* section of the *consolidated balance sheet*?
A. $ –0–
B. $ 200 debit
C. $ 200 credit
D. $2,000 debit
E. $2,000 credit

10. At the beginning of 2010, Bean Inc. had two assets: *Cash* of ¥30,000 and *Land* which originally cost ¥50,000 when acquired on June 30, 2008. On August 18, 2010, the company rendered services to a customer for ¥80,000, an amount that was paid in cash. On November 15, 2010, the company incurred an operating expense of ¥26,000, which was immediately paid. No other transactions occurred during the year. Currency exchange rates were as follows:

Date	Spot Rate
June 30, 2008	0.008850 = ¥1
January 1, 2010	0.009280 = ¥1
August 18, 2010	0.009350 = ¥1
November 15, 2010	0.009450 = ¥1
December 31, 2010	0.009680 = ¥1

Bean Inc. is a Japanese subsidiary of an American company, and the U.S. dollar is the *functional currency* of the parent and the subsidiary. What is the *remeasurement gain or loss* for 2010?

A. $ 32.42 gain
B. $ 32.42 loss
C. $278.40 gain
D. $245.70 loss
E. $813.12 gain

Items 11 and 12 are based on the following information:

A subsidiary of Parket Inc. purchased marketable equity securities and inventory on March 1, 2010, for 80,000 pesos each. Both of these items were paid for on May 1, 2010, and were still on hand at year-end. Inventory is carried at cost under average lower-of-cost-or-market valuation. Currency exchange rates are as follows:

Date	Spot Rate	
January 1, 2010	$0.0925 =	1 peso
March 1, 2010	$0.0920 =	1 peso
May 1, 2010	$0.0910 =	1 peso
December 31, 2010	$0.0895 =	1 peso

11. Assuming the peso is the subsidiary's *functional currency*, what balances are reported on the December 31, 2010 *consolidated balance sheet*?

	Marketable Securities	Inventory
A.	$ 7,160	$ 7,360
B.	$ 7,400	$ 7,360
C.	$ 7,400	$ 7,400
D.	$ 7,160	$ 7,160
E.	$893,855	$893,855

12. Assuming that the U.S. dollar is the subsidiary's *functional currency*, what balances are reported on the December 31, 2010 *consolidated balance sheet*?

	Marketable Securities	Inventory
A.	$ 7,160	$ 7,360
B.	$ 7,400	$ 7,360
C.	$ 7,400	$ 7,400
D.	$ 7,160	$ 7,160
E.	$893,855	$869,565

Problems

1. Nelson Inc. has a $2,500 translation loss due to foreign currency exchanges before any year-end adjustments on December 31, 2010. The following information exists at year-end and has not yet been taken into account:

    *   Nelson's wholly-owned foreign subsidiary, Jennings Inc., when translated, shows a $5,000 foreign currency translation loss for the year ended December 31, 2010.

    *   In transactions with an unrelated supplier, Nelson recognized a payable denominated in the currency of the supplier. In U.S. dollars, the payable was $19,000 on November 1, 2010, when the transaction originated; on December 31, 2010, the U.S. dollar equivalent of the payable was $19,750.

    Required:

    In Nelson's 2010 *income statement*, what amount should be shown as a *foreign exchange loss*?

2. Kent Inc. has a wholly-owned foreign subsidiary in Canada called Barbel Co. Barbel maintains certain accounts in Canadian dollars as follows:

	Canadian $
Depreciation on building acquired on August 1, 2010	$ 7,500
Equipment rental expense for 2010	6,000

    Assume that the Canadian dollar is Barbel Co.'s *functional currency*. Selected exchange rates are shown below:

	US $ Equivalent of Canadian $
August 1, 2010	$ .8750
December 31, 2010	$ .8540
Average for 2010	$ .8420

    Required:

    What dollar amount should be included in Kent's Income Statement on December 31, 2010 to reflect the expenses shown above?

Advanced Accounting – 10/e

3. On 1/1/2010, Awlamer, Inc., a U.S. company, acquires 90% of Justa Minuto Incorporato, located in a new country in South America. Justa Minuto was incorporated in 1993 when the exchange rate was $.520 = 1 bobb. Justa Minuto's only asset is 2,000 acres of land that was acquired in 1993 on the date of incorporation at a cost of 55,000 bobbs.

At 1/1/2012, Justa Minuto's Retained Earnings balance in U.S. $ was $19,975. At 12/31/2012, Awlamer must convert Justa Minuto's financial statements into $US for consolidation purposes. Justa Minuto's dividends were paid on 10/1/2012. On June 30, Justa Minuto sold land originally costing 20,000 bobbs for 23,000 bobbs. Justa Minuto uses the bobb for most of its transactions. Foreign currency exchange rates are listed below.

Exchange Rates:

1/1/2012	1 bobb = $ .850 US
10/1/2012	1 bobb = $ .800 US
12/31/2012	1 bobb = $ .660 US
6/30/2012	1 bobb = $ .640 US
Weighted Avg.	1 bobb = $ .785 US

Financial Balances

Revenues	84,000 bobbs
COGS	62,000 bobbs
Salaries Expense	11,000 bobbs
Gain on Sale of Land	3,000 bobbs
Other Operating Exp.	8,500 bobbs
Cash	14,000 bobbs
A/R	28,000 bobbs
Inventory	57,000 bobbs
Land	35,000 bobbs
A/P	10,000 bobbs
Common Stock (par)	100,000 bobbs
R/E (Beginning)	23,500 bobbs
Dividends Paid	5,000 bobbs

Required:

Prepare a *translated* Income Statement, Statement of Changes in Retained Earnings, and Balance Sheet for Justa Minuto Incorporato (in proper format) for the year ended December 31, 2012. Assume there were no intra-entity transactions and that Justa Minuto uses U.S. GAAP for accounting purposes.

Solutions to Multiple Choice Questions

1. **C**

2. **D** A translation is appropriate since the € is the *functional currency* of the subsidiary. All assets are translated and reported using the *current* exchange rate as of the balance sheet date.

   Translated value at 12/31/2010 (300,000 € x $.1.3650) = $409,500

3. **A** Shaw is exposed to net asset exposure, because assets translated at the current exchange rate exceed liabilities translated at the current exchange rate.

4. **A**

5. **B**

6. **A**

7. **A**

8. **B**

9. **D** Only changes in the *net assets* have an impact on the calculation of the *translation adjustment*. The equipment purchase does not change net assets since the increase in the *Equipment* account is offset by the reduction in the *Cash* account. The sale of inventory increases net assets by the amount of the gross profit.

Beginning cash balance	£ 500,000 × $1.8500 =	$ 925,000
Sale of merchandise for a gain	40,000 × $1.8500 =	74,000
Payment of cash dividend	(60,000) × $1.8450 =	(110,700)
Recording of depreciation	(50,000) × $1.8520 =	(92,600)
	£ 430,000	795,700

Actual value of net assets, 12/31/2010   £430,000 × $1.8550/ £= $797,650
Translation adjustment (**debit**) $ 2,000

10. **A**

Net monetary assets - cash	¥	30,000 ×	0.009280 =	$ 278.40
Increase in monetary assets - revenues	¥	80,000 ×	0.009350 =	$ 748.00
Decrease in monetary assets - expenses	¥	(26,000) ×	0.009450 =	$ (245.70)
Net monetary assets @ 12/31/20 - value				$ 780.70
Prior to rate change	¥	84,000 ×	0.009680 =	$ 813.12
Remeasurement gain				$ 32.42

11. **D** Translation of marketable equity securities (80,000 pesos × $.0895) $7,160
Translation of inventory (80,000 pesos × $.0895) $7,160

12. **A** Translation of marketable equity securities (80,000 pesos x $.0895) $7,160
Translation of inventory (80,000 pesos x $.0920) $7,360

Solutions to Problems

1.

Translation loss before adjustment	$ 2,500
Loss on transaction with supplier ($19,750 – $19,000)	750
Foreign exchange loss	$ 3,250

The loss associated with the wholly-owned foreign subsidiary would not be shown on the *income statement*; instead, that adjustment is shown in the *equity section* of the *balance sheet*.

2.

Depreciation in Canadian dollars	C$ 7,500
Equipment rental expense in Canadian dollars	6,000
Total expenses	C$ 13,500
Average exchange rate for 2010	.8420
Depreciation and equipment rental expenses included in Kent Inc.'s 2010 income statement in U.S. dollars	$ 11,367

3. This translation requires the application of the current rate method.

Justa Minuto

Statement of Income

For the Period Ending 12/31/2012

	bobbs	Exchange Rate	U.S. $
Revenues	(84,000.00)	0.7850	(65,940.00)
Cost of Goods Sold	62,000.00	0.7850	48,670.00
Gross Margin	(22,000.00)		(17,270.00)
Salaries Expense	11,000.00	0.7850	8,635.00
Other Operating Expense	8,500.00	0.7850	6,672.50
Gain on Sale of Land	(3,000.00)	0.6400	(1,920.00)
Net Income	(5,500.00)		(3,882.50)

The Statement of Changes in Retained Earnings and the Balance Sheet are on the following page.

Justa Minuto
Statement of Changes in Retained Earnings
For the Period Ending 12/31/2012

	bobbs	Exchange Rate	U.S. $
Retained Earnings, 1/1/2012	(23,500.00)	N/A	$ (19,975.00)
Add: Net Income	(5,500.00)	N/A	(3,882.50)
Less: Dividends	5,000.00	0.8000	4,000.00
Retained Earnings, 12/31/2012	(24,000.00)		$ (19,857.50)

Justa Minuto
Balance Sheet
12/31/2012

	bobbs	Exchange Rate	U.S. $
Assets			
Cash	14,000.00	0.6600	$ 9,240.00
Accounts Receivable	28,000.00	0.6600	18,480.00
Inventory	57,000.00	0.6600	37,620.00
Land	35,000.00	0.6600	23,100.00
Total Assets	134,000.00		$ 88,440.00
Liabilities and Owners' Equity			
Accounts Payable	(10,000.00)	0.6600	$ (6,600.00)
Common Stock	(100,000.00)	0.5200	(52,000.00)
Retained Earnings, 12/31/2012	(24,000.00)	N/A	(19,857.50)
Cumulative Translation Adjustment			(9,982.50)
Total Liabilities and Owners' Equity	(134,000.00)		$ (88,440.00)

Chapter 11

Worldwide Accounting Diversity and International Standards

Chapter Outline

Standards Mentioned in This Chapter:

- **FASB Exposure Draft,** *Earnings per Share – an Amendment of FASB Statement 128*
- **IAS 1,** *Presentation of Financial Statements*
- **IAS 2,** *Inventory*
- **IAS 8,** *Accounting Policies, Changes in Accounting Estimates and Errors*
- **IAS 12,** *Income Taxes*
- **IAS 16,** *Property, Plant and Equipment*
- **IAS 17,** *Accounting for Leases*
- **IAS 19,** *Revenue*
- **IAS 23,** *Borrowing Costs*
- **IAS 31,** *Interest in Joint Ventures*
- **IAS 33,** *Earnings per Share*
- **IAS 37,** *Provisions, Contingent Liabilities and Contingent Assets*
- **IAS 38,** *Intangible Assets*
- **IFRS 1,** *First-Time Adoption of IFRS*
- **IFRS 2,** *Share-based Payments*
- **IFRS 3,** *Business Combinations*
- **IFRS 5,** *Non-current Assets Held for Sale and Discontinued Operations*
- **IFRS 8,** *Operating Segments*
- **SFAS No. 13,** *Accounting for Leases*
- **SFAS No. 123 (revised 2004),** *Share-based Payments*
- **SFAS No. 133,** *Accounting for Derivative Instruments and Hedging Activities*
- **SFAS No. 141R,** *Business Combinations* (replaces SFAS 141)
- **SFAS No. 151,** *Inventory Costs – an Amendment of ARB 43, Chapter 4*
- **SFAS No. 153,** *Exchanges of Non-monetary Assets – an Amendment of APB Opinion No. 29*
- **SFAS No. 154,** *Accounting Changes and Error Corrections – a Replacement of APB Opinion No. 20 and FASB Statement No. 3*
- **SFAS No. 160,** *Noncontrolling Interests and Consolidated Financial Statements*

I.   **Evidence of Accounting Diversity**

A.   To function in today's changing world, business leaders must be able to utilize and assess information generated in many different countries.

B.   Accounting principles and applications are not uniform, because they have developed country by country. Differences include the:

1.   Format and presentation of financial statements.

2.   Measurement and recognition rules for preparing financial statements.

3.   Disclosures provided in the notes to financial statements.

4.   Terminology used to describe items in the financial statements.

II. **LO1 Reasons for Accounting Diversity**

A. **Legal system**

1. Countries with codified Roman law usually have a corporation law that establishes the basic legal parameters governing business enterprises.

2. In countries with a tradition of common law, the accounting profession or an independent, nongovernmental body representing a variety of constituencies establishes specific accounting rules. These countries, such as the U.S., tend to have much more detailed rules.

B. **Taxation**

1. In some countries, taxes are based on the financial statements.

2. In other countries, taxes are based on adjusted financial statements. Reports submitted to taxing authorities differ from reports sent to stockholders.

C. **Financing System**

1. Pressure for public accountability is less when families, banks or the state are the primary sources of funding.

2. Pressure for public accountability is greater when stockholders and capital markets serve as the primary sources of funding.

3. There can also be a difference in orientation:

   a. Stockholders may be more interested in profit – Income Statement orientation.

   b. Bankers may be more interested in liquidity – Balance Sheet orientation.

D. **Inflation**

1. Countries with high inflation adopt accounting rules requiring inflation adjustment of historical cost amounts. Historical cost becomes irrelevant in periods of double- and triple-digit inflation rates.

2. This has especially been true in Latin America.

E. **Political and Economic Ties**

1. Accounting rules have been transmitted from country to country through political and economic linkages.

2. Groups of countries with close historical political links tend to have similar accounting systems.

F. **Culture**

1. Four values used to describe similarities and differences in national cultures – individualism, uncertainty avoidance, power distance and masculinity – were identified by Hofstede.[1]

---

[1] Geert Hofstede, *Culture's Consequences: International Differences in Work-Related Values.* Beverly Hills, CA: Sage Publications, 1980.

2. A model suggesting societal values shape a country's accounting system in two ways was developed by Gray.[2]

    a. Values help to shape a country's institutions such as its legal systems and finance providers.

    b. Values (such as conservatism) help to shape the accounting values shared by members of the accounting sub-culture.

III. A General Model of the Reasons for International Differences in Financial Reporting

A. Nobes developed a simplified model of the reasons for international accounting diversity.[3]

    1. Two explanatory factors:

        a. National culture, including institutional structures.

        b. The nature of a country's financing system.

    2. This model divides financial reporting systems into two classes.

    Class A – Used in countries with a strong equity-outsider financing system. Accounting is less conservative, provides more disclosure, and does not follow tax rules.

    Class B – Used in countries with a weak equity-outsider financing system. Accounting is more conservative, disclosure is less extensive, and tax rules are more closely followed.

    3. Nobes suggests that as the financing system in a country evolves from weak to strong equity, the accounting system also evolves towards Class A accounting.

IV. *LO2* Problems Caused by Diverse Accounting Practices

A. One problem relates to the preparation of *consolidated financial statements* by companies with foreign operations – all of the foreign operations of a U.S. company must be converted from local GAAP to U.S. GAAP on the balance sheet date.

B. A second problem relates to companies obtaining access to foreign capital markets – a U.S. company that wants to obtain capital in a foreign country will usually be required to present financial statements prepared in accordance with the GAAP of the foreign country.

C. A third problem relates to the lack of comparability of financial statements among companies from different countries. This affects investment and lending decisions as well as foreign acquisition decisions.

---

[2] Sidney J. Gray, "Towards a Theory of Cultural Influence on the Development of Accounting Systems Internationally," *Abacus*, March 1998, pp. 1-15.

[3] Christopher W. Nobes, "Toward a General Model of the Reasons for International Differences in Financial Reporting," *Abacus*, September 1998, pp.162-187.

V. **International Harmonization of Financial Reporting**

    A. *Harmonization* is the process of reducing differences in financial reporting practices across countries, thereby increasing the comparability of financial statements. The ultimate goal is to have all companies around the world follow one set of international accounting standards.

    B. **European Union**

        1. The *European Union* (EU) endeavored to harmonize financial reporting practices within the EU.

        2. To do this, the EU issued directives that must be incorporated in the laws of member nations.

            a. The Fourth Directive (1978) – provides guidance for valuation rules, disclosure requirements, and the format of financial statements.

            b. The Seventh Directive (1983) – provides guidance on the preparation of consolidated financial statements.

        3. These directives did not create complete harmonization within the EU.

        4. 1990, the EU Commission indicated there would be no further accounting directives.

        5. In 1995, the commission indicated it would associate the EU with efforts by the International Accounting Standards Committee (IASC) towards broader harmonization.

        6. The desire to be competitive in the international capital market led the EU in 2005 to require all publicly-traded companies to use IFRS in preparing consolidated financial statements.

VI. **International Accounting Standards Committee**

    A. The *International Accounting Standards Committee* (IASC) was formed in 1973 in hopes of eliminating the diversity in accounting principles.

    B. The primary goal of the IASC was to develop international accounting standards (IASs).

    C. With the publication of IAS 39 in 1998, the IASC completed its core set of standards.

    D. The IASC was succeeded by the *International Accounting Standards Board* (IASB) in 2001.

    E. **The IOSCO Agreement**

        1. The International Organization of Securities Commissions (IOSCO) became a member of the IASC's Consultative Group in 1987.

        2. IOSCO's members include stock exchange regulators in more than 100 countries, including the U.S. SEC.

        3. One of its objectives is to facilitate cross-border securities offerings and listing by multinational issuers.

        4. In 2000, IOSCO recommended that securities regulators permit foreign issuers to use IASC standards to gain access to a country's capital market as an alternative to using local standards.

VII. International Accounting Standards Board (IASB)

A. The IASC restructured, and created the IASB in April 2001.

   1. The IASB has sole responsibility for establishing International Financial Reporting Standards (IFRS).

   2. The IASB does not have authority to require the application of IASB Standards.

   3. Members pledge to work toward adoption of IASB Standards in their own countries.

   4. Originally 14 members; 12 full time, 2 part time.

   a. Five members must have a background as practicing auditors.

   b. Three members must have a background as preparers of financial statements.

   c. Three members must have a background as users of financial statements.

   d. One member must come from academia.

   e. Full time members must sever all ties with former employers. They may not engage in any activities that might be a conflict of interest.

   5. Increased to 16 members in 2009.

B. *LO3* **International Financial Reporting Standards (IFRS)**

   1. The IASB adopted all IASC standards in 2001 and announced that its accounting standards would be called IFRS.

   2. As of July 2009, 29 of the 41 International Accounting Standards (IASs) and 8 International Financial Reporting Standards (IFRSs) were in force.

   3. These two sets of standards, along with several interpretations, are what the IASB calls IFRS and what can be thought of as IASB GAAP.

   4. The IASB cannot enforce its standards; they are made available to any organization or nation for their use.

   5. The IASB Framework identifies a wide range of financial statement users, however, the objectives of financial statements can be achieved by focusing on the information needs of investors because financial statements "that meet their needs also will meet most of the needs of other users that financial statements can satisfy (IASB)".

   6. With the emphasis on providing relevant information to investors, IFRS falls within the Class A accounting system as defined by Nobes.

C. *LO4* **Use of IFRS**

   1. A country can use IFRS in a variety of ways:

   a. Adopt IFRS as domestic GAAP.

   b. Require domestic companies to use IFRS for consolidated financial statements.

   c. Allow domestic companies to use domestic GAAP or IFRS.

   d. Require or allow foreign companies listed on a domestic stock exchange to use IFRS, instead of domestic GAAP.

2. IFRS adoption

   a. As of July 2009, 86 countries require domestic listed companies to use IFRS, including the 27 countries of the EU.

   b. All publicly traded companies in the EU have been required to use IFRS for consolidated financial statements since 2005, with only a few exceptions.

   c. Brazil and South Korea are scheduled to adopt IFRS in 2010.

   d. Canada and India are scheduled to adopt IFRS in 2011, and Mexico is scheduled to adopt IFRS in 2012.

3. Exceptions to IFRS adoption

   a. Most countries of economic importance require or allow domestic listed companies to use IFRS.

   b. The most important exceptions are China, Japan and the United States.

   c. In 2006, China adopted a completely new set of Chinese Accounting Standards based on IFRS.

   d. In 2007, the Accounting Standards Board of Japan and the IASB agreed on a convergence process between Japanese GAAP and IFRS. In June 2009, Japan indicated it would allow some Japanese companies to use IFRS beginning in 2010, with mandatory use of IFRS for public companies contemplated for 2015 or 2016.

   e. U.S. acceptance of IFRS is discussed in the following section.

VIII. *LO5* **FASB – IASB Convergence**

   A. *Norwalk Agreement* – at a joint meeting in Norwalk Connecticut in September 2002, the FASB and IASB agreed to "use their best efforts" to:

      1. Make their existing financial reporting standards fully compatible as soon as is practicable, and to coordinate their work program to ensure that once achieved, compatibility is maintained.

      2. This set the FASB and IASB along a path of convergence.

      3. Convergence can occur by:

         a. The FASB adopting an existing IASB standard.

         b. The IASB adopting an existing FASB standard.

         c. The IASB and FASB working together to develop a new standard. This is done when existing standards need improvement.

      4. Convergence means similar, but not necessarily identical standards. Convergence, as pursued by the FASB, is different than outright adoption of IFRS (done by many countries and the EU).

      5. An impetus for convergence is found in the Sarbanes-Oxley Act of 2002 which requires the FASB to consider "the extent to which international convergence on high quality accounting standards is necessary or appropriate in the public interest and for the protection of investors."

B.   There are six key FASB initiatives to further convergence between IFRS and U.S. GAAP:

    1.   **Short-term Convergence Project**

       a.   Eliminate differences where convergence is likely in the short-run.

       b.   Likely solution is the selection of either the FASB or the IFRS standard.

       c.   The project has resulted in changes to U.S. GAAP:

           (1)   Inventory costs: SFAS No. 151, *Inventory Costs – an Amendment of ARB 43, Chapter 4,* December 2004, issued to converge with IASB treatment.

           (2)   Asset Exchanges: SFAS No. 153, *Exchanges of Non-monetary Assets – an Amendment of APB Opinion No. 29,* December 2004.

           (3)   Accounting Changes: SFAS 154, *Accounting Changes and Error Corrections – a Replacement of APB Opinion No. 20 and FASB Statement No. 3,* issued in May, 2005.

           (4)   EPS: FASB revised Exposure Draft, *Earnings per Share – an Amendment of FASB Statement No. 128,* issued in August, 2008.

           (5)   SFAS No. 123 *Share-based Payment,* revised December 2004, though not part of the project, was justified partially through convergence with IFRS.

       d.   The project has also resulted in changes to IFRS:

           (1)   Discontinued operations: IFRS 5 converges with U.S. GAAP with respect to the timing of classification of discontinued operations and presentation.

           (2)   Segment reporting: IFRS 8 converges with U.S. GAAP.

           (3)   Borrowing costs: IAS 23 was revised to eliminate an option in which entities could expense borrowing costs even if eligible for capitalization. Now capitalization is required under certain criteria, similar to U.S. GAAP.

    2.   **Joint Projects**

       a.   **Business Combinations**

           (1)   The FASB and IASB together developed a common solution in 2007 with respect to the measurement of an acquired company's assets and liabilities at full fair value and the measurement and presentation of noncontrolling interests.

           (2)   SFAS 141R, "*Business Combinations,*" and *SFAS 160*, "*Noncontrolling Interests in Consolidated Financial Statements,*" were issued in the U.S.

           (3)   IFRS 3, "*Business Combinations*" was issued in 2008. The two sets of standards are not completely identical.

      b.   **Financial Statement Presentation** – considerations include whether the following should be required:

          (1)   Comprehensive Income Statement as a primary financial statement,

          (2)   Use of the direct method for cash flow,

          (3)   Cash equivalents being reported separately from cash on the balance sheet,

          (4)   Assets and liabilities being classified on the balance sheet as operating, investing, and financing, with income taxes in a separate section, and

          (5)   A similar classification for the statement of comprehensive income.

      c.   **Revenue Recognition Project** – the objective is to develop a common, principles-based comprehensive standard.

          (1)   IFRS has a single standard (IAS 19, *Revenue*)

          (2)   U.S. GAAP has more than 140 authoritative pronouncements related to revenue recognition.

          (3)   The project should result in a single standard that will eliminate inconsistencies in existing literature, fill in gaps from newer business models, and provide a conceptual basis for addressing new issues.

      d.   **Conceptual Framework Project**

          (1)   The objective is to develop a common conceptual framework that could be used as a basis for future standards.

          (2)   There are eight phases to this project.

      e.   In 2008 the Boards set milestones for joint projects to be achieved by 2011.

C. SEC Acceptance of IFRS

    1.   In November 2007, the SEC ruled that foreign companies using IFRS were no longer required to provide a reconciliation to U.S. GAAP in annual reports filed with the SEC for fiscal years ended after November 15, 2007.

    2.   Approximately 180 companies filed their 2007 annual reports without the reconciliation.

    3.   Foreign companies using foreign GAAP other than IFRS must continue to provide a U.S. GAAP reconciliation.

    4.   Thus, U.S. domestic companies are required to use U.S. GAAP, while foreign companies can use IFRS.

    5.   The SEC issued a Concept Release for comment in July of 2007 about allowing U.S. companies to choose between U.S. GAAP and IFRS.

    6.   A majority of the comments were not in favor of allowing a choice.

7. In November 2007, the chairs of the FASB and Financial Accounting Foundation (FAF) concluded in a letter to the SEC that investors would be better served if all U.S. public companies used a single set of global accounting standards to prepare financial reports.

8. They feel that this would be best accomplished by moving U.S. public companies to an improved version of IFRS, a complex, multi-year endeavor.

D. IFRS Roadmap

1. In November 2008, the SEC issued a proposed roadmap for the potential use of IFRS by U.S. public companies.

2. The roadmap identifies milestones which need to be achieved before IFRS will be required.

3. If significant progress has been made by 2011, the SEC will require mandatory adoption of IFRS for public companies over a three-year phase-in beginning in 2014.

4. The roadmap envisions providing a limited number of companies the opportunity to adopt IFRS as early as 2010. Two criteria would need to be met for early adoption:

   a. A company is among the 20 largest (measured by market capitalization) publicly-traded companies in its industry worldwide.

   b. More companies among the 20 largest in that industry use IFRS than any other set of accounting standards.

5. The SEC estimated at least 110 U.S. companies in 34 industries would be eligible for early adoption.

6. The milestones the SEC will monitor until 2011 are:

   a. Improvement in IFRS, including completion of joint projects.

   b. Accountability and funding for the IASB to help ensure independence in the standard setting process.

   c. Improvement in the ability to use interactive data for IFRS reporting by expanding the use of XBRL to provide interactive data in more detail than currently possible.

   d. Education and training in the U.S., including investor education.

7. Negative comments about the roadmap include:

   a. IFRS are an incomplete set of standards, and lack industry specific guidance.

   b. IFRS are not compatible with the U.S. litigation environment.

   c. The U.S. economy has more important issues to deal with (i.e. the financial crisis).

   d. Congress might not allow the SEC to designate the IASB as the U.S. standard setter.

E. First-Time Adoption of IFRS

1. Under the SEC's roadmap, large U.S. companies might be required to use IFRS in 2014.

2. Converting to IFRS is quite complex.

3. IFRS 1, *"First-Time Adoption of IFRS"*, establishes procedures to use.

4. An *opening balance sheet* is required at the *date of transition* (the beginning of the earliest period for comparative information).

   a. A company preparing financial statements for the year ended 12/31/2014 must provide comparative financial statements for 12/31/2013 under IFRS.

   b. January 1, 2013 is the beginning of the earliest period for which comparative information must be provided, so this is the *date of transition.*

   c. The company begins to use IFRS on 1/1/2013 in order to prepare IFRS financials for 2014.

5. Five steps to prepare the opening balance sheet:

   Step 1: Determine applicable IFRS accounting policies based on standards in force on the reporting date.

   Step 2: Recognize assets and liabilities required to be recognized under IFRS that are not recognized under previous GAAP, and derecognize assets and liabilities previously recognized that are not allowed under IFRS. Examples include:

   (1) Deferred development costs are assets under IFRS, not U.S. GAAP.

   (2) Restructuring related liabilities can be recognized at an earlier date under U.S. GAAP than IFRS, thus may need to be derecognized.

   Step 3: Retroactively apply IASB standards to measure assets and liabilities on the opening balance sheet in accordance with IFRS. Examples of changes include:

   (1) Companies using LIFO will have to select an inventory method acceptable under IFRS (FIFO or weighted average) and retroactively apply it.

   (2) This is a change in accounting principle, the effect of which under IFRS 1 is recognized in stockholders' equity in the opening balance sheet.

   Step 4: Reclassify items to comply with IFRS. Examples of changes include:

   (1) Deferred tax assets and liabilities are classified as current or noncurrent in U.S. GAAP, but are always classified as non-current under IFRS.

   (2) In some cases, convertible debt classified as a liability under U.S. GAAP would be reclassified as equity under IFRS.

   Step 5: Comply with all disclosure and presentation requirements.

6. There are several optional exemptions from complying with IFRS where retrospective application would be extremely difficult and the benefit is unlikely to exceed the cost.

7. Once the opening IFRS balance sheet is prepared, the company uses IFRS for the next two years so the company can include comparative information in its first IFRS financial statements.

8. Reconciliations of equity from the previous GAAP to IFRS are required in the first IFRS financial statements, as well as disclosures about the company's adoption of IFRS.

F. **IFRS Accounting Policy Hierarchy**

1. IAS 8, *Accounting Policies, Changes in Accounting Estimates and Errors,* establishes the following hierarchy of standards firms must use to determine appropriate accounting policies:

    a. Apply specifically relevant standards to the issue (IASs, IFRSs, or Interpretations).

    b. Refer to other IASB standards dealing with similar or related issues.

    c. Refer to the definitions, recognition criteria, and measurement concepts in the IASB *Framework.*

    d. Consider recent pronouncements of other standard-setting bodies that use a similar conceptual framework (including FASB standards), other accounting literature, and accepted industry practice to the extent they do not conflict with sources in b and c above.

2. In determining accounting policies to be used under IFRS, two extreme approaches are:

    a. *Minimize change* – adopt IFRS accounting policies that are most consistent with current accounting policies (less costly).

    b. *Fresh start* – ignore current accounting policies and adopt IFRS policies best reflecting economic reality. This is a unique opportunity to make improvements.

IX. *LO6* **Differences Between IFRS and U.S. GAAP**

A. **Recognition Differences** relate to whether an item is recognized or not, how it is recognized, or when it is recognized. Examples include:

1. R&D – Under U.S. GAAP, R&D costs are generally expensed immediately. IFRS allow capitalization of development costs if certain criteria are met.

2. Gains on sale and leaseback transactions.

3. Deferred tax assets.

B. **Measurement Differences** occur because different measurement methods are required under U.S. GAAP and IFRS. Examples include:

1. The different meaning of "market" in lower-of-cost-or-market rules for valuing inventory under U.S. GAAP and the IFRS.

    a. GAAP uses *replacement cost* for market.

    b. IFRS uses lower of cost or *net realizable value.*

2. LIFO is permitted under U.S. GAAP but not under IFRS.

3. IAS 16, *Property, Plant and Equipment* allows two approaches: (1) cost less accumulated depreciation and any impairment losses and (2) the revaluation model. U.S. GAAP requires the use of historical cost.

C. **Presentation and Disclosure Differences** relate to the manner in which items are presented in the financials or disclosed in the notes. Examples include:

    1. Extraordinary items as presented under U.S. GAAP are not allowed under IFRS.

    2. The definition of a discontinued operation is less restrictive under U.S. GAAP than under the IFRS.

    3. IFRS contain a single standard (*IAS 1*) that governs the presentation of financial statements. There is no U.S. GAAP equivalent.

D. *LO7* **U.S. GAAP Reconciliations** – prior to the SEC removing the U.S. GAAP reconciliation requirement for foreign companies using IFRS, the reconciliations provided a good source of information for understanding the differences between U.S. GAAP and IFRS.

E. Exhibit 11.8 in the book shows differences between IFRS and U.S. GAAP as of 7/1/ 2008.

X. Obstacles to Worldwide Comparability of Financial Statements

A. IFRS and U.S. GAAP are the dominant worldwide accounting standards.

B. The approaches used by IFRS and U.S. GAAP differ.

    1. The IASB has taken a principles-base approach to establishing accounting standards.

    2. The FASB in the U.S. has taken a "so-called" rules-based approach.

    3. The text contrasts leasing standards as an example (SFAS 13 and IAS 17).

    4. There have been concerns that the FASB-IASB convergence project might result in IASB standards becoming more rules based.

C. Several obstacles stand in the way of a common set of standards being interpreted and applied consistently.

    1. Translation of IFRS into other languages.

    2. The impact of culture on financial reporting.

Multiple Choice Questions

1. The International Accounting Standards Committee was replaced in April 2001 by the

    A. International Accounting Oversight Board.
    B. International Accounting Standards Board.
    C. European Union
    D. The Third Directive
    E. The United Nations Accounting Standards Committee

2. How many members currently serve on the IASB?

    A. 10
    B. 12
    C. 14
    D. 16
    E. 20

3. Which of the following are ways that a country could use IFRS?

    A. Adopt IFRS as domestic GAAP
    B. Require domestic companies to use IFRS for consolidated financial statements
    C. Allow domestic companies to use domestic GAAP or IFRS
    D. Require foreign stock exchange registrants to use IFRS instead of domestic GAAP.
    E. All of the above.

4. Which of the following is **not** one of the six common factors that influence a country's financial reporting practices?

    A. Legal system.
    B. Population.
    C. Inflation.
    D. Providers of financing.
    E. Taxation.

5. The process of reducing differences in financial reporting practices across countries is referred to as:

    A. Cooperation
    B. Reconciliation
    C. Joint Compromise
    D. Joint Adoption
    E. Harmonization

Brief Essay Questions

1. Describe the three major types of differences that generally exist between U.S. GAAP and IFRS. Give an example of each type of difference.

2. What are the six primary reasons that accounting rules differ from country to country?

Solutions to Multiple Choice Questions

1. B

2. D   Originally, there were 14 members of the IASB. In 2009, this was changed to 16.

3. E

4. B

5. E

1. The three major types of differences between U.S. GAAP and IFRS can be grouped into three major categories:

- **Recognition Differences** – Differences relate to (1) whether to recognize an item, (2) how it is recognized, and (3) when it should be recognized. An example of a recognition difference is the treatment of R&D costs. Under U.S. GAAP, R&D costs are generally expensed immediately. IFRS allow capitalization of development costs if certain criteria are met.

- **Measurement Differences** – The amount to be recognized is an issue with some items being recognized at cost and others at market value. In other cases, the different alternative treatments available will lead to significant differences in totals such as net income. One example is the alternative treatment allowed by IAS 16 where fixed assets can be revalued to fair market value. Another example of a measurement difference is in the use of LIFO. LIFO is permitted under U.S. GAAP but not under IFRS.

- **Presentation and Disclosure Differences** – These differences relate how items are presented and disclosed in the financial statements, and the amount of information that is disclosed. An example of a presentation difference is the treatment of extraordinary items under U.S. GAAP. U.S. GAAP requires the presentation of extraordinary items if certain criteria are met. IFRS do not allow the presentation of extraordinary items.

2. The primary factors that drive the differences in accounting rules between different countries are:

- **Differing legal systems** – Generally, countries using a code law system will differ from countries using a common law system.

- **Taxation** – Some countries base their tax collections on the financial statements. Other countries, such as the U.S., base taxes on a computation of net income that may differ from the net income presented in the financial statements.

- **Source of Financing** – Countries where corporate financing is primarily derived from the debt sector or from government will tend to have less disclosure and public accountability than countries where financing is primarily drawn from the capital markets.

- **Inflation** – Countries with high inflation will often have accounting policies that require adjustments for inflation.

- **Political and economic ties** – Accounting rule systems tend to be similar among groups of countries that have similar historical ties and similar types of government.

- **Culture** – A country's culture helps shape its institutions and its accounting values. For example, Gray hypothesizes that in a society with a low tolerance for uncertainty, greater emphasis will be on the accounting value of conservatism.

Chapter 12

Financial Reporting and the Securities and Exchange Commission

Chapter Outline

Standards Mentioned in This Chapter:

- **SAB 101,** *SEC Staff Accounting Bulletin No. 101*
- **SFAS No. 19,** *Financial Accounting and Reporting by Oil and Gas Producing Companies*
- **SFAS No. 86,** *Accounting for the Costs of Computer Software to Be Sold, Leased, or Otherwise Marketed*

I.   *LO1* **The Work of the Securities and Exchange Commission (SEC)**

    A.   The SEC is an independent agency of the federal government created by the Securities Exchange Act of 1934.

    B.   The primary mission of the SEC is to protect investors; maintain fair, orderly, and efficient markets; and facilitate capital formation.

    C.   The SEC's authority applies mainly to publicly held companies, but its guidelines and requirements are a major influence in the development of all U.S. GAAP.

    D.   The SEC is headed by 5 commissioners.

        1.   Appointed by the President.

        2.   Serve 5-year staggered terms.

        3.   The Chairman of the SEC is usually from the same political party as the President.

    E.   The SEC is composed of 18 offices and 4 divisions, including:

        1.   The *Division of Corporation Finance* has responsibility for ensuring that disclosure requirements are met by publicly held companies.

        2.   The *Division of Trading and Markets* oversees the securities markets in the U.S. and is responsible for registering and regulating brokerage firms.

        3.   The *Division of Enforcement* helps to ensure compliance with federal security laws by investigating possible violations of securities laws and recommends appropriate remedies.

        4.   The *Division of Investment Management* oversees the $15 trillion investment management industry and administers the securities laws affecting investment companies including mutual funds and investment advisers.

        5.   The *Office of Investment Technology* supports the SEC and its staff in all aspects of information technology. This office operates the Electronic Data Gathering Analysis and Retrieval System (EDGAR).

        6.   The *Office of Compliance Inspections and Examinations* determines whether brokers, dealers, and investment companies and advisors are in compliance with federal securities laws.

        7.   The *Office of the Chief Accountant* is the principal advisor to the commission on accounting and auditing matters that arise in connection with the securities laws. It works closely with the AICPA and the FASB.

F. **Purpose of the Federal Securities Laws** – four interconnected goals of the SEC:

1. Ensuring that full and fair information is disclosed to all investors before the securities of a company are allowed to be bought and sold.

2. Prohibiting the dissemination of materially misstated information.

3. Preventing the misuse of information, especially by inside parties.

4. Regulating the operation of securities markets such as the New York Stock Exchange and the American Stock Exchange.

G. *LO2* **Full and Fair Disclosure** – is a primary SEC responsibility. All publicly held companies unless specifically exempted must file periodic reports as a result of securities laws passed by Congress over the years.

1. The *Securities Act of 1933* – Regulates the initial offering of securities by a company or underwriter.

2. The *Securities Exchange Act of 1934* – Created the SEC, and regulates the subsequent secondary-market trading of securities through brokers and exchanges.

3. *Public Utilities Holding Company Act of 1935*

4. *Trust Indenture Act of 1939*

5. *Investment Company Act of 1940*

6. *Investment Advisers Act of 1940*

7. *Foreign Corrupt Practices Act of 1977*

8. *Insider Trading Sanctions Act of 1984 and Insider Trading and Securities Fraud Enforcement Act of 1988*

9. *Sarbanes-Oxley Act of 2002* (discussed later)

H. **SEC Requirements** – most disclosure requirements are in two basic documents:

1. *Regulation S-K* establishes requirements for all nonfinancial information contained in filings with the SEC.

2. *Regulation S-X* prescribes the form and content of the financial statements (as well as the accompanying notes and related schedules) included in the various reports filed with the SEC.

II. **The SEC's impact on Financial Reporting to Stockholders**

A. *Rule 14c-3* states that annual reports of public companies should include audited financial statements, called proxy *information* (because it is with management's request to cast votes for the shareholders at the annual meeting) to be included in annual reports.

B. Information required in the proxy statements, in addition to the financial statements includes:

1. 5-year summary of operations including sales, total assets, income from continuing operations, and cash dividends per share.

2. Description of the business activities, including principal products and sources and availability of raw materials.

3. Three-year summary of industry segments, export sales, and foreign and domestic operations.

4. Listing of company directors and executive officers.

5. Market price of the company's common stock for each quarterly period within the two most recent fiscal years.

6. Any restrictions on the company's ability to continue paying dividends.

7. Management's discussion and analysis of financial condition, changes in financial condition, and results of operations.

C. The SEC requires certain other disclosures (intended to help ensure auditor independence) regarding services provided by the company's independent auditor in proxy statements:

1. All nonaudit services provided by the independent auditing firm.

2. A statement as to whether the board of directors (or its audit committee) approved all nonaudit services after considering the possibility that such services might impair the external auditor's independence.

3. The percentage of nonaudit fees compared to the total annual audit fee.

4. Individual nonaudit fees that are more than 3% of the annual audit fee.

III. **LO3 Corporate Accounting Scandals and the Sarbanes-Oxley Act**

A. In response to large corporate accounting scandals in the early 2000's (Enron, WorldCom), the Sarbanes-Oxley Act (SARBOX) was passed in 2002 to reduce or eliminate future abuses and to restore public confidence in public companies and their accounting information.

B. **Creation of the Public Companies Accounting Oversight Board (PCAOB)** – eliminated self-regulation of the accounting profession.

1. Five-member board appointed to staggered 5-year terms.

2. Only 2 members can be accountants.

3. Enforces auditing, quality control, and independence standards and rules.

4. Operates under the oversight and authority of the SEC.

5. Funded from fees collected from publicly traded companies.

C. PCAOB's Standard-Setting Authority

1. The PCAOB is mandated to play a significant role in setting professional standards for the conduct of audits.

a. In the future, the PCAOB could take over setting of audit standards for public companies, currently set by the Auditing Standards Board (ASB) of the AICPA.

  b. ASB standards, unless later modified or superseded by the PCAOB, are adopted for audits of public companies.

  c. The PCAOB has taken an active role in developing its own standards and thus many new ASB pronouncements apply only to nonpublic entities.

 2. The FASB will likely still be the primary setter of accounting standards.

D. **Registration of Public Accounting Firms** – public accounting firms performing audits of publicly traded companies must be registered with the PCAOB.

 1. Fees are collected and used to fund the PCAOB.

 2. Inspections of Registered Firms – registered firms are subject to inspection.

  a. Firms that audit more than 100 publicly traded companies are inspected annually.

  b. Other firms are inspected every 3 years.

  c. Eliminates the need for *peer reviews*.

 3. The Oversight Board has the power to take disciplinary action as a result of inspection findings. Disciplinary actions include disclosure of deficiencies if not addressed within 12 months, suspension or revocation of registration, censure, and significant fines.

 4. Foreign firms that play a substantial role in the audit of companies with securities registered in the U.S. must also be registered with the PCAOB.

E. **Auditor Independence** – A significant goal of SARBOX is to ensure that public accounting firms are independent.

 1. Financial information system design and implementation, and internal audit outsourcing can no longer be provided to an audit client.

 2. The audit committee must preapprove any allowed services and disclose them in reports to the SEC.

 3. Audit Committees have expanded responsibilities:

  a. Appointing and compensating the external auditor.

  b. Members of the Audit Committee must be independent from management.

  c. The auditor reports directly to the Audit Committee, not to management.

  d. The lead partner of the auditing firm must be rotated off the job after 5 years.

IV. **LO4 The SEC's Authority over GAAP**

    A.   Sarbanes-Oxley's primary focus was on the regulation of independent auditing and auditing standards.

    B.   The SEC holds the legal authority for establishing accounting principles for most publicly held companies in the U.S.

        1.   The SEC has delegated much of its standards setting authority to the AICPA and the FASB, allowing the accounting profession to set its own standards.

        2.   On occasion, when the SEC disagrees with the profession, the SEC will effectively mandate a particular standard.

        3.   The SEC can amend accounting standards by amending Regulation S-X.

    C.   *Financial Reporting Releases* (FRRs) are issued by the SEC as needed to supplement Regulations S-K and S-X. By 2004, 72 FRRs had been issued.

    D.   The SEC staff published a series of *Staff Accounting Bulletins* (SABs) as a means of informing the financial community of its views on current matters relating to accounting and disclosure practices.

    E.   Other potential SEC actions:

        1.   Additional disclosure requirements if current rules are viewed as insufficient.

        2.   Moratorium on specific accounting practices

        3.   Challenging individual statements and forcing a specific registrant to change its filed statements.

        4.   Overruling the FASB.

V.   **LO5 Filings with the SEC**

    A.   The SEC reporting process can be divided into two broad categories.

        1.   *Registration statements* are required prior to the issuance of any new security (1933 Act).

        2.   Periodic filings with the SEC are required of registrants by a number of federal laws; the most important of which is the Securities Exchange Act of 1934.

    B.   The SEC is charged with ensuring full and fair disclosure of relevant financial information in registration statements.

        1.   The registrant is responsible for supplying the data.

        2.   The decision to invest must remain with the public.

    C.   **Registration Statements (1933 Act)** – The SEC seeks to ensure the filing's contents and disclosures comply with regulations. Depending on specific circumstances, a specific form is required:

        1.   **Form S-1** – Used when no other form is prescribed; usually used by new registrants or by companies that have been filing reports with the SEC for less than 36 months.

2. **Form S-2** – Used by companies that have filed with the SEC for 36 months or longer, but are not large enough to file a Form S-3.

3. **Form S-3** – Used by companies that are large in size and already have a significant following in the stock market.

   a. At least $75 million of its voting stock is held by nonaffiliates.

   b. Disclosure is reduced for these organizations because the public is assumed to have access to a considerable amount of information.

4. **Form S-4** – Used by securities issued in connection with business combination transactions.

5. **Form S-8** – Used as a registration statement for employee stock plans.

6. **Form S-11** – Used for the registration of securities by certain real estate companies.

7. **Form 1-A** – Used by small business issuers to register up to $10 million of securities but only if the company has not registered more than $10 million of securities in the previous twelve months.

8. **Form 1-B** – Used by small business issuers to register securities to be sold for cash.

D. *LO6* **Registration Procedures**

1. The Division of Corporation Finance reviews registration statements.

   a. The registrant receives a *letter of comments* from the SEC indicating the changes or explanations that are requested for the registration statement to proceed in the approval process.

   b. This letter is sometimes referred to as a *deficiency letter*.

2. When the Division of Corporation Finance is satisfied that all SEC regulations have been fulfilled, the registration statement is made *effective* and the securities can be sold.

3. Large companies are allowed to use a process known as *shelf registration*.

   a. The company files once with the SEC.

   b. The company can offer the securities at any time over the subsequent 2 years without having to go back to the SEC.

E. **Registration Statements**

1. Part I (also called the *Prospectus*) contains:

   a. Financial statements for the issuing company audited by an independent CPA along with appropriate supplementary data.

   b. An explanation of the intended use of the proceeds to be generated by the sale of the new securities.

      c.   A description of the risks associated with the securities.

      d.   A description of the business and the properties owned by the company.

  2.   Part II – Optional additional data such as marketing arrangements, expenses of issuance, sales to special parties, etc.

F.   **Securities Exempt from Registration** – not all securities require registration. However, these offerings may be subject to securities laws of the individual states. Exempt offerings include (but are not limited to):

  1.   Securities sold strictly to the residents of the state in which the issuing company is chartered and principally doing business.

  2.   Securities issued by governments, banks, and savings and loan associations.

  3.   Securities issued that are restricted to a company's own existing shareholders where no commission is paid to solicit the exchange.

  4.   Securities issued by nonprofit organizations such as religious, educational, or charitable groups.

  5.   Small offerings of no more than $5 million.

  6.   Offerings of no more than $1 million made to any number of investors within a 12-month period, with no specific disclosure requirements. General solicitations are allowed.

  7.   Offerings of no more than $5 million made to 35 or fewer purchasers in a 12-month period, with no general solicitation.

  8.   The private placement of securities to no more than 35 sophisticated investors that already have sufficient information available to them about the issuing company. General solicitation is not allowed.

G.   **Periodic Filings with the SEC** – are required for companies that have their securities publicly traded on an exchange.

  1.   **10-K** – An annual report filed with the SEC within 60 days of the end of a registrant's fiscal year end to provide information and disclosures required by Regulation S-K and Regulation S-X.

  2.   **10-Q** – Contains condensed interim financial statements for the registrant and must be filed with the SEC within 30 days of the end of each quarter.

  3.   **8-K** – Used to disclose a unique or significant happening. Must be filed within 2 days of the event. Examples include resignation of a director, changes in control of the registrant, changes in auditors and bankruptcy.

  4.   **Proxy statements** – Used to solicit votes to be used at stockholders' meetings. They must be filed with the SEC at least 10 days before being distributed.

H.   **Electronic Data Gathering, Analysis, and Retrieval System (EDGAR)**

  1.   Development began in 1984.

  2.   System not fully operational until 1994.

3. Virtually all public companies are required to file their SEC reports electronically.

4. Most statements are posted to EDGAR within 24 hours.

5. Allows financial information to be accessed via the Internet.

6. The EDGAR database has helped make financial reporting significantly more transparent.

Multiple Choice Questions

1. Which one of the following is **not** a major goal of the SEC?

   A. Protecting investors against financial losses.
   B. Ensuring that full and fair information is disclosed to all investors before the securities of a company are allowed to be bought and sold.
   C. Prohibiting the dissemination of materially misstated information.
   D. Preventing the misuse of information especially by inside parties.
   E. Regulating the operation of securities markets.

2. Which one of the following statements is correct?

   A. The U.S. Senate appoints the five commissioners of the SEC.
   B. Regulation S-K provides the regulations for all financial information including the form and content of financial statements.
   C. Regulation S-X establishes requirements for all nonfinancial information contained in filings with the SEC.
   D. The SEC's authority for financial accounting principles is only in the gray area of accounting where the FASB's rules are not clear.
   E. Companies issuing securities in connection with business combination transactions must file Registration Statement S-4 with the SEC.

3. A letter sent to a company by the SEC indicating needed changes or clarifications in a registration statement is known as a(n)

   A. Post-audit letter.
   B. Letter of comments.
   C. Staff accounting bulletin.
   D. Advisory letter.
   E. Memorandum of modifications.

4. Filing information with the SEC by indicating that the information is already available in another document is called

   A. Single reporting.
   B. Summary financial reporting.
   C. Incorporation by reference.
   D. Proxy information reporting.
   E. Reporting by referral.

5. What is the nickname of the system that was designed for the SEC to allow electronic filings?

    A. EDGAR
    B. MADONNA
    C. OCSAR
    D. FIONA
    E. CHARLIE

6. A registration statement is a(n):

    A. Annual filing made with the SEC.
    B. Required filing with the SEC before an outside party can obtain a large quantity of stock.
    C. Filing made with the SEC to indicate that a significant change has occurred.
    D. Document that must be filed with the SEC before a company can begin its initial offering of securities to the public.
    E. Form used for securities issued in connection with business combination transactions.

7. Which one of the following regulations prescribes the form and content of financial statements included in the various reports filed with the SEC?

    A. Regulation S-K
    B. Regulation S-1
    C. Regulation S-2
    D. Regulation 8-K
    E. Regulation S-X

8. A Form 10-K is filed with the SEC within:

    A. 90 days of the end of each quarter.
    B. 90 days of the end of the registrant's fiscal year.
    C. 45 days of the end of each quarter.
    D. 45 days of the end of the registrant's fiscal year.
    E. 60 days of the end of the registrant's fiscal year.

9. Which one of the following divisions or offices of the SEC helps draft rules for the form and content of financial statements and other reporting requirements?

    A. The Division of Corporation Finance.
    B. The Division of Enforcement.
    C. The Division of Investment Management.
    D. The Office of the Chief Accountant.
    E. The Office of Compliance Inspections and Examinations.

10. What is the purpose of Staff Accounting Bulletins (SABs)?

    A. To supplement Regulation S-K.
    B. To supplement Regulation S-X.
    C. To inform the financial community of the SEC's views on current matters relating to accounting and disclosure practices.
    D. To prescribe the form and content of financial statements filed with the SEC.
    E. To request clarifications or additional information from a company that is filing an incomplete registration statement.

11. The Public Companies Accounting Oversight Board (PCAOB) effectively minimizes the accounting professions' self-regulating process previously overseen by:

    A. The old Public Oversight Board
    B. The Securities and Exchange Commission
    C. The FASB
    D. The AICPA
    E. The Congress

12. How many years does a member of the PCAOB serve?

    A. 3
    B. 5
    C. 10
    D. 15
    E. 25

13. How often must the lead partner on an audit be rotated off the job?

    A. Every 2 years
    B. Every 3 years
    C. Every 4 years
    D. Every 5 years
    E. Every 6 years

14. Which form is used to disclose unique or significant happenings for a publicly traded company?

    A. Form 10-K
    B. Form 10-Q
    C. Form 8-K
    D. Form S-8
    E. Form S-1

Brief Essay Questions

1.   What are the four interconnected goals that the SEC has attempted to achieve?

2.   What are the eight common forms used in the filing of SEC registration statements?

3.   What kinds of stock issuances are exempt from filing with the SEC?

Solutions to Multiple Choice Questions

1.   A

2.   E

3.   B

4.   C

5.   A

6.   D

7.   E

8.   E

9.   D

10.   C

11.   D

12.   B

13.   D

14.   C

Answers to Brief Essay Questions

1.   The four interconnected goals are:

A.   Ensuring full and fair information is disclosed to all investors before the securities of a company are allowed to be bought and sold.

B.   Prohibiting the dissemination of materially misstated information.

C.   Preventing the misuse of information especially by inside parties.

D.   Regulating the operation of securities markets such as the New York Stock Exchange and American Stock Exchange.

2. The eight common forms are:

   A. **Form S-1** – Used when no other form is prescribed; usually used by new registrants or by companies that have been filing reports with the SEC for less than 36 months.

   B. **Form S-2** – Used by companies that have filed with the SEC for 36 months or longer, but are not large enough to file a Form S-3.

   C. **Form S-3** – Used by companies that are large in size and already have a significant following in the stock market. At least $75 million of its voting stock is held by nonaffiliates and disclosure is reduced for these organizations because the public is assumed to have access to a considerable amount of information.

   D. **Form S-4** – Used by securities issued in connection with business combination transactions.

   E. **Form S-8** – Used as a registration statement for employee stock plans.

   F. **Form S-11** – Used for the registration of securities by certain real estate companies.

   G. **Form SB-1** – Used by small business issuers to register up to $10 million of securities but only if the company has not registered more than $10 million of securities in the previous twelve months.

   H. **Form SB-2** – Used by small business issuers to register securities to be sold for cash.

3. The following stock issuances are exempt from filing with the SEC:

   A. Securities sold strictly to the residents of the state in which the issuing company is chartered and principally doing business.

   B. Securities issued by governments, banks, and savings and loan associations.

   C. Securities issued that are restricted to a company's own existing shareholders where no commission is paid to solicit the exchange.

   D. Securities issued by nonprofit organizations such as religious, educational, or charitable groups.

   E. Small offerings of no more than $5 million.

   F. Offerings of no more than $1 million made to any number of investors within a 12-month period, with no specific disclosure requirements. General solicitations are allowed.

   G. Offerings of no more that $5 million made to 35 or fewer purchasers in a 12-month period, with no general solicitation.

   H. The private placement of securities to no more than 35 sophisticated investors whom already have sufficient information available to them about the issuing company. General solicitation is not allowed.

Chapter 13

Accounting for Legal Reorganizations and Liquidations

Chapter Outline

Standards Mentioned in This Chapter:
- **AICPA SOP 90-7,** *Financial Reporting by Entities in Reorganization Under theBankruptcy Code*
- **SFAS No. 109,** *Accounting for Income Taxes*

I.   *LO1* **Accounting for Legal Reorganizations and Liquidations**

A.   For many different reasons, a company sometimes becomes *insolvent*, a state referred to as *bankruptcy*.

B.   **Bankruptcy Reform Act of 1978** – as amended, provides legal guidance with the two following goals:

    1.   Fair distribution of a debtor's assets.

    2.   The discharge of an honest debtor from debt.

C.   *LO2* **Voluntary and Involuntary Petitions** – Bankruptcy proceedings can be formally instigated by either the debtor or a group of creditors.

    1.   When the insolvent company petitions the court, this is referred to as a *voluntary* petition.

    2.   When a minimum number of creditors (in some cases, only one creditor is necessary) petitions the court, this is referred to as an *involuntary* petition.

        a.   When the number of creditors is > 12 creditors:

            (1)   At least three creditors must sign the petition.

            (2)   The three signing creditors must be holding combined unsecured debt of $13,475 (4/1/07).

        b.   When the number of creditors is < 12 creditors:

            (1)   Only one creditor has to sign the petition.

            (2)   The creditor must be holding unsecured debt of $13,475.

    3.   If the court accepts the petition, an *order of relief* is granted to halt all actions against the debtor, until the debtor either is liquidated or emerges from the protection of the bankruptcy court.

D.   *LO3* **Classification of Creditors** – determining the appropriate classification of all creditors is an important step in achieving a fair settlement.

    1.   *Fully secured creditors* hold a *collateral interest* in assets of the insolvent company. The collateral must be sufficient to cover the amount of the liability owed to the creditor.

a. Any excess over the amount owed to the creditor will be available to help cover unsecured liabilities in a liquidation.

b. The determination of whether the collateral is sufficient is based on the *net realizable value* of the collateral, not the book value.

2. *Partially secured creditors* (the net realizable value of the collateral is < the liability) also have a collateral interest in the assets of the insolvent company.

a. The uncovered part of the liability is included as part of the total unsecured liabilities of the company.

b. This situation may occur with assets that decrease in value over time, such as equipment, when the loan balance decreases at a slower rate than the decrease in value. This situation may also occur with inventory.

3. *Unsecured liabilities with priority* are a special group of liabilities for which there is no collateral interest, but that are given special treatment because of their nature.

a. Included in this category are:

(1) Claims for administrative expenses related to the bankruptcy process, including expenses of the trustee, lawyers, and accountants. Back rent is also included in this category.

(2) Obligations arising between the date that a petition is filed with the bankruptcy court and the appointment of a trustee or the issuance of an order for relief.

(3) Employee claims for wages earned, but not paid, during the 180 days preceding the filing of a petition. The claim is limited to $10,950 per employee. This group does not include salaries of company officers.

(4) Employee claims for contributions to benefit plans earned, but not paid, during the 180 days preceding the filing of a petition. The claim is limited to $10,950 per employee.

(5) Claims for return of deposits made by customers to acquire property or services that have not been delivered by the insolvent company. The claims are limited to $2,425 per deposit.

(6) Government claims for unpaid taxes.

b. Some of these liabilities are given priority to encourage individuals, firms, or companies to continue their business relationship with insolvent company while it attempts to sort out its finances. Without such encouragement, employees might leave, or accounting or law firms might refuse to lend their services when they are most needed.

4. *Unsecured liabilities* include all other liabilities of the insolvent.

    a. Creditors holding unsecured liabilities often only receive a portion of the total amount due to them in liquidation.

    b. The low likelihood of receiving full payment is often an incentive for unsecured creditors to look for ways to help the insolvent company stay in business.

5. *Equity shareholders* are paid only after all creditors have been paid.

E.   *LO4* **Liquidation versus Reorganization**

1. The most important decision in a bankruptcy filing is the method by which the debtor will be discharged from its obligations.

2. One option is to liquidate the company's assets and distribute proceeds to creditors based upon their secured positions and priority ranking (*Chapter 7 bankruptcy*).

3. Another option is to propose *reorganization* (*Chapter 11 bankruptcy*). Under most reorganizations, creditors agree to absorb a partial loss rather than force a liquidation.

F.   *LO5* **Statement of Financial Affairs** – is prepared by the debtor to assist in disclosing its current financial position. Because the business may close its doors at any time, the going concern assumption is no longer valid and the rules for disclosure change.

1. Assets are reported at net realizable value.

2. Assets are grouped and labeled as follows:

    a. Pledged with fully secured creditors.

    b. Pledged with partially secured creditors.

    c. Available for priority liabilities and unsecured creditors.

3. Liabilities are grouped and labeled as follows:

    a. Liabilities with priority.

    b. Fully secured creditors.

    c. Partially secured creditors.

    d. Unsecured creditors (including stockholders).

4. The statement of financial affairs can be useful at the beginning of the bankruptcy process to assist all parties in evaluating the prospective outcomes of the various alternatives.

5. Most of the asset balances are estimated projections of net realizable value, and do not usually represent firm commitments to sell by the company.

II.   *LO6* **Liquidation – Chapter 7 Bankruptcy**

     A.   In a Chapter 7 bankruptcy, proceedings conclude with the assets of the insolvent company being liquidated to satisfy creditor claims.

     B.   A trustee appointed by the court oversees the termination of business activities, liquidation of the noncash properties, and distribution of cash to the creditors and stockholders. The trustee's duties include:

         1.   Changing locks and moving assets and records to locations controlled by the trustee.

         2.   Posting notices that all assets of the insolvent company are in the possession of the U.S. Trustee.

         3.   Compiling all financial records and placing them in the custody of the trustee's own accountant.

         4.   Obtaining possession of all other corporate records.

     C.   **Role of the Trustee** – the trustee has wide ranging authority and must:

         1.   Recover all property belonging to the insolvent company.

         2.   Preserve the estate from further deterioration.

         3.   Liquidate noncash assets.

         4.   Make distributions to the proper claimants.

         5.   The trustee may need to continue operating the company to complete business activities that were in process at the time the order for relief was entered.

         6.   The trustee can void any transfer of property (called a *preference*) made by the debtor within 90 days prior to the filing of the bankruptcy petition if the company was already insolvent at the time.

             a.   The recipient must return these payments so they can be included in the debtor's free assets.

             b.   The 90 day limit is extended to one year if the transfer is made to an inside party such as an officer, director or affiliated company.

             c.   The one-year limit also applies to any transfer made with the intent to defraud another party.

             d.   Transfers of less than $5,000 cannot be challenged as preferences.

     D.   **Statement of Realization and Liquidation** –reports the major aspects of the liquidation process. The report conveys:

         1.   Account balances at the date on which the order for relief was filed.

2. Cash receipts generated by the sale of the debtor's property.

3. Cash disbursements the trustee made to wind up the business and pay secured creditors.

4. Any other transactions, such as the write-off of assets and the recognition of unrecorded liabilities.

III. *LO7* **Reorganization – Chapter 11 Bankruptcy**

A. In a Chapter 11 Bankruptcy, the insolvent company seeks to stay in business.

1. Control over the company is normally retained by the ownership (referred to as *a debtor in possession*).

2. The owners and managers are required to preserve the company's estate as of the date the order of relief is entered.

3. While under the temporary protection of the court from the actions of creditors, the company develops a plan to reorganize the business with hopes that the reorganized company will be profitable.

B. **The Plan for Reorganization** – the plan must be devised to win the approval of each class of creditors, each class of stockholders, and the court.

C. Reorganization plans often include the following elements:

1. Proposed changes in operations.

2. Plans for generating additional monetary resources.

3. Plans for changes in management.

4. Plans to settle the debts of the company that existed when the order for relief was entered. Proposals may take several forms:

   a. Assets can be transferred to creditors, who accept the assets as payment in exchange for extinguishing debt.

   b. Equity interest can be conveyed to creditors to settle outstanding debt.

   c. The terms of liabilities can be modified.

5. A recent development is the use of *prepackaged* or prearranged bankruptcies.

   a. The company and its debtors agree on some or all of the terms of the reorganization plan before the bankruptcy petition is signed.

   b. This avoids extensive legal fees and increases the likelihood of greater bankruptcy protection as the court is less likely to require extensive changes.

D. **Acceptance and Confirmation of the Reorganization Plan**

1. Each class of creditors must approve the plan with a vote that represents 2/3 of the dollar amount and more than ½ of the votes cast.

2. Each class of shareholders must approve the plan with a vote of 2/3 of the owners casting votes.

3. Court confirmation of a positive acceptance vote is required.

4. If the plan is not approved, but the court believes it to be a good plan, the judge can impose the plan over the objections of the owners and creditors in a *cram down* reorganization.

E. *LO8* **Financial Reporting during Reorganization** – *SOP 90-7* provides guidance for the preparation of financial statements by companies during Chapter 11 reorganization.

1. **Income Statement** – Income statements prepared during the period of reorganization should disclose operating activities separately from reorganization items.

    a. Any gains, losses, revenues, or expenses resulting from the reorganization must be reported separately before any income tax expense or benefit.

    b. Reorganization items include gains and losses from the sale of assets necessitated by the reorganization.

    c. Professional fees incurred in connection with the reorganization must be expensed immediately.

    d. Interest expense usually does not accrue on debts owed at the date on which the order of relief is granted. Interest is recognized only if payment will be made during the proceeding or if the interest will probably be an allowed claim. Recognized interest expense is not reported separately as a reorganization item.

    e. Interest revenue during reorganization may be substantial because of increases in the company's cash reserves (it may have cash because the company is not forced to pay debts incurred prior to the order for relief). Thus, interest revenue is reported separately as a reorganization item.

2. **Balance Sheet** – a new entity is not created when a company moves into reorganization, therefore, traditional GAAP continues to apply.

    a. Assets are reported at their book value.

    b. Liabilities are reported at the amount owed, though some of those amounts may be reduced in the final reorganization plan.

    c. The current/noncurrent classification is not applicable during reorganization because due to the order of relief, payments may be delayed for years.

    d. During reorganization, liabilities are reported as either *subject to compromise* or *not subject to compromise*.

(1) *Liabilities subject to compromise* (liabilities that may be reduced by the court through acceptance of a reorganization plan) include all unsecured and partially secured debts that existed on the day the order for relief was granted.

(2) *Liabilities not subject to compromise* include fully secured liabilities and all debts incurred since the granting of the order for relief. These liabilities are reported in a normal manner as either a current or noncurrent liability, and as the expected amount of the allowed claims vs. the amounts for which those allowed claims may be settled.

F.   *LO9* **Financial Reporting for Companies Emerging from Reorganization**

   1.   *SOP 90-7* provides accounting guidance.

      a.   If certain conditions are met, *fresh start accounting* may be required when a company emerges from reorganization.

      b.   In *fresh start accounting*, the emerging company is viewed as a new entity for accounting purposes.

      c.   The emerging company adjusts its assets and liabilities to current value.

   2.   A company emerging from Chapter 11 Bankruptcy must use *fresh start* accounting if two criteria are met:

      a.   The *reorganization value* (which approximates the fair market value of the emerging company's assets) is less than the total of the allowed claims as of the date of the order for relief plus liabilities incurred subsequently.

      b.   The original owners are left with less than 50% of the voting stock of the reorganized company.

   3.   After the reorganization value is determined, an allocation to individual asset accounts is carried out in the same manner as with the purchase price that establishes a business combination.

      a.   Assets are reported based on individual fair values on the day it exits from reorganization.

      b.   Recognition of intangible assets and goodwill might be necessary.

   4.   To make the necessary asset adjustments to fresh start accounting, *additional paid-in capital* is normally increased or decreased. However, any write-down of a liability creates a recognized gain.

   5.   Because the company is viewed as a new entity, after the reorganization it has a zero balance in retained earnings.

   6.   Liabilities are reported at the present value of the future cash flows. Exception: deferred income taxes, which are accounted for according to *SFAS 109*.

Multiple Choice Questions

1. Information useful to the creditors of a business filing for bankruptcy is found in the

    A. Statement of Financial Affairs
    B. Charge and Discharge Statement
    C. Realization and Liquidation Statement
    D. Plan of Reorganization
    E. Statement of Bankruptcy

2. Under a voluntary Chapter 7 bankruptcy, the assets would

    A. Remain in the custody of the company.
    B. Be placed in the custody of the trustee.
    C. Be placed in the custody of the court.
    D. Be given to the creditors to satisfy their claims.
    E. Be sold at auction for cash.

3. Charles Turner Construction Inc. is a creditor of ABC Co. Turner constructed the office building in which ABC has its headquarters. At the time the building was constructed, Turner attached a lien on the building as security for the $80,000 note which Turner accepted. Now, ABC Co. has filed for bankruptcy and it is estimated that the building has a net realizable value of $70,000. Turner's status is

	Fully Secured	Partially Secured	Unsecured
A.	Yes	No	Yes
B.	No	No	Yes
C.	No	Yes	No
D.	No	Yes	Yes
E.	Yes	No	No

Items 4 through 6 are based on the following information.

Veltri Inc. has the following assets and liabilities (assets are stated at net realizable value).

Assets pledged with secured creditors	$ 80,000
Assets pledged with partially secured creditors	60,000
Other assets	150,000
Secured liabilities	40,000
Partially secured liabilities	95,000
Liabilities with priority	75,000
Unsecured liabilities	225,000

4. In a liquidation, what is the amount of free assets after payment of liabilities with priority?

    A. $190,000
    B. $120,000
    C. $ 75,000
    D. $ 95,000
    E. $115,000

5. In a liquidation, what percentage of unsecured liabilities will be paid?

   A.   84%
   B.   34%
   C.   54%
   D.   44%
   E.   64%

6. In a liquidation, how much money would be paid on the partially secured liabilities?

   A. $35,400
   B. $65,200
   C. $75,400
   D. $95,200
   E. $67,800

Items 7 through 9 are based on the following information.

ABC Co. is beginning the process of liquidation. ABC has prepared a statement of financial affairs that discloses the following data:

Assets pledged with secured creditors	$210,000
Secured liabilities	125,000
Assets pledged with partially secured creditors	290,000
Free assets (not including excess to be received from assets pledged on secured liabilities)	225,000
Unsecured liabilities with priority	121,000
Unsecured liabilities	450,000

7. What percentage of unsecured liabilities will be paid?

   A.   69%
   B.   37%
   C.   50%
   D.   48%
   E.   42%

8. ABC owes $45,000 to Wallace Co., an unsecured creditor (without priority). How much money can Wallace Co. expect to collect from ABC?

   A. $42,600
   B. $ -0-
   C. $21,800
   D. $18,900
   E. $17,200

9. ABC owes $90,000 to a bank on a note payable that is secured by a security interest attached to the property with an estimated net realizable value of $75,000. How much can the bank expect to collect?

   A. $81,300
   B. $37,800
   C. $75,600
   D. $45,500
   E. $60,100

10. Before a company can use fresh start accounting, which one of the following conditions must exist?

   A. The reorganization value of the company must exceed the value of the liabilities.
   B. The fair market value of the assets of the emerging company must be less than the allowed claims as of the date of the order of relief (plus liabilities incurred during reorganization).
   C. The original owners must hold at least 50% of the stock of the company when it emerges from bankruptcy.
   D. The reorganization value of the emerging entity's assets must exceed the sum of all postpetition liabilities and allowed claims.
   E. The reorganization value of the company must be less than the value of all liabilities.

Brief Essay Questions

1. The statement of financial affairs is prepared for the debtor and is especially important in assisting the unsecured creditors as they decide whether to push for reorganization or liquidation. The debtor's assets are reported according to the classifications relevant to a liquidation. Consequently, how are assets labeled?

2. The statement of financial affairs is prepared for the debtor and is especially important in assisting the unsecured creditors as they decide whether to push for reorganization or liquidation. The debtor's liabilities are reported according to the classifications relevant to a liquidation. Consequently, how are debts labeled?

3. A limited amount of unpaid wages to employees is given priority in a distribution of cash resulting from a liquidation of an insolvent company. What is that limit? What happens to the amount of unpaid wages to employees that exceed the limit and therefore do not get the priority treatment?

Solutions to Multiple Choice Questions

1. **A** The statement of financial affairs is the statement most useful for this purpose. The charge and discharge statement is associated with estates and the realization and liquidation statement is associated with Chapter 7 bankruptcies that have been approved by the court.

2. **B** All Chapter 7 bankruptcies, whether voluntary or involuntary, result in the assets being placed in the custody of either a permanent or interim trustee.

3. **C** The net realizable value of the asset is insufficient to cover the debt. This means that the creditor is partially secured rather than fully secured. A partially secured creditor joins the unsecured creditors without priority for an amount equal to the difference between the value of the loan and the amount realized from the sale of the asset.

4. E Free assets:

Other assets	$150,000
Excess from assets pledged with secured creditors ($80,000 – $40,000)	40,000
Total	$190,000
Liabilities with priority	(75,000)
Free assets after payment of liabilities with priority	$115,000

5. D The percentage of unsecured liabilities to be paid is 44%. This is determined by dividing free assets by the amount of total unsecured liabilities.

Excess of partially secured liabilities over partially pledged assets ($95,000 – $60,000)	$ 35,000
Unsecured creditors	225,000
Total unsecured liabilities	$260,000
Free assets (from #4 above)	$115,000
Total unsecured liabilities	÷260,000
Percentage of unsecured liabilities to be paid	44%

6. C

Assets pledged with partially secured creditors	$60,000
44% of partially secured liabilities not covered by pledged assets ($35,000 × 44%)	15,400
Total paid on partially secured liabilities	$75,400

7. E

Free assets - available to unsecured creditors	$ 225,000
Excess to be received from assets pledged on secured liabilities ($210,000 – $125,000)	85,000
Amount available for unsecured creditors	$ 310,000
Unsecured liabilities with priority	(121,000)
Net amount available for unsecured creditors	189,000
Unsecured liabilities	÷ 450,000
Percentage of unsecured liabilities that will be paid	42%

8. D Amount Wallace Co. can expect to collect ($45,000 × 42%) = $18,900

9. A

Security interest net realizable value	$75,000
Expected payment on unsecured remainder ($15,000 × 42%)	6,300
Amount bank can expect to receive	$81,300

10. E

Answers to Brief Essay Questions

1. The assets are labeled as:

    A. Pledged with fully secured creditors.
    B. Pledged with partially secured creditors.
    C. Available for priority liabilities and unsecured creditors (often referred to as free assets)

2. The debts are labeled as:

    A. Liabilities with priority.
    B. Fully secured creditors.
    C. Partially secured creditors.
    D. Unsecured creditors.

3. The wage limit for determining unsecured liabilities with priority is $10,950 per employee, covering the 180 days preceding the filing of the petition. Any excess over the $10,950 limit is included with unsecured liabilities without priority.

Chapter 14

Partnerships: Formation and Operation

Chapter Outline

I. *LO1* **Partnerships – Advantages and Disadvantages**

    A. **Advantages** of partnerships include:

        1. Ease of formation.

        2. Flexibility.

        3. Absence of double taxation.

            a. The partnership is not taxed.

            b. Revenue and deductions are passed through to the partners to be included on their tax returns.

    B. **Disadvantages** include:

        1. *Unlimited liability* – any partner can be held personally liable for the debts of the partnership.

        2. *Mutual agency* – each partner has the right to incur liabilities on behalf of the partnership.

        3. Partnerships rarely grow to a significant size (compared to large corporations) primarily due to the unlimited liability being assumed by each general partner.

    C. **Alternate Legal Forms** combine the benefits of partnerships and corporations.

        1. **Subchapter S Corporation** (*S corporation*)

            a. Owners must be individuals, estates, certain tax-exempt entities, or certain types of trusts.

            b. Limited to 75 stockholders and 1 class of stock.

            c. Created as a corporation.

            d. If certain regulations are met, S corporations are taxed as partnerships.

        2. **Limited Partnership (LP)**

            a. Ownership consists of general partners and limited partners.

            b. *Limited partners* contribute investment capital, but do not participate in management of the partnership. Their risk is limited to the amount they invest.

            c. *General partners* assume liability for all the obligations of the business.

3. **Limited Liability Partnership (LLP)**

    a. Same characteristics as a general partnership, except LLPs significantly reduce the partners' liability.

    b. Partners may lose their investment, and are responsible for the contractual debts of the partnership.

    c. **Advantage**: a partners' liability for damages is limited to their own acts and omissions and the acts and omissions of those who are supervised by them.

4. **Limited Liability Corporation (LLC)**

    a. Classified as a partnership for tax purposes.

    b. Depending upon the laws of the state, the owners risk only their investment (limited liability).

    c. In contrast to a Subchapter S, the number of owners is usually not restricted.

II. **Partnership Accounting – Capital Accounts**

    A. The unique aspects of partnership accounting lie primarily in the handling of the partners' capital accounts.

    B. Individual capital accounts record contributions, income allocations, and withdrawals for each partner.

    C. Unlike corporations, partnership capital accounts are not segregated by type of capital (i.e. contributed capital, paid-in-capital, etc.).

    D. The *Statement of Partners' Capital* shows changes to the individual capital accounts, and replaces the Statement of Retained Earnings used by corporations.

III. *LO2* **Articles of Partnership**

    A. Oral or written covenant between the partners that governs the operation of the business.

    B. Should Include:

        1. Name and address of each partner.

        2. Business location.

        3. Description of the nature of the business.

        4. Rights and responsibilities of each partner.

        5. Initial contribution to be made by each partner along with the method to be used for valuation.

        6. Specific method by which profits and losses are to be allocated.

        7. Periodic withdrawal of assets by each partner, and limits on those withdrawals.

8. Procedures for admitting new partners.

9. Method for settling partnership disputes.

10. Life insurance provisions for acquiring the interest of a deceased partner.

11. Method for settling a partner's share in the business upon the partner's withdrawal, retirement, or death.

C. Any area not covered by Articles of Partnership will usually be settled by referring to the *Uniform Partnership Act*.

IV. *LO3* Accounting for Capital Contributions

A. The accounting basis for capital contributions is the *Articles of Partnership,* which establishes provisions for contributions, withdrawals, admission of new partners, etc.

B. **Tangible contributions** made by the partners are recorded at fair market value.

C. *LO4* **Bonus and Goodwill Methods** – Two different approaches are available when one or more partners contribute *intangible assets* to the partnership (such as expertise, name recognition, or established clientele).

1. **The Bonus Method**

    a. Identifiable, tangible assets are recorded at their fair market value.

    b. The capital account balances for each of the partners are adjusted to indicate tangible and intangible contributions made by each partner.

2. **The Goodwill Method**

    a. The implied value of the business or intangible asset contributed is computed.

    b. The difference between the implied value and the fair market value of the tangible asset contributions is *goodwill*.

    c. Recognition of goodwill poses theoretical problems and should be viewed with professional skepticism.

D. **Additional Capital Contributions and Withdrawals**

1. Partners may choose to contribute additional capital during the life of the business. Contributions are recorded as an addition to the partner's capital account based on fair value.

2. The articles of partnership often allow withdrawals on a regular periodic basis as a reward for ownership or as compensation for work done.

    a. Often individual drawing accounts are used to record the withdrawals.

    b. Drawing accounts are closed to the individual partner's capital account at year-end.

3. Other amounts may be withdrawn on an occasional basis – for example due to a partner's need for money or desire to reduce their investment in the partnership.

    a. These amounts are often significantly higher than a partner's periodic drawing.

    b. The articles of partnership may require prior approval by the other partners.

V.   *LO5* **Allocation of Income or Loss**

A. At the end of each fiscal period, the revenue and expense accounts must be closed out with the resulting income figure being assigned to the individual capital accounts.

B. The method of allocating income to the capital accounts should be established in the *Articles of Partnership*.

   1. If no method has been specified, state partnership law normally holds that all partners receive an equal allocation of income or loss.

   2. *LO6* **Alternative Allocation Techniques** – partnerships can have different profit and loss sharing percentages for each partner based upon multiple factors such as capital invested, expertise or experience, and work performed. Essentially, these factors represent pre-allocations of the partnership's income/loss to the partners prior to applying the negotiated profit/loss sharing percentages.

    a. Partners may receive credit for "interest" based on their capital account balances. This reduces the amount of income available for allocation to the partners using the profit/loss sharing percentages.

    b. Partners may receive credit for "unpaid" compensation or bonuses. These "salary" or "bonus" allocations reduce the amount of income available for allocation to the partners using the profit/loss sharing percentages.

VI.   *LO7* **Accounting for Partnership Dissolutions**

A. **Legal Dissolution**

   1. Whenever the group of individuals making up a partnership changes its membership, including admission or withdrawal of a partner, there is a legal dissolution of the partnership.

   2. Actual operation of the partnership business often is not interrupted when a new partner is added to the partnership.

   3. However, partners may choose to terminate the partnership and liquidate the business when there is a change in the partners.

B. *LO8* **Admission of a New Partner through Purchase of a Current Interest**

   1. A partnership interest can be purchased directly from one or more partners.

   2. There are three primary rights that can be granted to a new partner:

    a. The right of co-ownership in the business property.

    b. The right to share in profits and losses as specified in the articles of partnership.

    c. The right to participate in management of the business.

3. Any partner can sell or assign the first *two* of the above rights to another party; however, the right to participate in management can be conveyed only with the permission of the other partners.

4. **Book Value Method** – Cash Paid Directly to the Partners

   a. Under this method, there is no effect on the overall capital of the partnership. The capital accounts are simply reallocated between the partners.

   b. Reduce the capital account balance of the selling partners by a percentage equal to the ownership percentage purchased by the new partner.

   c. Set up the new partner's capital account balance.

5. **Goodwill Method** – Cash Paid Directly to the Partners

   a. Under this method, the admission of a new partner is viewed as a transaction between two separate reporting entities, and thus, assets and liabilities are subject to revaluation.

   b. Determine the implied value of the partnership based on the new partner's payment to the partners and the percentage of the partnership acquired (Cash Payment ÷ Percentage Ownership Acquired).

   c. Determine the amount of Goodwill generated by the transaction. (Implied Value – Net Tangible Assets of the Partnership).

   d. Allocate the goodwill to the original partners based on the original partners' profit/loss sharing percentages.

   e. Reduce the capital account balances of the selling partner(s) by a percentage equal to the ownership percentage purchased by the new partner and create the new partner's capital account (equal to the amount paid to the "old" partners).

C. *LO9* **Admission of a New Partner by a Contribution Made to the Partnership**

1. **Bonus Credited to Original Partners**

   a. Under this method, since the amount of total capital in the partnership does not change due to revaluation, the capital accounts are merely reallocated to the existing and new partners.

   b. Debit the Cash account for the cash contributed to the partnership by the new partner.

   c. Credit the capital account balance of the new partner for the new partner's percentage of the tangible assets of the partnership (the tangible net assets of the partnership prior to the new partner's admittance plus the cash contribution).

   d. Any difference between "b" and "c" above should be allocated to the original partners based on the profit and loss sharing percentages established in the *Articles of Incorporation*.

2. **Goodwill Credited to Original Partners**

    a.   Under this method, the admission of a new partner is seen as a transaction between two independent reporting entities, thus, assets and liabilities are subject to revaluation.

    b.   Determine the *implied value* of the partnership based on the new partner's payment to the partners and the percentage of the partnership acquired (Cash Payment ÷ Percentage Ownership Acquired).

        (1)   If the implied value of the partnership is greater than the net tangible assets of the partnership, including the newly contributed cash, then there has been an implied increase in value of the partnership and goodwill will be recorded (continue with step d.).

        (2)   If the implied value is less than the net tangible assets + the new contribution, the intangible asset is attributable to the new partner (see 4c).

    c.   Determine amount of goodwill generated by the transaction (implied value – net tangible assets of the partnership, including the contributed cash).

    d.   Allocate the goodwill to the original partners based on the original partners' profit/loss sharing percentages.

    e.   Increase the assets by the amount of the contributed cash and establish the capital account balance of the new partner.

3. **Hybrid Method of Recording Admission of New Partner** – in this approach, identifiable assets are revalued, but no goodwill is recognized.

4. **Bonus or Goodwill Credited to New Partner**

    a.   The new partner may be contributing an intangible asset to the partnership. In this case, the bonus or goodwill is credited to the new partner.

    b.   **Bonus Method** – the total capital (including the new contribution) is allocated to the existing and new partners.

        (1)   Debit the Cash account for the cash contributed to the partnership by the new partner.

        (2)   Credit the capital account balance of the new partner for the new partner's percentage of the tangible assets of the partnership (the tangible net assets of the partnership prior to the new partner's admittance plus the cash contribution).

        (3)   Any difference between (1) and (2) above should be allocated (debited) to the original partners capital accounts based on the profit and loss sharing percentages established in the *Articles of Incorporation*.

    c.   **Goodwill Method**

        (1)   When the implied value of the partnership is less than the total capital (including the new contribution), either there is negative goodwill (a decline in the value of the business) or the new partner is contributing an intangible asset.

(2) If the new partner is contributing an intangible asset, the amount of the goodwill to be recorded has to be determined mathematically.

Where NP Cont. represents the amount of the new partner contribution, and NP% represents the % ownership the new partner is to receive, and GW represents goodwill, use the following formula to determine goodwill.

NP Cont + GW = NP%(Capital before NP Cont. + NP Cont. + GW)

NP Cont + GW = NP%(Capital before NP Cont. + NP Cont.) + NP%(GW)

The equation is then solved to determine GW (goodwill)

---

(3) The tangible asset and goodwill are debited, and the new partner's capital account is credited.

VII. *LO10* Dissolution – Withdrawal of a Partner

A. When a partner withdraws from the partnership, and the remaining partners continue with the business, assets are usually distributed to the withdrawing partner.

B. The amount of the distribution to the withdrawing partner is often determined by the Articles of Partnership.

1. **Bonus Method** – The difference between the amount distributed to the withdrawing partner and the withdrawing partner's capital balance is recorded as an adjustment to the remaining partners' capital accounts.

2. **Goodwill** (revaluation) **Method** – goodwill and all capital accounts are adjusted to fair market value. The fair value is indicated by the distribution amount.

3. A hybrid approach can also be applied. This approach recognizes asset and liability revaluations, but ignores goodwill.

Multiple Choice Questions

1. Which one of the following is a reason for the popularity of partnerships as a legal form for businesses?

   A. Partnerships avoid the double taxation of income found in corporations.
   B. Partnerships avoid limited liability.
   C. Partnerships often make it easy to raise capital.
   D. Partners are not subject to unlimited liability.
   E. Partnerships avoid mutual agency.

   Items 2 and 3 are based on the following information:

   John and Sarah formed a partnership on January 4, 2011. John invested cash of $150,000 as well as inventory costing $25,000, but with a current appraised value of $40,000. Sarah contributed land with a $60,000 book value and a $90,000 fair market value. The partnership also accepted responsibility for a $25,000 note payable held by Sarah in connection with the land. The partners agreed to begin operations with equal capital balances.

2. Assuming that the bonus method was used by this partnership, what was John's initial capital balance?

   A. $150,000
   B. $127,500
   C. $190,000
   D. $ 95,000
   E. $140,000

3. Assuming that the goodwill method was used by this partnership, what is the amount of goodwill and the amount of Sarah's initial capital balance?

	Goodwill	Sarah's Initial Capital Balance
A.	$ 0	$202,500
B.	$ 0	$190,000
C.	$125,000	$202,500
D.	$125,000	$190,000
E.	$100,000	$190,000

   Items 4 through 6 are based on the following information:

   The partnership of Albert and Beach decided to admit Collins as a partner with a 20% interest. Collins invested $75,000 in cash into the partnership. Albert's and Beach's capital accounts and their profit and loss sharing ratios are shown below:

	Capital	Profit and Loss Sharing Ratio
Albert	$120,000	40%
Beach	$ 80,000	60%

4. If the partnership used the goodwill (revaluation) method, how much goodwill should be recognized by this transaction?

A. $175,000
B. $200,000
C. $100,000
D. $375,000
E. $ 0

5. If the partnership used the goodwill (revaluation) method, what would be the capital balances for Albert, Beach, and Collins after Collins' investment was recorded?

	Albert	Beach	Collins
A.	$160,000	$140,000	$ 55,000
B.	$120,000	$ 80,000	$ 55,000
C.	$ 32,000	$ 28,000	$ 75,000
D.	$160,000	$140,000	$ 75,000
E.	$120,000	$ 80,000	$175,000

6. If the partnership used the bonus method, what would be the capital balances for Albert, Beach, and Collins after Collins' investment was recorded?

	Albert	Beach	Collins
A.	$120,000	$ 80,000	$75,000
B.	$134,000	$101,000	$40,000
C.	$120,000	$ 80,000	$40,000
D.	$120,000	$ 80,000	$55,000
E.	$128,000	$ 92,000	$55,000

Items 7 and 8 are based on the following information:

A partnership was formed on January 1, 2011 with the following capital balances:

Allen	$400,000
Dunn	$250,000
Gaw	$350,000

The Articles of Partnership stipulated that profits and losses are assigned as follows:

- Each partner is allocated interest equal to 8.5% of the beginning capital balance.
- Dunn is allocated a $52,000 salary
- Any remaining profits/losses are allocated on a 2:2:6 basis, respectively.
- Each partner is allowed to withdraw up to $15,000 per year.

Net income of $190,000 was earned by the business in 2011.

7. How much income is allocated to Dunn in 2011?

   A. $ 52,000
   B. $ 38,000
   C. $ 90,000
   D. $ 83,850
   E. $ 42,250

8. Assuming that each partner withdraws the maximum amount, what is each partner's capital account balance at the end of 2011?

	Allen	Dunn	Gaw
A.	$429,600	$318,850	$396,550
B.	$444,600	$333,850	$411,550
C.	$438,000	$288,000	$464,000
D.	$423,000	$273,000	$451,000
E.	$385,000	$235,000	$335,000

Items 9 and 10 are based on the following information:

As of December 31, 2011, the Algood Co. partnership had the following capital balances:

Delveaux, Capital	$ 420,000
Grinder, Capital	$ 360,000
Dockery, Capital	$ 120,000
Rand, Capital	$ 100,000

Profits/Losses are split on a 3:2:4:1 basis, respectively. Grinder decided to leave the partnership and was paid $390,000 from the business based on the original contractual agreement.

9. If the goodwill method is applied, what is the total amount of goodwill?

   A. $ 30,000
   B. $ 6,000
   C. $150,000
   D. $100,000
   E. $ 90,000

10. If the goodwill method is applied, what is Delveaux's capital after Grinder's withdrawal?

   A. $476,250
   B. $465,000
   C. $431,250
   D. $429,000
   E. $420,000

Items **11** and **12** are based on the following information:

The following condensed balance sheet is presented for the partnership of Cooke, Dorry, and Evans who share profits and losses in the ratio of 4:3:3, respectively.

Cash	$ 90,000
Other Assets	820,000
Loan Rec. - Cooke	30,000
Total Assets	$ 940,000
Accounts Payable	$ 210,000
Loan Payable - Evans	40,000
Cooke, Capital	300,000
Dorry, Capital	200,000
Evans, Capital	190,000
Total Liabs. & Capital	$ 940,000

11. Assume that Fisher is going to pay $300,000 to the partnership for her 25% interest. Using the goodwill method, what will Dorry's capital balance be after admitting Fisher?

   A. $ 290,000
   B. $ 63,000
   C. $ 263,000
   D. $ 360,000
   E. $1,200,000

12. Assume that Fisher is going to pay $300,000 to the individual partners for a 25% interest. Using the book value approach, what will Fisher's capital balance be?

   A. $ 75,000
   B. $ 300,000
   C. $ 235,000
   D. $ 172,500
   E. $ 247,500

Brief Essay Questions

1. How does *partnership accounting* differ from *corporate accounting*?

2. What are the meaning and purpose of the *Articles of Partnership*?

3. When a partner sells his or her interest in a partnership, what rights are conveyed to the new partner?

Problems

1. The Albright & Baker partnership had the account balances shown below on January 1, 2011 when the partners decided to admit Clark as a new partner. Clark was to contribute $20,000 cash to the partnership for a 25% interest in the firm.

Cash	$ 10,000
Other current assets	$ 40,000
Buildings and equipment – net	$ 50,000
Land	$ 20,000
Accounts payable	$ 40,000
Albright, Capital	$ 50,000
Baker, Capital	$ 30,000

    Required:

    A. What entry would have been made to admit Clark as a partner under the goodwill method?

    B. What entry would have been made to admit Clark as a partner under the bonus method if Albright and Baker had shared profits and losses according to their relative capital balances?

    C. If Clark was to receive a 40% interest in the partnership and if no goodwill or bonus was to be recognized, how much cash would Clark have contributed? Show supporting calculations.

2. The partners of the XYZ partnership had the following capital balances on January 1, 2011:

X, Capital	$ 52,000
Y, Capital	$ 82,000
Z, Capital	$ 92,000

    The *Articles of Partnership* provided that each partner might draw $1,000 per month and the profit and losses for the year would be allocated as follows:

    - Z would be allowed a $2,000 per month salary allocation.
    - Each partner would be allocated interest as income at the rate of 10% per year based on his or her end-of-year balance (after drawing but before income allocation).
    - Any remaining balance (positive or negative) is to be allocated based on the beginning capital balances of the partners.

    The XYZ partnership had sales of $312,000 and expenses of $231,000 for 2011 before any allocations to the partners. Each partner withdrew the maximum amount allowed under the articles of partnership.

    Required:

    For the year ending December 31, 2011, develop a *Schedule of Income Allocation* for the XYZ partnership. Also, show the entries necessary to close the *Profit and Loss Summary* account and the *Drawing* accounts into the capital balances.

3. A partnership has the following balances and profit/loss sharing percentages:

	Capital Balances	Profit/Loss Sharing %
Fesler	$ 80,000	50%
Swanson	$ 100,000	40%
Galbreath	$ 70,000	10%

Required:

A. Elmore is going to buy into the partnership by paying $100,000 to the partners in exchange for a 20% ownership in the partnership. Using the **book value method**, what are the four capital balances after admitting Elmore to the partnership?

B. Elmore is going to buy into the partnership by paying $100,000 to the partners in exchange for a 20% ownership in the partnership. Using the **goodwill method**, what are the four capital balances after admitting Elmore to the partnership?

C. Elmore is going to buy into the partnership by paying $100,000 directly to the partnership in exchange for a 20% ownership in the partnership. Using the **bonus method**, what are the four capital balances after admitting Elmore to the partnership?

D. Elmore is going to buy into the partnership by paying $100,000 directly to the partnership in exchange for a 20% ownership in the partnership. Using the **goodwill method**, what are the four capital balances after admitting Elmore to the partnership?

Solutions to Multiple Choice Questions

1. A

2. B Under the bonus method, all contributed property is recorded at fair market value. As specified by the *Articles of Partnership*, total capital is then divided equally between the partners. Total capital (net assets) is calculated as follows:

Cash	$ 150,000
Inventory	40,000
Land	90,000
Total assets	$ 280,000
Less: Notes payable	(25,000)
Total capital	$ 255,000
John's percentage	50%
John, Capital	$ 127,500

3. **D**   The fair market value of John's contribution is $190,000, whereas Sarah is investing only a net amount of $65,000 (the value of the land less the accompanying debt). Since John is contributing a fair value of $190,000 for a 50% share, the implied value of the partnership is $380,000 ($190,000 / 50%). Because the capital accounts are initially to be equal, Sarah is presumed to be contributing goodwill of $125,000 ($190,000 – $65,000). The initial capital balances can also be calculated as follows:

Cash	$ 150,000
Inventory	40,000
Land	90,000
Goodwill	125,000
Total assets	$ 405,000
Less: Notes payable	(25,000)
Total capital	$ 380,000
Sarah's percentage	50%
Sarah, Capital	$ 190,000

4. **C**

Implied value of the business ($75,000 ÷ 20%)	$ 375,000
Total capital ($120,000 + $80,000 + $75,000)	(275,000)
Goodwill	$ 100,000

5. **D**

	Albert	Beach	Collin
Original capital	$120,000	$ 80,000	
Goodwill ($100,000 × 40% & 60%)	40,000	60,000	
Collins' payment			$ 75,000
Capital balances	$160,000	$140,000	$ 75,000

6. **E**

	Albert	Beach	Collins
Original capital	$120,000	$ 80,000	
Allocation to Collins ($275,000 × 20%)			$55,000
Bonus to Albert & Beach ($20,000 × %)	8,000	12,000	
Capital balances	$128,000	$ 92,000	$55,000

7. **D**

	Allen	Dunn	Gaw	Total
Interest – 8.5% of Beginning Capital	$ 34,000	$ 21,250	$ 29,750	$ 85,000
Salaries		52,000		52,000
Allocation of remaining income ($53,000 allocated 2:2:6)	10,600	10,600	31,800	53,000
Total Income Allocation	$ 44,600	$ 83,850	$ 61,550	$ 190,000

8. **A**

	Allen	Dunn	Gaw	Total
Beginning Capital	$ 400,000	$ 250,000	$ 350,000	$ 1,000,000
Income allocation	44,600	83,850	61,550	190,000
Withdrawals	(15,000)	(15,000)	(15,000)	(45,000)
Ending Capital	$ 429,600	$ 318,850	$ 396,550	$ 1,145,000

9. **C** Goodwill ($30,000 ÷ 20% = $150,000)

10. **B**

	Delveaux	Grinder	Dockery	Rand
Original Capital	$ 420,000	$ 360,000	$ 120,000	$ 100,000
Goodwill Allocation	45,000	30,000	60,000	15,000
Capital Balances	$ 465,000	$ 390,000	$ 180,000	$ 115,000

11. **C**

Fisher's contribution	$	300,000
÷ Fisher's % ownership		25%
Implied value of the partnership	$	1,200,000
Implied value of the partnership	$	1,200,000
Less: Tangible partnership assets		(990,000)
Goodwill	$	210,000
Dorry, Capital – Beginning	$	200,000
Add: Dorry's share of the goodwill (30%)		63,000
Dorry, Capital – Ending	$	263,000

12. **D**

This question states that the individual partners will be paid, not the partnership. Therefore, Fischer's capital account is determined as follows:

Tangible Net Partnership Assets	$	690,000
× Fisher's % ownership		25%
Fischer's capital account	$	172,500

Answers to Brief Essay Questions

1. Partnership accounting issues focus on the equity (or capital) section of the balance sheet. In a corporation, stockholders' equity is divided between earned capital (retained earnings) and contributed capital. Conversely, for a partnership, each partner has an individual capital account which is not differentiated according to its sources. Virtually all accounting issues encountered in connection with the partnership format are related to recording and maintaining these capital balances.

2. The Articles of Partnership is a legal document that defines the rights and responsibilities of the partners in relation to the business and in relation to each other. Because the Articles of Partnership serves as a governing document for the partnership, it should be created as a prerequisite for the formation of a partnership. It may contain any number of provisions but should normally specify each of the following:

   A. Name and address of each partner.
   B. Business location.
   C. Description of the nature of the business.

D. Rights and responsibilities of each partner.

E. Initial investment to be made by each partner along with the method to be used for valuation.

F. Specific method by which profits and losses are to be allocated.

G. Periodic withdrawals to be allowed each partner.

H. Procedures for admitting new partners.

I. Method for arbitrating disputes.

J. Method for setting a partner's share of the business upon withdrawal, retirement, or death.

3. In selling an interest in a partnership, three rights are conveyed to the new owner:

A. The right of co-ownership of the business property.

B. The right to a specified allocation of profits and losses generated by the partnership's business, and

C. The right to participate in the management of the business.

No problem exists in selling or assigning the first two of these rights. However, *the right to participate in management decisions* can only be transferred with the consent of all partners.

Solutions to Problems

1. **A.**

Date	Accounts	Debit	Credit
	Cash	20,000	
	Goodwill	6,667	
	Clark, Capital		26,667

The key to the solution is to determine the net assets (total capital) of the partnership after Clark's contribution in order to determine his 25% share.

Assets before contribution	$ 120,000
Less: Liabilities	(40,000)
Net Assets (total capital before Clark's contribution)	$ 80,000
Clarks contribution	20,000
Projected Net Assets after Clarks's contribution	$ 100,000
Clark's percentage	25%
Clark's share of the partnership's net assets	$ 25,000

However, since Clark is contributing $20,000 for a 25% share, that indicates an implied value of the partnership of only $80,000. Thus, either negative goodwill appears to exist, or the new partner is bringing an intangible contribution (goodwill).

Thus, goodwill is attributable to Clark's capital account. Goodwill is determined algebraically, as follows:

$$\$20,000 + GW = 25\% \times (\$80,000 + \$20,000 + GW)$$
$$.75GW = \$5,000$$
$$GW = \$6,667 \text{ (rounded)}$$

B.

Date	Accounts	Debit	Credit
	Cash	20,000	
	Albright, Capital	3,125	
	Baker, Capital	1,875	
	Clark, Capital		25,000

In order to provide Clark with a 25% interest in the firm, Albright's and Baker's capital accounts must be reduced. The amount of the reduction for Albright is based on Albright's profit sharing ratio:

$$\$50,000 \div (\$50,000 + \$30,000) \times \$5,000 = \$3,125$$

C. Let X = Cash to be contributed by Clark

$$X = .4 \times (\$80,000 + X)$$
$$X = \$32,000 + .4\,X$$
$$.6X = \$32,000$$
$$X = \$53,333 \text{ (rounded)}$$

2. Schedule of Income Allocation:

XYZ Partnership
Schedule of Income Allocation
For Year Ending December 31, 2011

	Total	X	Y	Z
Income	$ 81,000			
Z's Salary	(24,000)			$ 24,000
Remainder	57,000			
Interest	(19,000)	$ 4,000	$ 7,000	8,000
Remainder	38,000			
Remaining balance	(38,000)	8,000	14,000	16,000
Totals	$ -	$ 12,000	$ 21,000	$ 48,000

Date	Accounts	Debit	Credit
	Income Summary	81,000	
	X, Capital		12,000
	Y, Capital		21,000
	Z, Capital		48,000
	to close Income Summary to the capital accounts		
	X, Capital	12,000	
	Y, Capital	12,000	
	Z, Capital	12,000	
	X, Drawing		12,000
	Y, Capital		12,000
	Z, Drawing		12,000
	to close Income Summary to the capital accounts.		

3. **A.** Book value method, cash paid to the partners:

Each partner gives up 20% of their current balance to Elmore.

Fesler, Capital			Swanson, Capital	
	80,000			100,000
16,000			20,000	
	64,000			80,000

Galbreath, Capital			Elmore, Capital	
	70,000			
14,000				50,000
	56,000			50,000

B. Goodwill method, cash contribution paid to partners:

Elmore's contribution	$	100,000
÷ Elmore's % ownership		20%
Implied value of the partnership	$	500,000
Implied value of the partnership	$	500,000
Less: Tangible partnership assets		(250,000)
Goodwill	$	250,000

The goodwill is allocated to the three original partners. Then 20% of each balance is allocated to Elmore.

Fesler, Capital			Swanson, Capital	
	80,000			100,000
41,000	125,000		40,000	100,000
	164,000			160,000

Galbreath, Capital			Elmore, Capital	
	70,000			
19,000	25,000			100,000
	76,000			100,000

C. Book value method, cash contribution paid to partnership:

Assets before contribution	$ 250,000
Elmore's contribution	100,000
Assets after contribution	$ 350,000

After identifying the total assets of the new partnership, cash is debited for $100,000. Elmore's capital account is credited for 20% of the total assets ($350,000 × 20%). The difference is allocated to the other partners.

Fesler, Capital			Swanson, Capital	
	80,000			100,000
	15,000			12,000
	95,000			112,000

Galbreath, Capital			Elmore, Capital	
	70,000			
	3,000			70,000
	73,000			70,000

D. Goodwill method, cash contribution paid to partnership:

First, compute the implied value of the new partnership, and the amount of goodwill to be recorded.

Elmore's contribution	$ 100,000
÷ Elmore's % ownership	20%
Implied value of the partnership	$ 500,000
Implied value of the partnership	$ 500,000
Less: Tangible partnership assets	(350,000)
Goodwill	$ 150,000

Second, allocate the goodwill to the three original partners. Then, credit Elmore's account for the amount of Elmore's contribution.

Fesler, Capital	
	80,000
	75,000
	155,000

Swanson, Capital	
	100,000
	60,000
	160,000

Galbreath, Capital	
	70,000
	15,000
	85,000

Elmore, Capital	
	100,000
	100,000

Chapter 15

Partnerships: Termination and Liquidation

Chapter Outline

I. **Termination and Liquidation – Protecting the Interests of all Parties**

    A. Reasons for the termination of a partnership and liquidation:

        1. The death, withdrawal, or retirement of a partner can lead to cessation of business activities.

        2. The bankruptcy of an individual partner or the partnership as a whole can also lead to the same conclusion.

    B. *LO1* **Termination and Liquidation Procedures**

        1. Partnership assets are converted into cash.

        2. Resulting gains and losses are allocated to the partners.

        3. Business obligations and liquidation expenses are paid.

        4. Any remaining assets are then distributed to the individual partners based on their final capital balances.

        5. The partnership's books are permanently closed since no general ledger accounts remain.

    C. *LO2* **Termination and Liquidation Journal Entries**

        1. As partnership assets are sold, partner capital accounts are debited for losses (credited for gains) according to the P&L distribution procedures. Cash is recorded and the asset is removed from the books.

        2. Liabilities are paid (debited) and cash credited.

        3. When liquidation expenses are paid, the partner capital accounts are debited for their share of the expenses. Cash is credited.

        4. Ultimately, remaining assets are distributed to the individual partners based on their final capital balances.

    D. The accountant's role in the process:

        1. The accountant provides timely financial information to all parties.

        2. The accountant works to ensure an equitable settlement of all claims.

II. **Schedule of Liquidation** – is prepared to disclose:

    A. Transactions to date.

    B. Property still being held by the partnership.

C.   Liabilities remaining to be paid.

D.   Current cash and capital balances.

III.   *LO3* **Deficit Capital Balance** – By the end of the liquidation process, one or more partners may have a negative capital balance (*deficit*), usually as a result of losses incurred in disposing assets.

A.   **Deficit Capital Balance – Contribution by Partner** – legally, any deficit should be eliminated by having that partner contribute enough additional assets to offset the amount of the deficit.

B.   **Deficit Capital Balance – Loss to Remaining Partners** – If a contribution from a partner with a deficit capital balance is not received immediately, the remaining partners may request a *preliminary distribution* of any partnership cash that is available.

1.   This payment is based on *safe capital balances* – the amounts that would remain in the individual capital accounts even if all deficits and other properties prove to be losses that must be absorbed by the remaining partners.

2.   If a portion (or all) of a deficit is subsequently recovered, a further distribution to the partners is made based on newly calculated *safe capital balances*.

3.   Any deficit that is not recovered is charged to the remaining partners based on their relative profit and loss ratio.

IV.   *LO4* **Preliminary Distribution of Partnership Assets**

A.   The liquidation process can extend for a lengthy period as business activities wind down and property is sold.

B.   More cash may be generated than the amount needed to extinguish all potential liabilities and liquidation expenses.

C.   Once all liabilities and expenses are paid, leftover cash can be distributed, even if some assets remain for disposal.

1.   The accountant may choose to produce a *proposed schedule of liquidation* periodically to determine the equitable distribution of available cash amounts.

2.   The proposed schedule of liquidation is developed based upon simulating the accounting recognition that would be required by a possible series of transactions: assets are sold, expenses are paid, etc.

a.   Anticipate maximum losses in each case.

b.   Noncash assets are assumed to have no resale value, maximum possible liquidation expenses are included, and all partners are considered personally insolvent.

c.   Since numerous capital distributions may be required, this process is often called a liquidation made in installments.

3. Ending capital figures that remain on a proposed schedule of liquidation are safe capital balances – the amounts that could be immediately paid to each partner without jeopardizing future payments.

4. Safe capital balances indicate that the partner currently has a sufficient interest in the partnership to absorb all potential losses even after a preliminary distribution.

V. *LO5* Predistribution Plan

A. The proposed schedule of liquidation indicates safe capital balances, but revised statements must be produced frequently.

B. Accountants often prefer to produce a single predistribution plan at the start of a liquidation to provide guidance for all payments made to the partners throughout this process.

C. Information for the predistribution plan is generated by assuming the occurrence of a series of losses, each just large enough to eliminate one partner's claim to any partnership property.

D. Once a series of losses has been simulated that would eliminate the capital balances of all partners, the actual plan is developed by measuring the effects that occur if the losses do not materialize.

E. By working backwards through this series of possible losses, a predistribution plan can be produced that will cover all payments made within the liquidation.

Multiple Choice Questions

1. In a partnership liquidation, how is the final allocation of business assets made to the partners?

   A. equally
   B. according to the profit and loss ratio
   C. according to the balances of the partners' loan and capital accounts
   D. according to the initial investments made by the partners
   E. according to the method stipulated by the partnership agreement

2. A partnership is in the process of liquidating and is currently reporting the following capital balances.

Marla, Capital (50% share of all profits and losses)	$ 80,000
Barbara, Capital (30%)	60,000
Roberta, Capital (20%)	(24,000)

   Roberta has indicated that the $24,000 deficit will be covered by a forthcoming contribution. However, the two remaining partners have asked to receive the $116,000 in cash that is presently available. How much of this money should each partner be given?

	Marla	Barbara
A.	$65,000	$51,000
B.	$81,000	$35,000
C.	$58,000	$58,000
D.	$85,000	$31,000
E.	$72,000	$44,000

3. A partnership is considering the possibility of liquidation because one of the partners, Thomas, is insolvent. Capital balances at the current time are as follows, and profits and losses are divided on a 6:3:1 basis, respectively.

George, Capital	$65,000
Stewart, Capital	82,000
Thomas, Capital	53,000

   Thomas' creditors have filed a $40,000 claim against the partnership's assets. The partnership currently holds assets reported at $300,000 and liabilities of $100,000. If the assets can be sold for $125,000, what is the minimum amount that Thomas' creditors would receive?

   A. $25,000
   B. $26,000
   C. $21,000
   D. $30,000
   E. $27,000

Items 4 and 5 are based on the following information.

The following condensed balance sheet is for the partnership of Andrews, Carroll, and Murray, who share profits and losses in the ratio of 6:2:2, respectively.

Cash	$ 80,000
Other assets	120,000
Total assets	$ 200,000
Liabilities	$ 140,000
Andrews, Capital	30,000
Carroll, Capital	25,000
Murray, Capital	5,000
Total liabilities and partners' equity	$ 200,000

4. Which partner is most vulnerable to a loss?

   A. Andrews
   B. Carroll
   C. Andrews and Carroll are equally vulnerable
   D. Murray
   E. Andrews and Murray are equally vulnerable

5. If the other assets are sold for $80,000, how should the available cash be distributed?

	Andrews	Carroll	Murray
A.	$ 6,000	$14,000	$ -0-
B.	$ 3,750	$16,250	$ -0-
C.	$16,250	$ 3,000	$ 750
D.	$ 3,750	$13,250	$3,000
E.	$ 7,350	$11,750	$ 900

6. Which one of the following statements is **incorrect** regarding a predistribution plan?

   A. A predistribution plan is developed by simulating a series of losses that are just large enough to eliminate, one at a time, all of the partners' claims to cash.
   B. A predistribution plan recognizes that the individual capital accounts exhibit differing degrees of sensitivity to losses.
   C. A predistribution plan serves as a guideline for all future cash payments in a liquidation.
   D. A predistribution is prepared at the end of a liquidation to confirm actual cash distributions.
   E. A series of absorbed losses forms the basis for the predistribution plan.

7. The following condensed balance sheet is for the Ashley, Bart, and Charles partnership. The partners share profits and losses in the ratio of 5:3:2, respectively.

Cash	$ 125,000
Inventory	100,000
Other assets	300,000
Total assets	$ 525,000
Liabilities	$ 270,000
Ashley, Capital	100,000
Bart, Capital	85,000
Charles, Capital	70,000
Total liabilities and partners' equity	$ 525,000

The partners have decided to liquidate the business. Liquidation expenses are estimated to be $8,000. The other assets are sold for $180,000. What distribution can be made to the partners?

	Ashley	Bart	Charles
A.	$14,000	$ 6,600	$ 6,400
B.	$ -0-	$ 8,200	$18,800
C.	$ 4,000	$ 6,400	$16,600
D.	$ -0-	$ 8,400	$18,600
E.	$ 4,500	$ 7,400	$15,100

8. A partnership has the following capital balances:

Monica, Capital (50% of profits and losses)	$100,000
Patricia, Capital (30%)	80,000
Susan, Capital (20%)	50,000

If the partnership is to be liquidated and $20,000 becomes immediately available, who gets the money?

	Monica	Patricia	Susan
A.	$5,000	$ 3,000	$12,000
B.	$7,000	$ 8,000	$ 5,000
C.	$ -0-	$14,000	$ 6,000
D.	$5,000	$ 6,000	$ 9,000
E.	$4,000	$ 8,000	$ 8,000

9. Stanley, a partner of the Newtown partnership, made a loan to the partnership. The partnership is now in liquidation. Which one of the following statements is **incorrect** regarding the status of this loan during the liquidation process?

    A. The loan must be repaid before any cash distribution is made to the other partners, even if Stanley does not have a sufficient amount of capital to absorb all possible losses.
    B. The loan has a lower priority than obligations to outside creditors.
    C. If the partner has a negative safe capital balance, a portion or even the entire loan should be retained as an offset against the capital account.
    D. The loan is accounted for in liquidation as if it were a component of the partner's capital.
    E. If Stanley is insolvent and reports a negative capital balance, the handling of the loan becomes significant.

Brief Essay Question

1. What four types of transactions must be recorded in regard to the termination and liquidation of a partnership?

Problems

1. The partners of ABC Partnership have decided to liquidate and terminate the partnership. Prior to liquidating, the partnership balance sheet is as follows:

ABC Partnership
Balance Sheet
May 15, 2011

Cash	$	10,000
Inventory		50,000
Property, Plant & Equipment - Net		80,000
Total assets	$	140,000
Liabilities	$	60,000
A, Capital		30,000
B, Capital		40,000
C, Capital		10,000
Total liabilities and partners' equity	$	140,000

The profit and loss sharing ratio is 6:3:1 for A, B, and C respectively.

Required:

A. Prepare a schedule of liquidation for ABC Partnership, given that the partnership sold the inventory for $20,000 and the property, plant, and equipment for $60,000.

B. Prepare a schedule of liquidation for ABC Partnership, given that the inventory was sold for $5,000 and the property, plant, and equipment for $50,000.

2. Richards, Kidd, Brown, and Marley are partners who share profits and losses on a 4:3:2:1 basis, respectively. On March 31, 2011, the partners were presently beginning to liquidate the business. At the beginning of this process, capital balances were as follows:

Richards, Capital	$50,000
Kidd, Capital	45,000
Brown, Capital	36,000
Marley, Capital	24,000

Required:

Based on the information that has been provided, prepare a predistribution plan for the partnership.

Solutions to Multiple Choice Questions

1. **C**

2. **A**

	Marla	Barbara	Roberta
Reported Capital Balances	$ 80,000	$ 60,000	$ (24,000)
Potential Loss from Roberta's Deficit (split on a 5:3 basis)	(15,000)	(9,000)	24,000
	$ 65,000	$ 51,000	$ -

3. **A**

	George	Stewart	Thomas
Reported Capital Balances	$ 65,000	$ 82,000	$ 53,000
Allocate loss on sale of assets ($175,000 split on a 6:3:1 basis)	(105,000)	(52,500)	(17,500)
Adjusted Balances	$ (40,000)	$ 29,500	$ 35,500
Potential Loss from George' Deficit (split 3:1)	40,000	(30,000)	(10,000)
Assignment of Stewart's Loss to Thomas		500	(500)
Minimum Cash Distributions	$ -	$ -	$ 25,000

4. **D** A loss of only $25,000 will completely eliminate Murray's capital balance.

Andrews	$30,000 ÷ 60% = $ 50,000 loss to eliminate capital
Carroll	$25,000 ÷ 20% = $125,000 loss to eliminate capital
Murray	$ 5,000 ÷ 20% = $ 25,000 loss to eliminate capital

5. B Schedules follow.

	Andrews	Carroll	Murray
Reported Capital Balances	$ 30,000	$ 25,000	$ 5,000
Allocate loss on sale of assets ($40,000 split on a 6:2:2 basis)	(24,000)	(8,000)	(8,000)
Adjusted Balances	$ 6,000	$ 17,000	$ (3,000)
Potential Loss from Murray's Deficit (split 6:2)	(2,250)	(750)	3,000
Minimum Cash Distributions	$ 3,750	$ 16,250	$ -

Reported cash balance	$ 80,000
Proceeds from sale of other assets	80,000
Adjust balance	$ 160,000
Cash used to pay creditors	(140,000)
Available cash	$ 20,000

6. D

7. B

	Ashley	Bart	Charles
Reported Capital Balances	$ 100,000	$ 85,000	$ 70,000
Allocate loss on sale of assets ($120,000 split on a 5:3:2 basis)	(60,000)	(36,000)	(24,000)
Adjusted Balances	$ 40,000	$ 49,000	$ 46,000
Anticipated liquidation expenses ($8,000 split on a 5:3:2 basis)	(4,000)	(2,400)	(1,600)
Anticipated loss on inventory ($100,000 split on a 5:3:2 basis)	(50,000)	(30,000)	(20,000)
Potential balances	(14,000)	16,600	24,400
Potential loss from Ashley deficit (split 3:2)	14,000	(8,400)	(5,600)
Current Cash Distributions	$ -	$ 8,200	$ 18,800

8. C

Since the partnership currently has total capital of $230,000, the $20,000 that is available would indicate maximum potential losses of $210,000.

Schedule follows.

	Monica	Patricia	Susan
Reported Capital Balances	$ 100,000	$ 80,000	$ 50,000
Allocate loss ($210,000 split on a 5:3:2 basis)	(105,000)	(63,000)	(42,000)
Potential balances	$ (5,000)	$ 17,000	$ 8,000
Potential loss from Monica's deficit (split 3:2)	5,000	(3,000)	(2,000)
Minimum Cash Distributions	$ -	$ 14,000	$ 6,000

9. A

Answers to Brief Essay Question

1. The four types of transactions that must be recorded in regard to the termination and liquidation of a partnership are:

A. The conversion of partnership assets into cash.
B. The allocation of the resulting gains and losses.
C. The payment of liabilities and expenses.
D. The distribution of any remaining assets to the partners based on their final capital balances.

Solutions to Problems

1. A.

ABC Partnership
Schedule of Liquidation
May 15, 2011

	Cash	Other Assets	Liabilities	A, Capital	B, Capital	C, Capital
	10,000	130,000	60,000	30,000	40,000	10,000
Inventory Sold	20,000	(50,000)		(18,000)	(9,000)	(3,000)
	30,000	80,000	60,000	12,000	31,000	7,000
PP&E Sold	60,000	(80,000)		(12,000)	(6,000)	(2,000)
	90,000	-	60,000	-	25,000	5,000
Creditors Paid	(60,000)		(60,000)			
	30,000	-	-	-	25,000	5,000
Cash Distributed	(30,000)				(25,000)	(5,000)
	-	-	-	-	-	-

B.

	Cash	Other Assets	Liabilities	A, Capital	B, Capital	C, Capital
	10,000	130,000	60,000	30,000	40,000	10,000
Inventory Sold	5,000	(50,000)		(27,000)	(13,500)	(4,500)
	15,000	80,000	60,000	3,000	26,500	5,500
PP&E Sold	50,000	(80,000)		(18,000)	(9,000)	(3,000)
	65,000	-	60,000	(15,000)	17,500	2,500
A's deficit (3:1)				15,000	(11,250)	(3,750)
	65,000	-	60,000	-	6,250	(1,250)
C's deficit					(1,250)	1,250
	65,000	-	60,000	-	5,000	-
Creditors Paid	(60,000)		(60,000)			
	5,000	-	-	-	5,000	-
Cash Distributed	(5,000)				(5,000)	
	-	-	-	-	-	-

2.

Richards, Kidd, Brown, and Marley Partnership
Predistribution Plan
March 31, 2011

	Richards	Kidd	Brown	Marley
Beginning Balances	$ 50,000	$ 45,000	$ 36,000	$ 24,000
Assumed loss of $125,000 (see Sch. 1; allocated 4:3:2:1)	(50,000)	(37,500)	(25,000)	(12,500)
Step one balances	$ -	$ 7,500	$ 11,000	$ 11,500
Assumed loss of $15,000 (see Sch. 2; allocated 3:2:1)		(7,500)	(5,000)	(2,500)
Step two balances		$ -	$ 6,000	$ 9,000
Assumed loss of $9,000 (see Sch. 3; allocated 2:1)			(6,000)	(3,000)
Step three balances			$ -	$ 6,000

Schedule 1

Partner	Capital Balance/Loss Allocation			Maximum Loss That Can Be Absorbed
Richards	$	50,000 ÷	40%	$125,000
Kidd	$	45,000 ÷	30%	$150,000
Brown	$	36,000 ÷	20%	$180,000
Marley	$	24,000 ÷	10%	$240,000

Schedule 2

Partner	Capital Balance/Loss Allocation			Maximum Loss That Can Be Absorbed
Kidd	$	7,500 ÷	50%	$15,000
Brown	$	11,000 ÷	33%	$33,000
Marley	$	11,500 ÷	17%	$69,000

Schedule 3

Partner	Capital Balance/Loss Allocation			Maximum Loss That Can Be Absorbed
Brown	$	6,000 ÷	67%	$9,000
Marley	$	9,000 ÷	33%	$27,000

The summary of the plan for distributing cash is created by backwards through the predistribution plan schedule created earlier. If there are known creditors, the amounts due them may be shown as the first debts to be paid.

Predistribution Plan

	Richards		Kidd		Brown		Marley
First $6,000	$ -	$	-	$	-	$	6,000
Next $9,000			-		6,000		3,000
Next $15,000	$ -	$	7,500	$	5,000	$	2,500

All further cash will be distributed according to the original profit and loss percentages

Chapter 16

Accounting for State and Local Governments (Part I)

Chapter Outline

Standards Mentioned in This Chapter:
- **GASB Concepts Statement No. 1,** *Objectives of Financial Reporting*
- **GASB Statement No. 33,** *Accounting and Financial Reporting for Nonexchange Transactions*
- **GASB Statement No. 34,** *Basic Financial Statements and Management's Discussion and Analysis for State and Local Governments*
- **GASB Statement No. 54,** *Fund Balance Reporting and Governmental Fund Type Definitions*

I. *LO1* **Introduction to Governmental Accounting**

   A. **Generally Accepted Accounting Principles for State and Local Governments**

      1. Prior to 1984, the AICPA and the National Council on Governmental Accounting established governmental accounting standards.

      2. Since 1984, the *Governmental Accounting Standards Board* (GASB) has set governmental accounting standards.

   B. **Governmental Accounting – User Needs** – There are three primary user groups of governmental accounting information:

      1. Citizenry.

      2. Legislative and oversight bodies.

      3. Investors and creditors.

   C. *LO2* **Two Sets of Financial Statements** –required to satisfy the broad demands of users.

      1. **Fund-based financial statements**

         a. These statements report individual activities and the amount of financial resources allocated to them each period and the use of those resources.

         b. The statements help citizens assess the government's fiscal accountability in raising and utilizing money.

         c. Primary measurement focus –the flow and amount of *current financial resources*, such as cash and receivables.

            (1) *Current financial resources* are resources that will be received soon enough in the future to be used in paying for current period expenditures.

            (2) Determining what is "soon enough" is up to the reporting government.

    d. Timing of recognition – in most cases based on *modified accrual accounting*, recognizing:

        (1) Revenues when the resulting current financial resources are measurable and available to be used, and

        (2) Expenditures when they cause a reduction in current financial resources.

2. **Government-wide financial statements** report a government's financial affairs as a whole.

    a. Measurement focus – all economic resources (not just current financial resources).

    b. Timing recognition – accrual accounting.

    c. These statements show *all* revenues and *all* costs of providing services each year as well as *all* assets and liabilities (comparable to business accounting).

D. **The Need for Two Sets of Financial Statements**

1. *GASB 34* expands the objective of governmental accounting to providing both fiscal and operational accountability.

2. Governmental financial statements attempt to answer three questions:

    a. Where did the financial resources come from?

    b. Where did the financial resources go?

    c. What amount of financial resources is presently held?

3. With two sets of financial statements, each user can select the most relevant information for their needs.

4. Summary of differences discussed:

	Fund-based Financial Statements (public service activity funds)	**Government-wide Financial Statements**
Emphasis	Individual activities (in current period)	Government as a whole
Measurement focus	Current financial resources (cash, investments, and receivables and claims to those assets)	All economic resources (all assets and liabilities)
General information	Inflows and outflows of current financial resources	Overall financial health
Timing of recognition	Modified accrual accounting	Accrual accounting

E. **LO3 Internal Record Keeping – Fund Accounting**

1. Fund accounting is used by state and local governments.

2. Each activity is monitored in a separate reporting unit called a *fund*.

   a. Each fund is a self-balancing set of accounts that is used to record data generated by an identifiable governmental function.

   b. All of the funds taken together make up the government's financial reporting system.

   c. Accounting for an entity as a group of funds may be the most unique element of not-for-profit accounting.

3. **LO4 Fund Accounting Classifications**

   a. **Governmental Funds** – These funds are used to account for the activities of a government that are carried out primarily to provide services to citizens, and that are financed primarily through taxes.

Governmental Funds	Account for and Report:
General Fund	All financial resources not in another fund. The general fund accounts for many of a government's most important services, which may include general government, public safety, social services, education, library, streets and highways, and sanitation.
Special Revenue Funds	Resource inflows that are restricted or committed for a specific purpose other than debt payments or capital projects. The legal or donor restrictions limit expenditures to specific operating purposes.
Capital Projects Funds	Financial resources restricted, committed, or assigned to cover costs in acquiring or constructing government facilities such as bridges, high schools, roads or buildings. Note that the asset being obtained is not reported here – just the money to finance the purchase or construction.
Debt Service Funds	Financial resources accumulated to pay long-term liabilities and interest as they come due, but not the long-term debt itself.
Permanent Funds	Financial resources restricted by an external donor, contract or legislation with the stipulation that the principal cannot be spent, but income can be used by the government, often for a designated purpose.

b. **Proprietary Funds** – These funds are used to account for government activities that charge users for their services and are similar to businesses.

Proprietary Funds	Account for and Report:
Enterprise Funds	Government operations open to the public and financed, at least in part, by a user charge. Examples: sewer and water services, public facilities, airports. Any activity charging a user fee *may* be classified as an enterprise fund, however, if the activity meets any *one* of the following, it *must* be designated as an enterprise fund: • The activity generates net revenues that provide the sole security for the debts of the activity. • Laws or regulations require recovering the activity's costs (including depreciation and debt service) through fees or charges.
Internal Service Funds	Operations that provide service to other units within the government on a cost-reimbursement basis.

c. **Fiduciary Funds** – These funds account for monies held by the government in a trustee capacity and are held for external parties.

Fiduciary Funds	Account for and Report:
Investment Trust Funds	The outside portion of investment pools when the reporting government has accepted funds from other governments in order to have more money to invest, and hopefully earn a higher return.
Private Purpose Trust Funds	Monies held in a trustee capacity when both the principal and interest are for the benefit of external parties such as individuals, private organizations, or other governments. Usually unclaimed property is recorded here.
Pension Trust Funds	Employee retirement systems.
Agency Funds	Resources a government holds as an agent for individuals, private organizations, or other government units. This fund maintains the money until it is transferred to the proper authority.

II. *LO5* **Overview – Government-wide Financial Statements** – there are only two government-wide financial statements

A. **Statement of Net Assets**

1. Uses separate columns for information related to governmental activities and for business-type activities (Proprietary Funds).

2. Due to the *economic resources* focus, *all* assets and liabilities are reported in three sections:

    a. Assets

    b. Liabilities

    c. Net Assets – this section indicates:

        (1)   The amount of capital assets less related debt,
        (2)   Restrictions on any net assets, and
        (3)   The total amount of unrestricted net assets.

B. **Statement of Activities** – reading across the statement, one sees direct expenses and program revenues for each government function.

1. It uses columns for Expenses, Revenues, Net (Expense) Revenue from Governmental Activities, and Net (Expense) Revenue from Business-Type Activities.

2. It includes three basic sections (reading down the statement):

    a. *Governmental Activities* – lists the revenues and expenses for each different fund.

    b. *Business-Type Activities* – lists the revenues and expenses for each different fund.

    c. *General Revenues* – records revenues not related to a specific fund (for example property taxes, interest, or grants).

III. Overview – Fund-Based Financial Statements

A. A number of fund based statements are produced, but only the two fundamental statements that most parallel the government-wide statements are examined at this point – the balance sheet and statement of revenues, expenditures and changes in fund balance.

1. The totals are not the same as shown on the government-wide statements.

2. Primary reasons for differences:

    a. *Grouping* – In government-wide statements, internal service funds are grouped with the funds they primarily benefit. In the fund based statements they are reported as proprietary funds, so the totals are different due to the different grouping.

    b. *Measurement focus* – Government-wide statements use the economic resources measurement focus whereas fund-based statements use the current financial resources measurement focus. Thus, different assets and liabilities are being reported.

    c. *Timing of recognition* – Government-wide statements use accrual accounting while fund-based statements use modified accrual accounting.

3. Because of these differences, reconciliations of the totals from the two different types of statements are reported (Chapter 17).

B. **Balance Sheet**

1. Includes columns for each major fund.

2. Includes three basic sections:

   a. Assets

   b. Liabilities

   c. Fund Balances

C. **Statement of Revenues, Expenditures, and Changes in Fund Balance**

1. Includes columns for each major fund.

2. Includes three basic sections, discussed later:

   a. Revenues

   b. Expenditures

   c. Other Financing Sources (uses)

D. **Fund Balances**

1. The balance sheets of governmental entities do not need a stockholders' equity section like for-profit businesses. Instead, it shows the "fund balance", which is the assets minus liabilities, or the net current financial resources at the time.

2. In February 2009, the GASB issued Statement No. 54, "*Fund Balance Reporting and Governmental Fund Type Definitions*" to standardize the reporting of the fund balance within five categories.

3. The purpose of the fund balance classifications is to show the *availability* of the net assets.

4. Summary of classifications:

Classification	Assets included in the category
Fund-balance – nonspendable	Assets that cannot be spent by government officials. 1. Some assets such as supplies and prepaid expenses are not in a spendable form. 2. Financial resources, for example a gift, may have externally imposed limitations.
Fund-balance – restricted	Assets held that must be spent in a manner designated by an external party.
Fund-balance – committed	Assets designated for a particular purpose by the highest level of decision-making authority in the governmental unit.

Classification	Assets included in the category
Fund-balance – assigned	Assets designated for a specific purpose without formal action by the highest level of decision-making authority. This is an internal designation and can be changed.
Fund-balance – unassigned	The net assets with no designated use. This money is available to government officials for any appropriate purpose.

5. This classification system must be used in state and local government financial statements for periods beginning after June 15, 2010.

IV. *LO6* Accounting for Governmental Funds

A. The Importance of Budgets and the Recording of Budgetary Entries

1. The budget enhances accountability and serves several important purposes:

   a. Expresses public policy.

   b. Serves as an expression of financial intent for the upcoming fiscal year.

   c. Provides control by establishing spending limitations for each activity.

   d. Offers a means of evaluating performance by comparing actual results to budget.

2. Fund-based Financial Statements – the budgetary entry records the budget for each fund with a debit to *Estimated Revenues* and credits to various *Appropriations* accounts.

Estimated Revenues	xxxx	
Appropriations – Salaries		xxxx
Appropriations – Utilities		xxxx
Appropriations – Other		xxxx

3. On occasion, original budget entries are adjusted for appropriations that have been modified.

4. These entries serve as controls during the period and are closed out at the end of the period.

B. Encumbrances

1. *Encumbrances* are financial commitments such as purchase commitments, contracts, or orders for goods. They are recorded in the funds before becoming legal liabilities.

2. Fund-based Financial Statements – entry to show an encumbrance (commitment):

Encumbrances Control	xxxx	
Fund Balance – Reserved for Encumbrances		xxxx

3. When the goods are received, or the services are performed, the entry is reversed and *replaced* by a legal liability. Note that the encumbrance amount and the liability amount may differ due to sales tax, freight or other adjustments.

Fund Balance – Reserved for Encumbrances	xxxx	
Encumbrances Control		xxx

Inventory, Supplies, etc	xxxx	
Voucher Payable		xxx

4. **Encumbrances at year-end** –

    a. GASB Statement No. 54, "*Fund Balance Reporting and Governmental Fund Type Definitions*" changed the handling of encumbrances at year-end.

    b. Any commitments that remain outstanding at year-end are removed from the accounting records by reversing the original entry. This is done because no transaction has occurred, and encumbrances are recorded to help prevent spending funds greater than the amount authorized for the period.

    c. If the fund balance has already been reclassified as restricted, committed, or assigned due to this eventual expenditure no further change is needed.

    d. However, if no fund balance has been reclassified as restricted, committed, or assigned, the amount of the encumbrance should be reclassified as either committed or assigned to show the anticipated use of the fund's assets.

C. *LO7* **Recognition of Expenditures for Operations and Capital Additions**

1. Because the emphasis in the funds is on measuring changes in *current financial resources, neither expenses nor capital assets are recorded in the fund-based financial statements*. This is likely the greatest distinction between fund-based statements and government-wide statements.

2. Outflows or other reductions of resources are recorded as expenditures.

3. **Operations** – When the government makes expenditures, expenses are **not** recorded. All expenditures are debited to an *Expenditures* account.

Expenditures – Salaries	xxxx	
Voucher Payable		xxx

4. **Capital Additions** – When the government makes capital acquisitions, fixed assets are **not** recorded. All expenditures are debited to an *Expenditures* account.

Expenditures – Building	xxxx	
Voucher Payable		xxxx

5. **Supplies and Prepaid Items** – Two methods are used for recording transactions, however, the reporting in the statements is the same.

       a.   **Purchases Method** – reflects modified accrual accounting.

          (1)   Initially records the cost as an expenditure.

          (2)   Unused supplies or unexpired prepaid items are debited to an asset account just prior to financial statement production. An offsetting amount is credited to an account such as *Fund Balance Reserved for Inventory of Supplies* (or *Prepaid Items*).

          (3)   Governments have traditionally used this method.

       b.   **Consumption Method** – parallels government-wide financial statements.

          (1)   Initially records the cost as an asset.

          (2)   As items are consumed, they are moved to an expenditure account.

          (3)   Because these assets cannot be spent, a portion of the Fund Balance account should be reclassified as reserved.

  6.   Virtually no assets other than current financial resources such as cash, receivables, and investments are reported.

  7.   All capital assets are recorded as expenditures when purchased or constructed, and the balance is closed out at the end of the fiscal period.

  8.   Consistent with this approach, depreciation is not recorded in government funds.

D.   *LO8* **Recognition of Revenues – Overview**

  1.   For most revenues, such as property taxes, income taxes and grants, there is no associated earning process similar to a for-profit business.

  2.   GASB Statement Number 33, *Accounting and Financial Reporting for Nonexchange Transactions*, provides a comprehensive system for recognizing many of the revenues of state and local government units.

  3.   *Nonexchange transactions* occur when the government either gives value (benefit) to another party without directly receiving equal value in exchange, or receives value (benefit) from another party without directly giving equal value in exchange.

  4.   Classification of *nonexchange transactions*:

       a.   *Derived tax revenues* – a tax is assessed or imposed when an underlying exchange takes place.

          (1)   Sales tax is assessed when a sale takes place.

          (2)   Income tax is assessed when income is earned.

       b.   *Imposed nonexchange revenues* – a tax is assessed with no underlying transaction.

          (1)   Property tax is taxed on ownership, not on a transaction.

          (2)   Fines and penalties.

c. *Government-mandated nonexchange transactions –*

    (1) A governmental unit mandates the conveyance of funds from one government to another.

    (2) Grants conveyed from one government to another to help cover the costs of *required* programs.

d. *Voluntary nonexchange transactions –*

    (1) Money is conveyed willingly to a government by an individual, another government or an organization, usually for a particular purpose.

    (2) Voluntary grants conveyed from one government to another to help cover the costs of *desired* programs.

E. Accounting for Nonexchange Transactions – Fund-based Statements

1. **Derived Revenues** such as income taxes and sales taxes are recognized when the resources become available for use. Because the resource must be available before the revenue can be recognized, a resource to be received during the year or soon after, or cash, must be in-hand to record the entry.

Cash (or Receivable)	xxxx	
Revenues – Taxes		xxxx

2. **Imposed Nonexchange Revenues** such as property taxes and fines are recorded as soon as the government has an *enforceable claim,* unless some portion of the future cash collection will not be available this period. Because property taxes are such a significant source of revenue, a specific 60-day period for recognition has been standardized.

Property Tax Receivable	xxxx	
Allowance for Uncollectible Amounts		xxxx
Revenues		xxxx

3. **Government-Mandated Nonexchange Transactions** and **Voluntary Nonexchange Transactions** including such items as grants or donations must be *available* for revenue recognition. Record a debit to *Cash* and a credit to *Revenues*.

Cash	xxxx	
Revenues – Grants		xxxx

F. *LO9* **Issuance of Bonds – Fund-based Statements**

1. Bonds serve as an important source of funds for government.

2. No revenues are recognized because the bond proceeds must be repaid. To emphasize that the inflow of money is not revenue, bond proceeds are recorded as *Other Financing Sources – Bond Proceeds*.

Cash	xxxx	
Other Financing Sources – Bond Proceeds		xxxx

G. Payment of Long-Term Liabilities – Fund-based Statements

1. Expenditure accounts are used to record the payment of the principal and interest (often paid for and recorded in a Debt Service Fund).

Expenditure-Bond principal	xxxx	
Expenditure-Interest	xxxx	
Cash		xxxx

H. Tax Anticipation Notes – Fund-based Statements

1. State and local governments often issue short-term debt referred to as *tax anticipation notes* to provide financing until taxes are collected.

2. As short-term liabilities, they are a claim on current financial resources and thus are recorded as a liability (in the same manner as in the government-wide statements).

Cash	xxxx	
Tax Anticipation Note Payable		xxxx

3. The liability is debited when payments are made. The interest is recorded as an expenditure when paid.

Tax Anticipation Note Payable	xxxx	
Expenditure-Interest	xxxx	
Cash		xxxx

I. Special assessments – Fund-based Statements

1. State and local governments occasionally provide improvements that directly benefit a particular property, such as sidewalks, paving streets, and water and sewage services. The government then assesses the costs to the owner.

2. The government usually issues debt and may place a lien on the property being improved to ensure reimbursement.

3. Neither the infrastructure nor the long-term debt is recorded in fund-based statements because the current financial resources measurement basis is used.

4. Upon payment, the liability is debited and interest is debited as an expenditure.

5. Example of journal entries for a special assessments project:

Capital Projects Fund

Cash	xxxx	
Other Financing Sources - Bond Proceeds		xxxx
To record resources provided by the bond issuance		

Expenditures - Special Assessment	xxxx	
Cash		xxxx
To record payment for the cost of the project		

Debt Service Fund

Taxes Receivable - Special Assessment	xxxx	
Revenue - Special Assessment		xxxx

To record the assessment to be used to pay the related debt

Cash	xxxx	
Taxes Receivable - Special Assessment		xxxx

To record the collection of the assessment by citizens,
to be used to extinguish the related debt

Expenditure - Special Assessment Bond	xxxx	
Expenditure - Interest	xxxx	
Cash		xxxx

To record payment of the bonds and interest

J. *LO10* **Interfund Transactions – Fund-based Statements**

1. It is important to keep track of transfers of cash between various funds.

2. Two types of transfers occur:

   a. *Intra-activity transactions* – occur between two governmental funds, or between two enterprise funds.

   b. *Interactivity transactions* – occur between governmental funds and enterprise funds.

3. An intra-activity transaction requires two entries – one entry to record the transfer from one account and an entry to record the receipt of the transfer by the other account.

   General Fund

Other Financing Uses - Transfer Out - Capital Projects Fund	xxxx	
Due to Capital Projects Fund		xxxx

   Capital Projects Fund

Due from General Fund	xxxx	
Other Financing Sources - Transfers in - General Fund		xxxx

4. An interactivity transaction also requires two entries – one entry to record the transfer from, for example, the general fund to an enterprise fund to help fund a subway system.

   General Fund

Other Financing Uses - Transfer Out - Subway System	xxxx	
Cash		xxxx

   Enterprise Fund

Cash	xxxx	
Capital Contributions		xxxx

5. *Internal exchanges*, for example, a city's payment to its own Enterprise Fund or Internal Service Fund for services or materials is equivalent to a transaction with an outside party. Thus, expenditures and revenues are recorded by the appropriate fund.

V. Accounting for Government-Wide Financial Statements

A. Budgets – budgetary entries are not made for the government-wide financial statements, which are more like for-profit financial statements.

B. Encumbrances

1. Encumbrances are not recorded for Government-Wide Financial Statements, because no liability has been incurred yet.

2. When the goods are received, or the services are performed for the government, a legal liability is recorded.

Inventory, Supplies, etc	xxxx	
Voucher Payable		xxxx

C. Recognition of Expenditures

1. **Operations** – When the government makes expenditures, expenses are recorded, just as in a business-type organization.

Salaries Expense	xxxx	
Voucher Payable		xxxx

2. **Capital Additions** – when the government makes capital acquisitions, capital (fixed) assets are recorded, just as in a business-type organization.

a. Newly acquired infrastructure items are capitalized (for fiscal years ending after June 30, 1980).

b. The book value of any infrastructure items acquired prior to the establishment of government-wide financial statements should also be approximated and capitalized. This is required for major general infrastructure assets acquired or significantly improved since June 30, 1980.

D. Recognition of Revenues – Overview – Government-Wide Financial Statements

1. **Derived Revenues** such as income taxes and sales taxes are recognized when the underlying transaction occurs. Thus, income tax revenue is recorded when a taxpayer earns income. Similarly, sales tax revenue is recognized when sales are made.

Accounts Receivable – Taxes	xxxx	
Revenues – Taxes		xxxx

2. **Imposed Nonexchange Revenues** are items such as property taxes and fines.

   a. The receivable is recorded as soon as the government has an enforceable claim.

   b. The revenue should be recognized when the resulting resources are required to be used or in the first period in which use is permitted.

   c. If there is a timing difference between the receivable and the recognition of the revenue, deferred revenue is recorded.

3. **Government-Mandated Nonexchange Transactions** and **Voluntary Nonexchange Transactions** such items as grants or donations are recognized at the time all eligibility requirements are met. General classifications of eligibility requirements:

   a. Required characteristics of the recipients.

   b. Time requirements.

   c. Reimbursement.

   d. Contingencies.

E. *LO9* **Issuance of Bonds – Government-Wide Financial Statements**

   1. Bonds serve as an important source of funds for government.

   2. Record just as with a business-type organization.

Cash	xxxx	
Bonds Payable		xxxx

F. **Tax Anticipation Notes – Government-Wide Financial Statements**

   1. The initial recording is the same as in the fund-based financial statements.

Cash	xxxx	
Tax Anticipation Note Payable		xxxx

   2. The liability and the related interest expense are debited when payments are made.

Tax Anticipation Note Payable	xxxx	
Interest Expense	xxxx	
Cash		xxxx

G. **Special Assessments – Government-Wide Financial Statements** – Debt and the subsequent construction are recorded in the same manner as a for-profit business.

H. **Interfund Transfers – Government-Wide Financial Statements**

   1. *Intra-activity transactions* are not recorded for government-wide financial statements as they occur solely within the governmental or business-type activities.

2. *Interactivity* transactions are recorded.

3. An *interactivity transaction* requires two entries – one entry to record the transfer from, for example, the general fund to an enterprise fund to help fund a subway system.

Governmental Activities

Transfers Out - Subway System	xxxx	
Cash		xxxx

Business-Type Activities

Cash	xxxx	
Transfers In - General Fund		xxxx

4. *Internal Exchange Transactions* – because Internal Service Funds are usually reported as governmental activities in the government-wide financial statements, these exchanges normally have no net impact on overall figures and should be omitted.

Multiple Choice Questions

1. Which of the following is **not** considered part of the primary group of users of governmental accounting information?

   A. Citizens
   B. Management
   C. Legislature
   D. Governmental Oversight Groups
   E. Creditors

2. A fund is:

   A. A term used for money collected and spent by a governmental unit.
   B. An account used to accumulate donations by non-profit groups.
   C. A self-balancing set of accounts used to record data generated by an identifiable governmental unit.
   D. Not used when preparing government-wide financial statements.
   E. Not used when preparing fund-based financial statements.

3. Which of the following group of funds uses the *current financial resources measurement focus* for the fund-based financial statements?

   A. Donated Funds
   B. Proprietary Funds
   C. Fiduciary Funds
   D. Charitable Funds
   E. Governmental Funds

4. Which of the following statements would show an account called *Expenditures*?

   A. Fund-Based Balance Sheet
   B. Fund-Based Statement of Revenues, Expenditures, and Changes in Fund Balance.
   C. Government-Wide Statement of Net Assets
   D. Government-Wide Statement of Activities
   E. Government-Wide Statement of Revenues, Expenditures and Changes in Fund Balance.

5. Which of the following statements would show an account called *Expenses*?

   A. Fund-Based Balance Sheet
   B. Fund-Based Statement of Revenues, Expenditures, and Changes in Fund Balance.
   C. Government-Wide Statement of Net Assets
   D. Government-Wide Statement of Activities
   E. Government-Wide Statement of Revenues, Expenditures and Changes in Fund Balance.

6. When preparing fund-based financial statements, what account should be debited when office supplies are ordered?

   A. Expenditures
   B. Vouchers Payable
   C. Fund Balance
   D. Encumbrances
   E. Appropriations

7. When preparing fund-based financial statements, what account should be debited when office equipment is purchased?

   A. Expenditures
   B. Vouchers Payable
   C. Fund Balance
   D. Encumbrances
   E. Appropriations

8. Property taxes are classified as what kind of revenues?

   A. Derived Revenues
   B. Imposed Nonexchange Revenues
   C. Voluntary Nonexchange Transactions
   D. Government-Mandated Nonexchange Transactions
   E. Earned Revenues

9. Federal grants for road construction are classified as what kind of revenues?

   A. Derived Revenues
   B. Imposed Nonexchange Revenues
   C. Voluntary Nonexchange Transactions
   D. Government-Mandated Nonexchange Transactions
   E. Earned Revenues

10. Which type of funds are **not** included in government-wide financial statements?

    A.   Donated Funds
    B.   Proprietary Funds
    C.   Fiduciary Funds
    D.   Charitable Funds
    E.   Governmental Funds

Brief Essay Questions

1. The following balances were included in the subsidiary records of Dartwell Village's Parks and Recreation Department at March 31, 2011:

Appropriations – Supplies	$ 125,000
Expenditures – Supplies	86,000
Encumbrances – Supply Orders	24,250

How much does the department have available for additional purchases of supplies?

2. Identify the three basic fund groups and the individual funds that are usually found in each group.

3. Are encumbrances recorded in the accounting process used to prepare government-wide financial statements? Why?

Problems

1. Examine the following 2011 transactions for Dwelling Township's General Fund.

    a.   On July 1, 2011, the city council approves the budget for the General Fund. Included in this budget is $4,900,000 in anticipated property taxes, $32,000,000 in anticipated sales tax revenues, $3,000,000 for utilities, $12,000,000 for salaries and wages, $1,400,000 for rent, 5,600,000 for administrative expenses, and $14,900,000 for capital improvements.

    b.   On July 5, the purchasing office orders $42,000 of office supplies.

    c.   On July 7, a cash transfer of $300,000 is made to the Public School Superintendent's office for a new roof on the town high school. The project will begin on August 1.

    d.   On July 12, $600,000 of computer equipment is purchased with payment due in 30 days. The computers will have an estimated useful life of 3 years.

    e.   On July 15, the office supplies ordered on July 7 arrive. The bill is for $43,700 and it is due in 30 days. The supplies are not considered assets, but are treated just the same as utilities.

    f.   On July 20, property tax bills totaling $5,200,000 are mailed to city residents.

    g.   On July 25, $78,000 in property tax payments are received by the city tax assessor's office.

    h.   On July 30, the city receives a payment from the state revenue office for June's sales taxes collections. The check is for $3,400,000.

Required:

Assume you are going to prepare fund-based financial statements. Prepare all the journal entries for the above transactions and events.

2.   Use the information for Problem 1.

   Required:

   Assume you are going to prepare government-wide financial statements. Prepare all the journal entries for the above transactions and events.

Answers to Multiple Choice Questions

1.   B

2.   C

3.   E

4.   B

5.   D

6.   D

7.   A

8.   B

9.   D

10. C

Answers to Brief Essay Questions

1.   The Recreation Department has $14,750 available for the purchase of supplies. Approved expenditures (appropriations) were $125,000. However, $86,000 of this amount has already been spent and an additional $24,250 is committed. Therefore, the available spending authority for supplies is equal to *Appropriations – (Expenditures + Outstanding Encumbrances).*

2.   The three groups of funds are *Governmental Funds, Proprietary Funds* (Business-Type), and *Fiduciary Funds.*

   General Funds include the General Fund, Special Revenue Funds, Capital Projects Funds, Debt Service Funds, and Permanent Funds.

   Proprietary Funds include Enterprise Funds and Internal Service Funds.

   Fiduciary Funds include Pension Trust Funds, Investment Trust Funds, Private-Purpose Funds, and Agency Funds.

3. Government-Wide Financial Statements are prepared primarily using accrual accounting principles. Implied in that approach is the traditional prohibition against recording commitments or contracts. Since Encumbrances are exactly that; commitments and contracts; they are not recorded for Government-Wide Financial Statements.

Solutions to Problems

1. The journal entries for the fund-based financial statements are as follows:

Date	Accounts	Debit	Credit
07/01/11	Estimated revenues - Property Taxes	4,900,000	
	Estimated revenues - Sales Taxes	32,000,000	
	Appropriations - Utilities		3,000,000
	Appropriations - Salaries		12,000,000
	Appropriations - Rent		1,400,000
	Appropriations - Administrative Expenses		5,600,000
	Appropriations - Capital Improvements		14,900,000
07/05/11	Encumbrances Control	42,000	
	Fund Balance - Reserve for Encumbrances		42,000
07/07/11	Other Financing Uses - Transfer to Capital Projects Fund	300,000	
	Cash		300,000
07/12/11	Expenditures - Computers	600,000	
	Cash		600,000
07/15/11	Fund Balance - Reserve for Encumbrances	42,000	
	Encumbrances Control		42,000
	Expenditures - Office Supplies	43,700	
	Voucher Payable		43,700
07/20/11	No entry until resources are available.		
07/25/11	Cash	78,000	
	Revenues - Property Taxes		78,000
07/30/11	Cash	3,400,000	
	Revenues - Sales Taxes		3,400,000

2. The journal entries for the government-wide financial statements are as follows:

Date	Accounts	Debit	Credit
07/01/11	Estimated revenues - Property Taxes	4,900,000	
	Estimated revenues - Sales Taxes	32,000,000	
	Appropriations - Utilities		3,000,000
	Appropriations - Salaries		12,000,000
	Appropriations - Rent		1,400,000
	Appropriations - Administrative Expenses		5,600,000
	Appropriations - Capital Improvements		14,900,000
07/05/11	No entry when preparing government-wide financial statements.		
07/07/09	No entry when preparing government-wide financial statements. Transfers are treated as simple internal transfers of cash.		
07/12/11	Computers	600,000	
	Cash		600,000
07/15/11	Office Supplies Expense	43,700	
	Voucher Payable		43,700
07/20/11	Receivables - Property Taxes	5,200,000	
	Revenues - Property Taxes		5,200,000
07/25/11	Cash	78,000	
	Receivables - Property Taxes		78,000
07/30/11	Cash	3,400,000	
	Revenues - Sales Taxes		3,400,000

Chapter 17

Accounting for State and Local Governments (Part II)

Chapter Outline

Standards Mentioned in This Chapter:
- **GASB Concepts Statement No. 1,** *Objectives of Financial Reporting*
- **GASB Statement No. 14,** *The Financial Reporting Entity*
- **GASB Statement No. 34,** *Basic Financial Statements and Management's Discussion and Analysis for State and Local Governments*
- **GASB Statement No. 35,** *Basic Financial Statements and Management's Discussion and Analysis for Public Colleges and Universities – An Amendment of GASB Statement No. 34*
- **SFAS No. 13,** *Accounting for Leases*
- **SFAS No. 116,** *Accounting for Contributions Received and Contributions Made*

I. *LO1* **Capital Leases**

    A.   If any *one* of the four criteria established in *SFAS 13* is met, the lease is held to be a capital lease. Otherwise, it is an operating lease. **Criteria**:

        1.   The lease *transfers ownership* of the property to the lessee by the end of the lease term.

        2.   The lease contains an option to purchase the leased property at a *bargain price*.

        3.   The *lease term* is equal to or greater than 75% of the estimated economic life of the leased property.

        4.   The *present value* of the rental or other *minimum lease payments* equals or exceeds 90% of the fair value of the leased property.

    B.   **Leases – Government-Wide Financial Statements**

        1.   Debit the asset account and credit the *Capital Lease Obligation* account for the present value of the minimum lease payments (as in for-profit businesses).

        2.   Thereafter, lease payments are recorded and broken down into Interest Expense and reduction of Capital Lease Obligation components.

        3.   If the leased item is a depreciable asset, depreciation is recorded over its life.

    C.   **Leases – Fund-Based Financial Statements**

        1.   *Proprietary funds* – accounting is the same as for government-wide statements.

        2.   *Government Funds* –

               a.   Generally, no asset or long-term liability is recorded at signing of the lease agreement. *Expenditures - Leased Asset* is debited, *Other Financing Source - Capital Lease* is credited.

        b.   Subsequent lease payments (for the interest and the reduction of the principal) are recorded as *Expenditures*.

        c.   Depreciation is ignored.

        d.   The fund-based journal entries may appear to be double counting the expenditures, but the accounting mirrors the accounting that would occur if the governmental entity had borrowed the funds to purchase the asset.

II.   *LO2* **Solid Waste Landfill**

    A.   Landfills require efforts to alleviate environmental contamination at the time the landfill is closed. Those costs must be initially estimated at the time the landfill is opened.

    B.   **Landfills – Government-Wide Financial Statements**

        1.   At the end of each period, an expense is recorded (along with a corresponding liability) to accrue a portion of the expected future cost of closing the landfill based on the percentage of the landfill that has been filled to date.

        2.   Any cash payments made in relation to the liability are recorded and charged against the liability.

    C.   **Landfills – Fund-Based Financial Statements**

        1.   *Enterprise Fund* – reporting is the same as in government-wide statements.

        2.   *General Fund* –

            a.   There is no periodic accrual of the expense.

            b.   Cash payments related to environmental clean-up costs are recorded as expenditures as they are incurred.

            c.   Despite the large future liability, it is considered too far in the future to warrant accounting.

III.   *LO2* **Compensated Absences** – In addition to regular wages and salaries, employees earn the right to take paid vacations and paid sick leave.

    A.   **Compensated Absences – Government-Wide Financial Statements**

        1.   Record an expense and a corresponding liability in the period that the compensated absences are accrued.

        2.   When the employees take the vacation or sick leave, reduce the liability and record the payment.

B. **Compensated Absences – Fund-Based Financial Statements**

    1. Record an entry in expenditures and a corresponding liability only for the compensated absences that are likely to be used by employees during the next period and that will be paid out of available resources.

    2. The remainder is not reported, as it is not a claim on current financial resources

    3. When the employees take the vacation or sick leave, reduce the liability and record the payment.

IV. *LO3* **Works of Art and Historical Treasures**

    A. State and local governments sometimes acquire works of art and historical treasures for display or research, rather than to generate revenue.

    B. *GASB 34* states "governments should capitalize works of art, historical treasures, and similar assets at their historical cost or fair value at the date of donation" except in certain specific cases.

    C. **Government-Wide Financial Statements – Acquisition of Historical Treasure**

        1. *Purchased asset* – the asset is recorded at its cost.

        2. *Donated asset* –

            a. Generally, the asset is recorded at its fair value and *Revenue from Donations* is credited.

                (1) The donation is viewed as a voluntary nonexchange transaction. Revenue is recognized when all eligibility requirements are met.

                (2) Until then a deferred revenue account is credited.

            b. However, when *three* conditions are met, the governmental unit may expense the item *immediately*, rather than capitalize the item. Those criteria are:

                (1) The asset must be held for public exhibition, education, or research in furtherance of public service, rather than financial gain.

                (2) The asset must be protected, kept unencumbered, cared for, and preserved.

                (3) The asset must be subject to an organizational policy that requires the proceeds from sales of collection items to be used to acquire other items for collections.

    D. **Fund-Based Financial Statements – Acquisition of Historical Treasure**

        1. *Purchased Asset* – the acquisition is recorded as an *Expenditure*.

        2. *Donated Asset* – no entry is made because *current* financial resources are unchanged.

V.　　*LO4* **Infrastructure Assets and Depreciation – Government-Wide Statements**

A.　　*Infrastructure Assets* – are long-lived capital assets that normally are stationary in nature and normally can be preserved for a significantly greater number of years than most capital assets (GASB 34).

B.　　Newly acquired infrastructure items are capitalized.

C.　　Many previously acquired infrastructure items acquired prior to the establishment of government-wide financial statements should also be capitalized.

　　　1.　　Those assets acquired in fiscal years ending after June 30, 1980, or

　　　2.　　Those assets that had major renovations, restorations, or improvements since June 30, 1980.

D.　　Governments tend to depreciate some of their infrastructure assets over extended periods such as 20 -100 years. The Brooklyn Bridge, for example, was constructed in 1883.

E.　　*Modified Approach* – if specific guidelines are met, *GASB 34* provides for the expensing of all maintenance in lieu of depreciation for assets that have a virtually unlimited life if maintained.

VI.　　*LO5* **Expanded Financial Reporting**

A.　　The GASB requires state and local governments to include a *Management Discussion and Analysis* (MD&A) document in their published financial statements. The MD&A is similar to the discussion found in the financial statements of publicly traded companies.

B.　　General purpose external financial statements of a state and local government are divided into three sections:

　　　1.　　Management's discussion and analysis

　　　2.　　Financial Statements

　　　　　a.　　Government-wide financial statements

　　　　　b.　　Fund-based financial statements

　　　　　c.　　Notes to the financial statements

　　　3.　　Required Supplemental Information

C.　　General purpose financial statements are presented to the public as part of a *comprehensive annual financial report* (CAFR).

D.   The CAFR of a state or local government must include three broad sections:

    1.   *Introductory Section* – includes a letter of transmittal from the appropriate government officials, an organization chart, and a list of principal officers.

    2.   *Financial Section* – presents the general purpose external financial statements, reproduces the auditor's report, and usually includes additional supplementary information.

    3.   *Statistical Section* – discloses a wide range of data about the government.

VII.   *LO6* **The Primary Government and Component Units**

A.   The *primary government* serves as the focus of a set of financial statements. All state and general-purpose local governments should be treated as primary governments.

B.   A *component unit* is a governmental unit which is legally separate but so closely connected to a primary government that omission from the statements of the primary government cannot be justified. A component unit must be included in the CAFR of the primary government if it meets either one of two criteria:

    1.   *Criterion 1* – fiscal dependency exists. This means the organization cannot do one or more of the following without the approval of the primary government: adopt its own budget, levy taxes or set rates, or issue bonded debt.

    2.   *Criterion 2* – first, the primary government appoints a voting majority of the governing board of the separate unit. Second, it can impose its will on the board, or the separate organization provides a financial benefit or imposes a financial burden on the primary government.

C.   **Reporting Component Units** – component units are reported in one of two ways:

    1.   *Discrete presentation* – reported at the far right side of the government-wide statements.

    2.   *Blended presentation* – component units are included as an actual part of the reporting primary government (included because the component unit, though legally separate, is highly intertwined with the primary government).

D.   **Special Purpose Governments**

    1.   Cities, counties, states, and the like are known as *general purpose governments*.

    2.   *Special purpose governments* carry out only a single function for the public, or a limited number of functions. Examples include a transit authority, a public school district, a college or university, utility, hospital, or library.

3. An activity or function qualifies as a special purpose government if it meets all three of the following criteria:

    a. Has a separately elected governing body.

    b. Is legally independent.

    c. Is fiscally independent of other state and local governments.

VIII. **LO7 Government-Wide and Fund-Based Financial Statements – Physical Structure**

A. The general-purpose financial statements are at the core of a CAFR. Government-wide statements present financial information for both governmental activities and business type activities. Fund-based statements separately present governmental funds, proprietary funds, and the fiduciary funds. Measurement and recognition depend upon the fund.

B. **Statement of Net Assets – Government-Wide Financial Statements**

1. This statement is designed to report the economic resources of the government as a whole (except fiduciary funds).

2. The measurement focus is the economic resources controlled by the government. Thus, all assets including capital assets are reported as well as long-term liabilities.

3. Capital assets are reported net of accumulated depreciation.

4. The primary government is divided into governmental activities and business-type activities (generally enterprise funds, but also internal service funds if they predominantly serve an enterprise fund).

5. Internal balances shown in the asset section come from receivables and payables between the governmental activities and business-type activities and are offset so that there is no net effect on the primary government totals.

6. Investments are reported at fair value.

7. These statements do not use the traditional GAAP accounting equation of assets = liabilities + stockholders' equity. Rather, on the government-wide statement, assets - liabilities = net assets.

8. Restricted net assets are shown if the usage of the assets has been specified by external parties or legislation.

C. **Statement of Activities – Government-Wide Financial Statements**

1. This statement presents a wide array of information with the same general classification of governmental activities, business-type activities and component units.

     Advanced Accounting – 10/e

2. Operating expenses are shown in the first column, classified by function rather than traditional accounts.

3. Interest expense on general long term debt is normally viewed as an indirect expense because it benefits many government operations, however, due to various factors, it is often shown as a separate "function".

4. *Program revenues* are revenues derived from the function, or from outsiders seeking to reduce the governments' cost for that function. They are classified as charges for services, operating grants and contributions, and capital grants and contributions.

5. Net revenue or expense is determined from each function's revenues and expense. This net figure is a measure of the financial cost or benefit of the function.

6. General revenues are reported as additions to either the governmental activities, business-type activities, or component unit. Taxes and other inflows such as the gain on sale of a capital asset are general revenues because they are obtained from the population as a whole vs. charges for service.

7. Transfers between governmental activities and business-type activities are also shown under the general revenues, but they offset each other, so there is no impact on the total primary government.

D. **Balance Sheet – Governmental Funds – Fund-Based Statements**

1. This statement measures only current financial resources and uses modified accrual accounting.

2. Only governmental funds are included. Proprietary funds, component units and fiduciary funds are not included.

3. Separate columns are shown for the General Fund and any other fund considered major within the governmental funds. The government can classify any fund as major if it believes it is important to statement users. However (chapter 16), a fund is considered major and therefore must be reported separately if it meets 2 criteria:

   a. Total assets, liabilities, revenues or expenses/expenditures of the fund are at least 10% of the corresponding total for all such funds.

   b. Total assets, liabilities, revenues or expenses/expenditures of the fund are at least 5% of the corresponding total of all governmental and enterprise funds combined.

4. Internal balances such as "due from other funds" and "due to other funds" are not offset.

5. The Fund Balance figures should reflect the nonspendable, restricted, committed, assigned, and unassigned categories (chapter 16).

E. Statement of Revenues, Expenditures, and Changes in Fund Balances – Governmental Funds – Fund-Based Statements

1. The General Fund and each of the major funds are shown in separate columns. Figures for all remaining nonmajor funds are then combined and shown together.

2. Because of the current financial resources measurement focus, expenditures (not expenses) are reported.

3. The modified accrual method of accounting is used.

4. No elimination of transfers between funds is made.

5. A reconciliation should be shown between the ending change in governmental fund balances and the ending change in net assets for governmental activities.

F. Statement of Net Assets – Proprietary Funds – Fund-Based Statements

1. Separate columns are shown for major enterprise funds and a single column is shown for the summation of all other enterprise funds.

2. Internal service funds are combined and exhibited.

3. Restricted cash and investments are listed under noncurrent assets when an external source or legislation has designated the use of the cash.

4. Amounts owed in connection with accrued compensated absences, liability for landfill closure and capital lease obligations are reported as current or noncurrent liabilities.

G. Statement of Revenues, Expenditures, and Changes in Fund Balances – Proprietary Funds – Fund-Based Statements

1. This statement provides more detail about the revenue and expenses for the proprietary funds.

2. Because this statement reflects all changes in the net assets of each activity, capital contributions as well as transfers in and out and special items are included at the bottom of the statement.

H. Statement of Cash Flows – Proprietary Funds – Fund-Based Statements

1. This statement is considered as important as the cash flow statement for businesses.

2. Unlike the statement for for-profit businesses, the proprietary fund statement of cash flows has four sections versus three:

   a. Cash flows from operating activities.

   b. Cash flows from noncapital financing activities.

     c.   Cash flows from capital and related financing activities.

     d.   Cash flows from investing activities.

  3.   Unlike for-profit businesses, the *direct method* is required. Most businesses use the indirect method.

IX.   *LO8* Reporting Public Colleges and Universities

  A.   Financial reporting for public colleges and universities is guided by *GASB 35*. Private colleges and universities follow FASB pronouncements.

  B.   Differences between operations of public and private colleges/universities:

     1.   State and local governments provide a significant source of funding for public colleges and universities.

     2.   Public colleges and universities have less of their funds from endowment funds.

  C.   GASB vs. FASB

     1.   The debate has been whether public colleges and universities should follow FASB standards for private not-for-profit organizations, or GASB standards for state and local governments.

     2.   *GASB 35* officially adopts the *GASB 34* approach for public colleges and universities.

     3.   *GASB 35* does not require both government-wide financial statements and fund-based financial statements, but a single set of financial statements using the reporting standards of *GASB 34*.

     4.   Many public schools view themselves as special purpose governments that are engaged only in business-type activities. Thus, they only need to present fund-based statements for a proprietary fund.

Multiple Choice Questions

1.   When a city signs a capital lease, which of the following entries would be made?

  A.   For government-wide financial statements, debit Encumbrances.
  B.   For fund-based financial statements, debit Encumbrances.
  C.   For fund-based financial statements, credit Capital Lease Obligation.
  D.   For government-wide financial statements, credit Capital Lease Obligation.
  E.   For fund-based financial statements, debit an Asset account.

2. When a city establishes a new landfill, which of the following entries would be made?

    A. At the time of establishing the landfill, for government-wide financial statements, credit a Liability for the future cost of closing the landfill.
    B. At the end of each period, for government-wide financial statements, credit a Liability for a pro-rata share of the cost of closing the landfill.
    C. At the time of establishing the landfill, for fund-based financial statements, credit a Liability for the future cost of closing the landfill.
    D. At the end of each period, for fund-based financial statements, credit a Liability for a pro-rata share of the cost of closing the landfill.
    E. For government-wide financial statements, no entry is ever made for the estimated costs of closing the landfill until the cost is actually paid.

3. If the City of Dayglow receives a priceless Van Gogh painting for display in the town hall, how should the gift be recorded?

    A. For government-wide financial statements, a credit is made to a fiduciary trust fund.
    B. For fund-based financial statements, a credit is made to a fiduciary trust fund.
    C. For government-wide financial statements, a credit is made to a Revenue account.
    D. For fund-based financial statements, a credit is made to a Revenue account.
    E. Such a donation is never recorded, because it is not considered as an available financial resource.

4. The City of Monroe has 120 employees. The employees have accumulated a combined total of 2,400 days of unused vacation time valued at approximately $396,000. Because the city's year-end is June 30, the city estimates that the employees will use 600 of those vacations days in the seven weeks before the school year begins. The cost to the city is estimated to be $99,000.

    A. In its government-wide financial statements, Monroe should record a $99,000 liability.
    B. In its government-wide financial statements, Monroe should record a $396,000 liability.
    C. In its fund-based financial statements, Monroe should record a $396,000 liability.
    D. In its fund-based financial statements, Monroe should record a liability only for the employees that work in an enterprise fund. No liability will be recorded for the other employees.
    E. In its government-wide financial statements, Monroe should record a liability that is less than $99,000, excluding a liability for those employees working in an enterprise fund.

5. Which of the following standards required that state and local governments provide a Management Discussion and Analysis section with their annual financial statements?

    A. GASB Concepts Statement No. 1
    B. GASB Statement No. 14
    C. GASB Statement No. 34
    D. CAFR

6. Which of the following is **not** a requirement necessary to identify a unit as a "special purpose government"?

    A. A special purpose government must have a separately elected governing body.
    B. A special purpose government must be legally independent.
    C. A special purpose government must have a limited life span.
    D. A special purpose government must be fiscally independent of other state and local governing bodies.

7. A prominent citizen donates a series of letters from historical figures dating back to the Revolutionary War to the town library in Hope City. The letters will be put on permanent display for the general public after being properly preserved and protected with a new security system. If the letters are ever sold by the city, the proceeds are to be used to acquire other items for the library's collection. The city is not required to pay for the letters, though the collection has been valued at over $2 million.

   A.   GASB No. 34 requires that the letters be capitalized at the fair value of $2 million.
   B.   GASB No. 34 allows Hope City to forgo the capitalization of the letters.
   C.   The letters should be capitalized in the government-wide financial statements, but donation of the letters should be treated as revenue and a corresponding expense in the fund-based financial statements.
   D.   GASB No. 34 recommends the capitalization of the asset and requires that all donated assets be depreciated, if the governmental unit chooses to capitalize them.

8. Which of the following is **not** a section that is included in the CAFR?

   A.   Introductory Section
   B.   Financial Section
   C.   Statistical Section
   D.   Compliance Section

Brief Essay Questions

1. What circumstances give rise to the accounting issues related to the future costs associated with closing a landfill? How are the future costs treated in the government-wide and fund-based financial statements?

2. Under what conditions can a governmental unit forego depreciation on an acquired asset?

3. Does GASB 34 *require* governments to capitalize works of art or historical treasures at cost or fair value at the date of donation?

Answers to Multiple Choice Questions

1. D

2. B

3. C

4. B

5. C

6. C

7. B

8. D

Answers to Brief Essay Questions

1. The government's environmental agencies impose very strict procedures related to any facility that handles hazardous waste materials. The closing and clean-up costs are very large, and the future nature of these costs dictates that for the purpose of government-wide financial statements, the expense for closing the landfill must be accrued based on accrual accounting principles and the economic resources measurement basis. Each year a portion of the expected future cost of closing the landfill is accrued based upon the percentage of the landfill that has been filled to date. Prior estimates of the cost are adjusted as information becomes available and used in the accrual.

    In fund-based statements because of the focus on current resources, the future liability is not recorded. Payments related to environmental clean-up costs are recorded as expenditures as they occur.

2. A governmental unit can elect to forego recording depreciation on a work of art or historical treasure if three conditions are met:

    A. The asset must be held for public exhibition, education, or research in furtherance of public service, rather than financial gain.
    B. The asset must be protected, kept unencumbered, care for, and preserved.
    C. the asset must be subject to an organizational policy that requires the proceeds from sales of collection items to be used to acquire other items for collections.

3. GASB No. 34 only says that the governmental unit *should* capitalize a work of art or historical treasure, but does not require it. In the event the asset is capitalized, it should be recorded at either its cost or the fair value at the date of donation.

Chapter 18

Accounting and Reporting for Private Not-for-Profit Organizations

Chapter Outline

Standards Mentioned in This Chapter:

- **SFAS No. 116,** *Accounting for Contributions Received and Contributions Made*
- **SFAS No. 117,** *Financial Statements of Not-for-Profit Organizations*
- **SFAS No. 124,** *Accounting for Certain Investments Held by Not-for-Profit Organizations*

I. **General Characteristics of Not-for-Profit Organizations**

    A.   They often receive significant amounts of contributed resources without providing a commensurate return (contributions are not *exchange transactions*).

    B.   Their operating purpose is not providing goods and services for a profit.

    C.   They do not have ownership interests like a for-profit business.

II.   *LO1* **Financial Reporting** – the FASB sets standards for private not-for-profit organizations. As discussed in previous chapters, the GASB sets standards for public not-for-profit organizations.

    A.   **Basic Goals:**

        1.   The financial statements should focus on the entity as a whole.

        2.   Private not-for-profit organizations have much in common with for-profit business entities with the exception of *three critical differences*:

            a.   Contributions that private not-for-profit organizations receive create transactions with no counterpart in for-profit businesses.

            b.   Contributions often have donor-imposed restrictions.

            c.   No single indicator describes performance in a not-for-profit organization as well as profit in a commercial entity, thus, other indicators are necessary.

    B.   *LO2* **Financial Statements for Private Not-for-Profit Organizations** – three financial statements are required for private not-for-profit organizations. A fourth statement is required of voluntary health and welfare organizations.

        1.   **Statement of Financial Position** – reports assets, liabilities, and net assets.

            a.   Asset and liability sections resemble for-profit businesses.

            b.   The concept of owners' equity does not apply.

            c.   In the place of owners' equity, the final section in the statement presents *total net assets*, (the excess of the organization's assets over liabilities).

      d.   Net assets are presented in three categories:

          (1)   *Unrestricted* – board designated or internally restricted assets are classified as unrestricted because donors from outside the organization must impose restrictions.

          (2)   *Temporarily Restricted* – assets designated by an external party for a particular purpose or use in a future period.

          (3)   *Permanently Restricted* – assets expected to remain restricted for as long as the organization exists, although some or all of the income may be available for general or specified use.

2.   **Statement of Activities and Changes in Net Assets** – reports revenues, expenses, gains and losses for the period.

      a.   Revenues and expenses are determined using the accrual basis of accounting, including depreciation of fixed assets.

      b.   The statement presents the change in each category of net assets for the period. The final totals agree with net assets in the statement of financial position.

      c.   One main purpose of the statement is to provide a clear picture of donations and any attached restrictions.

      d.   Includes columns for each category of net assets (unrestricted, temporarily restricted, and permanently restricted).

      e.   **Recognition of Pledges**

          (1)   Unconditional promises to give are recognized as both a receivable and as contribution revenue in the period promised.

          (2)   Conditional promises to give are not recognized until they become unconditional (conditions are substantially met).

      f.   **Expenses and Release of Temporarily Restricted Net Assets**

          (1)   All expenses are reported in the Unrestricted Assets column.

          (2)   Expenses related to temporarily restricted assets are also reported in the Unrestricted Assets column.

          (3)   When conditions meet donor requirements, a portion of the temporarily restricted assets are reclassified to the Unrestricted Assets category. For example:

              o   Funds were appropriately expended for an expense or an asset as designated by the donor, or
              o   A donor restriction based on time was satisfied.

      g.   Expenses are presented in two broad categories:

          (1)   **Program Services** are activities relating to the organization's mission, such as social services, research etc.

          (2)   **Supporting Services** consist of administrative costs and fund-raising costs.

h. Investments in securities with readily determinable market values and all debt investments are reported at fair value (*SFAS 124*).

    (1) Resulting unrealized gains and losses are reported in the statement of activities.

    (2) Gains and losses, along with dividend and interest income, are reported as increases or decreases in unrestricted net assets unless there is a donor restriction.

3. **Statement of Cash Flows** – uses the standard FASB classifications and format used for for-profit businesses:

    a. Cash flows from Operating Activities – can be prepared either using the direct or indirect basis.

    b. Cash flows from Investing Activities.

    c. Cash flows from Financing Activities.

4. *LO3* **Statement of Functional Expenses** – required only for voluntary health and welfare organizations, but allowed for all not-for-profit organizations – provides a detailed schedule of expenses by function and by object.

    a. Because donors are concerned about how their gifts are used, this statement specifically addresses the allocation of costs related to fund-raising activities.

    b. If certain criteria are met, some or all of the costs of fund-raising campaigns can be reported under Program Services, instead of under Fund-Raising:

        (1) The literature must include a specific call for action that would have been the same even without the fund-raising appeal.

        (2) The appeal cannot be directed purely at potential contributors.

        (3) The requested action must be specific and help accomplish the entity's overall mission.

III. *LO4* **Accounting for Contributions**

    A. *Contributions* are unconditional transfers of cash or other resources to an entity in a voluntary nonreciprocal transaction *(SFAS 116)*.

    1. Contributions, including unconditional promises to give, are recognized as revenue in the period received. The amount is based on the *fair market value* of the resources contributed.

    2. If the pledge statements allow the donors to change their minds about their intention to give, the revenue is not recognized until the resource is received.

    3. Contributions are recorded at fair value; therefore, they are presented at *net realizable value*. The estimated uncollectible portion of pledged amounts should be deducted from contribution revenue and an allowance account credited.

    4. Contributions that will not be fully collected within the fiscal period are carried at their *present value*.

B. **Conditional Promises to Give** are not recognized as revenue until the donor conditions have been met.

C. **Donated Supplies and Other Materials** (*in-kind* donations).

1. Donated supplies and other materials are recognized as revenue and recorded at fair market value.

2. Use of estimates and averages in establishing value are allowed if they approximate the results of detailed measurement.

D. **Donations of Works of Art and Historical Treasures** – recording is not required when three conditions are met:

1. The items are added to a collection for public exhibition, education, or research; and

2. The items are protected and preserved; and

3. They are subject to a condition that, if they are ever sold, any receipts will be used to acquire other collection items.

E. **Holding Contributions for Others**

1. Some organizations receive donations that by agreement are to be distributed to other parties (for example, the United Way collects money to be redistributed to needy organizations within the local community).

2. If the beneficiary is identified, then a liability called *Liability to [Beneficiary]* is created for the specific beneficiary.

3. If the donor has the right to revoke or redirect the gift, then a liability called *Refundable Advance from Donor* is recorded.

4. If the donor has not retained the right to revoke or redirect the gift, and has given the organization powers that allow it to change the beneficiary, then the organization controls the asset. In that case, it records contribution revenue in an account such as *Temporarily Restricted Net Assets - Contributions*. An expense is recorded when the contribution goes to the eventual beneficiary.

F. **Contributed Services**

1. **Donated services** include work done by individuals or organizations, including services such as advertising. These services are recognized only if specific criteria are met:

    a. The service must create or enhance a nonfinancial asset, or

    b. The service requires a specialized skill possessed by the contributor and would have to be purchased if not donated.

2. Qualifying services are recognized as contributed service revenue and as an appropriate expense or asset addition.

3. Other services are not recognized due to the difficulty in establishing their fair value.

G. Exchange Transactions

1. *Exchange transactions* are *reciprocal transfers* when both parties give and receive something of value (i.e. YMCA dues).

2. Record reciprocal transfers as *earned revenue* when earned (accrual accounting).

3. If the paying person receives little or no value, record as *contributed revenue*.

H. *LO5* Tax Exempt Status – tax laws and regulations are distinct for different tax-exempt entities. Three common tax-exempt statuses are:

1. **Section 501 (c)(3)** applies to charitable, education and scientific not-for-profit organizations.

   a. Federal income taxes – exempt for related business income.

   b. State taxes – in most cases exempt.

   c. Donors – may use charitable deductions to reduce taxable income.

   d. Nonprofit postal permit – these entities qualify for the permit.

2. **Section 501 (c)(4)** applies to advocacy groups.

   a. Federal income taxes – exempt.

   b. State taxes – often taxed.

   c. Donors – do not receive a tax deduction.

   d. Nonprofit postal permit – these entities do not qualify unless they are also educational organizations.

3. **Section 501 (c)(6)** applies to non-profit organizations including chambers of commerce, real estate boards and boards of trade, and professional football leagues, which are not organized for profit and where no part of the net earnings benefits any private shareholder or individual.

   a. Federal income taxes – exempt for related business income.

   b. State taxes – often taxed.

   c. Membership dues are tax deductible when they are ordinary and necessary business expenses.

   d. Nonprofit postal permit – these entities do not qualify unless they are also educational organizations.

4. Most tax-exempt organizations are required to submit a Form 990 tax return or Form 990 EZ each year. Groups that study and report on non-profits usually do so by gathering information from these forms.

I.   *LO6* **Mergers and Acquisitions**

1.   **Reasons for mergers and acquisitions:**

a.   More efficient use of resources.

b.   Cost cutting through efficiency.

c.   Attempts to rescue charities that are financially suffering.

d.   Expanding the scope of an organization's outreach.

2.   **Acquisitions**

a.   An acquisition in a not-for-profit organization occurs when one entity obtains control over another entity.

b.   The definition of control is broader than for a for-profit business: "the direct or indirect ability to determine the direction of management and policies through ownership, contract, or otherwise. (FASB)."

c.   In most respects, the accounting for an acquisition parallels the consolidation process of a for-profit business.

d.   Goodwill

(1)   The recognition of goodwill implies an unrecorded ability to generate high revenues and profits in the future.

(2)   This reporting is appropriate for organizations that generate large amounts of revenue, such as the YMCA.

(3)   However, where future operations are expected to be predominately supported by contributions and returns on investments, rather than earned revenue, any unexplained excess of the acquisition value is reported as an immediate reduction in unrestricted net assets on the statement of activities versus goodwill.

3.   **Mergers**

a.   A merger occurs if two or more not-for-profit organizations come together to form a new (third) not-for-profit and control is turned over to a newly created governing board.

b.   Since neither organization is being acquired, identifiable assets and liabilities are not adjusted to fair value.

c.   The *carryover method* is used, in which the newly formed organization reports all of the previously recognized assets and liabilities at their book values as of the merger date.

IV.   *LO7* **Accounting for Health Care Organizations**

   A.   **Third Party Payors**, such as insurance companies, are the most unique aspect to accounting for health care organizations.

      1.   In most businesses, the customer who benefits from the goods or services is the one who pays for them.

      2.   In most health care organizations, the patient receives the service, while an insurance company (or some other third party payor) pays the bill.

      3.   Examples of third party payors include insurance companies such as Blue Cross/Blue Shield, Medicare, and Medicaid.

   B.   **Accounting for Patient Service Revenues**

      1.   Patient revenues are initially recorded at standard rates regardless of collectability. Receivables are recorded as due from the third-party payors and the patients for their respective portions.

      2.   To account for the fact that health care entities often receive less than the total amount normally charged for patient services, *Bad Debt Expense, Contractual Adjustments* and changes to the *Allowance for Uncollectible and Reduced Accounts* must be recorded at the end of the period.

      3.   For receivables the non-profit does not intend to collect (for example due to patient poverty), patient service revenue and the related receivable are reduced.

      4.   Frequently there is a difference between the amount of revenue recorded and the amount that the third party payor will pay (based on a prior negotiated agreement). These *Contractual Adjustments* (debits) reduce net patient service revenues. The allowance account is credited.

      5.   An alternative method of determining the amount to be paid is known as a *prospective payment plan*. A set reimbursement amount is based on the diagnosis of the patient's illness or injury.

      6.   Reductions should be estimated and recognized in the same period as the patient service revenue.

Multiple Choice Questions

1. A hospital has the following account balances:

Amount charged to patients	$500,000
Revenue from newsstand	15,000
Undesignated gifts	40,000
Contractual adjustments	70,000
Interest income	12,000
Salaries expense - nurses	120,000
Bad debts	8,000

   What is the hospital's net patient service revenue?
   A. $422,000
   B. $430,000
   C. $500,000
   D. $540,000
   E. $473,000

2. Which one of the following is **not** a required financial statement for a voluntary health and welfare organization?

   A. Statement of Financial Position
   B. Statement of Activities and Changes in Net Assets
   C. Statement of Fund Balance
   D. Statement of Cash Flows
   E. Statement of Functional Expense

3. Which entry would be the correct entry to record pledges of $200,000 that were made during a public radio fundraiser? The public radio organization estimates that 5% of the funds will be uncollectible.

   A. Debit Pledges Receivable $200,000, credit unrestricted net assets-contributions $200,000
   B. Debit Pledges Receivable $200,000, credit unrestricted net assets-contributions $190,000, credit allowance for uncollectible pledges $10,000
   C. Debit Cash $200,000, credit unrestricted net assets-contributions $200,000.
   D. Debit cash $200,000, debit allowance for uncollectible pledges $10,000, credit unrestricted net assets-contributions $190,000
   E. Debit Pledges Receivable $190,000, debit allowance for uncollectible pledges $10,000, credit unrestricted net assets-contributions $200,000

4. Southside Medical Center, a not-for-profit hospital, provides its patients with services that would normally be charged at $600,000. However, a $70,000 reduction is estimated because of contractual adjustments. Another $30,000 reduction is expected because of bad debts. Finally, $100,000 will not be collected because the amounts are deemed to be charity care. Which of the following are correct?

	Patient Service Revenues	Net Patient Service Revenues
A.	$500,000	$430,000
B.	$600,000	$500,000
C.	$530,000	$400,000
D.	$500,000	$470,000
E.	$530,000	$450,000

5. The Green Tree Preservation Society received a donation of $3,000,000 from the estate of a wealthy supporter in 1995. The funds are permanently restricted. Only the income from the endowment can be used by the Society. During 2010, the Society incurred fund management expenses of $3,500 related to this endowment. How should those expenses be reported?

A. The management expenses should be recorded in the unrestricted column of the Statement of Activities and Changes in Net Assets.
B. The management expenses should be recorded in the Temporarily Restricted column of the Statement of Activities and Changes in Net Assets.
C. The management expenses should be recorded in the Permanently Restricted column of the Statement of Activities and Changes in Net Assets.
D. The Society should record the expenses as part of Cash Flows from Investing Activities.

6. The Hurricane Flood Awareness Fund focuses its activities on educating people on the dangers of floods that occur following hurricanes. In connection with its fund raising efforts, they send out literature to people on their mailing list describing the various dangers that people face after flood waters recede. In order to print and distribute information booklets to Gulf Coast residents, they are requesting donations. How should they report the costs of printing and mailing the fund raising brochures?

A. The costs should be recorded as part of Fund-Raising Services.
B. The costs should be recorded as part of Educational Services.
C. The costs should be recorded as part of Program Services.
D. The costs should be deferred and matched against any donations received.

7. Which method is used to account for mergers of two not-for-profit organizations?

A. The acquisition method.
B. The purchase method.
C. The carryover method.
D. The cost method.

8. A local voluntary health and welfare organization had the following expenditures:

Administrative Salaries	$ 20,000
Work to help elderly citizens	60,000
Fund-raising costs	5,000
Child care services provided for indigent familites	40,000

How should these items be reported by the organization?

	Program Service Expenses	Supporting Service Expenses
A.	$120,000	$ 5,000
B.	$100,000	$25,000
C.	$105,000	$20,000
D.	$ 80,000	$45,000
E.	$ 95,000	$30,000

9. Dora volunteers her time to answer the phones at Shelter House, a home for abused women. Her normal rate as a professional accountant is $100 per hour. Locally, phone receptionists earn approximately $7.00 per hour. She volunteers 20 hours a week. How should Shelter House account for Dora's contribution each week?

   A. Shelter House should record weekly revenue of $2,000.
   B. Shelter House should record weekly revenue of $140.
   C. Shelter House should not record any revenue related to Dora's volunteer hours.
   D. Shelter House should record both weekly revenue of $140 and a weekly expense of $140 related to Dora's volunteer hours

10. Preston Hamilton V has pledged to donate $1,000,000 toward construction of the new radiology center at the local hospital, if the hospital can raise a matching $1,000,000. How should the pledge be accounted for?

   A. The pledge should be accounted for as deferred revenue.
   B. The pledge should not be recorded as revenue until the conditions of the pledge have been met.
   C. The pledge should be recorded as conditional revenue.
   D. The pledge should be recognized as an "in-kind" donation.

Brief Essay Questions

1. What are the two major goals discussed in the text that form the framework for the FASB's standards for not-for-profit organizations? Why are these ideas important?

2. One of the major factors influencing the accounting practices of health care entities is the presence of third-party payors. What is a third-party payor, and how does the presence of third-party payors affect the financial reporting of a health care entity?

Problems

1. A not-for-profit hospital, Barnes Hospital, had the following transactions:

   A. Patients were charged $360,000 for services. Of this amount, $60,000 was actually charged to the patients. Hospital officials anticipate that $14,000 will be uncollectible. The remaining $300,000 was billed to insurance companies and other third-party payors. Officials believe that these companies will only pay $264,000 after determining reasonable costs for the procedures.

   B. Insurance companies and other third-party payors paid $224,000 to cover 80% of the charges in A. The remaining amounts from these charges were denied and are not expected to be collected.

   C. An unrestricted pledge for $48,000 was received from a wealthy individual, but the money cannot be spent for several years.

   D. A local volunteer contributed services to the hospital to replace a retired worker. The value of these services was $11,000.

Required:

Prepare journal entries for the above transactions.

2. During 2010, a voluntary health and welfare organization received unrestricted pledges of $120,000. 40% were payable in 2010 with the remainder payable in 2011 (for use in 2012). Officials estimate that 10% of these pledges will be uncollectible. In addition, a local medical technician earning $10 per hour working for a hospital, contributed 320 hours of time to the charitable organization. If not for these donated services, an additional staff person would have been hired by the organization.

    Required:

    A.   How much should the organization report as net public support for 2010?

    B.   How should the organization record the contributed services?

Solutions to Multiple Choice Questions

1. **B**
Amount charged to patients	$ 500,000
Contractual adjustments	(70,000)
Net patient service revenue	$ 430,000

2. **C**

3. **B**

4. **A**
Fair market value of patient services	$ 600,000
Uncollectible charity care amount	(100,000)
Patient service revenues	$ 500,000
Contractual adjustments	(70,000)
Net patient service revenues	$ 430,000

5. **A**   All expenses are recorded in the Unrestricted Assets Column

6. **C**

7. **C**

8. **B**
Program service expenses:	
Work to help elderly citizens	$ 60,000
Child care services provided for indigent families	40,000
Total	$ 100,000

Supporting service expenses:	
Administrative salaries	$ 20,000
Fund-raising costs	5,000
Total	$ 25,000

9. **C**

10. **B**

Answers to Brief Essay Questions

1. The two goals discussed in the text are:

   A. The financial statements should focus on the entity as a whole. This goal is important because the organization's financial statements should be centered on the entity, not the funds that are used for internal record keeping.

   B. Requirements for not-for-profit organizations should be similar to business entities unless there are critical differences in the information needs of financial statement users. This goal is important because not-for-profit entities use many of the same accrual accounting techniques used by business firms for recording and reporting transactions. Thus, existing FASB standards regarding many items do not have to be rewritten.

2. A third-party payor is any outside party who assumes responsibility for all or part of a patient's medical charges. The most commonly encountered third-party payors are insurance companies, Medicare, Medicaid, and Blue Cross/Blue Shield. Because these third parties bear such a significant portion of the medical costs in this country, they require extensive and accurate financial information. Health care entities must, therefore, develop and maintain accounting systems that provide this data.

Solutions to Problems

1. Entries for Barnes Hospital:

Entry	Accounts	Debit	Credit
A	Accounts Receivable - Patients	60,000	
	Bad Debt Expense	14,000	
	Patient Service Revenues		60,000
	Allowance for Uncollectible and		
	Reduced Accounts		14,000
	Accounts Receivable - Third-Party Payors	300,000	
	Contractual Adjustments	36,000	
	Patient Service Revenues		300,000
	Allowance for Uncollectible and		
	Reduced Accounts		36,000
B	Cash	224,000	
	Contractual Adjustments	16,000	
	Accounts Receivable - Third-Party Payors		240,000
C	Pledges Receivable	48,000	
	Contributed Support - Temporarily Restricted		
	Net Assets		48,000
D	Salaries Expense	11,000	
	Contributed Support- Unrestricted Net Assets		11,000

2. A. Net Public Support

Pledges	$	120,000
Uncollectible (10%)		(12,000)
Net Pledges	$	108,000
Usable in 2010		40%
Net Pledges - 2010 Support	$	43,200
Donated servcies (320 hours × $10 per hour)		3,200
Net public support for 2010	$	46,400

B. The contributed services are recorded as public support of $3,200 and as expenses of $3,200.

Chapter 19

Accounting for Estates and Trusts

Chapter Outline

I.   *LO1* **Accounting for an Estate**

    A.   Estate accounting encompasses the recording and reporting of events occurring from the time of a person's death until distribution of all the property that belonged to that person.

    B.   **Wills and Probate Laws**

        1.   An individual who dies with a legal will dies *testate*.

        2.   An individual who dies without a legal will dies *intestate*.

        3.   State probate laws govern wills and estates, and have three goals:

            a.   Gather and preserve all of the decedent's property.

            b.   Carry out an orderly and fair settlement of all debts.

            c.   Discover and implement the decedent's intent for the remaining property held at death.

        4.   Almost half of the states have adopted the *Uniform Probate Code* to create consistent treatment between states.

        5.   Where no will exists, the *laws of descent* (for real property) and the *laws of distribution* (for personal property) are applicable.

    C.   A will should name an *executor* (or *executrix*, if female) of the estate to oversee the distribution of property.

        1.   If an executor is not named or is not able to serve, the court will appoint an administrator.

        2.   The executor or administrator is normally responsible for fulfilling several tasks:

            a.   Taking possession of all the decedent's assets and completing an inventory of this property.

            b.   Discovering all the claims against the decedent and settling these obligations.

            c.   Filing estate income tax returns, federal estate tax returns, and state inheritance or estate tax returns.

            d.   Distributing property according to the provisions of the will, or according to state laws, if a valid will is not available.

            e.   Making a full accounting to the probate court to demonstrate that the executor has properly fulfilled the fiduciary responsibility.

D. **Property Included in the Estate** – the basis for estate accounting is the property the decedent held at death. These assets are used to settle claims and pay taxes, with any remaining property being distributed. All assets are shown at fair value. Normally, an estate includes assets such as:

1. Cash.

2. Investments in stocks and bonds.

3. Interest accrued to the date of death.

4. Dividends declared prior to death.

5. Investments in businesses.

6. Unpaid wages.

7. Accrued rents and royalties.

8. Valuables such as paintings and jewelry.

E. **Discovery of Claims against the Decedent** – an adequate opportunity needs to be given to the decedent's creditors so they can file claims against the estate. These claims against the estate must be paid in a specific order of priority:

1. Expenses of administering the estate. Without this preferential treatment, the appointment of an acceptable executor and the hiring of lawyers, accountants, and/or appraisers could become a difficult task in estates with limited funds.

2. Funeral expenses and medical expenses of any last illness.

3. Debts and taxes given preference under federal and state laws.

4. All other claims, such as unsecured obligations, credit card debts etc.

F. **Protection for Remaining Family Members**

1. State laws vary, so no absolute rules about probate laws can be given.

2. Normally, state laws provide some amount of protection for a surviving spouse and/or the decedent's minor and dependent children.

3. Small monetary allowances, such as *homestead allowances* or *family allowances,* may be conveyed to these parties prior to legal claims.

4. Family members are also entitled to a limited amount of exempt property such as cars, furniture and jewelry.

5. All other property is included in the estate to pay claims and to be distributed.

G. *LO2* **Estate Distributions**

1. Property remaining after settlement of claims is to be distributed according to the will or state law.

2. A gift of real property such as land or a building is referred to as a *devise*.

3. A gift of personal property such as stocks, jewelry or furniture is a *legacy* or a *bequest*. The identification of the type of legacy becomes especially important if the estate has insufficient resources to meet the specifications of the will.

    a. A *specific legacy* is a gift of personal property that is directly identified.

    b. A *demonstrative legacy* is a cash gift made from a particular source.

    c. A *general legacy* is a cash gift with the source being undesignated.

    d. A *residual legacy* is a gift of any remaining estate property.

4. **Insufficient Funds** – the debts and expenses of the administration are paid first in settling an estate. If the estate has insufficient assets to settle the claims, the process of *abatement* is utilized. Each of the following categories is exhausted completely to pay all of the claims before money is taken from the next category.

    a. Residual legacies – the first to suffer abatement and the last to receive an inheritance.

    b. General legacies.

    c. Demonstrative legacies.

    d. Specific legacies and devises.

II.   *LO3* **Estate and Inheritance Taxes**

    A.   **The federal estate tax** is an *excise tax* assessed on the right to convey property.

        1. The fair market value of estate property is taxed after reduction for several items:

        a. Funeral expenses.

        b. Estate administration expenses.

        c. Liabilities.

        d. Casualties and thefts during the administration of the estate.

        e. Charitable bequests.

        f. Marital deduction for property conveyed to the spouse.

        g. State inheritance taxes.

        2. The remaining value is taxed at graduated rates based on the year of death. For 2009, the highest estate tax rate is 45%, after an exemption of $3.5 million. The estate tax is repealed in 2010. The estate tax returns in 2011 with the highest estate tax rate of 55% in that year, after an exemption of $1 million.

        3. Note the astonishing difference on the estate tax as a result of death in 2009, 2010 and 2011 (unless additional legislation is passed by Congress to extend the repeal of the estate tax, make the repeal permanent, or reinstate the legislation that provided escalating exemptions).

4. The *valuation date* for the estate's assets is the date of death, or an alternate date (six months after the date of death or the date of disposition for any property disposed of within 6 months of death) which can be used if it reduces estate taxes.

5. **Gifts**

    a. Gifts made to individuals prior to death are tax-free as long as they do not exceed $13,000 per donee per year. This annual amount is periodically indexed to change with inflation.

    b. There is a lifetime exemption on tax-free gifts of $1 million as well as the annual $13,000 per donee gift tax exclusion.

B. **State inheritance taxes** are assessed on the right to receive property, with the levy and all other regulations varying based on state laws.

C. **Estate and trust income taxes** are based on the income earned by the estate (or trust) assets from the time of death until the ultimate resolution of the property.

1. The estate is viewed as a taxable entity. It must file a federal tax return if its gross income > $600.

2. Reductions are allowed for:

    a. Taxable income donated to charity, and

    b. Taxable income distributed to a beneficiary.

3. State income tax returns are also filed according to state law.

D. *LO4* **The Distinction between Income and Principal**

1. In many estates, the executor needs to differentiate between income and principal transactions because the recipients of the income and principal, and the way they are distributed, may differ.

2. The recipient(s) of the income is called an *income beneficiary*.

3. The recipient(s) of the principal is called a *remainderman*.

4. Two cash balances are often maintained to assist in the process of keeping income and principal transactions separate.

5. Some transactions are not easily categorized as income or principal. As fiduciary for the estate, the executor can be held legally liable if the amounts are distributed incorrectly.

E. **Recording the Transactions of an Estate**

1. All estate assets are recorded at fair market value to indicate the amount and the extent of the executor's accountability.

2. Debts, taxes, or other obligations are only recorded at the date of payment.

3. Income and principal have their balances and transactions separately identified; often two cash balances are used to assist in this process.

F.   *LO5* **Charge and Discharge Statement**

1.   The executor periodically files reports, known as *charge and discharge statements*, with the probate court to disclose the progress being made in settling the estate.

2.   The statement should indicate:

   a.   The assets under the control of the executor.

   b.   Disbursements made to date.

   c.   Any property still remaining.

III.   **Accounting for a Trust**

A.   A *trust* is created by the conveyance of assets to a *fiduciary* (or *trustee*) who manages the assets that will ultimately be distributed to one or more beneficiaries.

B.   **Reasons for creating a trust:**

1.   To ensure assets are protected and that their distribution is as intended.

2.   To reduce the size of the taxable estate (and thus estate taxes).

3.   The *trustor* (the person who funds the trust) believes that a chosen trustee will be able to manage the assets better than the beneficiary would (for example, a minor child or a person with disabilities).

4.   Trusts can be set up before death, or through the provisions of a will.

   a.   An *inter vivos trust* is one started by a living individual.

   b.   A *testamentary trust* is created by a will.

C.   *LO6* **Revocable living trusts** have become popular in recent years.

1.   Assets are turned over to the trust during the trustor's lifetime.

2.   The trustor manages the trust and receives most, of not all, of the income until death.

3.   The trust is revocable, so the trustor can change beneficiaries or other terms at any time.

4.   After death, future income and possibly principal payments are made to the named beneficiaries.

5.   Advantages:

   a.   The revocable living trust avoids the delay and expense of probate.

   b.   Publicity is avoided because the trust document is private – unlike a will, which is a public document.

D. *LO6* Other Common Types of Trusts

1. **Credit Shelter Trust** – also known as a *Bypass Trust* or *Family Trust,* is designed for couples. Each spouse agrees to transfer at death an amount up to the tax-free exclusion to a trust fund for the benefit of the other.

2. **Qualified Terminable Interest Property Trust** (QTIP Trust) – is frequently created to serve as a credit shelter trust. Property is conveyed to the trust with the income, and possibly a portion of the principal, being paid to the surviving spouse (or other beneficiary).

3. **Charitable Remainder Trust** – all income is paid to one or more beneficiaries identified by the trustor. After a period of time (or at the death of the beneficiaries), the principal is given to a stated charity.

4. **Charitable Lead Trust** – is the reverse of a charitable remainder trust. Income from the trust fund goes to benefit a charity for a specified time with the remaining principal then being given to a different beneficiary.

5. **Grantor Retained Annuity Trust** (GRAT) – the trustor maintains the right to collect fixed payments from the trust fund with the principal being given to a beneficiary after a stated time or at the death of the trustor.

6. **Minor's Section 2503(c) Trust** – is usually designed to receive a tax-free gift of up to $13,000 each year ($26,000 if the transfer is made by a couple). Over time, especially if enough beneficiaries are available, a significant amount of assets can be removed from a person's estate.

7. **Spendthrift Trust** – is established so the beneficiary cannot transfer or assign any unreceived payments, and is usually established in hopes of preventing the beneficiary from squandering the assets being held by the trust.

8. **Irrevocable Life Insurance Trust** – money is contributed to the trust to buy life insurance on the donor. If a couple is creating the trust, the life insurance policy is usually designed so that proceeds are paid only after the second spouse dies.

9. **Qualified Personal Resident Trust** – the donor's home is given to the trust, but the donor retains the right to live in the house for a period of time rent-free. This removes what is often an individual's most valuable asset from the estate.

E. **Record Keeping for a Trust Fund** – trust record keeping is similar to accounting for an estate, however, because of the many types of trusts and the extended time that might be involved the accounting process may be more complex.

1. Transactions and balances must be separately identified for the trust principal and income.

2. The trust agreement should specify the distinction between transactions to be recorded as income and those to be recorded as principal.

    a. If the agreement is silent, or if a transaction is incurred that is not covered by the agreement, state laws are applicable.

    b. GAAP is usually not considered appropriate.

3. **Adjustments to the Trust's Principal**

   a. Investing costs and commissions.

   b. Income taxes on gains added to the principal.

   c. Costs of preparing property for rent or sale.

   d. Extraordinary repairs (improvements).

4. **Adjustments to the Trust's Income**

   a. Rent expense.

   b. Lease cancellation fees.

   c. Interest expense.

   d. Insurance expense.

   e. Income taxes on trust income.

   f. Property taxes.

5. Trustee fees and the cost of periodic reporting (accounting and legal fees) are allocated between trust income and principal. The allocation is often based upon the relative value of the principal and income assets.

6. *Inter vivos* trusts report annually (or more frequently) to all beneficiaries.

7. *Testamentary* trusts come under court jurisdiction, so additional reporting may be necessary.

8. Normally, a statement resembling the charge and discharge statement of an estate is adequate for these purposes.

Multiple Choice Questions

1. The following statement appeared in Steven Jackson's will: "I leave $20,000 in cash to my niece, Sally Martin." Such a gift is a:

   A. Specific legacy.
   B. Demonstrative legacy.
   C. General legacy.
   D. Residual legacy.
   E. Major legacy.

2. Jay Jones believes that each individual should make his or her own way in life upon graduation from college. To help his children accomplish this goal, he created a trust, which will distribute income to his children until they graduate from college, at which time the principal of the trust will go to the American Red Cross. For this type of trust, the American Red Cross is the:

   A. Legatee.
   B. Remainderman.
   C. Grantor.
   D. Inheritor.
   E. Trustee.

3. If an estate has insufficient funds after paying administrative expenses to satisfy all gifts, a person who is to receive a demonstrative legacy would receive that gift ahead of individuals that are assigned to receive:

	Residual Legacy	Specific Legacy	General Legacy
A.	No	No	Yes
B.	Yes	Yes	No
C.	No	Yes	No
D.	Yes	Yes	Yes
E.	Yes	No	Yes

4. Which one of the following expenses of an estate would normally **not** be charged against income?

   A. Brokerage fees for the sale of investments.
   B. Ordinary repair expenses.
   C. Insurance expenses.
   D. Property taxes.
   E. Utility expenses.

5. Which one of the following is **not** a valid reason for creating a trust?

   A. To save on estate taxes.
   B. To provide management expertise.
   C. To provide for the education of minor children.
   D. To reduce income taxes since trusts are not taxable entities.
   E. To prevent the beneficiary from squandering the protected assets.

6. Which one of the following statements is correct?

   A. If an individual dies without leaving a will, the property will be distributed according to federal laws.
   B. An executor is named in a person's will, whereas an administrator is appointed.
   C. Because of the many accounting responsibilities involved such as filing federal income tax returns and federal estate tax returns, the administrator must be an accountant.
   D. If real property is distributed according to the provision of a will, it is called a legacy.
   E. The executor named in a person's will must be an attorney.

7. Which one of the following statements is correct?

    A.   Real property transferred under state law without being subject to probate is excluded from the gross estate on the federal estate tax return.

    B.   If a trust document is silent regarding the appropriate accounting treatment for some type of transaction, the trustee is bound to follow generally accepted accounting principles.

    C.   The executor must file periodic reports called charge and discharge statements with the heirs of an estate.

    D.   An individual may make tax-free, lifetime gifts totaling $1 million to as many different individuals as they like.

    E.   Trust accounting is quite different from estate accounting.

8. Catherine Miller died on March 1, 2011. All of her property was conveyed to several relatives on November 18, 2011. For federal estate tax purposes, the executor chose the alternative valuation date. On which of the following dates was the value of the property determined?

    A.   November 18, 2011.
    B.   December 1, 2011.
    C.   September 1, 2011.
    D.   December 31, 2011.
    E.   March 1, 2012.

9. The executor of an estate is filing an income tax return for the current period. Revenues of $36,000 have been earned. Which one of the following is a deduction allowed in calculating taxable income?

    A.   Funeral expense.
    B.   Administrative expense.
    C.   Accounting fees.
    D.   Executor's fee for managing the estate's assets.
    E.   Personal exemption.

10. Which one of the following is designed for married couples and is known as a *bypass trust*?

    A.   Credit shelter trust.
    B.   Charitable lead trust.
    C.   Charitable remainder trust.
    D.   Spendthrift trust.
    E.   Grantor retained annuity trust.

Brief Essay Questions

1. What three goals are probate laws usually designed to achieve?

2. What are the four types of legacies covered in the text?

Problems

1. An estate had the following income:

Rental income	$ 20,000
Interest income	10,000
Dividend income	12,000

    The interest income was immediately conveyed to the appropriate beneficiary. 75% of the dividends were given to charity as per the decedent's will.

    Required:

    What is the taxable income of the estate?

2. The estate of Albert Johnstone reported the following:

Value of estate assets	$ 1,600,000
Conveyed to spouse	800,000
Conveyed to children	325,000
Conveyed to charities	300,000
Funeral expenses	10,000
Administrative expenses	15,000
Debts	150,000

    Required:

    Assuming that Albert made no taxable gifts during his lifetime, what is the taxable estate value?

Solutions to Multiple Choice Questions

1. **C**   When a cash gift is made without the source being designated, a *general legacy* is created.

2. **B**   The recipient of the principal of a trust is known at a specified point in time as the *remainderman*.

3. **E**   If the estate has insufficient available resources to satisfy all claims, the process of *abatement* is used. Each of the following categories is completely exhausted to pay all debts and expenses before money is taken from the next: (1) residual legacies, (2) general legacies, (3) demonstrative legacies, and (4) specific legacies and devises.

4. **A**   Investment expenses are normally charged against the principal of an estate.

5. **D**   Trusts normally pay income taxes unless all income has been distributed; in which case, the recipient of the income pays the tax. However, the trust is required to file annually.

6. **B**

7. D

8. C

9. E

10. A

Answers to Brief Essay Questions

1. Probate laws are usually designed to achieve the following three goals:

   A. Gather and preserve all of the decedent's property.
   B. Carry out an orderly and fair settlement of all debts.
   C. Discover and implement the decedent's intent for the remaining property held at death.

2. The four types of legacies are:

   A. A specific legacy,
   B. A demonstrative legacy,
   C. A general legacy, and
   D. A residual legacy.

Solutions to Problems

1. The estate's taxable income:

Rental income	$	20,000
Interest income		10,000
Dividend income		12,000
Total revenue		42,000
Personal exemption		(600)
Gift to charity ($12,000 x 75%)		(9,000)
Distributed to beneficiary		(10,000)
Taxable income	$	22,400

2. Albert Johnson's taxable estate value:

Gross estate (fair market value)		$ 1,600,000
Funeral expenses	$ 10,000	
Administrative expenses	15,000	
Debts	150,000	
Charity bequests	300,000	
Marital deduction	800,000	(1,275,000)
Taxable estate		$ 325,000

In this problem, the amount of the marital deduction is the amount that was conveyed to the spouse. There is no limit on the amount of property that can be conveyed tax free to a surviving spouse; however, this is not a total avoidance of tax but rather a deferral of tax.

The taxable estate is the amount conveyed to the children. The taxes to be paid in this example will be $0 due to the current exemption amount.

Working Papers

Problems 1-1 to 1-12

Name _____

1. _____

2. _____

3. _____

4. _____

5. _____

6. _____

7. _____

8. _____

9. _____

10. _____

11. _____

12. _____

Problem 1-13

Problem 1-15

Journal Entries	Debit			Credit		

Problem 1-16

Journal Entries	Debit			Credit		

Problem 1-17

Name _____

Journal Entry to Defer Unrealized Gain:	Debit		Credit	

Problem 1-18

a.			

b.

c.

a.

b.

c.

d.

e.

f.

g.

h.

i.

a.

b.

c.

d.

e.

f.

g.

a.

b.

c.

d.

a.

b.			

Problem 1-24

Part a.1.			

Part a (continued)			
a.2.			

Journal Entry for restrospective adjustment		**Debit**	**Credit**

Part b.1.		
b.2.		
Part c		

Part a			
Part b			

Part b (continued)

Part c

a.

Problem 1-26 (continued)

Name _____

Part a (continued)			
Part b			

Problem 1-27

Name _____

Journal Entries	Debit	Credit

Computations

Working Papers

a.

b.

Problem 1-30

Journal Entries	Debit	Credit

Journal Entries	Debit		Credit	

Journal Entries	Debit	Credit

Name _____

Problems 2-1 to 2-12

Name _____

1. _____

2. _____

3. _____

4. _____

5. _____

6. _____

7. _____

8. _____

9. _____

10. _____

11. _____

12. _____

Problem 2-13

a.
b.

Problem 2-14

Journal Entries	Debit			Credit		

Problem 2-15

Journal Entries	Debit			Credit		

Problem 2-16

Name _____

Consolidated Balances			
Inventory			
Land			
Buildings and Equipment			
Franchise Agreements			
Goodwill			
Revenues			
Additional Paid-in Capital			
Expenses			
Retained Earnings, 1/1			
Computations			

Problem 2-17

Computations			
Consolidated Balances			
Net Income			
Retained Earnings 1/1			
Patented Technology			
Goodwill			
Liabilities			
Common Stock			
Additional Paid-in Capital			

Pinnacle Corporation and Strata Corporation			
Consolidated Balance Sheet			
January 1, 2011			
ASSETS			
Total Assets			
LIABILITIES			
Total Liabilities			
EQUITY			
Total Equity			
Total Liabilities and Equity			

Computations			

Consolidated Balances			
Cash			
Receivables			
Inventory			
Land			
Buildings (net)			
Equipment (net)			
Investment in Tucker			
Goodwill (if any)			
Total Assets			
Accounts Payable			
Long-term liabilities			
Common Stock - $1 par value			
Common Stock - $20 par value			
Additional paid-in capital			
Retained Earnings 1/1			
Total Liabilities and equity			

Accounts		Debits		Credits		Consolidated Balances	
Cash							
Receivables							
Inventory							
Land							
Buildings (net)							
Equipment (net)							
Investment in Tucker							
Total Assets							
Accounts Payable							
Long-term Liabilities							
Common Stock - $1 par							
Common Stock - $20 par							
Additional Paid-in Capital							
Retained Earnings							
Total Liabilities and Equity							

Accounts	Debits	Credits			Consolidated Balances
Cash					
Receivables					
Inventory					
Investment in Spider					
Computer Software					
Buildings (net)					
Equipment (net)					
Total Assets					
Accounts Payable					
Notes Payable					
Common Stock					
Additional Paid-in Capital					
Retained Earnings					
Total Liabilities and Equity					

Computations			

Pratt Company and Subsidiary Spider, Inc.

Consolidated Balance Sheet

December 31, 2011

ASSETS			
Total Assets			
LIABILITIES			
Total Liabilities			
EQUITY			
Total Equity			
Total Liabilities and Equity			

Case 1

Journal Entry

Case 2

Journal Entry

Name _____

a.

Journal Entry

b.

Journal Entry

a.

b.

c.

d.

e.

f.

g.

h.

Problem 2-24

Name _____

a.

Journal Entry

ASSETS			
Total Assets			
LIABILITIES			
Total Liabilities			
EQUITY			
Total Equity			
Total Liabilities and Equity			
b.			
See worksheet on following page			

Working Papers

Accounts			Debits			Credits			Consolidated Balances
Cash									
Receivables									
Investment in On-the-Go									
Trademarks									
Record Music catalog									
Capitalized R&D									
Equipment									
Goodwill									
Total Assets									
Accounts Payable									
Notes Payable									
Common Stock									
Additional Paid-in Capital									
Retained Earnings									
Total Liabilities and Equity									

c.

Problem 2-25

Journal Entries	Debit			Credit		
a.						

Problem 2-25 b. and c.

Name _____

Accounts	b. Pacifica		Seguros		Debits		Credits		Consolidated Balances	

a.

b.

c.

d.

e.

f.

g.

h.

i.

j.

Name _____

a.

b.

c.

d.

Problem 2-28

a.

b.

c.

d.

Problem 2-29

Name _____

a.			
b.			
c.			
d.			
e.			

a.

Journal Entry	Debit		Credit	

Journal Entries	Debit			Credit		
b.						

Accounts				Debits			Credits			Consolidated Balances
Cash										
Receivables										
Inventory										
Investment in Harriss										
Land										
Buildings										
Equipment										
Patent										
Goodwill										
Total Assets										
Accounts Payable										
Long-term Liabilities										
Common Stock										
Additional Paid-in Capital										
Retained Earnings										
Total Liabilities and Equity										

Problem 2-31 _____

Problem 2-32

a.

b.

c.

a.

	Purchase			Pooling		
Inventory						
Land						
Buildings						
Unpatented Technology						
Goodwill						
Total						

b.

c.

Problem 3-1 to 3-11

Name _____

1. _____

2. _____

3. _____

4. _____

5. _____

6. _____

7. _____

8. _____

9. _____

10. _____

11. _____

Problem 3-12

a. Consolidated Retained Earnings - Equity Method			
Consolidated Retained Earnings - Partial Equity Method			
Consolidated Retained Earnings - Initial Value Method			

b.	**Investment in Rambis - Equity Method**			
	Investment in Rambis - Partial Equity Method			
	Investment in Rambis - Initial Value Method			
c.	**Entry *C**			
	Equity Method			
	Partial Equity Method			
	Initial Value Method			

a.

b.

c.

d.

Calculation of Goodwill

a. Journal Entry

b. Goodwill Impairment

Goodwill Impairment Test - Step 1			
Goodwill Impairment Test - Step 2			

b.	Tangible assets, net		
	Goodwill		
	Customer List		
	Patent		

a. Goodwill Impairment Test - Step 1			
b. Goodwill Impairment Test - Step 2			
c.			

Consolidation Journal Entries	Debit		Credit	
ENTRIES FOR 12/31/11				

Consolidation Journal Entries	Debit			Credit		
ENTRIES for 12/31/12						

Consolidation Journal Entries	Debit		Credit	
ENTRIES FOR 12/31/11				

Consolidation Journal Entries	Debit			Credit		
ENTRIES for 12/31/12						

Working Papers

Name _____

Consolidation Journal Entries	Debit	Credit
ENTRIES FOR 12/31/11		

Consolidation Journal Entries	Debit			Credit		
ENTRIES for 12/31/12						

a. 1. Initial Value Method			
2. Equity Method			
b.			
c.			
d. 1. Initial Value Method			
2. Equity Method			

e. Worksheet Entry *C - Initial value method							
f. Worksheet entry S							
g.							

Working Papers

a.

b.

c.

d.

a.	**Consolidated Balances**			
	Depreciation Expense			
	Dividends Paid			
	Revenues			
	Equipment			
	Buildings			
	Goodwill			
	Common Stock			

b.

c.

d.

e. Initial Value Method R/E - 1/1/13

Partial Equity Method R/E - 1/1/13

Equity Method R/E - 1/1/13

a.

b.   Consolidated Balances

Revenues			
Cost of Goods Sold			
Depreciation Expense			
Amortization Expense			
Income from O'Brien			
Net Income			
Retained Earnings, 1/1			
Dividends Paid			
Retained Earnings, 12/31			
Cash			
Receivables			
Inventory			
Investment in O'Brien			
Trademarks			
Customer Relationships			
Equipment			
Goodwill			
Total Assets			
Liabilities			
Common Stock			
Retained Earnings, 12/31 (from above)			
Total Liabilities and Equities			

Accounts	Patrick	O'Brien	Debits	Credits	Consolidated Balances
Revenues					
Cost of Goods Sold					
Depreciation Expense					
Amortization Expense					
Income of O'Brien					
Net Income					
Retained Earnings, 1/1					
Net Income					
Dividends					
Retained Earnings, 12/31					
Cash					
Receivables					
Inventory					
Investment in O'Brien					
Trademarks					
Customer Relationships					
Equipment (net)					
Goodwill					
Total Assets					
Liabilities					
Common Stock					
Retained earnings, 12/31					
Total Liabilities and equity					

Accounts	Michael	Aaron	Debits	Credits	Consolidated Balances
Revenues					
Depreciation Expense					
Amortization Expense					
Dividend Income					
Net Income					
Retained Earnings, 1/1					
Net Income					
Dividends Paid					
Retained Earnings, 12/31					
Cash					
Receivables					
Inventory					
Investment in Aaron Co.					
Copyrights					
Royalty Agreements					
Trademark					
Total Assets					
Liabilities					
Preferred Stock					
Common Stock					
Additional Paid-in Capital					
Retained Earnings, 12/31					
Total Liabilities and equity					

a.   Calculations

b.

c.

d.

a.

b.	Consolidated Balances			
	Revenues			
	Cost of Goods Sold			
	Depreciation Expense			
	Equity in Income of Small			
	Net Income			
	Retained Earnings, 1/1/13			
	Dividends Paid			
	Retained Earnings, 12/31/13			
	Current Assets			
	Investment in Small			
	Land			
	Buildings			
	Equipment			
	Goodwill			
	Total Assets			
	Liabilities			
	Common Stock			
	Retained Earnings, 12/31/13 (from above)			
	Total Liabilities and Equity			

c.   See Worksheet on the next page

d.		Debits	Credits

Accounts	Debits		Credits		Consolidated Balances	
Revenues						
Cost of Goods Sold						
Depreciation Expense						
Equity Income of Small						
Net Income						
Retained Earnings, 1/1/13						
Net Income						
Dividends						
Retained Earnings, 12/31/13						
Current Assets						
Investment in Small						
Land						
Buildings (net)						
Equipment (net)						
Goodwill						
Total Assets						
Liabilities						
Common Stock						
Retained Earnings, 12/31/13						
Total Liabilities and equity						

a.

Revenues			
Cost of Goods Sold			
Depreciation Expense			
Amortization Expense			
Buildings (net)			
Equipment (net)			
Customer List			
Common Stock			
Additional Paid-In Capital			

b.

c.	Debits	Credits

a.

Gain on Bargain Purchase

Equity Earnings from Santiago

Investment in Santiago

Problem 3-27 (continued)

Name _____

Accounts	Peterson	Santiago	Debits	Credits	Consolidated Balances
Revenues					
Cost of Goods Sold					
Gain on Bargain Purchase					
Depr. and Amortization					
Equity Income of Santiago					
Net Income					
Retained Earnings, 1/1					
Net Income					
Dividends					
Retained Earnings, 12/31					
Current Assets					
Investment in Santiago					
Trademarks					
Patented Technology					
Equipment (net)					
Total Assets					
Liabilities					
Common Stock					
Retained Earnings, 12/31					
Total Liabilities and equity					

Name _____

Journal Entries	Debit			Credit		
a.						
b.						
c. Equity Method						
d. Initial Value Method						

Problem 3-28 (continued)

Name _____

	Debits		Credits	

Problem 3-29

a.			
b. See worksheet on separate page			
c. Push-down Accounting			

Accounts	Palm	Storm	Debits	Credits	Consolidated Balances
Revenues					
Cost of Goods Sold					
Depreciation Expense					
Equity Income from Storm					
Net Income					
Retained Earnings, 1/1					
Net Income					
Dividends					
Retained Earnings, 12/31					
Current Assets					
Investment in Storm Co.					
Land					
Building and Equipment					
Formula					
Total Assets					
Current Liabilities					
Long-term Liabilities					
Common Stock					
Retained Earnings, 12/31					
Total Liabilities and equity					

a.	Investment in Jasmine Company (on Tyler's individual financial records)		
b.	Equity in subsidiary earnings (on Tyler's individual financial records)		
c.	Consolidated Net Income		

d.	Consolidated Equipment (net)			
e.	Consolidated Buildings (net)			
f.	Consolidated Goodwill (net)			
g.	Consolidated Common Stock			
h.	Consolidated Retained Earnings 12/31/11			

a.

b.   **A worksheet for Part b is included on the next page.**

Accounts	Picante	Salsa	Debits	Credits	Consolidated Balances
Sales					
Cost of Goods Sold					
Depreciation Expense					
Subsidiary Income					
Net Income					
Retained Earnings, 1/1					
Net Income					
Dividends					
Retained Earnings, 12/31					
Cash					
Accounts Receivable					
Inventory					
Investment in Salsa					
Land					
Equipment (net)					
Goodwill					
Total Assets					
Accounts Payable					
Long-term Debt					
Common Stock					
Retained Earnings, 12/31					

a.				
b.				
c.				
d.				
e.				

Problem 3-32 f. WORKSHEET   Name _____

Accounts	Prine	Lydia	Debits	Credits	Consolidated Balances
Revenues					
Operating expenses					
Equity in Lydia Earnings					
Impairment Loss					
Net Income					
Retained Earnings, 1/1					
Net Income					
Dividends					
Retained Earnings, 12/31					
Cash					
Receivables (net)					
Investment in Lydia, Co.					
Broadcast Licenses					
Movie Library					
Equipment (net)					
Goodwill					
Total Assets					
Current Liabilities					
Long-term Debt					
Common Stock					
Retained Earnings, 12/31					
Total Liabilities and equity					

Problem 4-1 to 4-19   Name _____

1. _____   11. _____

2. _____   12. _____

3. _____   13. _____

4. _____   14. _____

5. _____   15. _____

6. _____   16. _____

7. _____   17. _____

8. _____   18. _____

9. _____   19. _____

10. _____

Problem 4-20

a.			
b.			

a.

b.

c.

d.

e.

e.   (continued)

f.

g.

a.

b.

Consolidated Figures:			
Noncontrolling interest in subsidiary income			
End of year noncontrolling interest			
Machine			
Process Trade Secret			

Problem 4-24

a.			
b.			
c.			
d.			

a.

b.

c.

a.		Debits		Credits	

b. (continued)	Debits			Credits		
c.						
d.						

a.

b.

c.

d.   (1) Equity Method

(2) Partial Equity Method

(3) Initial Value Method

e.   (1) Equity Method

(2) Partial Equity Method

(3) Initial Value Method

f.				
g.				
h.	**Consolidated Balances:**			
	Common Stock			
	Additional Paid-in Capital			
	Retained Earnings			

Calculations			
Consolidated Balances			
Sales			
Expenses			
Noncontrolling Interest in Subsidiary's Net Income			
Consolidated Net Income			
Retained Earnings, 1/1			
Trademarks			
Goodwill			

a.

b.

c.

d.

Problem 4-29 (continued)   Name _____

e.			
f.			
g.			

Problem 4-30

a.	Worksheet follows			
b.				

Account Titles	Pierson	Steele	Debits	Credits	Noncontrolling Interest	Consolidated Balances

Account Titles	Krause	Leahy	Debits	Credits	Noncontrolling Interest	Consolidated Balances

b.

c.

Account Titles	Father	Sam	Debits	Credits	Noncontrolling Interest	Consolidated Balances

a.

b.

c. Consolidated Balances

Revenues			
Cost of Goods Sold			
Depreciation expense			
Amortization expense			
Interest expense			
Investment income			
Consolidated net income			
Income to noncontrolling interest			
Income to controlling interest			

Retained earnings, 1/1			
Net income			
Dividends paid			
Retained earnings, 12/31			
Current assets			
Investment in Barstow			
Land			
Buildings			
Equipment			
Patents			
Goodwill			
Notes payable			
Common stock			
Noncontrolling interest			

Account Titles	Father	Sam	Debits	Credits	Noncontrolling Interest	Consolidated Balances

Computations			
a. **Consolidated Income Statement**			
b. **Consolidated Balances**			
Goodwill			
Equipment			
Common Stock			
Buildings			
Dividends Paid			

Problem 4-35

a.

b.

c.

Problem 4-35 (continued)   Name _____

Account Titles		Debits		Credits		Noncontrolling Interest		Consolidated Balances

a.

b.

Account Titles	Allan	Sysinger	Debits	Credits	Noncontrolling Interest	Consolidated Balances

Problem 4-37

a.

b.

Account Titles				Debits	Credits	Noncontrolling Interest	Consolidated Balances

a. **Calculations**

b.

Account Titles			Debits	Credits	Noncontrolling Interest	Consolidated Balances

a.

b.

c.

d.

e.

f.

g.				
h.				

Calculations			

Problem 4-40 (continued)   Name _____

Account Titles		Debits	Credits	Noncontrolling Interest	Consolidated Balances

Problem 5-1 to 5-15

Name _____

1. _____	6. _____	11. _____
2. _____	7. _____	12. _____
3. _____	8. _____	13. _____
4. _____	9. _____	14. _____
5. _____	10. _____	15. _____

Problem 5-16

Inventory			
Sales			
Cost of Goods Sold			
Operating Expenses			
Noncontrolling Interest in the Subsidiary's Net Income			

Problem 5-17

a.			

b.	Journal Entries	Debit			Credit		

a.

b.

c.

d.

e.				
f.				
g.				

h.		Debits	Credits
	Noncontrolling interest in Kane's net income:		

Problem 5-19

Name _____

a.

b.

	Debits	Credits

Problem 5-20

a.

b.

c.

a.

Calculations:

b. | Income Statement

a.

	Debits			Credits		

b.

	Debits			Credits		

Journal Entries	Debit		Credit	

Problem 5-23

Calculations	

Journal Entries	Debit		Credit	

Name _____

a.

b.

c.

d.

CONSOLIDATED BALANCES			
Sales			
Cost of Goods Sold			
Operating Expenses			
Investment Income			
Inventory			
Equipment (net)			
Buildings (net)			

Problem 5-26   Name _____

a.	Consolidation Entries	Debit			Credit		

Working Papers

a.	(continued)	Debit			Credit		
b.	**Computation of Noncontrolling Interest**						

Name _____

a.

b.

c.

d.

e.

f.

g.							

h.	Entry S:	Debits			Credits	

i.	**CONSOLIDATED BALANCES**		
	Sales Revenue		
	Cost of Goods Sold		
	Expenses		
	Investment Income - Brey		
	Net Income		
	Noncontrolling Interest in Subsidiary's Net Income		
	Consolidated Net Income to Parent		
	Retained Earnings, 1/1		
	Net Income (above)		
	Retained Earnings, 12/31		
	Cash and Receivables		
	Inventory		
	Investment in Brey		
	Land, Buildings, and Equipment		
	Patented Technology		
	Total Assets		
	Liabilities		
	Noncontrolling Interest in Brey		
	Common Stock		
	Retained Earnings, 12/31		
	Total Liabilities and Stockholders' Equity		

Calculations			
CONSOLIDATED BALANCES			
Sales			
Cost of Goods Sold			
Operating Expenses			
Dividend Income			
Noncontrolling Interest in Consolidated Income			
Inventory			
Noncontrolling Interest in Subsidiary, 12/31/11			

Working Papers

Calculations			
CONSOLIDATED BALANCES			
Sales			
Cost of Goods Sold			
Operating Expenses			
Dividend Income			
Noncontrolling Interest in Consolidated Income			
Inventory			
Noncontrolling Interest in Subsidiary, 12/31/11			

Problem 5-30

Name _____

Calculations			

Account Titles			Debits	Credits	Noncontrolling Interest	Consolidated Balances

Name _____

a.

Account Titles			Debits	Credits	Noncontrolling Interest	Consolidated Balances

a.

Account Titles		Debits	Credits	Noncontrolling Interest	Consolidated Balances

Name _____

1.	CONSOLIDATION ENTRIES	Debits			Credits		
2.	Noncontrolling interests share of subsidiaries net income						

Working Papers

Name _____

Consolidation Journal Entries	Debit	Credit

a.	Calculations & Consolidation Journal Entries	Debit		Credit	

Problem 5-35 (continued)   Name _____

Consolidation Journal Entries	Debit	Credit

Account Titles								Debits						Credits					Noncontrolling Interest					Consolidated Balances			

Problem 5-35 (continued)

Name _____

b.	Consolidation Journal Entries	Debit			Credit		

a.

Calculations & Journal Entries	Debit		Credit	

Working Papers

Account Titles					Debits		Credits		Noncontrolling Interest	Consolidated Balances

Problem 6-1 to 6-21

Name _____

1. _____   8. _____   15. _____

2. _____   9. _____   16. _____

3. _____   10. _____   17. _____

4. _____   11. _____   18. _____

5. _____   12. _____   19. _____

6. _____   13. _____   20. _____

7. _____   14. _____   21. _____

Problem 6-22

Problem 6-23

a.

b.

c.

d.

Problem 6-24

a.

b.

a.

	Debit	Credit

b.

	Debit	Credit

c.

Problem 6-26

Name _____

CONSOLIDATED BALANCES			
Revenues and Interest Income			
Operating and Interest Expense			
Other Gains and Losses			
Loss on Retirement of Debt			
Net Income			

Problem 6-27

a.

	Debit		Credit	

b.

	Debit		Credit	

a.

b.

c.

	Debit	Credit

Problem 6-29

Problem 6-30

a.

b.

c.	Debits		Credits	

	Debits			Credits		

Name _____

Problem 6-34

Name _____

Name _____

Working Papers

Name _____

Working Papers

Problem 6-38

Problem 6-39

		Debit			Credit		
a.							
b.							

JOURNAL ENTRIES	Debit			Credit		

Problem 6-41   Name _____

Account Titles			Debits	Credits	Noncontrolling Interest	Consolidated Balances

JOURNAL ENTRIES	Debit			Credit		
a.						

Problem 6-42 (continued)   Name _____

JOURNAL ENTRIES	Debit		Credit	
a. (continued)				

b.

c.

	Debits	Credits

JOURNAL ENTRIES	Debit			Credit		
a.						
b.						
c.						
d.	Consolidated Franchises					

d.	(continued)			
	Consolidated Fixed Assets			
	Consolidated Accumulated Depreciation			
	Consolidated Expenses			

Working Papers

Problem 6-44

Irwin/McGraw-Hill
Advanced Accounting, 10/e

Problem 6-45

Problem 6-46

Name _____

Account Titles														Debits								Credits								Noncontrolling Interest			Consolidated Balances	

Name _____

1. _____

2. _____

3. _____

4. _____

5. _____

6. _____

7. _____

8. _____

9. _____

10. _____

11. _____

12. _____

13. _____

a.

b.

c.

d.

e.

f.

Problem 7-15

Name _____

a.

b.

Problem 7-16

Name _____

a.

b.

Problem 7-17

CONSOLIDATED BALANCES			
Sales			
Cost of Goods Sold			
Expenses			
Dividend Income			
Net Income			
Noncontrolling Interests in Subsidiaries' Income			

a.				
b.				

Problem 7-19

a.	CONSOLIDATED BALANCES			
	Sales			
	Cost of Goods Sold			
	Operating Expenses			
	Dividend Income			
	Noncontrolling Interst in Down's Income			
	Net Income			
b.				

Problem 7-20

Name _____

a.

b.

c.

d.

e.

a.

b.

a.

b.

c.

Problem 7-23

Name _____

a.				
b.				
c.				
d.				

Problem 7-24

Accounts Receivable			
Inventory			
Land			
Buildings			
Equipment			
Liabilities			
Deferred Tax Liability			
Assigned to Specific Accounts			
Purchase Price			
Goodwill			

Working Papers

Problem 7-25

Name _____

Journal Entries						

Journal Entries					

Working Papers

Account Titles						Debits	Credits	Noncontrolling Interest	Consolidated Balances

Account Titles					Debits	Credits	Noncontrolling Interest	Consolidated Balances

Acquisition Price Allocation & Amortization

Journal Entries	Debit	Credit

Calculation of Non-controlling Interest in subsidiary net income

JOURNAL ENTRIES and CALCULATIONS	Debits			Credits		
a.						

JOURNAL ENTRIES and CALCULATIONS	Debits	Credits
b.		

	JOURNAL ENTRIES and CALCULATIONS	Debits			Credits		
c.							

Problem 7-27 WORKSHEET   Name _____

Account Titles							Debits						Credits					Noncontrolling Interest					Consolidated Balances			

b.

c.

d.

	Debits			Credits		

a.

b.

c.

d.

e.

f.

g.

h.

i.

j.

	Debits			Credits		

k.

Working Papers

JOURNAL ENTRIES and CALCULATIONS	Debits			Credits		

JOURNAL ENTRIES and CALCULATIONS	Debits			Credits		

Working Papers

Problem 7-29 (continued)

Name _____

JOURNAL ENTRIES and CALCULATIONS	Debits			Credits		

Problem 8-1 to 8-33

Name _____

1. _____

2. _____

3. _____

4. _____

5. _____

6. _____

7. _____

8. _____

9. _____

10. _____

11. _____

12. _____

13. _____

14. _____

15. _____

16. _____

17. _____

18. _____

19. _____

20. _____

21. _____

22. _____

23. _____

24. _____

25. _____

26. _____

27. _____

28. _____

29. _____

30. _____

31. _____

32. _____

33. _____

Irwin/McGraw-Hill
Advanced Accounting, 10/e

© The McGraw-Hill Companies, Inc., 2011

8-1

Name _____

Segments	Revenues from Outsiders			Intersegment Transfers			Operating Expenses			Profit			Loss		

Revenue Test

Segments	Revenues			Percent			Reportable? Yes/No

Profit or Loss Test

Segments	Revenues			Expenses			Profit (Loss)			Reportable? Yes/No

Asset Test

Segments	Assets			Percent			Reportable? Yes/No

a.

b.

c.

d.

Revenue Test

Segments	Revenues			Percent			Reportable? Yes/No

Profit or Loss Test

Segments	Revenues			Expenses			Profit (Loss)			Reportable? Yes/No

Asset Test

Segments	Assets			Percent			Reportable? Yes/No

Problem 8-37 (continued)

Name _____

Problem 8-38

Revenue Test (sales to unaffiliated parties)

Segments	Sales to Outsiders			Percent			Material? Yes/No

Long-lived Asset Test

Segments	Balance			Percent			Material? Yes/No

a. Determination of Income Tax by Quarter - Estimated Annual Tax Rate 40%

Account	1st Quarter		2nd Quarter		3rd Quarter		4th Quarter	

b. Determination of Income by Quarter - Change in Estimated Annual Tax Rate

	1st Quarter		2nd Quarter		3rd Quarter		4th Quarter	

Problem 8-40

Name _____

	2010											2011	
	1st Quarter		2nd Quarter		3rd Quarter		4th Quarter				1st Quarter		

	3-Months Ended June 30				6-Months Ended June 30			
	2010		2011		2010		2011	

Problem 8-41

Journal Entries	Debits		Credits	

Working Papers

Problem 9-1 to 9-22

1. _____

2. _____

3. _____

4. _____

5. _____

6. _____

7. _____

8. _____

9. _____

10. _____

11. _____

12. _____

13. _____

14. _____

15. _____

16. _____

17. _____

18. _____

19. _____

20. _____

21. _____

22. _____

Problem 9-23

Problem 9-24

Name _____

Problem 9-25

	JOURNAL ENTRIES	Debit		Credit	

Problem 9-26

JOURNAL ENTRIES	Debit		Credit	

Problem 9-27

JOURNAL ENTRIES	Debit			Credit		

a.

b.

c.

JOURNAL ENTRIES	Debit			Credit		

JOURNAL ENTRIES	Debit	Credit
b.		

Problem 9-31   Name _____

	JOURNAL ENTRIES	Debit	Credit
a.	CASH FLOW HEDGE		

JOURNAL ENTRIES	Debit			Credit		
b. **FAIR VALUE HEDGE**						

JOURNAL ENTRIES	Debit			Credit		
a. **CASH FLOW HEDGE**						

Working Papers

JOURNAL ENTRIES	Debit	Credit
b. FAIR VALUE HEDGE		

JOURNAL ENTRIES	Debit			Credit		
a. CASH FLOW HEDGE						

JOURNAL ENTRIES	Debit	Credit
b. FAIR VALUE HEDGE		

JOURNAL ENTRIES	Debit	Credit
a. CASH FLOW HEDGE		

	JOURNAL ENTRIES	Debit			Credit		
b.	FAIR VALUE HEDGE						

JOURNAL ENTRIES	Debit			Credit		
a.						
b.						
c.						

JOURNAL ENTRIES	Debit	Credit
a.		
b.		
c.		

JOURNAL ENTRIES	Debit			Credit		
a. **FOREIGN CURRENCY RECEIVABLE**						

Working Papers

	JOURNAL ENTRIES	Debit			Credit		
b.	FOREIGN CURRENCY FIRM SALES COMMITMENT						

JOURNAL ENTRIES	Debit	Credit
a.		
b.		
c.		

JOURNAL ENTRIES	Debit	Credit
a.		
b.		
c.		

JOURNAL ENTRIES	Debit			Credit		
a.						

JOURNAL ENTRIES	Debit	Credit
b.		

JOURNAL ENTRIES	Debit	Credit
a.		
b.		

JOURNAL ENTRIES	Debit		Credit	
a.				
b.				

JOURNAL ENTRIES	Debit	Credit
c.		

JOURNAL ENTRIES	Debit	Credit
d.		

JOURNAL ENTRIES	Debit	Credit
e.		

1. _____

2. _____

3. _____

4. _____

5. _____

6. _____

7. _____

8. _____

9. _____

10. _____

11. _____

12. _____

13. _____

14. _____

15. _____

16. _____

17. _____

18. _____

19. _____

20. _____

Name _____

a.	**Rent Expense**
b.	**Dividends Paid**
c.	**Equipment**
d.	**Notes Payable**
e.	**Sales**
f.	**Depreciation Expense**
g.	**Cash**
h.	**Accumulated Depreciation**
i.	**Common Stock**

Problem 10-22

Working Papers

Problem 10-23

Name _____

	Translation			Remeasurement		
Accounts Payable						
Accounts Receivable						
Accumulated Depreciation						
Advertising Expense						
Amortization Expense						
Buildings						
Cash						
Common Stock						
Depreciation Expense						
Dividends Paid						
Notes Payable						
Patents (net)						
Salary Expense						
Sales						

Problem 10-24

a.			
b.			

Problem 10-25

Name _____

	LCU	RATE	US$

	LCU	RATE	US$

	LCU	RATE	US$

Working Papers

Problem 10-26

Name _____

		LCU			RATE			US$		

Problem 10-27

		LCU			RATE			US$		
a.										

		LCU			RATE			US$		
b.										

Problem 10-28

		LCU			RATE			US$		
a.										
b.										
c.										

Problem 10-29

Name _____

Account	(a) Translation			(b) Remeasurement		
Sales						
Inventory						
Equipment						
Rent Expense						
Dividends						
Notes Receivable						
Accumulated Depreciation - Equipment						
Salary Payable						
Depreciation Expense						

Problem 10-30

		Kites		RATE		US$	
a.							
b.				Debit		Credit	
c.							

Name _____

		KQ			RATE			US$		
a.	Cash									
	Accounts Receivable									
	Equipment									
	Accumulated Depreciation									
	Land									
	Accounts Payable									
	Notes Payable									
	Common Stock									
	Dividends Paid									
	Sales									
	Salary Expense									
	Depreciation Expense									
	Miscellaneous Expense									
b.	Cash									
	Accounts Receivable									
	Equipment									
	Accumulated Depreciation									
	Land									
	Accounts Payable									
	Notes Payable									
	Common Stock									
	Dividends Paid									
	Sales									
	Salary Expense									
	Depreciation Expense									
	Miscellaneous Expense									

Working Papers

		Goghs		RATE		US$	

		Goghs		RATE		US$	

		Goghs		RATE		US$	

		KR			RATE			US$		
a.										
b.										

	Pesos	RATE	C$
a.			

b. Prepare F/S in the functional currency		c. Translate into U.S. $	
Income Statement	C$	RATE	US$

b. Prepare F/S in the functional currency		c. Translate into U.S. $	
Statement of Retained Earnings	C$	RATE	US$

	b. Prepare F/S in the functional currency		C$			c. Translate into U.S. $		
	Balance Sheet		C$			RATE		US$

Problem 10-35

Name _____

Translation Worksheet									
Accounts		Egyptian Pound			RATE		US$		

Consolidation Worksheet

Accounts	Cayce (US$)			Simbel (US$)			Debits			Credits			Consolidated Balances		

JOURNAL ENTRIES	Debit	Credit

Problem 10-36

Name _____

PART I (a)		KCS		RATE		US$	
	Accounts						

Problem 10-36 (continued)

Name _____

PART I (b)												
Accounts			KCS			RATE			US$			

Problem 10-36 (continued)   Name _____

PART I (c)				
Accounts		KCS	RATE	US$

Problem 10-36 (continued)

Name _____

PART II

Problem 11-1 to 11-14

Name _____

1. _____
2. _____
3. _____
4. _____
5. _____
6. _____
7. _____

8. _____
9. _____
10. _____
11. _____
12. _____
13. _____
14. _____

Problem 11-15

a.

b.

a.

b.

Problem 11-18

Name _____

Working Papers

1. _____

2. _____

3. _____

4. _____

5. _____

6. _____

7. _____

8. _____

9. _____

10. _____

11. _____

12. _____

13. _____

14. _____

15. _____

16. _____

17. _____

18. _____

a.   **Blue Sky Laws**

b.   **S-8 Statement**

c.   **Letter of Deficiencies**

d.   **Public Company Accounting Oversight Board**

e.   **Prospectus**

Problem 12-22

Problem 12-23   Name _____

10-K
10-Q
8-K
Proxy Statement

Problem 12-24

Form S-1
Form S-3
Form S-4
Form S-8
Form S-11
Form SB-1
Form SB-2
Form F-3

Problem 12-25

Name _____

Problem 12-26

a.   **Staff Accounting Bulletins**

b.   **Wrap Around Filing**

c.   **Incorporation by Reference**

d.   **Division of Corporate Finance**

e.   **Integrated Disclosure System**

f.   **Management's Discussion and Analysis**

g.   **Chief Accountant of the SEC**

Problem 13-1 to 13-21

Name _____

1. _____
2. _____
3. _____
4. _____
5. _____
6. _____
7. _____
8. _____
9. _____
10. _____
11. _____
12. _____
13. _____
14. _____
15. _____
16. _____
17. _____
18. _____
19. _____
20. _____
21. _____

Name _____

Problem 13-24

Problem 13-25

Name _____

Problem 13-26

Working Papers

Problem 13-27

a.

b.

Problem 13-28

Problem 13-28 (continued)

Name _____

Problem 13-29

Problem 13-31

Problem 13-32

		Debit			Credit		

Working Papers

a.

b.

c.

JOURNAL ENTRIES	Debit			Credit		

Working Papers

JOURNAL ENTRIES	Debit			Credit		

a.

b.

Book Value			Assets	Available for Unsecured Creditors		

Book Value			Liabilities and Stockholders' Equity	Available for Nonpriority Liabilities		

Problem 13-40

Name _____

a.

b.

	JOURNAL ENTRIES	Debit			Credit		

c.

Name _____

Account Titles	Cash	Noncash Assets	Liabilities with priority	Fully Secured Creditors	Partially Secured Creditors	Unsecured, nonpriority liabilities	Stockholders' Equity (Deficit)

Working Papers

Problem 13-42 (continued)

Name _____

b.

Problem 13-43

	JOURNAL ENTRIES	Debit			Credit		

a.

Book Value			Assets	Available for Unsecured Creditors		

Book Value			Liabilities and Stockholders' Equity	Available for Nonpriority Liabilities		

b.

c.

d.

Book Value			Assets	Available for Unsecured Creditors		

Book Value			Liabilities and Stockholders' Equity	Available for Nonpriority Liabilities		

Account Titles	Cash	Noncash Assets	Liabilities with priority	Fully Secured Creditors	Partially Secured Creditors	Unsecured, nonpriority liabilities	Stockholders' Equity (Deficit)

Problem 13-46 (continued)

Name _____

b.			

Problem 13-47

JOURNAL ENTRIES	Debit		Credit	

JOURNAL ENTRIES	Debit	Credit

Problem 14-1 to 14-15

Name _____

1. _____

2. _____

3. _____

4. _____

5. _____

6. _____

7. _____

8. _____

9. _____

10. _____

11. _____

12. _____

13. _____

14. _____

15. _____

a. **Goodwill Method**			
b. **Bonus Method**			

Working Papers

JOURNAL ENTRIES	Debit		Credit	
a.				
b.				
c.				

Problem 14-18

a.	Capital Balances:			
	Nixon			
	Hoover			
	Polk			
	Grant			
b.	Capital Balances:			
	Nixon			
	Hoover			
	Polk			
	Grant			

Problem 14-19

Name _____

		Debit	Credit
a.			

		Com	Pack	Hal	Total
b.					

Problem 14-20

		Jones	King	Lane	Total

ALLOCATION OF INCOME	Purkerson		Smith		Traynor		Total	

STATEMENT OF PARTNERS' CAPITAL								
	Purkerson		Smith		Traynor		Total	

Name _____

INCOME ALLOCATION - 2010	Left			Center			Right			Total		

STATEMENT OF PARTNERS' CAPITAL - December 31, 2010												
	Left			Center			Right			Total		

INCOME ALLOCATION - 2011	Left			Center			Right			Total		

STATEMENT OF PARTNERS' CAPITAL - December 31, 2011												
	Left			Center			Right			Total		

INCOME ALLOCATION - 2012	Left			Center			Right			Total		

STATEMENT OF PARTNERS' CAPITAL - December 31, 2012												
	Left			Center			Right			Total		

Working Papers

Problem 14-23

Name _____

a.

Partner	Capital Balances After Withdrawal										
	Original Balance			Goodwill Allocation			Withdrawal			Final Balance	
Lennon											
McCartney											
Harrison											
Starr											

b.

Problem 14-24

a.

b.

Journal Entries	Debit			Credit		
c.						

Problem 14-24 (continued)

Name _____

	Journal Entries	Debit			Credit		
c.	(continued)						
d.							

Problem 14-25

a.				
b.	Allocation of Goodwill			

b. (continued)

Individual Capital Balances Following E's Investment of $36,000, Goodwill

		A			B			C			D			E		
	Balance																

c.   **Allocation of Goodwill**

Individual Capital Balances Following E's Investment of $42,000, Goodwill

		A			B			C			D			E		
	Balance																

d.   **Calculation of Bonus**

Individual Capital Balances Following E's Investment of $55,000, Bonus

		A			B			C			D			E		
	Balance																

e.   **Calculation of Bonus**

Problem 14-25 (continued)

Name _____

Individual Capital Balances Following C's Retirement		A		B		C		D	
Balance									

Problem 14-26

ALLOCATION OF INCOME - 2009	Boswell		Johnson		Total	
Total Allocation						

STATEMENT OF PARTNERS' CAPITAL - December 31, 2009	Boswell		Johnson		Total	

WALPOLE INVESTMENT - January 1, 2010

ALLOCATION OF INCOME - 2010	Boswell		Johnson		Walpole		Total	
Total Allocation								

STATEMENT OF PARTNERS' CAPITAL - December 31, 2010				
	Boswell	Johnson	Walpole	Pope	Total

POPE INVESTMENT - January 1, 2011

ALLOCATION OF INCOME - 2011				
	Boswell	Johnson	Walpole	Pope	Total

STATEMENT OF PARTNERS' CAPITAL - December 31, 2011				
	Boswell	Johnson	Walpole	Pope	Total

ALLOCATION OF INCOME - 2009												
a.	Gray			Stone			Lawson			Total		

CAPITAL ACCOUNT BALANCES 12/31/09												
	Gray			Stone			Lawson			Total		

Calculation - Monet Investment

ALLOCATION OF INCOME - 2010															
		Gray			Stone			Lawson			Monet			Total	

CAPITAL ACCOUNT BALANCES 12/31/10															
		Gray			Stone			Lawson			Monet			Total	

ALLOCATION OF INCOME - 2011		Gray			Stone			Lawson			Monet			Total		

CAPITAL ACCOUNT BALANCES 12/31/11		Gray			Stone			Lawson			Monet			Total		

b.

		Gray			Stone			Lawson			Totals		

	JOURNAL ENTRIES	Debit			Credit		
a.							
b.							
c.							
d.							
e.							
f.							

JOURNAL ENTRIES	Debit			Credit		
a.						

JOURNAL ENTRIES	Debit			Credit		
a. (continued)						
b.						

JOURNAL ENTRIES	Debit	Credit
b. (continued)		

1. _____

2. _____

3. _____

4. _____

5. _____

6. _____

7. _____

8. _____

9. _____

10. _____

11. _____

Problem 15-12

		Nixon		Cleveland		Pierce	

Problem 15-13

Name _____

	a. Land is sold for $25,000	Brown			Fish			Stone		
	b. Land is sold for $15,000									
	c. Land is sold for $5,000									

Problem 15-14

		ALLOCATION OF RASPUTIN'S CASH										
		Atkinson			Kaporale			Dennsmore			Rasputin	

Problem 15-15

Name _____

		PRELIMINARY CASH DISTRIBUTION							
		Ace		Ball		Eaton		Lake	

Problem 15-16

		PRELIMINARY CASH DISTRIBUTION											
		Cash		Other Assets		Accounts Payable		Hardwick, Loan & Capital		Saunders, Capital		Ferris, Loan & Capital	

Problem 15-17

Name _____

Problem 15-18

Problem 15-19

Name _____

Partner	Share of Loss	New Balance		

Problem 15-20

a.

Partner	Share of Loss	New Balance		

b.

Partner	Share of Loss	New Balance		

c.

Partner	Share of Loss	New Balance

d.

	Adams	Baker	Carvil	Dobbs

Assumed Loss Schedules

Partner	Loss Allocation	Max. Loss that can be absorbed

	Larson		Norris		Spencer		Harrison	

Assumed Loss Schedules

Partner	Loss Allocation	Max. Loss that can be absorbed		

a.   Predistribution Plan

	Able			Moon			Yerkl		

b.

Problem 15-23

	Simpson		Hart		Bobb		Reidl	
Predistribution Plan								

Problem 15-24

Part A
a.
b.
c.

Problem 15-24 (continued)

Name _____

Part B	
a.	
b.	
c.	

Problem 15-25

JOURNAL ENTRIES	Debit	Credit
a.		
b.		
c.		
d.		

JOURNAL ENTRIES	Debit			Credit		
e.						
f.						
g.						
h.						
i.						

Predistribution Plan				
	W	**X**	**Y**	**Z**

Assumed Loss Schedules		
Partner	**Loss Allocation**	**Max. Loss**

Van, Bakel, and Cox Partnership											
Safe Installment Payments to Partners											
January 31											
	Van			Bakel			Cox			Total		

Computation of Actual and Potential Liquidation Losses			
	Actual Losses		Potential Losses

	Van			Bakel			Cox			Total		
Van, Bakel, and Cox Partnership												
Safe Installment Payments fo Partners												
February 28												

	Van			Bakel			Cox			Total		
Van, Bakel, and Cox Partnership												
Safe Installment Payments fo Partners												
March 31												

Problem 15-28

Name _____

	Part A	Simon, Capital		Haynes, Loan and Capital		Jackson, Capital	

	Part B	Hough, Loan & Capital		Luck, Loan & Capital		Cummings, Capital	

	Part C	Hough, Loan & Capital		Luck, Loan & Capital		Cummings, Capital	

	Part D	Hough, Loan & Capital		Luck, Loan & Capital		Cummings, Capital	

Account Titles	Cash	Noncash Assets	Liabilities	Frick Capital (60%)	Wilson Capital (20%)	Clarke Capital (20%)

Predistribution Plan									
		Frick			Wilson			Clarke	

Assumed Loss Schedules				
Partner	Loss Allocation		Max. Loss that can be absorbed	

	Part A			
	Predistribution Plan			

Part A

	Wingler, Capital		Norris, Capital		Rodgers, Loan & Capital		Guthrie, Capital	

Supporting Schedules

Problem 15-30 (continued)

Name _____

Part B JOURNAL ENTRIES	Debit		Credit	

Problem 15-30 (continued)

Name _____

b. JOURNAL ENTRIES (continued)	Debit		Credit	

		Wingler, Capital			Norris, Capital			Rodgers, Loan & Capital			Guthrie, Capital		
Capital Balances															

Problem 16-1 to 16-28

Name _____

1. _____

2. _____

3. _____

4. _____

5. _____

6. _____

7. _____

8. _____

9. _____

10. _____

11. _____

12. _____

13. _____

14. _____

15. _____

16. _____

17. _____

18. _____

19. _____

20. _____

21. _____

22. _____

23. _____

24. _____

25. _____

26. _____

27. _____

28. _____

Problem 16-29

Name _____

JOURNAL ENTRIES	Debit			Credit		
Beginning of Year - Recording of Budget						
End of Year - Removal of Budget						

Problem 16-30

JOURNAL ENTRIES	Debit			Credit		
Government-Wide Financial Statements						
Fund-Based Financial Statements - General Fund						

JOURNAL ENTRIES	Debit			Credit		
Government-Wide Financial Statements						
Fund-Based Financial Statement						
General Fund						
Capital Projects Fund						

JOURNAL ENTRIES	Debit			Credit		
Fund-Based Financial Statements						
a.						
b.						
c.						
d.						
e.						
f.						
g.						
h.						

JOURNAL ENTRIES	Debit		Credit	
Fund-Based Financial Statements				
i.				
j.				
Government-Wide Financial Statements				
a.				
b.				
c.				
d.				
e.				
f.				
g.				
h.				

JOURNAL ENTRIES	Debit			Credit		
Government-Wide Financial Statements						
i.						
j.						

Problem 16-33

JOURNAL ENTRIES	Debit			Credit		
Fund-Based Financial Statements						
a.						
b.						
c.						
d.						
e.						

JOURNAL ENTRIES	Debit	Credit
Fund-Based Financial Statements		
f.		
g.		
h.		
Government-Wide Financial Statements		
a.		
b.		
c.		

JOURNAL ENTRIES	Debit		Credit	
Government-Wide Financial Statements				
d.				
e.				
f.				
g.				
h.				

JOURNAL ENTRIES	Debit		Credit	
Fund-Based Financial Statements				
a.				
b.				
c.				
d.				
e.				
f.				
g.				

JOURNAL ENTRIES	Debit			Credit		
Government-Wide Financial Statements						
a.						
b.						
c.						
d.						
e.						
f.						
g.						

a.

b.

c.

d.

e.

f.

g.

h.

i.

j.

Fund-Based Financial Statements

a.

b.

c.

d. Fund-Based Financial Statements - journal entries	Debit	Credit
e.		

f.

g.

h. Fund-Based Financial Statements	Debit			Credit		

JOURNAL ENTRIES	Debit	Credit
Fund-Based Financial Statements		
a.		
b.		
c.		
d.		
e.		
f.		
g.		

JOURNAL ENTRIES	Debit			Credit		
Fund-Based Financial Statements						
h.						
i.						
Government-Wide Financial Statements						
a.						
b.						
c.						
d.						
e.						
f.						

Problem 16-37 (continued)

Name _____

JOURNAL ENTRIES	Debit		Credit	
Government-Wide Financial Statements				
g.				
h.				
i.				

Problem 16-38

CITY OF JENNINGS		
GENERAL FUND		
Statement of Revenues, Expenditures, and Changes in Fund Balance		
(Condensed)		
Year Ending December 31, 2010		

CITY OF JENNINGS		
GENERAL FUND		
Balance Sheet (condensed)		
December 31, 2010		

JOURNAL ENTRIES	Debit			Credit		
Government-wide Financial Statements						
1.						
2.						
3.						
4.						
5.						
Fund-based Financial Statements						
1.						
2.						
3.						
4.						
5.						

a. Statement of Activities			

a. Statement of Net Assets			

b. Fund-Based Financial Statements		
Statement of Revenues, Expenditures, and Changes in Fund Balance		

b. Fund-Based Financial Statements		
Balance Sheet (condensed)		

Name _____

JOURNAL ENTRIES	Debit		Credit	
a.				
b.				
c.				
d.				
e.				
f.				
g.				
h.				
i.				

Working Papers

City of Lost Angel		
GENERAL FUND		
Statement of Revenues, Expenditures, and Changes in Fund Balance		

Problem 16-41

Name _____

JOURNAL ENTRIES	Debit		Credit	
a.				
b.				
c.				
d.				
e.				
f.				
g.				

Working Papers

JOURNAL ENTRIES	Debit	Credit
h.		
i.		

City of Lost Angel		
Government-Wide Financial Statements		
Statement of Net Assets		

Problem 16-42

Name _____

a.

b.

c.

d.

e.

Problem 16-43

a.

b.

c.

d.

e.

Working Papers

a.

b.

c.

d.

e.

f.

g.

h.

Problem 16-45

Name _____

a. _____

b. _____

c. _____

d. _____

e. _____

Problem 16-46

a. _____

b. _____

Working Papers

Problem 16-47

Name _____

Problem 16-48

a.

b.

c.

a.

b.

Problem 16-50

a.

b.

Problem 16-51

Name _____

a.

b.

Problem 16-52

a.

b.

Name _____

1. _____   14. _____

2. _____   15. _____

3. _____   16. _____

4. _____   17. _____

5. _____   18. _____

6. _____   19. _____

7. _____   20. _____

8. _____   21. _____

9. _____   22. _____

10. _____   23. _____

11. _____   24. _____

12. _____   25. _____

13. _____   26. _____

Problem 17-27   Name _____

Government-Wide and Fund-Based Financial Statements	
Enterprise Fund Lease	

Government-Wide Financial Statements - General Fund Lease	

Fund-Based Financial Statements - General Fund Lease	

Working Papers

JOURNAL ENTRIES	Debit	Credit
a. Government-Wide Financial Statements		
b. Fund-Based Financial Statements		

JOURNAL ENTRIES	Debit			Credit		
a. **Government-Wide Financial Statements**						
b. **Fund-Based Financial Statements**						
c. **Fund-Based Financial Statements**						

Problem 17-30

Name _____

JOURNAL ENTRIES	Debit			Credit		
a. **Enterprise Fund - Government-Wide Financial Statements**						
b. **General Fund - Government-Wide Financial Statements**						
c. **Enterprise Fund - Fund-Based Financial Statements**						
d. **General Fund - Fund-Based Financial Statements**						

a.	Government-Wide Financial Statements	
b.	Fund-Based Financial Statements	

Problem 17-32

	JOURNAL ENTRIES	Debit			Credit		
a.	Government-Wide Financial Statements						
b.	Fund-Based Financial Statements						
c.	Fund-Based Financial Statements						

Problem 17-33

Name _____

a. Government-Wide Financial Statements	
b.	
c.	

Problem 17-34

a. Government-Wide Financial Statements	
b. Fund-Based Financial Statements	

Problem 17-35   Name _____

Problem 17-36

a.

b.

c.

d.

e.

f.

g.

JOURNAL ENTRIES	Debit			Credit		
Enterprise Fund						

JOURNAL ENTRIES	Debit			Credit		
Enterprise Fund (continued)						

				a. CITY OF WILLIAMSON		
			STATEMENT OF ACTIVITIES			
			For Year Ended December 31, 2010			
Functions/Programs	Expenses	Charges for Services	Operating Grants and Contributions	Capital Grants and Contributions	Governmental Activities	Business-Type Activities	Total

Problem 17-38 (continued)   Name _____

	Governmental Activities	Business-type Activities	Total
a. CITY OF WILLIAMSON			
STATEMENT OF NET ASSETS			
December 31, 2010			

	General Fund	Total Governmental Funds
b. CITY OF WILLIAMSON		
STATEMENT OF REVENUES, EXPENDITURES, AND CHANGES IN FUND BALANCES		
Governmental Funds		
For Year Ended December 31, 2010		

Name _____

b. CITY OF WILLIAMSON			
Balance Sheet			
Governmental Funds			
December 31, 2010			
		General Fund	Total Governmental Funds

Problem 17-39

Name _____

a. CITY OF BERNARD							
STATEMENT OF ACTIVITIES							
For Year Ended December 31, 2010							
Functions/Programs	Expenses	Charges for Services	Grants and Contributions		Governmental Activities	Business-Type Activities	Total

Working Papers

Name _____

a. CITY OF BERNARD STATEMENT OF NET ASSETS December 31, 2010		
	Governmental Activities	Totals

b. CITY OF BERNARD			
STATEMENT OF REVENUES, EXPENDITURES, AND CHANGES IN FUND BALANCES			
Governmental Funds			
For Year Ended December 31, 2010			

b. CITY OF BERNARD			
Balance Sheet			
Governmental Funds			
December 31, 2010			

JOURNAL ENTRIES	Debit	Credit
a.		
b.		
c.		
d.		
e.		
f.		
g.		
h.		

JOURNAL ENTRIES	Debit			Credit		
h. (continued)						
i.						
j.						
k.						
l.						
m.						
n.						

JOURNAL ENTRIES	Debit			Credit		
o.						
p.						
q.						
r.						
s.						
t.						
u.						

Name _____

JOURNAL ENTRIES	Debit	Credit
u. (continued)		

			Net (Expenses) / Revenues			
City of Pfeiffer						
STATEMENT OF ACTIVITIES						
Government-Wide Financial Statements						
For Year Ended December 31, 2010						
	Expenses	**Program Revenues**	**Grants and Gifts**	**Governmental**	**Business-type**	**Total**	**Component Unit**

City of Pfeiffer			
STATEMENT OF NET ASSETS			
Government-Wide Financial Statements			
December 31, 2010			

JOURNAL ENTRIES	Debit			Credit		
a.						
b.						
c.						
d.						
e.						
f.						
g.						

JOURNAL ENTRIES	Debit	Credit
h.		
i.		
j.		
k.		
l.		
m.		

JOURNAL ENTRIES	Debit	Credit
n.		
o.		
p.		
q.		
r.		
s.		
t.		

JOURNAL ENTRIES	Debit		Credit	
u.				

City of Pfeiffer				
STATEMENT OF REVENUES, EXPENDITURES, AND CHANGES IN FUND BALANCES				
Fund-Based Financial Statements - Governmental Funds				
For Year Ended December 31, 2010				

City of Pfeiffer				
Balance Sheet				
Fund-Based Financial Statements - Governmental Funds				
December 31, 2010				

City of Pfeiffer	
STATEMENT OF REVENUES, EXPENDITURES, AND CHANGES IN FUND BALANCES	
Fund-Based Financial Statements - Proprietary Funds	
December 31, 2010	

City of Pfeiffer	
STATEMENT OF NET ASSETS	
Fund-Based Financial Statements - Proprietary Funds	
December 31, 2010	

Name _____

a.

b.

c.

d.

e.

f.

g.

h.

Working Papers

Problem 17-43 Name _____

a.

b.

c.

Problem 17-44

a.

b.

Problem 17-45

Name _____

Problem 17-46

a.

b.

Problem 17-47

a.

b.

c.

Problem 17-48   Name _____

a.

b.

Problem 17-49

a.

b.

c.

d.

e.

f.

g.

h.

Problem 17-50

a.

b.

c.

d.

e.

f.

Problem 17-51

a.

b.

c.

d.

Problem 17-52

Name _____

a.

b.

c.

d.

e.

Problem 17-53

a.

b.

c.

d.

Problem 18-1 to 18-31   Name _____

1. _____   18. _____

2. _____   19. _____

3. _____   20. _____

4. _____   21. _____

5. _____   22. _____

6. _____   23. _____

7. _____   24. _____

8. _____   25. _____

9. _____   26. _____

10. _____   27. _____

11. _____   28. _____

12. _____   29. _____

13. _____   30. _____

14. _____   31. _____

15. _____

16. _____

17. _____

a.

b.

c.

Problem 18-34

Name _____

Working Papers

Problem 18-36

a. Statement of Activities									
	Unrestricted Net Assets			Temporarily Restricted Net Assets			Permanently Restricted Net Assets		

b. Statement of Financial Position						

Problem 18-37

JOURNAL ENTRIES	Debit			Credit		

JOURNAL ENTRIES	Debit	Credit

Calculation of Changes in Net Assets	Unrestricted Net Assets			Temporarily Restricted Net Assets			Permanently Restricted Net Assets		

Problem 18-38

Name _____

JOURNAL ENTRIES	Debit			Credit		

JOURNAL ENTRIES	Debit			Credit		

Working Papers

	Unrestricted Net Assets			Temporarily Restricted Net Assets			Permanently Restricted Net Assets			Total		

University of Danville
Statement of Activities

a.

b.

c.

d.

e.

f.

g.

Name _____

(1)

(2)

(3)

(4)

(5)

(6)

(7)

(8)

(9)

(10)

(11)

(12)

(13)

Part (1)

Part (2)

Part (3)

JOURNAL ENTRIES	Debit	Credit

JOURNAL ENTRIES	Debit	Credit

Watson Foundation Statement of Activities For the Year Ended 12/31/10									
	Unrestricted Net Assets			Temporarily Restricted Net Assets			Permanently Restricted Net Assets		

Watson Foundation						
Statement of Financial Position						
December 31, 2010						

a. Computations			

Help & Save - Balances on Consolidated Statement of Financial Position **January 1, 2010**			
Cash			
Pledges Receivable (net)			
Investments			
Buildings & Equipment (net)			
Goodwill			
Total Assets			
Accounts Payable and Accrued Liabilities			
Notes Payable			
Total Liabilities			
Net Assets:			
Unrestricted			
Temporarily Restricted			
Permanently Restricted			
Total Liabilities and Net Assets			

b. Computations			

Help & Save - Balances on Consolidated Statement of Financial Position
January 1, 2010

Cash			
Pledges Receivable (net)			
Investments			
Buildings & Equipment (net)			
Total Assets			
Accounts Payable and Accrued Liabilities			
Notes Payable			
Total Liabilities			
Net Assets:			
Unrestricted			
Temporarily Restricted			
Permanently Restricted			
Total Liabilities and Net Assets			

c. Help-Swim-Save - Balances on Consolidated Statement of Financial Position			
January 1, 2010			
Cash			
Pledges Receivable (net)			
Investments			
Buildings & Equipment (net)			
Total Assets			
Accounts Payable and Accrued Liabilities			
Notes Payable			
Total Liabilities			
Net Assets:			
Unrestricted			
Temporarily Restricted			
Permanently Restricted			
Total Liabilities and Net Assets			

Problem 18-44

a.
b.

a.

b.

c.

Problem 18-46

a.

b.

c.

Problem 18-47

Name _____

Problem 18-48

a.

b.

c.

Problem 18-49

a.

b.

Working Papers

Problem 19-1 to 19-29

Name _____

1. _____   16. _____

2. _____   17. _____

3. _____   18. _____

4. _____   19. _____

5. _____   20. _____

6. _____   21. _____

7. _____   22. _____

8. _____   23. _____

9. _____   24. _____

10. _____   25. _____

11. _____   26. _____

12. _____   27. _____

13. _____   28. _____

14. _____   29. _____

15. _____

a. **Will**

b. **Estate**

c. **Intestate**

d. **Probate Laws**

e. **Trust**

f. **Inter vivos trust**

g. **Charitable Remainder Trust**

h. **Remainderman**

i. **Executor**

j. **Homestead Allowance**

Problem 19-32

a.	**Remainderman**
b.	**Trustor**
c.	**Demonstrative Legacy**
d.	**General Legacy**
e.	**Specific Legacy**
f.	**Life Tenant**
g.	**Testator**

Problem 19-33

a.

b.

Problem 19-34

Problem 19-35

Name _____

a.

b.

Problem 19-36

a. JOURNAL ENTRIES	Debit			Credit		

a. JOURNAL ENTRIES	Debit		Credit	

b.

Estate of Rose Shield						
Charge and Discharge Statement						
As to Principal						
As to Income						

Estate of Gina Purcell					
Charge and Discharge Statement					
As to Principal					
As to Income					

JOURNAL ENTRIES	Debit	Credit

a. JOURNAL ENTRIES	Debit			Credit		

a. JOURNAL ENTRIES	Debit	Credit

b.		
Estate of Lennie Pope		
Charge and Discharge Statement		

JOURNAL ENTRIES	Debit			Credit		

JOURNAL ENTRIES	Debit			Credit		

Working Papers